Security after the unthinkable

Manchester University Press

New Approaches to Conflict Analysis

Series editors: Peter Lawler (School of Social Sciences, University of Manchester) and Emmanuel-Pierre Guittet (Centre for Conflict, Liberty and Security, CCLS, Paris)

Until recently, the study of conflict and conflict resolution remained comparatively immune to broad developments in social and political theory. When the changing nature and locus of large-scale conflict in the post-Cold War era is also taken into account, the case for a reconsideration of the fundamentals of conflict analysis and conflict resolution becomes all the more stark.

New Approaches to Conflict Analysis promotes the development of new theoretical insights and their application to concrete cases of large-scale conflict, broadly defined. The series intends not to ignore established approaches to conflict analysis and conflict resolution, but to contribute to the reconstruction of the field through a dialogue between orthodoxy and its contemporary critics. Equally, the series reflects the contemporary porosity of intellectual borderlines rather than simply perpetuating rigid boundaries around the study of conflict and peace. *New Approaches to Conflict Analysis* seeks to uphold the normative commitment of the field's founders yet also recognises that the moral impulse to research is properly part of its subject matter. To these ends, the series is comprised of the highest quality work of scholars drawn from throughout the international academic community, and from a wide range of disciplines within the social sciences.

PUBLISHED

Christine Agius   *Neutrality, sovereignty and identity: The social construction of Swedish neutrality*

Tim Aistrope   *Conspiracy theory and American foreign policy: American foreign policy and the politics of legitimacy*

Eşref Aksu   *The United Nations, intra-state peacekeeping and normative change*

Michelle Bentley   *Syria and the chemical weapons taboo: Exploiting the forbidden*

M. Anne Brown   *Human rights and the borders of suffering: The promotion of human rights in international politics*

Anthony Burke and Matt McDonald (eds)   *Critical security in the Asia-Pacific*

Ilan Danjoux   *Political cartoons and the Israeli–Palestinian conflict*

Lorraine Elliott and Graeme Cheeseman (eds)   *Forces for good: Cosmopolitan militaries in the twenty-first century*

Clara Eroukhmanoff   *The securitisation of Islam: Covert racism and affect in the United States post-9/11*

Greg Fry and Tarcisius Kabutaulaka (eds) *Intervention and state-building in the Pacific: The legitimacy of 'cooperative intervention'*

Anna Geis, Maéva Clément and Hanna Pfeifer (eds) *Armed non-state actors and the politics of recognition*

Emmanuel-Pierre Guittet *Counter-terror by proxy: The Spanish State's illicit war with ETA*

Sophie Haspeslagh *Proscribing peace: How listing armed groups as terrorists hurts negotiations*

Naomi Head *Justifying violence: Communicative ethics and the use of force in Kosovo*

Charlotte Heath-Kelly *Death and security: Memory and mortality at the bombsite*

Richard Jackson *Writing the war on terrorism: Language, politics and counter-terrorism*

Tami Amanda Jacoby and Brent Sasley (eds) *Redefining security in the Middle East*

Matt Killingsworth, Matthew Sussex and Jan Pakulski (eds) *Violence and the state*

Jan Koehler and Christoph Zürcher (eds) *Potentials of disorder*

Matthias Leese and Stef Wittendorp (eds) *Security/mobility: Politics and movement*

David Bruce MacDonald *Balkan holocausts? Serbian and Croatian victim-centred propaganda and the war in Yugoslavia*

Adrian Millar *Socio-ideological fantasy and the Northern Ireland conflict: The other side*

Jennifer Milliken *The social construction of the Korean War*

Ami Pedahzur *The Israeli response to Jewish extremism and violence: Defending democracy*

Johanna Söderström *Living politics after war: Ex-combatants and veterans coming home*

Maria Stern *Naming insecurity – constructing identity: 'Mayan-women' in Guatemala on the eve of 'peace'*

Virginia Tilley *The one state solution: A breakthrough for peace in the Israeli–Palestinian deadlock*

Security after the unthinkable

Terror and disenchantment in Norway

J. Peter Burgess

MANCHESTER UNIVERSITY PRESS

Copyright © J. Peter Burgess 2024

The right of J. Peter Burgess to be identified as the author of this work has been asserted in accordance with the Copyright, Designs and Patents Act 1988.

Published by Manchester University Press
Oxford Road, Manchester M13 9PL

www.manchesteruniversitypress.co.uk

British Library Cataloguing-in-Publication Data
A catalogue record for this book is available from the British Library

ISBN 978 1 5261 6634 0 hardback
ISBN 978 1 5261 8006 3 paperback

First published 2024

The publisher has no responsibility for the persistence or accuracy of URLs for any external or third-party internet websites referred to in this book, and does not guarantee that any content on such websites is, or will remain, accurate or appropriate.

Typeset by Newgen Publishing UK

Jon Bing
in memoriam

Contents

Acknowledgements	*page* x
Introduction	1

Part I: Theory of disenchantment

1 Terror and disenchantment	29
2 The enchantment of security	49
3 The invention of vulnerability	85
4 Our coming security	110

Part II: Making security sense of Oslo/Utøya

5 22 July 2011: event, meaning and affect	135
6 The report of the 22 July Commission	161
7 There is no alternative to security	186
8 Giving and taking responsibility for terrorism	215
After thought	242
References	258
Index	277

Acknowledgements

A four-word resumé of this book would read something like this: security is about people. Nowhere is this clearer than in my debt to the many people who have helped this work along its way.

This book is dedicated to the memory of Jon Bing, a prodigious figure on the Norwegian cultural landscape who I am most fortunate to be able to say was also a mentor and a friend. Jon, who disappeared in 2014, much too young, was a science fiction author a whole generation ahead of his contemporaries and an ICT lawyer working at the forefront of his field. He was a gentle and generous soul who understood both the irreducible humanity of digital technological development and the cultural implications of our rush to seek security in technological solutions.

I also wish to acknowledge the contribution to this book made by Bjørg Ofstad. Bjørg was a pioneer in the development of security research in Norway in the 2000s, both through her work as a science officer at the Research Council of Norway and in the European Commission. When the Twin Towers fell on 11 September 2001, Bjørg was working in Brussels, seconded to the European Commission's Directorate General for Research. While the world was still spinning around the demonising discourse of terrorism served up by the Bush II Administration, Bjørg set in motion a European Science Foundation Cooperation in Science and Technology (COST) Action presciently called 'The Social Construction of Terrorist Threats', the first and most important European research endeavour on the meaning and experience of terrorism. This book is a direct result of that initiative. Back home in Norway, Bjørg was for me the original 'tough love'. Throughout our fifteen-year association, she worked uncompromisingly to clear an institutional space for new and innovative ways of thinking about security while remaining equally uncompromising in her insistence on the need for clarity, meaningfulness and practical relevance of research, writing and public speaking about security. European security research is poorer after her retirement in 2014; Norwegian security research may never have got off the ground without her. She remains for me today a decisive reference and inspiration as a philosopher, researcher, writer and citizen.

I am grateful to the institutional support for this work provided by the Peace Research Institute Oslo (PRIO). The PRIO Security Research Group powered and lifted this project by the intelligence, rigour, friendship and care of, among many others, Kristoffer Lidén, Mareile Kaufmann, Maria Gabrielsen Jumbert, Rocco Bellanova, Elida Jakobsen, Nina Boy, Stephan Davidshofer, Médéric Martin-Mazé and Anthony Amicelle.

Equally important is the friendship and support I have found at the Ecole normale supérieure (ENS), Paris, where I have had the honour of developing, with the support of the AXA Research Fund, the Chair in Geopolitics of Risk, and where I now work together with an uncommonly able team of young doctoral and post-doctoral researchers, all of whom have read and commented on one or several chapters of this work. Among these are Sarah Perret, Jan Wörlein, Dakota Root, Aisha Kadiri, Ellen Emile Henriksen, Jeta Abazi Gashi, Viktoria Akchurina, Willy Delvalle, Daniele Cavalli, Mélanie Pinet, Adrien Estève and Marie Kwon.

A special thanks to Cassandra Windey for her meticulous review of the final manuscript and for generating the book's index.

My warm thanks go to former Director of the ENS, Marc Mézard, who had the insight and the courage to support the project of the Chair in Geopolitics of Risk, and to the present ENS Director Frédéric Worms, whose friendship and support have lightened the work of the Chair and made completion of this book possible. I am indebted to Emmanuel Cunningham-Sabot, former Director of the Department of Geography at the ENS, who had the original genius to think the thought of the Chair, and the grit and courage to carry it to the robust reality it has become.

The research and writing of this book benefited directly from a generous award from the Bergesen Foundation. I am grateful to its Board of Directors and in particular to its now retired Administrative Director Ole Jacob Bull for friendship and support.

Thanks to Jørgen Watne Frydnes for wise advice and to Jonas Dahlberg for kind permission to use the maquette image of his magnificent *Memory Wound* for the cover of the book.

Finally, as always, it is not possible to sum up the contribution to this work made by Karen Lieve Ria Hostens. Every twist of plot and turn of phrase in these pages can be tracked, in daylight and darkness, to a moment of life that inevitably involved her.

All translations from Norwegian in this book are my own. Parts of Chapter 2 appeared earlier in 'An ethics of security' (Burgess, 2015).

Introduction

> I want you to panic.
> Thunberg (2019)

An inward turn

On 22 July 2011, Norway became the target of the most horrendous terrorist attack on its soil since the end of World War II. The perpetrator was a 32-year-old Norwegian man named Anders Behring Breivik. He was born and grew up in Oslo, was confirmed into the Lutheran Church of Norway, graduated secondary school and studied business at the Oslo Commerce School (Borchgrevink, 2013).

The attack happened in two separate events that took place over the course of about six hours. The first part of the attack was carried out using a car bomb, which detonated in front of the seventeen-storey government building that housed the Prime Minister's offices in the governmental quarter in central Oslo. The bomb, which was made of a mixture of artificial fertiliser and fuel oil, was estimated to weigh approximately 950 kilograms. It was placed in a large van that was parked immediately outside the main entrance of the building and detonated with a ten-minute fuse (Anderson *et al.*, 2002), which gave the attacker ample time to walk 100 metres to another car and escape injury. The explosion killed 8 people outright and injured 209, 12 of them seriously, while causing heavy damage to several buildings in the quarter. The second event was an armed attack on a summer camp of the Labour Party's Youth League (AUF) on Utøya, an island in the Tyri Lake just outside of Oslo. The summer camp was an annual event organised by AUF every summer since World War II. It was designed as a kind of summer school where aspiring young politicians could convene, discuss and debate, and meet the many leaders of its mother organisation, the Labour Party. Dressed as a police officer and displaying false identification, the attacker took the one-kilometre ferryboat ride to the island. He approached a number of the young activists grouped together and explained that he was there to secure the site after the explosion in Oslo, news of which had begun to reach the island. After a brief exchange, he opened fire at random on anyone he could find. His gun attack was stopped only when he was apprehended over an hour after the shooting began. He was charged with, then later confessed to, having committed the attacks. It became clear during subsequent study and testimony in his trial that the perpetrator had acted alone, inspired by a mixture of xenophobia, anti-Muslim, anti-Jewish sentiment and a wide variety of culturally conservative positions. Of the over 600 people on the island, 68 were killed and 110 were injured, 55 of them gravely. One additional victim died in hospital two days later.

In Norway, a relatively small and close-knit society, the attack was experienced as a moment of acute national crisis, but also one of remarkable unity and solidarity (Skjeseth, 2011). A number of spontaneous manifestations took place all over the country in the days and weeks after the attacks. Some were memorials for the dead or manifestations of support for the injured, or simply expressions of national unity. The most notable was the so-called 'Rose March', which took place three days after the attack, gathering 200,000 people in the centre of Oslo to hear speeches and performances by politicians, luminaries and others, calling for tolerance, openness and love. As we will see, these sentiments were echoed by a unified political class as well as by public opinion.

In the first days after the attack, one could observe an uncanny reaffirmation and even intensification of the political and moral values of the tolerant Norwegian society, a society by any measure already quite liberal. Societal values and the kind of security and comfort provided by social bonds, uniformly shared national culture and a low degree of social inequality seemed to hold the day. This was, at least at first glance, an apparently open and liberal society, in stark contrast to the anti-liberal reflex of the US and other countries in the wake of their own horrendous terror attacks during the previous decade, in addition to any number of other European and non-European states. However, as I will show in Chapter 5, only several days later, signs began to appear that the discourse of the open and liberal society, exemplified by the 'streets full of love' pronounced by the Crown Prince at the culmination of the Rose March and the assurances of the Prime Minister that the terrorist violence would be answered with 'more democracy, more openness, more humanity, but never naïveté', was beginning to show cracks. This discourse would find itself tamed by a parallel discourse of security of a different kind, the security offered by forces of order, reduced civil liberties, surveillance and extraordinary powers (Haakon, 2011; Stoltenberg, 2011a).

The trial of Anders Behring Breivik began nine months later, after extensive logistical and juridical preparation. Like the attack itself, the trial was widely covered by the international media. The arrangements surrounding it broke many norms and models for the unassuming and soft-spoken

Norwegian society, intensifying the already unprecedented experience of the attack and its aftermath. The live-televised trial had many remarkable moments. Most stunning to many observers, in particular those in the foreign press, was the respect and dignity with which the mass murderer was treated, the political rights and moral freedoms that the court took nearly clumsy pains to assure. The trial began with a medical assessment of the accused man's legal-psychological competence to stand trial. A team of court-appointed psychologists examined him and determined that he was not legally sane and was therefore not legally accountable under ordinary standards for the crime committed. As a consequence, there would be no trial or punishment, only commitment to a psychiatric facility. The public outcry was thunderous. The streets that were previously said to be filled with love took on a mood of vindictiveness. After a process and public debate that I will analyse in Chapter 8, the report was revised, the accused deemed competent and responsible and required to stand trial.

The ongoing criminal investigation revealed two disconcerting realities. First, Breivik was well supplied for the attacks in terms of raw materials for bomb fabrication, a stock of weapons and equipment, and second, he was well prepared in terms of ideas and arguments. Yet, what is most remarkable about the case from the point of view of the extreme event that it represents is that the activities Breivik undertook in preparation for the attacks all fell more or less within the margins of the law, and were protected by the freedoms of a liberal State. Norwegians were shocked to learn that Breivik's preparations for the attacks took place within the limitations set by Norwegian law and international conventions in place for the regulation of the flow of both weapons and the nitrogen-based fertiliser used to make the bomb. The mash-up of ideological elements that formed the basis for the perpetrator's own extreme views were already circulating widely in the Norwegian and international public spheres, protected by Norwegian and European norms and standards for free speech and for the free exchange of ideas.

Uncertainty as danger

In this sense, all the elements of what can be called a new 'age of uncertainty' are present: the dangers we confront today, in particular the threat of terrorist violence, are not exogenous, external or foreign to the societies they threaten. They are not alien corpuscles to a body politic that is already safe and secure, spiritually sound and morally righteous in its own right. On the contrary, they are already inherent in it. By the same token, the threats we face cannot be prevented from becoming reality through a strategy of holding them at bay, blocking their contact with the sanctity of the society they threaten. As disconcerting as it may seem, the threat to society is, in the case of Breivik and many others, a creation of that society, a symptom of its own malaise, spillover from its own excesses, penury from its own insufficiencies. In other words, from a societal point of view – setting aside the relatively extraordinary personal psychological situation that surrounded the perpetrator during his upbringing and youth – he was a product of Norwegian society, its culture, welfare, values, religion and customs (Berntzen & Sandberg, 2014; Leonard et al., 2014; Melle, 2013). He paradoxically benefited in his misdeeds from the social conventions, political liberties and legal permissiveness enjoyed by any modern liberal society, but most markedly by Norwegian society.

Long before the extraordinary legal process against Breivik began in April 2012, a range of far more pragmatic processes was set in motion in order to respond to the perceived political exigencies generated by the attacks. As many journalists underscored in the immediate aftermath of the catastrophe, a certain experience of geopolitical innocence was lost forever, even if that loss might seem to contradict at first glance the blushing idealism of the Rose March. An instinct of neighbourly tolerance and liberal empathy flourished in parallel with a drive for instrumentalisation, for analysis and explanation, cause and effect, responsibility and retribution, administration and control, safety and security.

In this spirit, on 12 August 2011, three weeks after the attack, the sitting Norwegian Government named a commission (the 22 July Commission) whose task was to 'undertake a review and evaluation in order to draw lessons from the events with the aim of making the Norwegian society better equipped to prevent and confront possible future attacks while at the same time preserving central values in Norwegian society such as openness and democracy' (NOU, 2012). In the immediate wake of the catastrophe and with Norway still in shock, naming an independent commission was a prudent political decision. It would not only seek to cast light on the background causes of the attack but also help reaffirm the principles of accountability of a well-ordered society, and reassert the legitimacy of its institutions and government, providing responsible recommendations for revising State practices in order to prevent such an attack from happening again.

The 22 July Commission, to which we will return in detail in Chapter 6, was only one in a long line of governmental initiatives that sought to capture and control the political trajectory of the unthinkable events, to, first, translate them into concrete strategies aimed at assuring Norway's 'societal security' – the core concept to which we will return many times in this book, starting with the conceptual instruction in Chapter 1 – and, second, to enact new policy intended to prevent or reduce the possibility of similar attacks in the future. These initiatives continue to this day. Unfortunately, so does the instrumentalising grip they hold on society's relation to its own vulnerability. Though political processes linked to reforming Norwegian anti- and counter-terrorism have varied across a span of over a decade and a major ideological shift between the centre-left Stoltenberg II Government that ended after the 2013 parliamentary elections and the centre-right Solberg Government that succeeded it, this basic ideological premise of security-making remains. Battling terrorism in Norway was and continues to be unexpectedly non-partisan. As we will see, in the political rationality that comes to govern anti- and counter-terrorism measures, and what will come to be called 'the societal security effort', traditional political oppositions seem to be irrelevant. In the traversal from socialist-left to a neoliberal-right government apparatus, there is little change in the perception of the methodology of societal security. Threat knows no ideology; insecurity dissolves politics. In this way, uncertainty emerged from the strange, organic, pastoral self-care in force in Norway, and the threat to society was displaced from its traditional position as the threatening other and internalised, rediscovered as a component, perhaps even the core essence, of society itself. Uncertainty became an endogenous, self-generated threat.

Yet, as this book will argue, ambivalence persisted in Norway, and indeed, if one seriously considers the notion of the security and insecurity of societies, will always persist. The double structure of this ambivalence can be generalised as follows. On the one hand, society's robustness is rooted in the organic cohesion that underpins its existence as a community. On the other hand, the available means, perhaps the only conceivable means, to enhance, to encourage, to stabilise or increase this robustness is through the forcibly instrumental political policy that undermines organicity.

Thus, on the one hand, the approach to the security of society, in Norway as elsewhere, comprises, among other things, a relatively significant empowerment of the police and security services, the introduction of an ensemble of data collection strategies and surveillance practices already common in Europe following the requirements of the US Patriot Act and existing European Union (EU) terrorism plans of action. On the other hand, this general methodology builds on two markedly Norwegian particularities. First, it carries a distinct focus on organisational responsibility and reform. The central investigative analyses of the 2011 attacks gave considerable, sometimes exclusive, attention to organisational and institutional culture, organisational structures, leadership, cooperation, competence and effectiveness. As we will see, this emphasis, first presented in the analyses of the 22 July Commission and others, continues across the board and at all levels. Second, this Norwegian approach makes use of a particularly Scandinavian *dispositif* already in place and easily adaptable to the needs of a new form of governmentality: the discourse of *societal security*. I will try to show in this book that the concepts and analytic perspectives of societal security had been developed in a unique post-World War II constellation of concerns about the comprehensive and cross-sectoral security of society, only to find their primary applications in the field of industrial safety in the meteoric evolution of the oil industries during the post-1970s boom.

Disenchantment and re-enchantment

In the first weeks and months after the Oslo/Utøya attacks – I will refer to them going forward as 'Oslo/Utøya' – a unique mood of community, solidarity, care, humanity, perhaps one might even dare to say love, reigned in the Kingdom of Norway. The first terrorist attack on Norwegian soil since World War II was experienced as an attack against the deep-felt humanity of Norwegian culture. The virtue of Norwegian social ties was constantly evoked in an appeal to the chosen response of a deeply democratic society like the Norwegian: 'more democracy, more openness, more humanity, but never naïveté', as Prime Minister Stoltenberg movingly formulated two days after Oslo/Utøya (Stoltenberg, 2011d). Yet, nearly a decade later, this response rings distantly naive. Long ago and far, far away is the encouragement of the Prime Minister – now moved on to become, of all things, Secretary General of NATO, the greatest military alliance in the history of the planet – to 'bake a cake, invite someone over for coffee, go for a walk together' (Stoltenberg, 2011c). It was, to use Weber's terms, a time of enchantment. Instead, as we will see in this book, the fight against terrorism and in defence of the Norwegian society takes the most bureaucratic forms imaginable. Anti-terror policy in the name of the societal security of Norway has been honed into a regime of neoliberal calculability, where political values like democracy, justice, equality, rule of law are recast and applied in their most instrumental forms, where social values like solidarity, community, individuality are operationalised through mechanical instruments of public institutions, and cultural values like religious ideas, language, heritage, nature, etc. are translated into administrative policies.

And yet, as I will try to show, there remains a grain of enchantment in the Norwegian rush to join the Euro-American instrumentality of prophylactic anti-terrorism strategies of neoliberal governance, identifying the terrorist threat as though it were a distinct object, cut off from affect and spirit, and putting in place the mechanical tools for cleansing the nation of it. In every attempt at bureaucratisation in the broad Norwegian approach to societal security, we can find that grain of enchantment resisting the imperative to bureaucratic accountability. Throughout the long decade since the attacks, this thorn in the side of Norwegian neoliberal societal security policy has remained a stone in the sandal of those who desire for bureaucratic streamlining as an answer to the drive to master and manage this or any society's endless vulnerability. I will try to argue in this book that this grain of enchantment at the heart of neoliberal self-understanding is actually not simply a thorn in the side, a stone in the sandal, an impurity in an otherwise smoothly running societal system, but, paradoxically, the precondition for that system itself. As a consequence, societal security as disenchanted, disembodied, rational, scientific calculability depends for its force on the enchanted other, the spirit of society's cultural and moral bonds, to do its work.

Disenchantment follows from the corruption of the relation behind mind and spirit, the link that makes Norwegians, or anyone, feel secure, we will see, is not just social engineering. Indeed, it cannot be engineered. It has agency and a certain kind of political subjectivity as well. The disenchanted neoliberal subject speaks, decides, securitises. It enacts its agency in accordance with a very attractive and even seductive set of means, of the kind to which any organisation would aspire: calculability, accountability, responsibility, professionalism. These virtues constitute the power of disenchanted thought in Norway and other modern social democracies, enacted through the structure, transparency, administration and decision-making of non-elected and thus theoretically disinterested agents. In the overall architecture of social democratic administration, the bureaucracy plays the role of implementing the political decisions handed down to the political superstructure. Political positions are clarified, then implemented, by the bureaucracy in order to be put in place according to the structural possibilities and organisational horizons as they are available. These possibilities and horizons are, of course, by no means neutral. Indeed, they are themselves products of political decisions adopted, the specific hierarchy of the bureaucratic structure, the specialisation and particular competencies, the division of labour and accepted procedures. This standard neoliberal narrative, which provides more to Norway's modern conformism rather than to its special Nordic character, was utterly disrupted at Oslo/Utøya. Not only did the disenchanted neoliberal business-as-usual completely fail to provide security for the Norwegian people but the rather remarkable success story of the horrendous event was, as many have noted, the informal, primeval, soulful unity of 'the Norwegian' that provided what security was on offer that day.

This book does not have the ambition of proposing a documentation and analysis of the facts of what happened at Oslo/Utøya. Many well-documented and rigorous works have already done this vital service, starting with the widely read but little-debated Report of the 22 July Commission, published in August 2012, just over one year after the events (NOU, 2012). Nor does it aim to reconstruct the events, in either a short or extended time frame, drawing conclusions about what provoked or even caused the events. Here, too, a range of sources are available, defending more or less well-founded hypotheses about what past events and elements led to the attacks (Borchgrevink, 2013; Bromark, 2014; Englund, 2012; Seierstad, 2015).

Instead, this book is designed as an *anti-history* of the attacks. It deals not with the question of what made a certain constellation of past conditions and events collate into a meaningful order and culminate in the Oslo/Utøya attacks. Rather, it deals with what *began* on that day, at that moment. What was created that had not existed before, and what was destroyed to never appear again? What changes were spontaneously initiated? What processes were set in motion? What was thought and what could never be thought again? What was experienced and what was never experienced again? Finally, what was lived, and what – death itself notwithstanding – would not be lived again? Here, too, a considerable body of scientific research has been generated; indeed, research on the 'aftermath' is far more voluminous than research on the 'sources'. An important body of research has emerged in the fields of risk analysis (Jore, 2019; Lindaas & Pettersen, 2016; Pursiainen, 2018); crisis communication (Englund, 2012; Goodman & Falkheimer, 2014); terrorism studies (Bangstad, 2014, 2016; Christensen & Aars, 2017; Hemmingby & Bjørgo, 2016; Malkki *et al.*, 2018); immigration studies (Jakobsson & Blom, 2014); psychology (Aakvaag *et al.*, 2014; Dyb *et al.*, 2014; Filkuková *et al.*, 2016; Nordanger *et al.*, 2013); law (Gröning *et al.*, 2019; Løvlie, 2019); economics (Gröning *et al.*, 2019; Løvlie, 2019); media studies (Kalsnes *et al.*, 2014; Kalvig, 2016); even tourism studies (Wolff & Larsen, 2014), among others. This book takes a perspective that is different from these conventional 'scientific' documentary and empirical approaches generated in both high quality and volume by the different scientific communities. In addition to seeking a metaphysical background for scientific research and discoveries about the Oslo/Utøya attacks, it seeks to look beyond the critical knowledge, insight and knowledge of the practitioners of crisis management, civil engineering, civil authorities, first responders, health workers and police services, charged in a variety of ways with providing exactly the security they were unable to provide. This publication will try to describe the affective and spiritual experience of seeking and finding security in the long shadow of the catastrophic, unthinkable event.

The material sources of knowledge and their analysis form the essential foundations on which mainstream knowledge on terrorism is built and through which practical approaches to the mitigation of terrorist threats are scientifically supported, politically legitimated and given popular currency.

Surprisingly, both the methodologies of scientific discovery and practical operationalisation are made possible, albeit in different ways, by the implicit bracketing, dissimulating or simply erasing of those qualities of life that are demonstrably the conditions of security but which in their vocation of providing robustness are both delicately invisible but also, as I will show, the only substance able to survive the catastrophe of Oslo/Utøya, and persist in the background of the intensely bureaucratic quest for security.

Methodology for studying the unthinkable

For these reasons, this book will methodologically invert classical security studies by examining security at the moment of its obliteration, at the conceptual and experiential ground zero of security: 22 July 2011 at 3:25 p.m. By staking out the frame of this book around the notion of what began at that moment, it will try to let itself be defined and delimited by all that ceased at that moment, surrendering in a certain sense to what was left, what was still there when everything else was gone, to all that could not and still cannot be accounted for by scientific means, by modes of thought, conceptualisation and analysis, and scopes of action. My methodological hypothesis, if I can speak of such in this context, is that by discovering, describing and analysing what is left of security after the catastrophe, we will be able to learn something more about what the irreducible kernel of security actually 'is'. By force of habit, we assume increasingly in our neoliberal environment that security can and should be the object of 'science'. Instead, for example, it could be thought of as art or philosophy, or, even more audaciously, that it should be no 'object' at all but rather some kind of yet-to-be-articulated, non-determinate form of being, a thesis that a certain reading of Heidegger's early work might support (Burgess, 2021; Dillon, 1996). More plausible, and representing the substantive hypothesis of this book, the irreducible core of security reveals itself – to use a formulation that will be further clarified as we go on – as spirit.

The *methodological* question to be asked throughout this book is: what are the means marshalled and mobilised by those charged, by formal mandate or informal expectation, with the responsibility of providing 'security'? What are the agents against disaster, against catastrophe, against the unthinkable? Who (or what) are the actors who conscientiously carry out their security mandates in a consistent, coherent, admirable and even heroic manner? What are the mandates and remit of first responders, police and civil defence officers, rescue and health workers, overseers of societal security, legislators, leaders and politicians, sworn to give body and movement to the will of the people and its need and desire for security? Charged with this ultimately impossible task, it is fair to ask what these agents of the people are capable of doing, in legal terms, of course, but more so in technical, logistical and operational terms. What, indeed, is in their remit to do in order to carry out their responsibilities? What lies within the scope of their responsibility, to the law and to the directives of their agency?

Security in Western societies is not a concept or ambition, not even a need that exists prior to the bureaucratic assignment of the competences, rights, duties and responsibilities of the regally sanctioned servants of the society. Security is what is created within the contours of the space of the qualities opened by this desire. What is more, and more complicating when it comes to the methodology needed to study it, security lies just beyond those contours, receding with every instrumental advance in the bureaucratic functions of the State. Security is, by its nature and by its very conceptual bounds, beyond the reach of State. Any threat that falls within the purview of the State's competences, rights, duties and responsibilities is conceptually containable and materially manageable by existing or envisageable security measures. The transition from an awareness of threat to its overcoming is merely a question of technical adjustment, adaptation, material or human resources and time. In short, if a threat can be thought and understood from within the finite bureaucracy of the State's security apparatus, then it can, and eventually will, be neutralised. Concretely, had the Oslo/Utøya disaster been more than remotely possible, its potential reality more closely within reach, had it been possible to concretely imagine it, then it would not have constituted a threat and essentially would not have happened. As the 2013 report of the 9/11 Commission underscored, from the point of view of the US government, the 11 September 2001 attack was not the result of a lack of security capability but rather of a lack of imagination (9/11 Commission, 2004: 339–50; see also Cerulo, 2008).

What can be thought about Oslo/Utøya, what can be articulated as the provision of security and thereby what can be researched and plausibly interpreted are, in a certain sense, governed by the aggregate of the remits and mandates, capacities and competencies, of those mobilised for the purpose of addressing the events of that day. The collective crisis management principles and practices have the function of carrying out an irrepressible ontological function in that they create and, importantly, sustain the reality of what happened and, in what will be key to our analysis, what began on 22 July 2011. The aggregate crisis managers did what they did with more or less appropriate competence and authority, and hence *created* for us today the reality of *what was to be done*. We can do nothing more or less in our analysis and assessment of their discursive utterances surrounding their actions than appraise them in relation to, in the shape of continuity or rupture, what is for us here and now, what is to be done, given what is given, and given the fact that what was given for them belonged to another horizon of threat and another world of danger.

'The borders of my language mean the borders of my world,' wrote Wittgenstein in the *Tractatus Logicus Philosophicus* in 1921 (1961: 56). Clearly, beyond the border of the world constituted by the language of security, there is insecurity, threat and danger. However, it is not an a priori world of objective danger waiting to be articulated and thus internalised through the discourse of security. It is the limit of the State's security discourse, the sum of its remits, competences, rights, duties and responsibilities. It is the relation to this border, this limit of security, this delimitation of threat, that this book tries to capture. It will always be fleeting, most often receding, inevitably, unpredictably, refusing patterns and resisting the kind of totalising conceptualisation that leads security thinking into inept limbo, anchoring itself, as we will see, in places where no security is to be found. Even the pages and pages of hindsight penned by all those who reviewed, analysed, critiqued and revised the measures that were taken after Oslo/Utøya could not do their analyses from a place beyond the horizon of security, the only place where danger actually lies, and from whence any threat that eventually can emerge will emerge. No one can re-live what they lived. To be sure, what actually happened can only have come into being in a world that can never be reconstituted. Hindsight is all powerful in the security world and yet utterly incoherent in the world beyond the horizon of security. Danger is danger only because it lies beyond the 'event horizon' of the security world, in other words, beyond what is thought. It is therefore not for lack of good will, competence or authority that authorities do not protect us from unimaginable threats.

In formulating the problem in these philosophical terms, this book tries to take a step in the direction of understanding the metaphysical problem of security, and the distinct way that danger in the West derives its power – its 'dangerousness' – not from its factual, objective or 'scientific' character but rather from its other-worldliness or enchantment. It is not the dangers that are familiar to us that generate insecurity, as threatening, even perilous, as these dangers might be, but rather the special form of *being* that danger constitutes: it does not *exist* in any plain, substantial sense. It exists as a kind of potential, as a *coming into being* of something dreadful. It is this 'coming into being' of danger, not the danger itself, that lies beyond the insecurity to which conventional security authorities, in Norway and elsewhere, respond with matter-of-factness.

I have no interest in this book in reproaching Norwegian security authorities for what they should have known but did not know – as reams of reports and political briefs have done over the course of the last decade – for not looking for answers where they could not know to look, for not asking meaningful questions about matters for which they could not plausibly have been curious or for not understanding that they did not know what they did not know, when there is no intelligible way of knowing that one does not know what one does not know. How can we expect a modern, rational, soberly managed, conscientiously organised social democratic bureaucracy to grasp dangers for which there is no extant evidence aside from what might gather in the near and far reaches of one's imagination?

Sense-making and informatisation: epistemological bureaucracy

Following Wittgenstein, we can, of course, only look for danger in a world already defined as one where there is danger. The tools and techniques of security goverannce, its principles and theories, concepts and data, both collected and stored and to be collected, have co-created the world of instrumental security threats if only by virtue of the fact that security thought takes place within an instrumental epistemological framework. It deploys rational scientific methods that enable it to study the objects governed by that reason, objects whose admission into the field of study are likewise governed by that reason. The limits of this field are organised and limited by the bureaucratic reason that polices them. As in most Western States, an epistemological bureaucracy governs both security research and the public policy about managing risk and security threats. By this I mean that security is understood to be a finite resource: we know what it is, where to get it, how to keep it and how to lose it. In the bureaucratic epistemology, we know how much security we have, how much we need, what it costs, what its trade-offs are.

Although one might expect that the field of study of the analytic tools of the system are defined by the objects in which it takes interest, it is in effect the analytic tools, logics, measures and methods that, in the very strongest ontological sense, create the objects of bureaucratic interest. The consequence for the work done in the pursuit of security is that only the threats that are expected to be detected are indeed detected. Scientific expectations are governed not by the empirical reality of the world but by the existing scientific reality, which consists of an assemblage of tools, technologies, institutions, culture and social, economic and political organisation (Kuhn, 1972; Latour, 1987; Stengers, 2000). The governance of security in any neoliberal democratic society is governed by a constellation of civil servants, public officials and private actors, operating under the more or less unquestioned certainty that the provision of security is to be assured through the application of concrete, finite, set tools, principles and procedures, itself embedded in the bureaucracy of the neoliberal State. This 'security bureaucracy' is, like the State bureaucracy mother ship, a complex system governed by a rationality of order, stability and predictability in the production, reproduction, of what is regarded as knowledge.

In his ground-breaking 1966 *The Order of Things*, Foucault first used the term *epistemē* to refer to the 'genealogical' context of knowledge, the principles that support it, the objectives that permit it to be applied, the methods used to affirm it, the teaching that transmits it, etc. (2002: xxiii, 336–419). This now classic concept can be applied to the way knowledge-based political action is enacted in harmony with the scientific premises of the modern State. Just as the scientifically and technologically validated foundation of the modern State assures conformity, predictability and, collaterally, the smooth functioning of the free market, the 'security *epistemē*' is characterised by uniformity and control of the institutionalised adjudicators of scientific knowledge and by distinct power structures that govern the reproducibility, redistribution and division of its outputs. It can be identified by semi-formal and regulated hierarchical procedures for decisions about the application of knowledge and closed circuits of authority and accountability with regard to the legitimacy of knowledge generated and consumed (Burgess, 2011: 2–4) This epistemological bureaucracy overshadows the organisational one, a theme we will return to in detail in the next chapter. The well-governed functions of a modern democratic bureaucracy cannot function in the absence of an equally well-governed organisation of the ecosystem of knowledge.

As noted above, security bureaucracy, like neoliberal bureaucracy in general, only sees what it is cultured, trained and equipped to see. The risks it detects and the uncertainties it manages are naturally those it is programmed to detect and manage. In the world of the neoliberal modern State, the key to bureaucratic accountability, stability, continuity, well-anchored hierarchies and continuity of authority is a stable platform of science and technology whose political incontestability was anchored in the post-war scientific miracle of progress, welfare and democracy.

The spirit of security

As Weber richly observed, the rise of bureaucracy is inseparable from the advancement of a certain kind of science, that is, the modern science that sprang forth at the dawn of the twentieth century from the new ethos of the laboratory and the seemingly endless innovations connected to the high era of industrialisation. The elements of the new scientific consciousness observed by Weber are the raw materials of the security bureaucracy and the tools and technologies of the instrumental governance of security. *Instrumental rationality* – the critique of which we will return to in detail in the next chapter – is a form of reason that functions as a means to its own end. It exists in order to fulfil its own aims, endemic to its goals. We would even be justified to claim that its aims are no more, no less, than its means.

Thus, on the one hand, there is no finality, no purpose or meaning beyond the execution of the operation for which it was conceived and, on the other hand, the purposefulness of modern science is to reaffirm the legitimacy of the social reality that invokes it. The conception of the tool is the conception of the completion of the work of the tool. The finitude of its meaning lies in the thought of its execution. In short, there is nothing outside of instrumental rationality. There is neither immanence nor transcendence. Instrumental security rationalities neither aspire to find *meaning*, nor are they equipped to find it. It is simply not proper to their epistemological disposition. We understand meaning as the referent or signified whose value, merit, sense or ultimate good surpass the concrete sign that refers to it. It is the significance or special quality of something, its worth, validity or value, import or essence. We typically say of objects of human purport that they have meaning: a painting, a poem, a story, a song, a building, a theatre play, but also more trivial items that touch our lives: the cufflinks my grandmother gave me, my first fountain pen, the morning light in the summer, the flavour of baklava, etc. In other words, the meaningful comprises any object of human experience that takes a special part of our consciousness. Some philosophers claim that this principle can and should apply to any object at all.

This book takes as a premise that this principle applies to *security*. Security touches us all; it is arguably the most intimate, the most personal, the most individual of qualities. It expresses what is more cherished to us, what we fear the most, we value. What we hope for, what we find abhorrent, what we will engage ourselves for. It should then come as a surprise that the security bureaucracy of any modern liberal State is conceived, constructed and executed in order to specifically not have meaning. In its scientific, bureaucratic forms, it is built to regard the correlates of security – the material, logistical, organisational, regulative measures – that are within their remit to turn to in order to operationalise the political injunctions that are given to them. They do not regard their tools as representations of future security, to be realised by human subjects. Indeed, they have no particular meaning at all. They are well embedded in Western liberal societies that proudly claim their modern humanism; they do not take humans, to borrow the Kantian formulation, as the finality of their action. There is no transcendental security that is within their reach either materially or spiritually. The spirit of security does not come into question in the execution of the bureaucratic function. The bureaucratic operational fulfilment is an end in itself.

This insight may come across like an indictment. It is not. The instrumental rationality inherent in any range of technologies is indispensable for any number of governance functions that require one form or another of self-effacing instrumental governance. My argument is that the provision of security is not among them. This book, thus, does not aim to deprecate or diminish the premises, processes and outcomes that are proper to the world of instrumental neoliberal bureaucracy, the measures taken, the principles applied or even the results obtained. It rather aims to ask what *happened* at Oslo/Utøya in the world beyond these confines: what happened in the world that these skilled and experienced agents of order did not consider, not because they in some way failed to, far from it, but rather because that world was not and is not their own. That world, the world of *meaning*, of danger, threat, risk and the vulnerabilities they co-determine, does not fall under the logic, the ethos or the ontology of the world as such, not only because it *should* not but because it *cannot*.

And yet, as we will see throughout the analysis, the frontier between these two worlds, these two ontologies, is a contested one, dotted with border skirmishes and incursions. The presence and tenacious insistence of this tension across the frontier between security governance, risk analysis and crisis management on the one hand and sense-making on the other is the anchoring and point of correlation of this book's fundamental argument: that meaning – at once rapturous and dark as a moonless night – and the reasoned management of the crisis that is somehow at its heart are ultimately inseparable. As much as I will argue to keep the worlds distinct, I will also have to admit that they are inseparable. At the same time, I will seek to ask what happened at Oslo/Utøya, in the security world *beyond* this one, beyond these metaphysical confines; what happened in the security world that these skilled and experienced agents of security did not, could not, consider, not because they failed to but because that security world was not, and is still not, their own.

In other words, this book asks: if the modern social welfare State is modelled on a notion of disinterested professionalism, how does it tackle the challenge of the horrendous catastrophe of mass terrorism? The case of the terrorist attack in Norway on 22 July 2011 presents itself as a test. Never before had an affect been generated that was so far away from the neutral, object and rational ethos of bureaucracy, and yet, it was the bureaucracy that received the bulk of the work of implementing societal security measures aimed at averting future terrorists and, not least, making sense of the terrorism of the recent past.

The book argues that the bureaucratic disenchantment of the Oslo/Utøya attacks, the narration of the events in terms of the bureaucratic reason, replaces the sense-making of interpretative humanising approaches, potentially capable of engaging with the spirit of security, and essentially prevents them from being *meaningful*. Instead of making sense of the attacks, the bureaucratisation of both the analysis of and the response to the attacks essentially results in an *unmaking* of sense. What is left in the narrative of terror today has neither to do with the intensely human experience of insecurity and uncertainty that constituted the attacks nor with the intensely human experience of security that was produced as a result of them. Again, it is crucial to underscore that the de-spiritualisation of the terror of Oslo/Utøya is not the trivial result of the indifference of agents of the State, of the sleepy complacence of bureaucratic agents nor of the blindness of technologically myopic security geeks. The conclusion that this book supports is that there simply is no discourse in which terror can be adequately narrated. There are neither words nor concepts nor rationality through which to adequately document the events, coherently carry out an analysis and meaningfully draw political conclusions. Yet, despite the operational absence of an enchanted spirit in the management of crisis and the analysis of Oslo/Utøya, sporadic signs of the original enchantment persist, emerging here and there in the discourses of political crisis management, without letting themselves be absorbed and homogenised by the bureaucratic rationality (see Stiegler, 2014). This book will aim to pick them up and weave them back into the story of terror. In order to do so, a clarification and critique of the historical concept of bureaucracy and its contemporary mutations are needed.

The evolution of bureaucratic rationality

The concept of bureaucracy has had an unusual life cycle in the twentieth century. It flourished in published literature during the late 1960s and 1970s. This was, as the late David Graeber explains it in *The Utopia of Rules*, a result of the rise of post-war social democracies, consolidated State-centred public administration and the growth of a certain scientificisation of administrative practices. Then, starting in 1973 and over the course of a decade or so, it declined considerably and, for the most part, disappeared altogether. Graeber proposes a double explanation for the rapid disappearance of the concept. The first argument points to the fact that starting in the 1970s, a marked decline in the principles and social and political institutions of social democracy, including its acute dependence on extensive bureaucratic norms and procedures, occurred in Western Europe. The second argument is that the principles hastily developed in the 1970s either became internalised in the everyday language of public management or were passed on to the myriad of private-sector actors who took over the traditional tasks of administering European social democracy through massive privatisations, tendencies that became mainstreamed and normalised in the course of the 1980s and 1990s (2016: 4–7).

While the origins of the concept of bureaucracy are somewhat unclear, its first of two nineteenth-century manifestations is often traced back to Marx's analysis of State bureaucracy in Hegel's *Philosophy of Right*, published in 1843–4. Marx identifies a distinct stratum in Hegel's analysis of the dialectical evolution of the modern State responsible for the administration of public affairs. At that point in the historical evolution of the State, the administration of justice assumed the more or less technical function of embodying, through the system of law, the moral character assumed to be condensed in the citizens, members of civil society (1991a: 240–58). It is this solidification of the administrative (or 'bureaucratic', as Marx famously expressed it) functions that became the unifying core of the State that prompted Marx to argue that the universal function of the administrative stratum is actually a false universal, one which imagines its serving of particular interests as serving the interests of all: 'The bureaucracy is ... the state's consciousness, the state's will, the state's power, as a corporation. ... [it] must thus defend the imaginary universality of particular interests, i.e. the corporation mind, in order to defend the imaginary particularity of the universal interests, i.e. its own mind' (1970: 46). In his analysis of the implicit structure of Hegel's State, Marx squarely situates the bureaucracy, the public administration, at the service of the dominant class. Bureaucracy is part of society but not in a general way that serves all equally. Its function is rather to express the configuration of power or domination in society, which at the same time makes it the useful target for suppression in the revolutionary struggle (Beetham, 1987: 78–9; Lefort, 1986: 90).

An entirely distinct but parallel view of bureaucracy's character and function is formulated in Weber's influential *Economy and Society*, published posthumously in 1922. Unlike Marx, who understands bureaucracy as a structure component of the State, Weber regards it far more as a problem of the architecture of 'domination and legitimacy'. Domination in Weber's view should be understood as one of three distinct types of power derived from economic power or authority, direct democracy or rule by notables or by organisational structure as the basis of legitimacy (2013: 941–54). These forms, Weber claims, form the rational basis for any legitimate domination of peoples in the organisation of rational governance. The 'typical' expression of '[r]ationally regulated association within a structure of domination', says Weber, 'finds its typical expression in bureaucracy', whereas traditionally prescribed social action corresponds to what Weber calls 'patriarchalism', and the 'charismatic' structure of domination is linked to individual authority uncoupled from both tradition and authority. The most familiar – and most rational – form of regulated association is 'modern bureaucratic association' (2013: 954).

Written nearly 100 years ago, Weber's pages on bureaucracy are stunningly precise in their description of the particular character of modern bureaucracies. Both in terms of its administrative structures and its relation to power and authority, legitimacy, rationality and knowledge, we can use the bureaucratic ideal type as a starting point for understanding Nordic post-industrial bureaucracies, even though the term has somewhat disappeared from the public discourse. Indeed, the word has only remained as a popular pejorative, with roots reaching back to the Marxist critique of the bureaucracy as an extension of an oppressive capitalist State. In Norwegian scholarly and official terminology, 'bureaucracy' has been supplanted with 'administration' or 'public administration', with the consequence that enmeshing of the bureaucrat and the object of his or her grip of bureaucratic power is tempered, and an association with a more impersonal servant of the people takes its place. By the same token, the notion of power has evolved and found new references and new expressions in the social sciences (Graeber, 2016).

From bureaucracy to disenchantment

Weber identifies a number of basic characteristics of modern bureaucracies. Their primary property is their clearly delimited 'jurisdictional areas': zones of influence, interaction and communication stipulated by clearly articulated laws, rules and regulations, which precede, structure and provide the overall organisational ethos for bureaucracy. These laws, rules and regulations not only regulate what takes place in the bureaucratic setting but, through the practice of jurisdictional regulation, they provide the very sense or meaningfulness of the regulating activity. It is not the rules that are in themselves meaningful but rather the fact that they provide the space for the emergence of meaningful activity. This means, in the case of the public sector, the meaningfulness of work in service of the State. Yet, these rules and regulations lay out not only what is required for meaningful activity but for any activity at all. The other central component of bureaucratic jurisdiction is, of course, the actual authority of the instance or person who pronounces the order. The bureaucracy also includes its own internal authority, giving the coordinated commands necessary to discharge the duties in a well-structured, properly distributed and stable way (2013: 956–8). The means of enacting the authority, and the forms of force, coercion or compulsion it might take, are thus, in Weber's view, embedded in any given bureaucratic logic. By the same token, it is indispensable for the continuous transformation of jurisdictional orders into operative bureaucratic functions that a set of concrete provisions be available for carrying out the order given by the authority with regularity and consistency. This first, jurisdictional structure is essentially the same for both public and private bureaucracies, though it takes different names and slightly different concrete forms.

To the determination of jurisdiction, Weber adds the prevalence of organisational hierarchy in bureaucracies. This includes a standard system of flows of both authority and appeal reaching in full continuity from one end of the organisation to the other. The presence of a firm internal hierarchy of authority is also key to the function of bureaucracy. In addition, the operationalisation of the authority through the institution's jurisdictional functions is essentially self-preserving by virtue of the presence of structures of self-maintenance such as protocols for the filling of vacancies, for succession and demission.

Bureaucracy also implies an entirely *material* dimension: files. The management of a modern bureaucracy, Weber points out, is based upon the existence and active use of 'written documents' and upon a staff of 'officials and scribes of all sorts' who are tasked with organising and managing a natural, hierarchical organisation of the creation, exchange and stockage of these documents. Indeed, Weber goes as far as to state that a 'bureau' is constituted by the collective apparatus of the material documentary infrastructure and the corps of officials working to directly accompany the documents, create and curate them, all within the constraints of a certain discourse of norms, standards, authorities and means. In short, what we might today, following Actor–Network Theory, call an 'assemblage'. In structural terms, there seems to be no reason to suggest that scriptural character of bureaucratic file-keeping should not extend in all its dimensions to the age of electronic communication and the advent of the digital document. The logic of the establishment, legitimacy, juridical force, stockage and exchange of digital files applies in every essential way to digital documents and files. Indeed, the natural expansion of the 'bureau' by digital means naturally extends the scope and reach of bureaucracy while maintaining its homogeneity.

Bureaucracy appears together with a specific form of *specialisation* of its component actors. The differentiation of the different elements of the structural hierarchy is itself determined and supported by the differentiation of expertise among the agents who occupy the nodes of the bureaucratic structure. It is essential that these agents work in full capacity. By this, he means that the bureaucrat is, by definition, not a clock-puncher: he or she is there to fulfil the vocation of the bureaucrat, a vocation which has no time, no temporality, on performance. Finally, the sixth characteristic is the operation of 'office rules', that is, a kind of internal jurisdictional logic that harmonises the task-level practices through a synthesis of certain management rules and guidelines.

The aforementioned components converge in what Weber considers to be a specifically modern form of politics, one which he experienced directly in the form of the Prussian social democracy of the end of the nineteenth century. In his analysis, bureaucracy took the unprecedented form of the fusion between social control and hierarchical organisation. Of course, the function of social control, and even the imposition of social norms, was well understood and documented by observers of the early modern public sphere. A decisive contribution is the step towards what Foucault calls the *homo œconominus* – 'one who is eminently governable' (2010: 274; Laval, 2019: 62–7). The *homo œconominus*, like the neoliberal subject, is characterised by its malleability. It is one that has suffered what Weber calls the 'disenchantment of the world' (2004: 13), the detachment of human experience from a certain kind of human value. The path towards this detachment is modern science, which turns the individual away from a spiritual experience of value, one based in metaphysical, 'enchanted' sources of meaning and significance, towards a rationalised form of value, one properly epitomised by the rise and generalisation of a new form of validation, a new way of making sense of the world, ascribing meaning and understanding our place in relation to it:

> Thus the growing process of intellectualization and rationalization does not imply a growing understanding of the conditions under which we live. It means something quite different. It is the knowledge or the conviction that if only we wished to understand them we could do so at any time. It means that in principle, then, we are not ruled by mysterious, unpredictable forces, but that, on the contrary, we can in principle control everything by means of calculation. That in turn means the disenchantment of the world. Unlike the savage for whom such forces existed, we need no longer have recourse to magic in order to control the spirits or pray to them. Instead, technology and calculation achieve our ends. This is the primary meaning of the process of intellectualization. (2004: 12–13)

Because of the new mode of scientific thought – 'intellectualization and rationalization' – we are no longer required to surrender before the mysteries of the world as did our predecessors. The world has been disenchanted, demystified, through the advent of science. But at what cost? Weber wisely draws attention to the fact that we are not witness to some kind of triumph of scientific rationality now capable of mastering, thus demystifying, the world that was once a mystery. It is not the wisdom of science that has grown to overpower the world. On the contrary, it is the world that has been reconceived in our day as that which lets itself be mastered by scientific rationality. It is no longer that we define ourselves in relation to reality;

rather, we define reality in relation to ourselves. Social reality is redrawn, restructured, reconceived according to the rationality of scientific logic. That logic, as Foucault develops in *The Birth of Biopolitics* and elsewhere, is the logic of economic calculability – neoliberalism (Dean, 2010; Foucault, 2010; Reid, 2013; Sparke, 2006).

Liminal analysis and the terror event horizon

This book will therefore seek to contribute to the analysis of terrorism as a phenomenon by focussing on the frontier between the world of bureaucratic security sensibility and the enchantment of collective meaning. It proceeds by confronting the presumed hermetic integrity of this border between these two ideas. As with any border, signs of leakage begin to appear, hinting at how very problematic the opposition between inside and outside relative to the problems of reference inevitably is. These signs and indices reveal not only the co-penetration and mutual contamination of any two opposed fields or worlds; they both, more importantly, define themselves and anchor their realities precisely in relation not to themselves but to the frontier and to what lies beyond it.

Euclidean geometry teaches us that the line drawn as a frontier between two fields does not, strictly speaking, exist as a substance or a being beyond its function of correlating two points (neither of which can belong to the line). In the same way, the experience of catastrophe, and of the frontier that governs the ontological difference between the world of catastrophe as the making of horrific meaning and catastrophe as a terminology for analytic explanation, reveals to us a 'thick' frontier, a dividing line. This zone is rich with depth and breadth, a heterogeneous symbolic space governed by antagonistic sources and discourses about what the world consists of and what reason organises the changes that shape it in its evolution through time. Indeed, the ontological frontier that marks the opposition between the catastrophe as meaning and the analysis of the catastrophe by the security bureaucracy – as a reduction to instrumental logic and practice – is so deep and broad that it expands to envelop the instrumental world like the billowing cloud of pulverised cement coursing at the speed of sound through the streets of lower Manhattan on the morning of 11 September 2001, filling every space with the horror of what was happening, leaving just enough air for those who were still breathing to reassert and reinflate the space where instrumental reason pushed back the intruding calamity.

This book is an attempt to condense the complex experiences and political processes of technical translation between agencies and authorities, technical reviews and ideological adaptation, analysis, negotiation and action. What we interpret in our analysis as the collapse of spiritual or moral sense-making through bureaucratic sense-making must follow complex and highly nuanced transfers and dispersions of the spirit. It will also have to contend with the profound matter of the 'disappearance' of human spirit through processes of security bureaucratisation. The process can be best described through a well-known metaphor, that which astronomers call the 'event horizon'.

The term refers to a range of paradoxes and experiences stemming from the fact that information cannot, according to the theory of special relativity, travel faster than the speed of light. Any event that takes place while moving away from an observer at close to or in excess of the speed of light can never be known to us because information will never reach us. It will never become an event for us. Its 'eventuality' lies beyond a horizon, the event horizon. In the case of black holes, whose gravitational force is so strong that they draw in light itself, a certain horizon thus appears beyond which neither information nor any other form of influence or causality can reach. There are thus phenomenological 'non-events' beyond this horizon. Taking some metaphorical liberties, a catastrophe, such as Oslo/Utøya, similarly lies beyond a kind of metaphorical event horizon.

The catastrophic in the catastrophe, the terror in the terrorism, is produced not by the 'facts' of the event that reach our senses and are processed by our brains but rather by virtue of its excess – following the metaphor of the event horizon, by virtue of the excessive intensity of its taking place. The force of terrorism is not ultimately derived from the aggregation of a given number of concrete, definable, limited facts, any one of which, or together which, creates the effect of terror – we read and hear about these every day. There are shootings and bombings, flooding and drought, food shortages and disease, internet attacks and internet failures. What marks Oslo/Utøya and other events like it is that it was not thinkable and thus not possible. It was effectively beyond the possible, beyond the conceivable, beyond the imaginable. This impossibility was the explosive spiritual force that, while not seeking to trivialise the harm and damage done by the physical attacks, nonetheless dwarfed the damage caused by the 950-kilogram bomb or the hundreds of rounds fired by the terrorist on Utøya. These same individual, concrete events are today thinkable, thus possible, envisageable, and thereby through the perverse logic of terror, they will never happen again; they are impossible.

However, at Oslo/Utøya, the exact collusion of facts, people, places, ideas, traditions, values and symbols did not, could not, would never have converged to form an event. Oslo/Utøya lay beyond the event horizon – the imagination of such a convergence of ideas and acts, humans and facts, that the imaginary gravitational force of its darkness sucked away the spiritual substance of the event – in its factual executability, which, as it happens, was well within the reach of the skills and ambitions of an intellectually and morally mediocre suburban drifter – beyond the event horizon.

And yet, it became an event. Indeed, it became multiple, even countless, continuous events still unfolding. It was experienced, conceptualised and acted upon as though its existence was self-evidently finite. Individuals – victims, family members, loved ones, friends, acquaintances, compatriots, fellow humans – lived the event, struggling to make sense of it, from the first inkling of violence. Collective groups – the AUF youth organisation, associations and clubs, local organisations, circles of friends – all experienced associated but distinct events. Government officials – the Prime Minister, Cabinet members, Parliament – took up and carried again a different event. All of these subjects of the event lived, negotiated and told the story of the violent transition from an event beyond the event horizon to one that rushed into the channels of their imaginaries, attached itself to the signs and symbols through which they make sense of life and actuated the levers of their enlightened reason permitting them to respond, sometimes humbly, sometimes arrogantly and forcefully, to the question of *what to do*.

This book tries to plot that conversion from non-event to event, from cataclysm to two-feet-on-the-floor-and-get-out-of-bed everydayness. Western philosophy has long grappled with what I am calling the non-event, the experience of excess that defies the senses, of an act so unnatural that it upsets nature, of a thought so horrifying that it upsets reason.

If security bureaucracy functions by disenchanting terrorism, neutralising its meaning by bringing it under the power of its reason, then this analysis aims at the re-enchantment of meaning in bureaucratic disenchantment of the events. It attempts to move into the world of disenchanted crisis management, not to re-enchant it like a hapless missionary but to follow the hypothesis and the hunch that the disenchanted experience of terrorism is energised by a dark but enchanted force of possibility.

Conventional theories of security take as their objective to make sense of security threats and nourish the formulation or reformulation of appropriate counter-measures against potential future threats. They seek to conceptualise and explain the measures taken in the past, the discourse and arguments engaged in order to face perceived dangers. This book, by contrast, does not aim to address future dangers but rather begins where the catastrophe left off. It begins with the catastrophic event, the attacks by a Norwegian right extremist in Oslo/Utøya on 22 July 2011, in order to analyse how security and risk are understood and managed when the worst has already happened. I propose in what follows a *post-security theory*, a theory of lost, or failed, security, a theory to explain how security can be envisaged after the moment of radical insecurity, how actors and objects are understood, how loss is unaccounted for, justified, moralised, in the immediate wake of all these traditional principles of what security actually is having been severely shaken, if not destroyed. This book tells the story of a security reboot, a politically tenuous, logistically distressing, morally ambiguous and spiritually heart-wrenching second thought of what is important, what should be protected, what is dispensable and exactly what is indispensable to those who were touched by the crime. It analyses the attempt to address something that it is too late to address. This book attempts to answer a tacit invitation to answer the question: what are we doing when we are doing security? What is a threat and what or who is actually threatened? What does it mean to threaten something that counts? What is it that counts? Beyond the slogans and political clichés, what does it mean to say that a national way of life is under threat? The answers to these questions and others make up a theory of security for *when the worst has already happened*. When having nothing left to secure means, paradoxically, having everything still to secure.

Three methodological conundrums

Three methodological conundrums present themselves in working through the research and reflection behind this book.

The *first* methodological conundrum concerns the exemplarity of the Norwegian case. Does one set of isolated and undoubtedly unique experimental findings permit us to draw general conclusions about the experience of terrorism and the transformation of that experience into operational conclusions, conclusions that could be deployed in the service of the prevention or dissuasion of a repetition of the same attack? Surely not. By any social scientific methodological standard, a theory cannot rest on one set of data and one operational conclusion alone. Indeed, a theory cannot rightly be called a theory if it can only be used once – even less so when its unique window of application lies in the past. I consequently cannot in this book lay claim to the establishment of a theory of terrorism. And yet from a meta-theoretical point of view, this affirmation offers a discovery of its own. If the necessary condition of terrorism in its ideal form is that it cannot be presaged, cannot be imagined or even thought, then the fundamental quality of terrorism – beyond the materiality of the death and destruction it causes – is its imagined impossibility, or perhaps the impossibility of imagining it. In other words, the condition of theorising terrorism is the ability to ascertain that it cannot be theorised. Terrorism cannot be condensed into a theory that would grant it, following scientific methodological ideas, predictive powers. To claim that this book seeks to formulate a theory of terrorism would be the equivalent of saying that it is not *about* terrorism.

The *second* methodological conundrum arises from the insight that what I qualitatively wish to conceptualise as the ontology of terrorism – the world that was created, then extinguished, at 3:25 p.m. on 22 July 2011 – does not consist of substantive qualities. If it were to be described in positivist terms, it could only be in terms of negatives, of collapses of the qualities, the rationale, the metrics and the discourse that at present permit us to identify a phenomenon in scientific terms. Terrorism can only rightly be described as one form or another of the eclipse of reason, the collapse of morality, the destruction of value, the denaturalisation of nature, the pulverisation of aesthetics, etc.

The *third* conundrum involves the problem of bridging between the two ontologies I have just described. To be clear, bridging the experience of terror and its operational theorisation was not our idea; it was the nonchalant ambition of the bureaucratic neoliberal State, and it will be the concrete objective of this book to interrogate the State about exactly how it intends to do this. This is not a book about rationality but about pathos, not about the pathos associated with the immense loss suffered at Oslo/Utøya, though that would be a right and important task for a study to come. Rather, it is about the pathos of trying to transform terror into hard, instrumental science, the only kind of bureaucratic science there is. It is about trying to express an experience, take action upon an experience when there are no words and there are no actions. It attempts to generously but critically give an account of the unforgiving and thankless task faced by political leaders, policy-makers and public officials to pronounce, first, 'what happened' in operational terms and, second, the 'what do we know about it' in epistemological terms. The moral drama of this book consists in observing as though in a drama of Ancient Greece, the actors of the play, honest, moral, competent, dignified and worthy, striving to formulate the best response to a question which, tragically, by the will of the capricious gods, has no answer. This third conundrum, teetering as a construction of one of the first two, is what this book essentially aims to describe.

Part I

Theory of disenchantment

1

Terror and disenchantment

> It was a way of recognizing places of enchantment:
> people falling asleep like this.
> Franzen (2010)

Oslo/Utøya didn't happen

Terrorism exceeds us, not only as an experience that conjures phenomena so rarely thought of that they test the limits of our imagination but also as a kind of political action that demands the expansion of our everyday political concepts and the scope of admissible political actions. We are *never* prepared for terrorism, neither intellectually, ethically, spiritually or emotionally. Terrorism rattles all these platforms: world views, political concepts, values and affective experiences. It exceeds what we know and blows the fuses of our experiential circuits. It thrusts upon us emotional evidence that what we are capable of understanding falls far short of what is real. It destabilises our attachment to our perceptions and puts into question the rational processes by which we govern our lives. It scrambles our childish, limited conception of what devastation can mean, the scope of violence that is actually possible and the depth of the fear and anguish that these existential disorientations are capable of producing. The ensemble of categories we use to *understand* the world, the rational and emotional charts we keep and use to navigate the waters of our experience of the world, our stock of well-travelled moods and feelings, the moral pathways we have repeatedly followed, the ruts of our civilisational habits, refined and polished in order to sensibly manage our experience-based judgement of the beneficent and the horrific, and our aesthetic discernment of the beautiful and the hideous. In other words, from the point of view of experience and ready-at-hand concepts adequate to capture it, Oslo/Utøya didn't happen at all.

As a consequence, the 'security work', so often evoked in the gently pragmatic approaches to danger taken by official Norwegian security policy-makers and practitioners, means ordinary citizens are forced to generate explanations, categorisations, operational and political responses, juridical actions, social measures to a phenomenon that as yet had no reality for them, 'the thought of what is not thought' (Rancière, 2009: 14). Neither the wealth of political and historical studies of terrorist atrocities, nor the interminable ivory tower controversies about the empirical attributes of the phenomenon of terrorism, nor the countless volumes of analysis of actual terrorist attacks can raise us to the point of cracking this uncrackable kernel. The crux of the matter, the invisible force that arrests us and leaves us dumbfounded before the object of study, lies precisely in the fact that both academic 'terrorism studies' and policy-orientated analysis indeed treat terrorism as exactly that: a nut to be cracked. It is an object that is clearly at hand in the present and the past, governed by rational, if occult, mental algorithms connecting research inputs with research outputs. These all take for granted, conceptually and pragmatically, the cessation of terrorism, letting this end point, this sunset of terrorism studies, shape both thought and action, the legitimate world view according to which the end of terror is a simple function of its existence, and then of its having existed. According to this quixotic view, once the correct counter-terrorist recipe can be identified, mass-produced and globally deployed, terrorism will disappear without a trace.

What we indeed find if we only scratch the surface of this pretence is that terror's excess, in effect, obeys none of these logics and responds to none of the remedies that might potentially be derived from them. This is because it exceeds *causal rationality*, leaving us only with the heart-breaking imaginary, the unbearable aesthetic and the moral eschatology in order to diagnose terrorism and to prescribe remedies that will have a predictable and dependable impact on the ambition of hindering it. It exceeds the *aesthetic* parameters that we commonly apply in order to understand a phenomenon as undesirable, unpleasant or unwanted. And, finally, it exceeds the *ethical* parameters, the virtuous, refined intelligence and the presumed purity of the *res cogitans*, the thinking being, nestled safely in complete Cartesian distinction from the body and its affective range of expressions. These are the three terms – rationality, aesthetics and ethical affect – whose collapse in the experience of terrorism it is the aim of this book to capture with the term *disenchantment*.

Disenchantment is the name we give to the process by which the unthinkable is made thinkable. The process takes many different shapes and forms but happens on every level of society, each with its own force and momentum, each with its own degree of imbrication with existing structures, each with its interaction with existing cultural ethos and mood. This book's aim, both in theory-building and practical analysis of Oslo/Utøya, is to develop an understanding of *disenchantment* that better accounts for the inevitably self-referential and self-serving political analysis that studies what is not starting from what is. This book responds in admitted clumsiness, by attempting to study what is *not* on the basis of what *is*, in both cases: *security*.

By essentially all common-sense accounts – excluding those of the decision-makers actually tasked with managing security in the public interest – security is only loosely related to scientific and administrative rationality. And yet we have no alternative but to cling to the shaky scientific rationality that is the heartbeat of the modern Welfare State, disregarding or disdaining the beauty, ethical substance and spirit that ultimately provide us with an unexplainable ability to resist it.

It is uncontroversial to claim that the experience of terrorism is dreadful, terrifying, horrendous, atrocious, etc. Yet, somehow, we quickly gain a sense that this list of always inadequate terms for the unthinkable could go on and still we would not capture the experience. Without undertaking a quantitative analysis of the discourse of testimonies of terror, the arc of such cliché-trodden, identifiable chains of superlatives for what is witnessed when terrorism is witnessed hints towards something unspeakable, unfathomable, unimaginable, incomprehensible, etc. In short, the experience of terrorism as described through the testimony of its victims and its immediate witnesses tends to be one that is not a simple object of experience. Rather, it is the experience of something that cannot be experienced, that surpasses experience, surpasses all measure of concepts and all character of description, all measures of value, aesthetics or reason (see Heath-Kelly et al., 2014). It is *anti-experience*.

The political question that immediately follows the assertion of an oddity like 'anti-experience' is: what kind of pragmatic consequences does this non-experiential experience of terrorism have? What kinds of measures can or should be taken against it? What reaction should we have taken at Oslo/Utøya? What kind of reaction should we expect or demand of public authorities in the future? Can or should our security officials be held to account for an event that surpassed what can reasonably be expected to be expected? Should authorities be obliged to anticipate and prepare for what exceeds us, for what erupts beyond our own expectations, escapes any imagination of what could possibly become reality, generates horrors beyond what we think possible, causes pain beyond our experience of pain, overturns any norms of civility that we might have nurtured and surpasses what we thought to be the abominable?

Thus from a certain, admittedly esoteric, ontological point of view, a terrorist event does not happen. Since it is not registered in our stock of memories, nor in the catalogue of our planning for the future, nor in the logistical scenarios responsibly prepared by our bureaucracies of security, not even in the library of our imaginations, how can it be said to happen? The answer is that the events of Oslo/Utøya are qualified as 'terrorist' exactly *because* they could never happen, because they were beyond the scope of what was thinkable. This is, of course, tragically, *why they took place*. They took place precisely because they were impossible. Had they been firmly lodged in our experience of the past or in any probable or imaginable scenario of the future, they would not have had the same terrorising force, security officials would not have been to such an extent unprepared for them and the sensibilities of those touched by them would not have been so stricken, so stung or so scarred by them. As we will see, myriad cycles of reproaches and recriminations of the North Buskerud Police Department, the Delta Special Forces Unit, the National Police, the military, the Ministry of Justice, did not, will never, erase the metaphysical reality of the double attack: that it terrorised because it was simply not regarded as possible.

Moreover, all the 'after-work', which forms the empirical object of this book, falls blithely into the same paradoxical imperative of planning for the impossible. Swept along by political forces that wash against the boat whose *spiritual* – not logistical – buoyancy, in the immediate wake of the double attack and beyond, saved the Norwegian people from themselves, the Norwegian bureaucracy has set about – as only a rational, well-organised and responsible democracy can – arduously, meticulously, rigorously preparing for the future terrorist event that will, alas, *never take place*. Oslo/Utøya will never happen again because a recurrence would contradict the metaphysical paradox of any terrorist attack: it will never, ever happen again because it has already happened once. The ineffable force of Oslo/Utøya sprang precisely from its ineffability. Paradoxically, Oslo/Utøya, in the form in which it happened, is now henceforth *impossible* precisely because we now know it was *possible*. This book tries to capture this strange, even paradoxical, being-in-excess of terrorism by examining the work of the conceptual, bureaucratic, cultural, moral and spiritual aftermath of Norwegians following Oslo/Utøya.

Disenchantment and mourning

In a famous article published nearly a century ago, Freud distinguished between 'mourning' and 'melancholy'. His aim in the short article was to clarify two distinct, though at times interdependent, psychic reactions to cataclysmic loss. 'Mourning', he explains, is the reaction to the loss of a loved one or to the abstraction that has taken its place. 'Melancholy', by contrast, is more complex: it is in part characterised by the loss of a cherished object but complicated by loss of a more 'ideal' kind. In some cases, the object is not completely lost; in others, one believes it to be lost when it is not entirely lost. It is, in Freud's terms, 'an object-loss which is withdrawn from consciousness, in contradistinction to mourning, in which there is nothing about the loss that is unconscious' (Freud, 1953: 243–6). For this reason, the melancholic, in contrast to the mere mourner, is taken to be suffering from a mental condition, characterised by self-reproach, self-critique and ambivalence about his or her own ego.

The opposition between mourning and melancholy can help us to understand the fundamental characteristics of the experience of terrorism, particularly in the case of Oslo/Utøya. Certainly, the aftermath of any terrorist attack is characterised by the concrete loss of irreplaceable human lives, objects of material value, practices and symbols and images. Much is lost. The work of grief over this loss, to use Freud's opposition, would commonly be carried out in terms of mourning. The object of loss is finite, identifiable, characterisable, recognisable, understandable. These are objects of consciousness whose loss we can regret and reflect upon, gradually realising their loss, condensing them into cherished memories, objects of conscious longing, irreplaceable, yet graspable, entities. As such, they are processed through mourning, considered and cherished, tensions resolved, meaning totalised, all to be tucked away as memory; their meaning and the emotions they provoke are our own. This is surely part of the grief experience of terrorism.

The problem is that terrorism makes grieving impossible. It disrupts precisely those cultural, religious, spiritual and moral ties that are required in order to grieve, to establish and nurture a relationship to what is absent. The experience of disorientation relative to a lost object is what we call *disenchantment*. Beyond the loss of human lives, and material objects, something more is lost, something unresolved, something whose essence we struggle to grasp. Our relation to this loss is ambivalent. It contains elements of identity, a story about who we were and never can be again, a story about who we have become, having passed through the alienating and violent sensory experience of terrorism; it contains components of a self-image, how we thought and now think we were seen by others and how we will never appear to them again. It contains a component of some complex constellation of our relationship to our finitude, our vulnerability or insecurity, both alone and collectively. It contains the traces of a naiveté or self-certainty, perhaps weakened, about our ability to defend ourselves, both individually and collectively, about what it means to defend ourselves, what exactly we defend when we defend 'ourselves', about where our vulnerabilities come from and about how and what they expose, about what is valuable to us and was valuable before in terms of a targeted attack, about where it hurts not only to be exposed but to learn, too late, always too late, that we were wrong about thinking we were secure. Forever changed in ways we cannot understand. This is the ambivalence of terrorism's melancholy. It is within this complex of ambivalent loss that we will search for insights in terms of *disenchantment*.

In her 2009 *Frames of War: When Is Life Grievable?*, Judith Butler circumnavigated what remained of that cross-section of post-Foucauldian biopolitics literature that still regarded some kind of 'normal' life – even one that itself is the product of one form or another of subjectification – as the plenum for understanding urgency, emergency, state of exception, etc. The biopolitical anthem 'making live, letting die' can only be considered coherent on the assumption that something called 'life' is fully alive, fully existent, present, centred around itself, morally and biologically sustainable, self-initiating.

An authentic thought of life can only be accomplished by thinking the thought of its end. The end of life, and thus the precariousness of life in the present, is thus implicit in life. Butler has gone so far as to argue, in *Precarious Life*, the book that immediately preceded *Frames of War*, that vulnerability is primordial, that fragility precedes the self, individuation and the 'I' (2004: 31). We can thus only conceive of life in the future anterior, through which:

> 'A life has been lived,' is presupposed at the beginning of a life that has only begun to be lived. In other words, 'this will be a life that will have been lived' is the presupposition of a grievable life, which means that this will be a life that can be regarded as a life, and be sustained by that regard. (2009: 15)

Already at the beginning of life, we are mourning the life that is not yet lived but rather 'will have been lived'. If Butler's ontological analysis of grievability of life as a kind of account of life far before it has a chance to be lived outpaces Freud, it shares with him a sense for what he calls the melancholic: the *irrecoverable* loss, the origin or meaning of life that cannot be adequately reconstructed because its meaning, if we can all it that, precedes the subject position from which meaning can be ascertained. The melancholy is so deep, so distant, that it has lost the very referent of its own melancholy. Any experience of life is, as fresh and new as it may be, sullied by the very uncertainty of its being.

I will attempt to document and cast light on the complex ambivalence of disenchantment by charting the official reactions to Oslo/Utøya, first, in the minutes, hours and days of the aftermath, then, through a more elongated analysis of the political reaction throughout the months and years that followed. I will begin with the immediate responses and political statements, look forward to the appointment of the 22 July Commission tasked with carrying out a one-year independent investigation of the events of the day, then widen and lengthen the analysis to examine how Norwegian officials understood the events and the horizon they presented, and gradually mutated, for carrying out politics in the name of Norway, Norwegian society and the Norwegian people. In order to do this work of overcoming the past, a kind of historical grieving, we have to let terrorism lose its power, its sinister magic, its terrifying other-worldly power. We have to let it be disenchanted. In so doing, we will never be able to study it, process it and grieve the loss it provokes. We will not be able to see the excesses it rests upon: beyond reason, beyond judgement, beyond emotions.

Terror and neoliberal violence

In exceeding our experiential boundaries, terror also exceeds our concept of violence. Terror most often takes the form of physical violence, but it is, as we know, more than physical violence, more than force applied with the aim of causing a specific type of material damage, physical pain, abuse or destruction. Such violence is disruptive, to be sure, destabilising, disconcerting and disorientating. But what does it disrupt? To answer this question, we must look more closely at the material and immaterial character of disruption.

A disruption intervenes in a continuity. It breaks, in one way or another, a continuous stream of substance, something substantial, something significant, something valuable, essential and real. It shatters and breaks the trajectories of our minds, our hearts, and in the worst case, our lives. In the socio-economic context, this notion of the continuity of value – and its potential disruption – has been widely thematised as the core function of neoliberalism. The continuity of flow of economic value is supported by the neoliberal value chains of late capitalism, the near universally institutionalised and virtually omnipresent system of norms and governance ever imagined. Neoliberalism is a complex and contested concept that emerges from century-long processes, beginning in the birth of the modern individual as the primary object of the benevolence of God and the beneficiary of natural law (Siedentorp, 2014: 208–24). The primordiality of liberty of the individual has dominated the evolution of Western culture since it was formulated in the philosophies of Hobbes and Locke, and became the guiding principle of modern market economics through the contrasting adaptations of Smith and Ricardo into basic premises for the general theorisation of economics in the industrial age. If the political, cultural, social and moral shocks of World War I threw into crisis classical economics, it was reshaped through post-war economic theories (the ordoliberalism of the 1940s, Hayek's evolutionism in the 1940s and Friedman's monetarism in the 1970s). With the quantitive innovations of New Public Management, it was transformed, in part through the audaciousness of Thatcherism and Reaganism, into a perfect storm of ideology, economics and control.

Dillon and Reid, among others, have shown how political violence has become not only a feature of late-modern society but its constitutive feature. The classical philosophy of liberalism has been transformed into a means of rule. The explicit primordiality of the circulation of value has transcended its original application to the governance of material values, goods, services, labour, etc. to an all-encompassing focus on the governance of life (Dillon & Reid, 2009: 15–18). Life has become 'informationalised', with the result that the flow of human value is optimised (54–9). In his remarkable analysis of the attacks of 11 September 2001, Reid reaches the pivotal insight that terrorism itself is not a phenomenon that appears as a response to neoliberalism, or even an external enabler, but rather that it emerges from its very logic. Terror can thus be understood 'not as a force born from outside the orbit of liberal modernity but … as very much a product of the development of liberal modernity' (Reid, 2006: 87).

One of the keys to maintaining this equilibrium of flow in our neoliberal societies is to enable and maintain the insight that 'equilibrium' in the global terror imaginary is not obtained by eliminating violence but rather by *internalising* it in such a way so as to make it align and harmonise with neoliberal social, economic and political norms and ends (Neal, 2008, 2012). Neoliberal violence is not merely structural in the sense exposed by Galtung in the 1960s as part of a comprehensive philosophy of peace but rather the very precondition of the equilibrium (Galtung, 1990). By this argument, and despite the considerable pathos released by the catastrophe of Oslo/Utøya, the underlying flow of continuous value that is the most stable, and yet the most sensitive to disruption, is that of the neoliberal value system that supports the Western model of living (see Brown, 2015; Zamora, 2016).

In addition to the mechanisms of domination in neoliberal societies born of the fusion of ideology, economics and governance, violent extremism is dependent upon neoliberalism in more concrete ways (Striegher, 2015). We know that certain extremists have claimed that their campaigns are provoked by and directed against liberal modernity and its decadence. Among these is the perpetrator of Oslo/Utøya (Carle, 2013; Richards, 2014). They see liberal institutions as objects of a campaign of emancipation, and violence as the only way to transcend the failure of democracy. Second, violent extremism is, from a logistical point of view, made possible by the nature of the liberal open society. The free access, free circulation, freedom of expression and, not least, availability of a range of goods have certainly been crucial for plotting and carrying out virtually all the extremist violence of recent memory. Yet, somehow, these explanations do not go far enough since they do not answer the question of how extremist ideas and violent extremism can emerge in the name of liberal democracy (Chalk, 1995, 1998; Dunne,

2009; Wilkinson, 2006). What indeed is the difference between 'extremism' and 'violent extremism'? Are they natural or accidental partners?

Three intermediate observations about violent extremism must be made at the outset of any answer to this question. First, no argument claiming violence as a necessary and unavoidable means to advance society's ends can, in the end, be coherent. This is because violence as an end is at odds with society as an end. Second, violence cannot coherently and adequately promote any views, let alone extreme views. Violence simply does not communicate doctrines or messages. Third, violence can never go far enough. There is not enough violence in the world to overcome the dissent that will be generated by the violence. The economy of societal violence is an open, not a closed, one (see Žižek, 2008).

Nonetheless, for better or worse, these questions remain purely philosophical. Violence, in a large number of its forms, among these terrorism, is already illegal, already thoroughly dealt with by police and investigative agencies. It is also important to note that a certain kind of extremism corresponds with an acute need for unity and coherence. Extremism dismisses compromise. It sees impurity in compromise, an acceptance of moral or technical standards that are beneath those that a given matter is worthy of. Violent extremism dialogues with no one and nothing. Despite the perception of perpetrators that they are 'sending a message', violence is neither a language nor a message. We can talk of violent language, we can talk of a message of violence and we can even talk about a violent message. In a certain narrow sense, it is true that language can do violence; and we must also admit that, in general, language and social relations channel power. Nonetheless, violence does not, in itself, communicate, because its target is the subjective, human relations that make language, communication and social relations possible at all (Jayakumar, 2019).

What measures are available to society to address extreme violence? To what extent is the unthinkable violence of Oslo/Utøya, following Reid, Dillon and others, the product, and not the antithesis, of neoliberal Norway? What is it that threatens such an idyllic society? How do the mundane powers of everyday Norwegian values, clearly embodied by the perpetrator of Oslo/Utøya, transmute into the unthinkable, the unthought Norwegians and many others? How can a harmonious plan society, a model of the Welfare State by any measure, transform unimaginable, literally unimaginable, violence? And how can security of heart and mind – Norwegians might call this *sjelefred* – be constructed on this unthinkable foundation. The dilemma is disconcerting: either we admit that the unthinkable is possible and thus lies somewhere, sometime on our horizon, or we reconstruct a security ethos based on the patently illogical assumption that what happened, the unthinkable, was impossible, and thus need not be fully planned for.

In order to answer this question, we need to take one step back. The most general background for the emergence of violent extremism from liberalism on a more or less global scale is a certain kind of globalisation of security and insecurity. As we will see in detail in Chapter 2, near the end of the Cold War, we began to see a shift in the way security was experienced in Western societies. Instead of a global preoccupation with the East Bloc/West Bloc ideological battle for national security, the concept of security began to take on new meaning on a number of levels, from the individual and local group level to regional and transnational group level. Horizontally, an array of thematic understandings of security and insecurity, from religious security to identity security, food security, health security, etc., became visible. The 1994 *Human Development Report* famously launched the concept of *human security*, providing the first of a number of institutional arrangements that would support and advance this new way of understanding security (UNDP, 1994).

The consequences of this significant paradigm shift have been slow but clear in coming. During the Cold War, the threats to our security were threats to the sovereignty of the nation-state and sovereignty was the primary mode of understanding the right to security. Threats were external: they came from outside a border, outside a wall or window. Today, certain globalisation processes have led us to a situation where this model no longer holds. Today, threats are among us. They surround and penetrate us. The next health crisis is already brewing in our midst, climate change touches entire regions, pollution is not limited to national interest areas and the most feared terrorists are the homegrown ones. Insecurity has become a challenge to society because it has become a product of our society. The challenges to our security do not come from outside but rather from within society. It is by being who we are, perfecting the ideals of the modern liberal society, that we become complicit in our own insecurity. It is in this logic that we must locate terrorism of the kind experienced in Norway at Oslo/Utøya for violent extremism is the ultimate *reflexive* social problem for liberal society. Violent extremism must be considered as a symptom of our own society and not as some foreign aberration.

What, then, can be the political response to the insecurity caused by violent extremism? We live in a world far beyond the Cold War logic of prevention and protection, of security understood as an effort directed towards an enemy that we seek to keep our society free from. It can no longer be a question of keeping our societies clear of the dangers that threaten them. For the threats are already here, already present. They are indeed the necessary by-product of our own societies.

Preventing unthinkable terrorism is seemingly not an option, both for empirical and for principled reasons. We must not seek to restructure our societies so that dangers are kept outside or somehow ghettoised. Our political objectives must revolve far more around living with dangers and developing societal resilience against them. Indeed, to purify our societies from terrorism, to eliminate all danger of terrorist attacks, exclude foreign menaces, is only to repeat the extremist logic and gesture at the heart of terrorism, the very one that cancels the principles of liberal society. In line with the changes in our world, we need to update our views on what it means to secure our societies: instead of a logic of 'us' against 'them', a more realistic approach would focus on the relation between society and the inner dangers it is required to harbour in order to be itself, in order to remain liberal, tolerant and free.

Thinkable and unthinkable violence

It is a trivial tautology to assert that nothing can be thought about the unthinkable. And yet, from the unthinkable events of Oslo/Utøya, experienced analysts, engineers and technicians, psychologists and medical doctors, forensic scientists, military experts, police investigators, historians, political scientists, risk analysts, security specialists and many others, even before the dust had settled over the quiet forest of Utøya and the empty streets of Oslo, resolved to take on the arduous task of documenting and, above all, trying to *understand* what had happened.

The production of scientific knowledge, political analysis, police policy and public debate skyrocketed in the weeks and months after the attacks. Investigative questioning in various degrees of desperation and clear-headedness spanned the range of human emotions, from the concrete and mundane – 'how did the radio link to police car X fail at moment Y?' (C-REX, 2022) – to the all-embracing, despondent – 'why us?'. The questions multiplied, evolved, flowed, disseminated, generating sub-questions, counter-questions, meta-questions. Research carried out in the pathos-driven, soon ten-year enterprise of exhausting such inexhaustible questions, questions of utter importance, has not produced any visible sign that such questions, or questioning in general, are reaching their end, that the heavy, emotion-filled riddles are receding into the background. From the absolutely unacceptable truth of the horror of the attacks, the fullness, the intensity, the totality or completion of its wickedness, only partial answers, statistical patterns, empirically based generalisations, innocuous inductions, informed projections and self-indulgent indictments can be offered.

Has the terrorist 'won'? Is the rational, moral tinkering of well-intended agents of 'the Norwegian' vanquished by the completeness of the horror? It would seem so. It would seem that the incontrovertible modus tollens logic ('if not, then not') – a centrepiece of obligatory philosophy education for Norwegian high school pupils – has prevailed: if a certain rationality has brought us a meaningful world, and if that world is negated, so too is the rationality that made that world a necessity destroyed. For how can rationality be reconstructed? Where do we start? Or, rather, when do we start? For we have indeed started. How can security again be recreated from this perfect insecurity? What can, or should, be changed in order to gain security back, where it has been so violently lost?

A complete answer to these questions is impossible to give. Nonetheless, headway can be made in answering the question of where to go from the unthinkable, what might be possible starting from the impossible, what can be secured from the security void. We have used the term 'unthinkable' to describe the events of Oslo/Utøya. This is, of course, partly in order to capture the empirical reality that the attacks were indeed unforeseen by those whose vocation it is to foresee and protect against such things. Thus, in a narrow sense, the events were unthinkable for a specific class of public servants charged with the task of 'thinking' and understanding which concrete, logistically possible ways of harming Norwegians and damaging Norwegian property are plausible, therefore preventable. The experiential and imaginary frames of this task are narrow, built on police and paramilitary training scenarios, risk analysis and experience, from Norway and abroad, of what other terrorists have done or imagined doing. Yet, the events were 'unthinkable' in a broader, more ambiguous, even ambivalent, way. This 'unthinkability' refers to the experience of those also beyond the security and civil preparedness communities, those for whom it was and remains unthinkable in a deeper moral, spiritual, even religious, sense. It corresponds to the still ongoing wait for a kind of question whispered to the heavens: 'what is a world in which such a thing is possible?' The addressee of this question is one form or another of the absolute, the power or force that unites and transcends us. The question is one of *meaning*. What does it mean? Why did this happen? Even beyond the question of responsibility, to which we will return in Chapter 6, there is a question of the human, of what it means to be a human, of what a human is who can behave so utterly 'inhumanly' towards other humans.

Aesthetics of terror

And if the finality of terrorism were not to be thought but rather felt? Terrorism operates to a considerable degree through aesthetic force. This insight can be traced quite far back in modern history to Burke's *Enquiry into the Origin of our Ideas of the Sublime and Beautiful* (1757), a turning point for modern aesthetics and a key reference for the understanding of political violence in aesthetic terms. Simply put, Burke understood extraordinary aesthetic experience as terror. Burke's *Enquiry* sets out the terms for raising the sublime from a concept reserved for literary aesthetics to a political concept, allowing us, as we will see, to deepen our reading of terrorism and political violence.

For Burke, 'pleasure' and 'pain' are the twin pillars of aesthetic experience. But the relation between these two experiences in Burke's thinking is notable because he describes them as entirely independent of each other (Burke, 2008: 30). Increasing the one will not decrease the other. Pain does not remove pleasure and pleasure does not remove pain. This absence of a closed economy of pain and pleasure opens a path to Burke's notion of the sublime and to its special relation to terror. For there is no hydraulic regulation of pain, no relief or easing of suffering by virtue of pleasure, no moral economy of goodness and evil. This figure of the open economy or non-zero-sum game will be crucial in what follows of the analysis of what security cannot do, and why instrumentalist approaches to security have no other moral, institutional or practical avenues available. The prophylactic approach to security that opposes the secure and the insecure within a closed economy of security cannot apply when the security to which 'the secure' refers and the insecurity to which 'the insecure' refers are asymmetrical in their intensity, violence and harm. Worse, the asymmetry is itself a source of insecurity, a second-order catastrophe that parasites on the first living from it, yet refusing to let it die.

Burke is thereby among the first to aestheticise pain. Among the human passions, he places pain and danger as the most powerful, those generating the greatest intensity. The reason is simple: of all the passions known to human experience, these two are existential. They are the ones that engage the very existence of the one who experiences them, and for this reason, they are the most powerful:

> Whatever is fitted to excite the ideas of pain, and danger ... whatever is any sort terrible or is conversant about terrible objects, or operates in a manner analogous to terror, is a source of the sublime, that is, it is productive of the strongest emotion the mind is capable of feeling. (2008: 36)

By bringing pain and death under the purview of aesthetics, Burke introduces a fundamental innovation into the thought of the sublime and a new understanding, both in the eighteenth century and today, of terror.

Kant was an avid reader and admirer of Burke. But though Kant's *Critique of Judgement*, published in 1790, only three years after Longinus's *On the Sublime*, had an agenda quite different from Burke's, its section 'Analytic of the Sublime' was explicitly indebted to Burke's formulations on the sublime.

Kant saw Burke as developing a 'physiological' theory of the sublime, a theory that explains the relation of the body to the experience of the sublime, how its power passes through an intense corporal reaction. As we noted, this conception of the sublime stands as a precursor to affect theory that has emerged in the last decades in the work of, among many others: Berlant (2011), D'abashi (2012), Grosz (2020), Massumi (1993, 2010), Wetherell (2012) and many others. In Burke's theory, according to Kant, we can see 'where merely empirical exposition of the sublime and the beautiful' can bring us (2007: 107). If Kant is inexact in characterising Burke's presentation of the sublime as an 'empirical exposition', it is this pigeon-holing of Burke which permits him to oppose his own 'transcendental' theory of the sublime.

Where Kant's first of the critiques was to set out the terms of a revolutionary new metaphysics, and the second was to provide a rational grounding for moral decision-making, the *Critique of Judgement* took the task of bridging the metaphysical and the moral. The bridge is aesthetic judgement. What quickly presents itself as the fundamental challenge of the critique of aesthetic is what drives our analysis of the experience of terror: the limited aesthetic experience and the question of what lies beyond, the question of the limits of experience and the way we experience this limit.

The discussion of total knowledge and absolute reason is the outcome of distinct political processes and the entryway into others. The question of the epistemological universality or rationalism flows into the political question of the democratic universality of reason. Coupled with the advances of technologies of reproduction and media, the rise of the European public sphere and its particular concrete culmination in the violent revolutions in the North American colonies and France revealed, if there was any doubt, the universal principles of European society as intensely political. The Reign of Terror that followed the first phase of the French Revolution in the wake of the destruction of the oppressive feudal order cast new doubt on the humanity and thus the rationality of the Revolution, considered by many as the pinnacle of human progress.

As Walter Benjamin poignantly noted in 1936 as he watched the momentum of the Third Reich build all around him, '[t]he logical result of fascism is the introduction of aesthetics into political life' (Benjamin, 1968: 241). The convergence of a political mobilisation of communication technologies, in the form of mass spectacle and technologies of violence that made possible the two World Wars, enabled a new mediated representations of the horrors of war. Not only the grandeur of visually mediated political spectacles but also the never before experienced industrial-scale murders of the Nazi concentration camps, the technologically driven production of weapons of extreme violence, the epitome of which was, of course, the atom bomb, making possible the visually documented annihilation of countless innocents. The force of the unthinkable in the form of aesthetic experience was already deniably present through the experience of inhumanity and destruction that characterised, more than others, the World Wars I and II.

Other early-twentieth-century critical theorists like Bloch, Brecht, Lukács and Adorno sought to understand the meaning of what they analysed as the rise of the 'aestheticisation of politics'. Aestheticisation, for these thinkers, led to violence and war as a consequence of the way it derailed political rationality. When politics became mixed with aesthetic phenomena, 'reasonable' political discourse, analysis, argumentation and decision-making became impossible, disrupting the safeguards of conventional politics and leading to the sometimes spiralling rise of violence (Simons, 2014: 227–8). The self-alienation of mankind 'has reached such a degree that it can experience its own destruction as an aesthetic pleasure of the first order' (Benjamin, 1968: 242; Jay, 1992). For all these authors, however, Hitler's monumental political spectacles are only one example – and, moreover, only the outer sign – of a deeper logic governing the general relationship between aesthetics, politics and political rationality. Each in his own way transcends the basically Marxist critical standpoint that anchors their analyses. As Rancière's intervention into the literary aesthetics has shown, the exploration of aesthetics reaches into questions of rationality itself, ethics, metaphysics, history and spirituality, to name but a few (2009, 2013a, 2013b). The study of the imbricated relation between aesthetics and politics will be the point of insertion for studying the political valences of the sublime and the role of the sublime in understanding the insecurity generated in the wake of terrorism.

The concept of the aesthetic has historically been accompanied by that of the *sublime*. In aesthetic theory, the sublime is considered variously as a kind of pinnacle of aesthetic experience. In classical aesthetic theory, this is formulated in the vivid debates around the turn of the eighteenth century as the maximum attainable sensory experience of beauty. These debates primarily happened in the literary sphere, to some degree following from the rhetorical orientation given to the study of the sublime by the ancient philosopher and rhetorician Longinus in his third-century treatise *On the Sublime*. For Longinus, the sublime produces 'ecstasy'. It is the reader's experience of going outside oneself, of being cast out or aside from what he or she is. It marks, in the words of Doran, a 'singular commitment to an aesthetics of transcendence, to an experience resembling or analogous to mystical religious experience' (Doran, 2015: 41). Sublime is the name of an out-of-body experience, a spiritual encounter, which opens reference to an entire complex of religious references, questions of the incarnation of the soul, embodiment and disembodiment. Indeed, what becomes of the self in the moment of the sublime? What are we when we are not our bodies? What is experience when it is not sensorially embodied? Such emotional response is variable, changing as a function of the rhetorical qualities and 'force' mentioned above. A continuum of aesthetic response reaches from ecstasy as pleasure or as pain, and on to the uncanny fusion of the two in expressions of bliss. The sublime is a disembodied relation to the self that encompasses pleasure and pain. In the end, terror presents itself as a mode of the sublime, one referred to in classical texts, one through which the observer experiences a form of transcendence (Doran, 2015: 43; Halliwell, 2012: 332).

My aim in this book is to isolate and identify the elements that will cast light on and give thickness to our reading of the aftermath of the Norwegian terror, in particular the evolving 'reading' of the catastrophe made by security officials. It might be more evident at first glance to identity the experience of terrorism with the efflorescence of emotions researched, described and eventually proselytised by the Romantics. However, it is the rapid reformulation of the movement into a kind of aesthetic politics that lets it shine light on our understanding of the Oslo attacks.

Enchanted security

The main question in what follows is straightforward, even if its analysis often proves complex: what does it mean to govern society's security when the threats we face are nothing if not beyond the pale, beyond the thinkable? How can social institutions, both formal and informal, be directed such that they increase the security of a society when the future secure society is systematically unimaginable? Indeed, what makes a society secure and how much of the security is drawn from the sensible, rational, predictable application of well-travelled practices? How can that security be governed, channelled, enhanced and exploited, when terrorist attacks are essentially bewildering? This book attempts to assess the means and measures thought to be available in an extraordinary case of societal security governance. It is extraordinary for two reasons. First, the attack of 22 July 2011 was of an intensity and singularity that was practically unimaginable, both by Norwegians and non-Norwegians. More than most catastrophes, it came out of nowhere. Second, Norwegian society is widely considered, again by both Norwegians and non-Norwegians, perhaps for different reasons as uncannily secure.

This book tells the story of the tension between social practices with a solid footing, the cultural and spiritual identity of the Norwegian people, and relations that provide security on many levels, and the administrative tools and practices available to exploit them. The Norwegian experience of 2011 and afterwards is taken as an example and a means of explaining the deep cultural and spiritual sources of security. It tries to suggest that cultural and spiritual values form the basis for a deeply resilient attitude to danger and threat, one which simultaneously generates veneration for terrorism and other threats to the security of society and provides a community-based defence against them.

We argue that terrorism draws its terrible force from the dark and destructive spell of enchantment it casts over both life and death, and that true security is inevitably drawn from equally enigmatic forces for good. *Enchantment* is the deepest continuity through the shift and flow of unknown dangers. Like the internationally acclaimed 'war on terror', there is no criteria for determining when what has not yet happened will ever happen, and what once happened will never happen again. This overarching enchantment of the world, to use the famous Weberian phrase to which we will return, takes place at all levels of the State apparatus. At times, we have only the anti-terror *dispositif* that can serve as a meaningful measure of the presence of the terrorist threat, thus confirming the principle of the next-generation security dilemma: the presence of measures of the security against invisible foes assures the presence of their danger (Bangstad, 2014; Borchgrevink & Puzey, 2013; Seierstad, 2015).

Conceptualising terrorism is a science unto itself. Debates have raged, volumes have been written, empirical studies and classifications have been compiled about the appropriate definition of the term, its scope and reach. Far more than related terms, terrorism has consistently appeared and operated as the object of a distinct conceptual politics. By this, we mean that the term is used to tap into the power of using the term to seek an impact upon a different, though perhaps adjacent, object. Though this is no place for a complete demonstration, there is little doubt that the postmodern era of terrorism – the one commencing with 11 September 2001 – revolves around the discovery that terrorism is discursive violence, that behind, and in addition to, its nearly arbitrarily targeted carnal victims, a world of violence, damage and pain is exercised by those whose disdain for the terrorist is seemingly unending. By either disastrous fate or the cynical design of the political imaginary, today's terrorism draws its enormous force not from the anger and fear of the terrorists but from the anger and fear of its targets. Terrorism is a mystifying recruitment and radicalisation machine. It plants the virus of fear and hate into its victims, then lets the liberal-democratic machine tear itself asunder. It is a new form of spellbinding sabotage, a new 'shoe' cast into the works of the neoliberal machine.

Like security, terrorism appeals to an uncanny metaphysical force, the ability to mobilise people or groups, to influence public opinion, to generate funding, to justify or legitimate political violence, to change or enact law, etc. The declaration of 'terrorism' is the ultimate securitising speech act. Terrorist or freedom fighter? Indeed, perpetrators of what are regarded by others as terrorist acts are seldom self-proclaimed terrorists. Most often, they regard themselves crusaders, warriors, soldiers, etc. This is the case for the Breivik who thought of himself as engaging in a noble and entirely legitimate cause. As the manifesto *2083: A European Declaration of Independence*, to which we will return, explicitly proclaims, Norway is at war, indeed, at a turning point in a war against Islam and the multiculturalism brought about by global migration (Breivik, 2011).

Clearly, terrorist attacks are carried out with a wide range of aims and motivations, producing a wide range of results. For our purposes, it is enough to note that a defining property of terrorism is that it essentially never targets the State itself in a way that presupposes the legitimate existence and sovereignty of that State. Terrorism does not belong to the international system, does not communicate through diplomatic channels and does not address the nation-state in itself. Its object or addressee is something else, something more or perhaps less. In many cases, it targets something more punctual: an imprisonment, an occupation, a policy or practice. In many cases, it addresses and idea or principle. Terrorism is non-specific in the sense that the concrete violence it delivers is both material violence to its immediate victims and affective violence on others. Indeed, its addressees are often less the immediate victims of its kinetic destruction than the extent of those who witness that violence while being materially untouched by it. Who are these victims by extension? Under what conditions do they suffer the extended violence associated with the murderous destructive violence? From a certain point of view, and perhaps somewhat idealistically, all human beings suffer the extended violence of the suffering of other human beings. In other words, to meet the criteria for being a victim of the extended violence of a terrorist act, it is enough to belong to the human family, to share a kind of basic human decency. Indeed, in uncommonly large, significantly mediated or particularly heinous terrorist attacks of recent history, a kind of global public sphere is self-constituted and impact is essentially universal.

Surely, this was the case after the Norway attacks. Public outcry and expressions of sympathy were noted around the world. Nonetheless, the addressee of the attack and the extended victim, alongside those murdered or maimed, is the community of Norwegians. As might be expected, the bulk of the international condolences were directed at that community by the intermediary of its political leaders. What is it that the community of Norwegians was injured more than or differently to the community of men and women, of humanity? How are the characteristics of that group that makes it more exposed or specially exposed to terrorist harm? As explicitly named in the terrorist's manifesto, the community targeted by the terrorist is the one shaped by the shared values and shared concrete experience of a particular kind of cultural and political liberalism. The liberalism of the community of surviving Norwegians touched by the attack is indeed so liberal that it arguably would have likely made space to entertain the terrorist's extreme views in a non-violent way. However, as in most liberal societies, liberalism ends abruptly where violence, even violence in the name of principles, begins, or where one version or another of the social contract is broken (Connolly, 1991; Cooper, 2004).

Of course, approaches to understanding violent extremism vary almost as widely as approaches to conceptualising terrorism. Psychological approaches seek to understand violent extremism as part of an internal determinism or linked to group influence. Sociological approaches try to draw lessons from group interactions and institutions. Cultural analyses focus on cultural interactions and, above all, conflicts. Political approaches underscore the channels of political expression and the availability of political institutions for enacting changes. Legal approaches focus on the function of local, national and international regulatory measures. Even so, like most scholarly approaches, these attempts to come to grips with violent extremism reflect as much their own starting points, premises and values as they do the object they seek to study. What is, however, a constant is that violent extremism in essentially all of its forms grows in a paradoxical way out of the evolution of the modern liberal society. It is paradoxical because, in more or less all cases, it is, on the one hand, a reaction to the values of liberalism and, on the other hand, made possible by the channels of free self-expression that are in turn made available by liberal society. The link between liberalism and extremism becomes clear when we consider the paradox at the heart of liberalism.

This book asks: if the Norwegian version of the 'war on terror' is modelled on a notion of disinterested security professionalism, how does it tackle the challenge of the horrendous catastrophe of mass terrorism? The case of the terrorist attack in Norway on 22 July 2011 presents itself as a test. Never before had an affect been generated that was so far away from the neutral, object and rational ethos of bureaucracy, and yet, it was the bureaucracy that received the bulk of the work of implementing societal security measures aimed at averting future terrorism and, not least, making sense of the terrorism of the recent past. The book will walk at a slow pace through the shifting media discourse in the hours, days and weeks after Oslo/Utøya (Chapter 5), the level-headed bureaucratic analysis of the attack against the Norwegian security landscape in the *Report of the 22 July Commission* (Chapter 6), the official government follow-up of that report and other officially mandated enquiries (Chapter 7) and the quest for 'responsibility' for the attack (Chapter 8).

Beyond the raw violence and brutality of the attacks, the assault was deeply experienced as an assault on a set of values and a way of life. The perception of an affront to Norway's cultural identity has for more than a decade translated into a crisis for Norwegian societal security policy. The Norwegian neoliberal societal security policy that emerged after 22 July 2011 has remained consistent in the near decade since the attacks, fueling a desire for bureaucratic streamlining as an answer to the challenge of securing society's complexity. Indeed, with little more than incomplete and circumstantial evidence to support the claim, I will try to argue that this grain of enchantment at the heart of neoliberal bureaucratisation is actually not simply a thorn in the side, a stone in the sandal, an impurity in an otherwise smooth-running bureaucratic system, but, paradoxically, the precondition for bureaucracy itself. I will try to convince the reader that societal security as disenchanted, disembodied, rational, scientific calculability depends for its force on the enchanted other, the spirit of society's moral bonds, to do its work.

Disenchantment, we will see, is not just social engineering. It has agency and a certain kind of political subjectivity as well. Disenchanted bureaucracy speaks, decides, securitises. It enacts its agency in accordance with a very attractive and even seductive set of means, of the kind to which any organisation would aspire: calculability, accountability, responsibility, professionalism. These virtues rest upon the nature of bureaucratic thought in Norway and other modern social democracies: structure, transparency, administration and decision-making through non-elected and thus theoretically disinterested agents. In the overall architecture of social democratic administration, the bureaucracy plays the role of implementing the political decisions handed down by the political superstructure. Political positions are clarified, then handed down to the bureaucracy to be implemented according to the structural possibilities and organisational horizon as they are available. These possibilities and horizons are, of course, by no means neutral. Indeed, they are themselves products of political decisions made, the specific hierarchy in place in the bureaucratic structure, the specialisation and particular competencies, the division of labour and accepted procedures.

2

The enchantment of security

> Stories matter in an enchanted forest.
> Coombs (2010)

What is security?

Obviously, in so many ways, the story of Oslo/Utøya is a story of security. But it's not about security Norwegians have; it's about the security Norwegians *thought* they had, the form security took in their minds and their imaginations, the emotions it produced, the reactions it generated. But it's even more about the spontaneous *insecurity* that exploded out of the events of that day and, of course, out of what critics would later call the complacent naiveté that was at the heart of the security before the event (Borchgrevink, 2013: 291; Burgess, 2020: 242; Døving, 2020: 191). We must also account for the equally spontaneous security that *emerged*, in part thanks to wise coaxing by political leaders, in the days and weeks following 22 July, the intensity and extravagance, of a feeling of security that then waned again and was gradually pushed aside by a more bureaucratic security, one that was thin like a cigarette paper, this security again to be replaced by a cultural insecurity that has endured until today.

In short, security has lived a thousand lives – it always has.

This is in part because it has lived from a thousand positions. It is used in public discussions, political debates and academic discourses with the greatest self-evidence. Everyone seems to know what it means, what it refers to, what its content is, how it can be delimited and, above all, what it can be used for. Everyone seems to know where it comes from, what can give it and how to lose it, who has it and who does not, who has a claim to it and who has no right to it. Everyone knows what it is worth, what can and should be paid for it, even sacrificed for it, and, likewise, where the limit goes. Everyone seems to know what the real source of security is, what it implies about our values, our heritage, our shared traditions and the priorities we should have, how we should organise society and which costs should be borne by the collective in the name of collective security. All this, in myriad debates and conversations, holds the unique privilege of self-evidence (Huysmans, 1998). Why is this so?

'Few concepts pack the metaphysical punch' of security, once proclaimed James Der Derian (1993). If there was ever any doubt about the power of concepts, about their ability to produce real consequences, that doubt can hardly have survived the attacks in the US on 11 September 2001, the twin attacks in Spain in 2004, the Oslo/Utøya attacks in Norway. The concept of security moves the world, changes society, puts life to serious test, justifies political reprioritisation and more reassessment. Trillions of dollars are spent every year on a shaky foundation of unclear and uncritical understandings of security. We organise our lives to an extraordinary and even shocking degree according to a certain set of assumptions about our own security and an invisible, perhaps even unconscious, attitude about insecurity. Infants and adolescents are schooled in it, public authorities are organised following it, commerce is framed by it, police officers are deployed for it and men and women are sent into battle in its name (Baldwin, 1997; Bubandt, 2005; Rothschild, 1995; Ullman, 1983; Wæver, 2011; Williams, 2007; Williams, 1998).

In other words, there are very few, perhaps no other, concepts that have as much political firepower as security. This is the case not only for Norway but for anywhere we may look in the Western world, any place where the relationship of the individual and collectivity to the 'dangerous other' is taken as the starting point for national geopolitics (Coaffee & Wood, 2006; Culcasi & Gokmen, 2011; Eckert, 2008; Marable, 2002). The concept of security touches all levels of society and all sectors of the State. Nevertheless, security remains unclear in our political, scientific and personal discussions in spite of the enormous power of the concept. This ambiguity is in part due to the fact that a certain understanding of security is applied to several different objects in the same way. Although there is much evidence to suggest that these social, cultural, ethical and political differences, that should be taken into account when determining security policy of one kind or another, are simply ignored, the variations in the assumptions behind these different areas can give massive variation in the way that security is seen as an object for policy.

What do we mean, then, by 'security'? What do we know about it? What is our understanding of security based on? How do we identify threats to security? What is threatened, and by whom? Can one understanding of security apply to all regions in the world? Is there a particular Norwegian concept of security that applies exclusively to the horrendous events of Oslo/Utøya?

Security is, of course, many things for many people. Among other things, it is a discourse, that is, a set of concepts, ideas, values, structures and paradigms that steer the way in which we conceive the horizon of our own understanding of the world, or what is possible for us in terms of thought and action (Dalby, 2002; Hansen, 2006; Shepherd, 2008). A discourse is a world view. It is not a simple concept but rather a *dispositif*, an apparatus whose function extends far beyond simple communication. A discourse is a toolbox that permits us to operate in the world in a very specific way, while at the same time leaving the impression that that is the only way. It is a toolkit that permits us to organise the way we see the different components that make up what we call 'reality'. It is an invisible set of informal guidelines for what is allowed to be thought and to be said, delimiting our possible interpretations of the world and our understandings of it. The discourse of nature, for example, is particularly strong in Norwegian culture. It implicitly affirms what nature is and what it is not, what is natural and unnatural, how we should behave towards nature and how nature relates to society, to non-nature. All this is wrapped up and affirmed in one term: nature (Sagarin, 2010).

Security is also a mighty discourse in Norway. As noted, it calls for a kind of power to designate and govern things and matters that lie beyond itself, beyond security and beyond politics. It impacts culture and social life, individuals and groups, organisations and institutions, shapes our relationship to political processes, to international politics, to processes and procedures, to security technologies and security measures. What is it, or who, that steers the discourse of security? Who decides what relation we will have to law and order, to technology, culture, society, etc.? The question is open and will not be answered here. From a certain point of view, the only possible task of an analysis like this one is to map the underside of security, to cast light upon it, to present it as the raw materials of the potential critique of power to be undertaken by others. Who or what is another question altogether. The army, the Prime Minister? Industrial leaders? The arms industry? The press?

Obviously, the possibilities for escaping the gravity of the US security black hole – especially after 11 September 2001 and the launch of the war against terror – are few (Shearman & Sussex, 2004). The genius of Bush II's rhetorical hat trick is not to be underestimated. It serves rather as the model of the power of concepts. The first step in an alternative understanding of security is the insight that security is implicitly linked to human beings and to human values. It can be shown that security is about an attempt to maintain a certain way of being. It is the expression of a set of values, an understanding of life, of individual and collective hopes and fears, of expectations of what can be sacrificed and what is worth preserving (Roe, 2008; Tusicisny, 2007). Security is an expression for what one is willing to pay, for what one is willing to fight and perhaps die for. In other words, security is a social, cultural and even ethical concept. The extent to which these values can be said to be national and when they are shared internationally is central. In a multicultural society like the Norwegian one, which way of living should be the one that counts? Which one should be valorised and put into everyday practice (Andrews *et al.*, 2015; Dalby, 2009; Van Ham, 2001)?

Security is often associated with the material and technical aspects of life because these have a greater tendency to be incorporated into or sometimes even replace human values. Nonetheless, these material and technical values should not be confused with life itself. Security does not concern only things; indeed, it does not concern things at all. It concerns human beings who value things and have a need for certain things as a means to live life.

Solid, rigorous and effective security measures must therefore account for the cultural and social forces that give shape to our conception of what security and insecurity are, what threatens what has value for us and what should govern our response in crisis and catastrophe. The aim of this chapter is to return to the concept of security and map its genealogy and foundations in order to better understand how and with what political coherence it can be applied in our time and in the Norwegian context.

We begin by putting the concept of security into a general historical perspective. As we will see, this perspective immediately links the security problematic to the international context and to a range of globalisation processes that unavoidably leave their mark on the events of Oslo/Utøya in Norway. I will then attempt a reconstruction of the concept of societal security and again seek to chart its field of application and relevance. Finally, the chapter will undertake a critical analysis of the use of the concept of security in those ministries that have the most central role in the work of assuring security in Norway.

The revolution in security thinking

The concept of national security emerges, of course, from the rise of the modern nation-state. The sovereignty of the State is guaranteed by its position in a more or less unified international system made up, in its essence, of a web of mutual recognitions of sovereign States. Sovereignty itself is linked in its foundations to the coincidence of some form of culturally determined national collective linked to the institutions of the State. Yet, even if the classical history of ideas contains a long and rich development around a certain understanding of security (as well as the relationship between security and the nation-state and society), the concept's scope and meaning first became politically meaningful, that is, politically contentious, as a consequence of the changes in the modern concept of politics, and not least in terms of the tools and means of politics. If security has become a concept both interesting and meaningful over the years, it is because it is increasingly articulated with the group dynamics of those who understand their own relationship to threats and dangers that might be present in a complex world. This conceptual history has been documented and lucidly analysed by practitioners of the movement that came to be called critical security studies, starting in the 1990s (Baldwin, 1997; Krause & Williams, 1997; Møller, 2000; Smith, 2005; Wæver, 1997).

How is the opposition between the secure and the insecure, the dangerous and the innocuous, the safe and the unsafe, marked, specified and manipulated? This opposition reveals quite a bit about the security subject's position, values, culture and self-image. At the same time, it says a lot about the implications of security ontology, that is, what the understanding of security reality is. And, of course, it speaks volumes about how normality in relation to dangers is defined, and how progress towards more security, more safety, is understood as a deployment – through political and social means – towards something more normal.

While today's concept of security is the immediate inheritor of the academic field of international relations, the term 'security' was, oddly enough, hardly even used before the turn of the twentieth century in connection with questions of international relations or political science. As late as 1940, interest (or concern) for security was completely different compared with the dominant role the concept was to assume only a few years later. The turning point for this development was, of course, the end of World War II and the dawn of the Cold War when security became identical to national security, understood not only as the security of State borders and State sovereignty but also as the security of the nationality of nation-state borders and sovereignty (Wæver, 2012).

Of course, in Norway, as in other Western countries, the concept of security has gone through a particularly turbulent development since 1989 when it was disconnected, as with everywhere else in the West, from the geopolitical, bipolar logic of the Cold War. Between 1947, when the varying ideologies of deterrence were first taken into us, and the fall of the Berlin Wall in 1989, the anti-Soviet and Soviet opposition had a stranglehold on how the concept could and would be understood and used (Wæver, 2012). From being a precise term in international politics, 'security' has developed to become a collective concept for a multiplicity of threats in our time, becoming today one of the most widely used and politicised terms of all time.

In 1994, the United Nations Development Programme (UNDP) presented its annual 'development report' in which the concept of 'human security' was firmly formulated and conceptualised (UNDP, 1994). The presentation of the concept in such a widely recognised, international forum led to a considerable pluralisation of what was previously a narrow geopolitical security concept. This, in turn, led to an increasing distinction between both the different levels of security (from individual, to group, to region, to the global level, etc.) and a range of thematic focuses (economic security, food security, health security, etc.). Then, through the 1990s, a range of theoretical positions were developed in a variety of attempts to make conceptual sense of the new security landscape. Some chose to develop a new theoretical horizon for what security could mean and its conceptual relevance. These new approaches all tried to put a fresh perspective on the term by developing a more critical approach to understanding security. Suddenly, it became possible to see security and insecurity unfolding in new ways, and being used in many new manners for both good and bad.

Inscribed in a complex way in the short history of the concept of security since the 1990s, the notion of societal security emerged at a time when the division between inner and outer security was becoming more and more difficult to uphold, and at a time when Norwegian authorities began to recognise the degree to which we live in a global world where threats and crises that emerge far away can, and often do, have relevance for local-national politics of security (C.A.S.E Collective, 2006; Walker, 1993). In Norway, as elsewhere, media, the internet and increased mobility have led to the world being experienced as smaller and events that take place far away becoming part of our immediate, proximate, everyday life. Technological development continuously creates new possibilities for more effective and integrated cooperation beyond national borders. Norwegians travel more often abroad and immigration to Norway has grown considerably, not least because of increased mobility, global consciousness and a globalised circulation of resources, capital and people.

A range of perceptions of international terrorism, the spread of weapons of mass destruction and threats of pandemic, some justified, others less justified, have emerged as a result of a globalised society. Processes of globalisation have two sides: they impact what we regard as threats against society, and they carry the consequence that the threats that we regard as relevant have roots beyond national borders. However, if we now attempt to retrace the concept of security even further back in time, we discover a completely unexpected story. In antiquity, security as a concept was primarily connected to spirits and spirituality, and thus with theology (Wæver, 2012).

In ancient times, security was understood as a state of mind, a world view and a spiritual or moral state with both psychological and moral significance. The Greek word *ataraxie* – spiritual fear – was used to describe the state of security. What is particularly interesting is that the expression 'security' had a negative connotation. It was understood precisely as the absence of emotional or spiritual worry or concern. Security was not an objective quality connected to an immediate, concrete situation but rather a subjective matter, connected to one's relation to oneself.

This stands in strong opposition to the political reality of today in which objective security, that is, security in relation to objective factual, real and observable threats, is front and centre. In addition, the social dimension of security, that which made it possible to speak of collective security at all, was not part of the discussion. Security was a personal matter, a concern that had little to do with the State, society or any other collective entity.

When the time came for the transition from ancient Greek to Latin terminology, *ataraxie* was translated in one of two different ways: on the one hand, by *certitudo*, on the other hand, by *securitas*. For the latter term, the connotation was much closer to what we today call safety, that is, stability, solidity, etc. This means that the Roman version of security has a much more objective character (Burns *et al.*, 1992; Waldron, 2011). Certitude, on the other hand, emerged as an epistemological or knowledge-based dimension of security, linked to insight or understanding into the sense or meaning of objective facts (Buzan *et al.*, 1990; Gros, 2008, 2012; Szpyra, 2014; Wæver, 2012; Walters, 2010).

This historical point of departure leads us to observe an odd interaction between moral status and security, an interaction that is completely different from the one we know today. According to the conception of the Middle Ages, one is said to be in a secure state when one is free of grief, without reflection, with care. This also means, in other words, without care for others, without care for or self-insight into oneself, with attention to or respect for oneself or others. To be in a state of *securitas* means to be in the absence of doubt, without reflection, above all, convinced of the existence and well meaning of God, a kind of arrogance in relation to other humans and in relation to the self-evidence of one's own existence. In the feudal period, this understanding was translated into an economic discourse about service and redemption. Security could be bought and sold. The function of the feudal prince was in some sense to offer security to those who could afford it. The first State-economic thought was constructed as a system of defence (Gros, 2012).

The millennium-long evolution of the concept of security accelerated abruptly and took on a new and modern aspect during the Cold War, which exposed this concept to a rigorous narrowing (Wæver, 1996, 1997, 2012). Already from the 1940s and up until the 1970s, 'security' was understood in a relatively limited way. First and foremost, it was, of course, the nuclear threat that shifted the security discourse in play in the general public to the presuppositions and consequences of nuclear threat and nuclear deterrence. All other conceivable threats stood in the shadow of the nuclear threat which became overnight the centre of a new thermonuclear balance (Beres, 2019). Moreover, it became quickly clear that security was a national matter, both in its scope and reach, and that the lesser (but also greater) security questions did not have the same significance as those that were directed towards the superpowers of the period. Before World War II, the concept of 'national security' was nearly unknown. This all changed suddenly when Truman signed the US National Security Act in 1947 (Demarest & Borghard, 2018). The Cold War's conceptual power of 'security' was overtaken by 'national security'. This conception subsequently held a stranglehold on the discourse of security for nearly forty years (Wæver, 2012: 65–7). Security experienced an extraordinary renaissance through the experience of a real or perhaps constructed threat against the nation-state. It acquired the meaning of a kind of state of play without threat from the other end of the bipolar spectrum, a potential threat (Stuart, 2008). Security was thus the relationship with a certain kind of invisible or unperceived threat, in opposition to the threats that became the objects for geo-military actions, politicised and structured hierarchically.

This politics of discourse can be illustrated by evoking an interesting linguistic phenomenon: the rise of the concept of safety in the Norwegian industrial sector in the years after World War II. The interesting question, which to some degree began to arise in the 1970s in Norway and accompanies us today, is how this concept relates to the concept of 'security'. The difference between 'safety' and 'security' can be observed in a variety of European languages in a way that parallels the split between *certitudo* and *securitas* mentioned above. This distinction corresponds, on the one hand, to an emphasis on psychological, intellectual or affective security (*certitudo*), and, on the other hand, to a focus on the secular and purely scientific (*securitas*). 'Safety' has become a key term for describing threats of the most objective type: at home, on the street, at work. In the Norwegian post-war period, there was an early conceptualisation and institutionalisation of 'societal security', security after the Cold War. It was a matter of daily life and daily tasks, for a certain level of everyday safety was needed and expected. The focus was on safe food, a safe workplace, safety in traffic, etc. Safety was used to refer to known, objective threats to everyday life. Safety, it was thought, came from protection from dangers that were clear, known and observable. It was all about identifying, analysing and understanding everyday threats, through research, science, innovation and new technological discoveries and insights, and transferring this understanding to institutions involved in State management in order to coordinate and further develop instruments and tools for the benefit of citizens in everyday life (Lægreid & Serigstad, 2006; Lango et al., 2011; Morsut, 2020).

'Security', on the other hand, appealed to the human experience of the unknown, of unknown threats, ones that invited speculation about what was or might be to come, fantasising and forecasting about what the future would bring. 'Security' opened the space of the human, of human pathos, human values, aspirations, fears, concerns, trepidations, hopes, etc., all such matters that will form the core of my reasoning in what follows about how terrorism and the future threats it conjures are digested in the intimate connection between State bureaucracy, cultural values and national spirit in the Nordic social democracies. The notion of security, I will try to show, will nourish this space in between bureaucracy and spirit in the age of uncertainty. This space is supported and nourished by technologies of governance, of which bureaucracy is exemplary, but it is also nourished by the unknown itself, by the absence of objective knowledge about concrete dangers and, of course, by our vivid capacities of imagination.

In this sense, security is a reference not to the world of *facts* but to the world of *possibilities*. It is also a reference to our most general level of vulnerability, a synthesis of both our material vulnerability – the physical fragility of human life and the improbability of its very existence – and the vulnerability of our social and moral selves, of our values and principles, the things that make any given society what it is. Insecurity is not, as most would claim, a reference to specific, concrete threats. It does not refer to actual dangers but rather to the fact that we are exposed to danger, that we know this and that we only approximately have some idea of what kind of danger it might be, when it eventually might be realised and how. In other words, security is far more a question about *us* than about the unknown danger lurking out there. It points less directly to the insecurity of the dangerous unknown than it does to ourselves who are exposed to the unknown dangers. Security is, in this sense, reflexive in that it expresses the relation of a human being or human beings in their relation to themselves. Philosophers would say in this context that it is through insecurity that the human experiences life, that insecurity – not security – is humanity itself: passion, sensitivity, sensibility. We will return to this theme repeatedly in these pages.

The globalisation of insecurity

Classical national security expresses a relation to a physically and geographically determined space. The nation-state is a territorial entity. Even the sovereignty of the State is ordinarily understood in territorial terms. When a State, through its domestic or international activities, violates the geographical borders of another State, we say that that State's territorial sovereignty has been violated. This geographical or spatial structuring of the relation between the threatening and the threatened, between the security subject and the object of security, makes an imprint on the way that the danger, threats and insecurity are even understood, let alone experienced (Philo, 2012).

And yet, security expresses an even older structure in the relation between the subject and the object, or, more concretely, between one individual and another, between one group and another, between cultures, social entities, religions, economic systems, sexualities, etc. (Walker, 1997). The structure is simple, nearly banal, but at the same time bottomlessly complex in its implications for the way we understand ourselves and our world. It presupposes a proximate or physically present object that is exposed to or potentially exposed to dangers, and the distant, the foreign, the absent, the threatening thing that is the source of danger. The essence of danger does not spring out of concrete, specific content but from its very otherness. Alterity arises and presents as danger itself.

This logic enables, at the same time, a *value-based* conceptual framework: us–them, secure–dangerous, good–evil, beautiful–ugly, authentic–inauthentic, etc. This binary structure has proved itself extraordinarily powerful, particularly, but certainly not exclusively, in recent times (Der Derian, 1985, 1993). This is true not only in the traditional security thinking of Western metaphysics. It is far more true among the most dominant structures organising our thinking, our understanding of ourselves and our understanding of what might potentially threaten us. It seems to be exceedingly difficult, though not impossible, to think of ourselves in other terms outside of this structural opposition. This is particularly important for this new generation's security. Security today, and increasingly, can only be thought of in terms of threats that are both here and there, intensely present and somehow vaguely absent, present in our society and absent in the sense that we do not manage to deal with the threats connected to them.

What today is called 'risk governance' is precisely a technical and social methodology for transcending the geopolitical opposition of security that presumes that, in order to live in security, we must live in the absence of security threats (Renn, 2008). The discourse of risk and risk management builds upon a significantly different kind of assumption, namely, that security understood as the pure absence of danger is not an option, and that the more appropriate question is how to coexist with the dangers that are already present and which surround us in every aspect of our lives. There is a clear empirical foundation for suggesting there is a gradual and ongoing transition from a prophylactic conception of security based on an external relation to security threats to a more reflexive conception of security based on the continuous management of the constant, unavoidable presence of threats. This is what is meant by the globalisation of security.

In the new, globalised security landscape, the most relevant threats have little, if anything, to do with territorial sovereignty. Today's threats – terrorism, of course, but also pandemic diseases, cybercrime, food security, financial criminality, etc. – all represent non-State-based, non-territorial threats, which prove more or less indifferent to State borders. They are not interested in national, or for that matter any other, borders, nor do they originate from within any particular State borders. They are global threats, threats that do not discriminate national States or have as their aim to weaken or overthrow national States. Today's threats do not follow the traditional binary security paradigm that opposes that threatened and the threat. The new threats are not 'out there'. On the contrary, their essence as threats stems from the very fact that they are difficult or impossible to locate physically. In fact, they are everywhere: in the air, in our blood, on our hard disk, in our food and among us in our society. Today's terror threats do not come from outside. The future terrorist is *already* here, *already* equipped with naturally acquired (or naturalised) values and ways of living that implicitly protect him or her.

The technologisation of security

Over the last twenty years, the number of expressions for and forms of security has risen considerably. Just as the Inuits are purported to have countless names for varieties of what we call snow, an apparently irrepressible need has increased for new categorisations of security. We have financial security, data security, food security, airport security, ICT security, human security, societal security, health security, home security and, of course, the traditional national security. This inflation in the concept of security has left a significant mark on the way we as individuals experience and manage ourselves, our place in society, in relation to the multiple groups we might belong to, and the world at large. The most dynamic driver behind the development of the concept of security is perhaps its continuous commercialisation.

For many criss-crossing reasons, the security industry in the West has grown enormously in the last decades. This process began long before the terrorist attacks of 11 September 2001, though it most certainly accelerated under the force of the shocks felt in the wake of them. Although the attacks were expressly directed against Western modernity understood as a set of liberal cultural values and world views, the decision was made immediately after the event that the best response was a material one, a physical or technical approach to an event that was actually a form of cultural war (Lacy, 2014). Technology had always been an expression of Western competence and progress, and that was precisely the expression that would mark a new era of insecurity (Bigo et al., 2008).

In the wake of 9/11, continually more and more sophisticated technological solutions have been used to confront our new security challenges. This has a number of consequences, to which we will return below, but it is important to underscore first and foremost the economic aspect of this very particular reaction to a wide-ranging security challenge: technology and technological solutions to security problems are understood as portable. That is, they have no implicit or organic roots in any specific social, cultural or moral geopolitical context. They can be used anywhere and under basically any conditions. This is in part because security has gradually evolved to be regarded as a purely technical challenge rather than a human one. Indeed, human beings are gradually but incessantly moved out of the security equation. Security problems are formulated and solved in technological terms with the help of technological developments, hard scientific research and innovation, all aimed at developing better, more precise, more comprehensive, more invisible tools for handling a problem which belongs more or less entirely to a different domain of reality: the human. Human beings, who are unique by their particular relationship to their own insecurity, are increasingly regarded as inessential, secondary or, most extraordinarily, as part of the problem.

The industrialisation of security

Security as a concept and practice thus developed primarily within a technology imaginary, nourished by an ever-receding horizon of technology-driven innovation and commerce. Intertwined with the liberal logic of industrialisation, a new practice of privatising security measures and service began to take hold. In the course of only a few years, security tasks that were traditionally reserved for public institutions in the service of citizens became transformed from a matter of public organisation and community ethos to one of commercial engagement, industrial innovation and private corporate governance. This phenomenon took form under the long arc of Eisenhower's 'military–industrial complex', formulated in 1961, and Der Derian's 'military–industrial–media–entertainment network' from 2001 (Der Derian, 2001). Security guards replaced police officers, mercenaries took over an increasing number of tasks from national armies, security consultants gave advice at all levels of public organisation, just to name a few of the evolutions. For reasons that need to be fully analysed, security has adopted the logic of commerce: the world can today increasingly be divided into security providers and security consumers. No longer an experience of personal well-being, or of spiritual serenity, security is fungible substance, marketable, exchangeable without any remainder. Security can be bought and sold, moved and delivered, exchanged and replaced. In some cases, security consumers in one setting are security providers in another. Finally, in accordance with the principle of globalisation, security circulates in the same way as goods, services, information and currency, criss-crossing the globe with little or no attachment to place, society, State, institution, organisation or local culture, interests or loyalty.

Furthermore, in line with the inner logic of market capitalism, the logic of industrialised security naturally leads to a discourse of security product differentiation. Just as the availability of mass-produced consumer articles varies less as a function of demand than as one of supply, demand for security grows not as a function of growing insecurity but as one of increasing supply. Paradoxically, insecurity varies not as a function of the dangers in the world but rather as one of the available response to new dangers, real or imagined. The need for security always grows with the availability of responses – preferably technology-orientated responses – to insecurity. The security industry generates continuously new responses to security needs that consumers did not yet know they had (Bigo & Jeandesboz, 2010; Cockayne & Mears, 2009).

Industrialised, technology-fixated security ultimately leads to a certain production of insecurity itself. In other words, insecurity grows proportionally to the accelerated thinking about and response to insecurity. Fighting the various new kinds of threat most often leads to instrumental solutions that remove humans and the human from the picture. We build walls, fences, gates and barriers, and develop detection systems. Such systems have multiple functions and certainly deflect dangers in a certain sense and to a certain degree. Yet, they also have a tendency to reduce confidence and trust in others, in society, in public officials and public institutions. Reduced trust leads to less security or more insecurity, something standing in stark contrast to the desired effect.

In Norway, the EU and the United Nations, security practices are increasingly characterised by their technological ambitions. This tendency finds itself justified in at least two distinct ways. First, technological solutions to security challenges (and other tasks which are relevant for security organisation and management of society) are increasingly regarded as more rational and more effective in terms of their use of public resources. Second, the use of security technologies by those who wish to violate our own security, whoever 'we' may be, are becoming more and more sophisticated. Criminals and terrorists are becoming more and more skilled at using the security technologies of their own. This general observation has been operationalised in the context of the EU through comprehensive industry-dominated security research programmes, now in their second decade.

Border control on the European level and data collection and storage in general have become enormous technological areas of investment.

New technologies are used in Europe and Norway based on a more or less simple assumption that surveillance and the collection and storage of personal data increase our security, an assumption far from unambiguously demonstrated. These security-orientated information technologies do not actually offer protection against current threats or criminal activities (Hayes, 2006). Such technologies rather take their point of departure in the gathering of aggregate data that permits the diagnosis of future threats. As a consequence of this temporal change in security thinking, the centre of gravity for security and our understanding of it is moved from the present to the future. Security measures are more and more future-orientated and the knowledge base of security measures becomes more and more speculative. It relies ever more often on notions of the possible instead of assessments of the factual. This future orientation has a clear political consequence: today's policy is constantly pressured to enact visible measures in the face of dangers that are themselves calculations of the future. Today, we need a knowledge basis in order to justify or legitimate political action.

Security and market liberalism

The need for speedy political decision-making also drives the broader technological development in security governance, as well as the need for accelerated innovation and excellence in technological thought. The need to assure more political measures tends to depend more intensely on the ability to deliver more advanced technological measures. Speed as a goal in itself is increasingly integrated with evolving technologies of national defence and defence institutions, despite the privatisation tendency noted above (Virilio, 1986). The fateful political decision by George W. Bush Jr in the wake of the US attacks of 11 September 2001, to categorise the attacks as acts of war – thus automatically triggering the international law of war, the Geneva Convention and other international agreements – contributed not only to shaping US and allied foreign policy for the still unforeseeable future, the legal, political and moral relationship to terrorism, and the very concepts of crime, war, civil and human rights, but also strengthened the technological dependence on time and the acceleration of events in security governance in the West and all over the world. The more or less permanent pre-emptive war that has been fought by multiple US governments since that day have created an even greater need for quick development of security technologies, technologies that make it possible to gaze even farther into the future, predict actions and events and manage risks that have not even begun to present themselves concretely.

The rise of security technologies also has a strong connection, in both Europe and the US, to the apparent need for a new type of public–private cooperation, in particular when it comes to the enormous and growing security industries. This need is discussed in detail in the following section. Its principal foundation is clear, namely, that public investments will not be able to keep apace with the technological developments of the present and future in a way that can satisfy coming security needs. The belief that they ever could has all but disappeared. A more current assumption is that a robust and future-orientated security industry will be necessary in order to meet continuously expanding needs.

This rapidly developing technological situation, particularly in the areas of surveillance and border control, has changed how citizens experience security. Surveillance technologies, like security technologies in general, are more and more frequently presented as security solutions that make it possible to differentiate between 'good' and 'bad' citizens in order to give the 'good' – or 'bona fide', as they are called in the EU parlance – more freedom of movement. The new social contract becomes, thus: 'if you permit yourself to be surveilled, you will be freer to live your life and realise your interests'. Increased security is in this way packaged and presented as increased freedom.

Eventually, society became increasingly dependent upon the various infrastructures and societal functions. The threat landscape inherited from the Cold War created the framework for the security measures of today. After the Cold War, the development and use of infrastructure and societal functions were first and foremost driven forward by market forces, technological development and a desire for effective and economical operation (Bigo & Jeandesboz, 2010). Society's rapid pace of change and high demand for profitability and production make it all the more important to have the ability to retool itself in relation to the new technological and organisational challenges and activities. At the same time, the ability to change is not only limited to these issue areas. It is equally important to preserve the concern for security of and through change itself. The good operation of a good security culture must have the ability to assimilate the changing security landscape in aggregate or in its entirety. For political authorities, it is important to be sure that the sum of the different change measures across or within a sector does not reduce the collective security of society.

Public ownership as a means by which to secure critical infrastructure and critical societal functions must be assessed in concrete terms within each activity and sector. The choice of ownership must take place on the basis of an overall assessment of the desirability of public control weighed against the eventual operational advantages of private ownership. The very aim of focussing on societal security and preparedness must be measured in terms of the criticality of critical infrastructure, a calculation to which we will return repeatedly in the pages that follow.

Clearly, market values make a fundamental impression on our understanding and experience of security (Berman, 2004). We live in a liberal market society. There is no doubt that society in general benefits immensely when things run smoothly, particularly in terms of security. This implies the free flow of goods, services, capital and people. We are accustomed to goods and services being delivered as expected and that these are safe. We are accustomed to accidents, when they happen, being minor and manageable, to their damage not being 'critical' to essential societal functions, and that incidents can be put back in order quickly such that everyday life continues as before. It is these liberal market expectations that most mark our understanding of societal security today. Then, where does one draw the line between these expectations and the expectation of some sort of social, cultural, even moral, 'security'?

The production of secondary insecurity

The strong relationship between the commercialisation of security, the inflation of insecurity and the growing differentiation between the many kinds of security threats and security solutions, and not least the security measures that operate with any solid anchoring in relation to unknown threats and an unknown future, leads to an unintentional and undesirable secondary production of insecurity. Initiating security measures without a full overview of what the potential secondary dangers actually are ends by aggravating the primary insecurity, creating questions, unease and concern about which threats or dangers are actually being avoided.

This is by no means the consequence of bad planning, lesser still of poor security management. Indeed, it lies in the very logic of security itself. Security threats inevitably arise from the presence of a suspicion or assumption of danger but without the certainty of being able to determine exactly what that danger is, where it is, how it will materialise. Paradoxically, we already know something about any given security threat; we already know something or perhaps even a lot about what must be done to confront it, to prevent it or reduce its impact, whether we are conscious of it or not. Indeed, to invert the logic of pre-emption, the security threat is already realising itself through its presence as an imaginary. The insecurity lies in the very uncertainty or partial knowledge about what can happen. This is valid for both social authorities responsible for measures in support of social security and for the public sphere which experiences the insecurity, both in its official announced form and on a personal level, and often in relation to a much less informed or less scientifically based situational analysis.

Moreover, it is increasingly the case that security authorities are operating under the sign of confidentiality – in the name of security – and when knowledge of the actual situation surrounding the presumed threats, risk or uncertainty are secret. In Norway and elsewhere, we have become accustomed to trust – without any informational grounds – the information, analyses and conclusions of public authorities. High-impact political decisions are taken and policy is deployed without any form of public accountability or democratic control, on the grounds that publication of such information about security threats might compromise the ability of authorities to act in order to manage the threats. The experience of insecurity and information about insecurity are inseparable (Eriksson & Giacomello, 2006; Levi & Wall, 2004).

As a consequence of this complex constellation – insecurity information, future threats – we easily experience a secondary type of insecurity in relation to just about any type of security preparedness. For example, increased police presence in the public space, based on entirely undisclosed information or threat assessment, leads us to question why authorities need to increase police activities (and thereby also problematises the public's trust of the judgement and intentions of the authorities), but also increases unease in local communities by means of the material violence represented by police presence. Increased surveillance through video cameras in public spaces, digital means and data processing can, of course, also naturally lead to a reduction of the possibility for the implementation of functioning security measures. Additionally, these tools create insecurity through their simple presence. Tougher border control in the name of security produces, in the very best of cases, this effect. The same goes for preventive efforts for natural catastrophes. Preventive measures create and nourish thoughts and images of a possible coming catastrophe. Dikes, roadblocks, emergency alarms, life preservers, security exercises, etc. form the basis for safety while, at the same time, generating questions, uncertainty and unease. Security experts claim that this unease is healthy, that it creates a useful attentiveness, which is itself the key to security in the long run.

The value function of security

It nearly goes without saying that the attacks of 11 September 2001 put the notions of 'security' and 'insecurity' on the lips of the Western world. First, in relation to the US-led 'war on terror', then, after the Madrid bombings of 11 March 2004 and, again, after the London bombings of 7 July 2005, Europe was forced to embrace a new global discourse of security.

Security, however, has not always been a central issue for Europe and for European research. The idea of security has had a unique history in this part of the world. Like many things European, it is bound to a certain set of traditions, a distinct historical experience and a repertoire of ideas, customs and traditions. At the moment of the birth of the EU, the threats were of a different kind to those we face today. The core issues that have marked European construction over the past fifty-five years have been dominated by economic concerns and largely organised by a kind of economic rationality (Burgess, 2012, 2014).

Yet, the EU we see today was conceived and has evolved largely as a project of peace. With the horrors of World War II freshly in mind, Robert Schuman, together with Jean Monnet and with the support of German Chancellor Konrad Adenauer, formulated in 1951 the basic idea that the only sure way to prevent future armed conflict on European soil – and, in particular, between France and Germany – was not to shelter the nations from each other but rather integrate them (Ghervas, 2021). The path to that integration was economic. In this sense, Europe's most clear historical enemy was its own historical divisions. European 'security' politics in the early years of the EU's construction was formed around the 'insecurity' caused by Europe's own internal oppositions, cultural differences and historically shaped animosities. The quest for peace and security was based on a perceived need for overcoming these divisions. Today, at the end of the long and sometimes haphazard path of European construction, we must ask a basic question: what does this uniquely European institutional evolution imply for the security of Europe (Leucht *et al.*, 2021; McCormick, 2020)?

Is there a distinctiveness in European history and culture with implications for how we confront security challenges? What indeed is 'European security'? What would it mean to say that Europe is insecure? What does it mean to say that Europe is threatened (Burgess, 2009b)? Is it the subways, bridges and railways, nuclear plants and other buildings that are under threat? Is it the ships and harbours, the sea lanes from the oil-exporting Middle East, that are in danger? Is it the oil and gas installations in the North Sea? Is it Europe's communications infrastructure that is exposed to attack? Is it Europe's 'borders' or its political leaders who are endangered? Or do threats concern something else, something more fundamental?

The challenge in answering these questions lies in our basic understanding of what threat is, what it means to predict it, what it means to react to it and what special challenges are brought by the new era of transnational terrorism. The purpose of this chapter is to indicate the shape of complexity involved in conceptualising European security today. These difficulties, I want to suggest, are not merely technical. Rather, the challenges emerge from the meeting between the human values that make European life what it is and the security technologies required to secure it. The challenge for European security research, I will argue, is to calibrate technological research to human needs, aspirations and fears of the citizens of Europe.

It is essential to not paint a picture here of a kind of irreducible opposition between technology and human values. Indeed, the reality is the contrary. Technology and human values are deeply interlinked. Yet, through educational traditions, scientific paradigms and institutional inertia, they are historically ghettoised. The conceptual bridge between them is value. Both technologies and human society and life are dependent upon their own understanding of value. Thus, value is the starting point of our analysis. What, then, is value (Burgess, 2011: 136–46)?

There is a wide range of theories of value. For our purposes, I wish to simply differentiate between a technical, economics-based notion of value and a culturally or socially based notion of value. According to neoclassical economics, the value of a thing is identical to the price it would bring in an open market. It is the worth of something relative to other things. Historically, the debate on economic value has revolved around the degree to which things have intrinsic value and the degree to which such value can be added or transformed. According to more culturally or socially based conceptions of value, the value of a thing is based on the particular quality of that thing that makes it valuable, i.e. either principles or standards that are socially accepted or moral ideas about what is good and right.

Thus, in social terms, it is not the materiality of a technical installation or structure that determines its value to society; it is rather the socially and culturally determined ideas of value that are attached to it, the historically, geographically, environmentally and also economically determined standards and measures which give it meaning in our lives. It is, therefore, not sufficient to refer solely to material or economic measures of value when considering technological objects. This is true for at least three reasons (Burgess, 2007). First, the market value of commodities produced, converted or transported by technical infrastructures varies as a function of a number of non-objective variables such as confidence, trust, fear, political climate and current events. The variation in oil prices is a significant example of this, but not the only one. Second, the cost of financing, or refinancing (and, not least, insuring), infrastructures also varies as a function of non-rational or non-material factors, with fear, mistrust and insecurity at the forefront. Third, threat is in part created, or at the very least supported, by the existence of infrastructures. The construction of infrastructure entails the construction of threat. Therefore, the value of critical infrastructure is in part determined by the potential danger of its destruction. There is, thus, a need for a kind of return to conceptual basics, to the basic ideas, concepts and definitions surrounding both human and technological values in Europe, in order to adequately bring safety and security to Europe.

The central principle is that threat involves an assessment of value and value is a fundamentally social, cultural and ethical term. To determine a threat is to situate a thing – in this case, European infrastructures – in a system of values that is structured and determined by the sphere of European society and culture. In order to move a step closer to this aim, let us look more closely at the value function of threat.

Threat and societal value

A threat is not simply an unknown danger lying in wait, ready to be launched upon us in some unknown way at some unspecified time. Threat is not incidental or accidental, or at least not entirely so. Nor is the effect of a threat independent of those targeted by it. Threat is not determined by others alone; it is codetermined by those who are under threat. This is why one can say that it is the existence of infrastructures which creates threat by virtue of creating value.

Threat is implicitly linked to what has value for us. It is linked to the possibility that what we hold as valuable could disappear, be removed or be destroyed. Objects of no value cannot be threatened in the same sense as those that do have value. The key to understanding threat therefore lies in understanding the systems which link human interests, values and things, such as infrastructures.

What, then, is the threat of terrorist attack? Terrorism goes well beyond ordinary threat by aiming at the fear of loss of what has value, and by striving to produce a signal effect of meanings from the very insecurities we already possess, insecurities that are already within us. These insecurities often have their origins in other contexts, in other times. They breed and mature in the hearts and minds of all of us. They have their roots in both past events and current vulnerabilities. Insecurities are caused both by the real, objective presence of threat and by the very effort of our authorities to protect us from threat. The disconcerting experience of security control and the presence of heavily armed security forces at all international airports is only one illustration of this.

How are value, threat and fear linked? The ideal terrorist act tries to find a fit between what we value, the fear of its loss implicit in that value and the political interests sought by those who carry out the act, though this link is never perfect or ideal. While infrastructure experts know and understand technical weaknesses in infrastructures, threat analysis must also take into account the human dimensions of loss associated with these infrastructures.

This naturally includes the consideration of how our lives would be practically changed by the destruction of such infrastructures. However, it also includes consideration of how our lives would be changed by the fear and insecurity created by such events, and how such fear asserts control on our lives and implants insecurity into our relation to both other potential targets and other aspects of our daily existence (Burgess, 2010).

It is not the disrupted train services, or oil production, not even the poisoning of a local water supply, in themselves which is significant for the terrorist, as horrible as these things may be. Rather, it is the loss of confidence in rail services, oil production, water supply and infrastructural services in general. It is not the reality of a computer virus in itself that we have to fear and which a terrorist might use as a tool but rather the fear of the release of a virus, the presence of a kind of symbolic virus, if you will permit me the metaphor, the contagion of insecurity, which disseminates distrust and fear, both in the world of private commercial services around which the European society is organised and also in terms of international trust and faith in a globalised market system (Burgess, 2007, 2008, 2009a).

We must, therefore, not fall back into a logic of the military fortress, in which the protection of material supplies is key to victory. We must remain aware of the socially and culturally determined systems of meaning which are the central concern of terrorist threat. It is less our physical security that must be assured as it is our moral security.

Classical war, terrorism and the value of destruction

According to the disconcerting logic of terrorism, destruction is, of course, a central value. Nothing is worth protecting or even saving if it does not have value. Nothing that serves or unites what we hold to be important can be separated from a certain kind of value. The valued thing is indispensable precisely because there is a cost associated with its loss. Perhaps more crucially in regard to possible responses to terrorist threat, one can say that nothing is worth attacking if it has no value (Schmid, 2004).

As absurd or uncivilised as terrorism might seem to us, it has a distinct function and logic. Indeed, it is this logic which assures the force of its name. If we know something to be terrorism – and all the signs of our public discourse would indicate that we do – then there is a distinct structure or form to it, and thereby a distinct predictability.

By the same token, terrorism respects a certain logic of threat. Terrorism formulates a relatively clear and instrumental aim, that of causing fear, weakening social and political solidarity, disrupting the institutional function of society and interrupting the exercise of the casually expected freedoms of liberal society. No part of the terror project has the destruction of infrastructure as its final goal, only as a means to another goal: the disruption of a culturally and socially determined way of life. Terrorism is a means to a non-technical end. Judging as one must both its ends and means, it obeys, more or less efficiently, an instrumental, goal-orientated rationality, which is, in the big picture, little interested in the technical values of Europe.

Terrorism, thus, chooses its targets and its means of attack in a manner that lends itself to predictability. The central axis of this logic is, for the terrorist as it is for civil society, a certain notion of value. Terrorism is without effect if it does not affect what has value for others. Both the ability of terrorism to successfully weaken society by attacking its infrastructure and our ability to protect society by protecting its infrastructure depend on a certain calculus of value, both human and technical.

Unfortunately, the technical-economic-material view of value is, in addition, particularly inept at seizing the value of spectacle implicit in today's terrorism. Through the virtues of global communication and our media-saturated society, the new generation of terrorism creates the spectre of a new kind of destruction, namely, the spectacular. While terrorism has a long prehistory prior to 11 September 2001, one of the great innovations of the attacks on New York and Washington was that they were orchestrated in order to take place before the eyes of millions. The menace was based on a carefully orchestrated spectacle.

Can the concept of war help us to understand the relation between security and values? The function of conventional war and warfare is instrumental. The function of a terrorism is psychological and symbolic. Its logic must therefore be understood differently. It is clear that European infrastructure is under threat. However, the logic of this threat is entirely different to the kind of threat produced and expected in wartime settings.

Where a critical infrastructure, let us say an oil refinery, contributes to the economic or technological nourishment of an enemy combatant, in this case, by producing fuel and other petroleum-based products to be used in the prosecution of war, destroying or damaging the installation shifts the balance of the conflict in the favour of the attacker. The function of the conventional war target is, in this sense, instrumental. The purpose of war is to interrupt the ability of the enemy to make war. The function of a terrorist target is psycho-symbolic. Its logic must be understood differently.

The terrorist logic of threat differs from this conventional one in a number of crucial aspects. First, the primary value of the target for the terrorist is symbolic, not material. Second, the primary value of the target is not determined by its use value. The material, economic and strategic consequences of destroying or not destroying the target cannot be directly correlated or calculated with any particular geopolitical aim. Third, the value of the target has political and social consequences in fields and domains not associated with the target. The consequences of terrorist threat are not military but social and cultural. Terrorist threat is affected by and causes changes in social and cultural values. Fourth, the value of the target is not stable or fixed. The determination of value of a target cannot be transferred or repeated from one target to another. The risk and value basis of risk, the danger and the value consequences that the threat implies vary from one social setting to another. Like the value itself, they cannot be determined objectively and consistently. Fifth, the determination of the value of a terrorist target has a second-order dimension. In other words, the determination of a target and the means of attack are derived from perceptions of the symbolic significance of both. These vary according to the public mood, to the political ambiance, to the economic conditions and to the sense of freedom, of patriotism, etc. Sixth, the determination of the consequences of an attack – the presupposition of any consequence management – is also of second order. The emotional, even moral, disruption such an attack would cause in a population, the ideological or symbolic effect it has, will depend upon a number of factors not objectively present or even associated with the attack itself. Rather, these are determined by previous experience, previous fears, allusions, associations and meanings. They depend upon already-existing fears, on political tendencies. They depend on the social, cultural and moral values of the population. Lastly, they depend on the vision of the future, the scenarios of fear created by the present attack.

What terrorism means

The aim of a terrorist attack is to create a certain kind of meaning. The successful terrorist attack is meaningful and projects enduring meaning. Terrorist threat to material infrastructure is not about infrastructure; it is about threat. The aim is not to disrupt electrical supply, computer networks or water and oil supplies; it is to disrupt confidence in these things. Threat, or rather more threat, will also be the desired result of terrorism. That is what sets it aside from classical war combat.

The notion of European safety and security protection thus clearly grows out of two lines of reflection, more or less at odds with each other. These two lines of reflection are, I believe, unifiable. One is an extrapolation of the essential economic freedoms embedded in the long-term project of European construction: subsidiarity, autonomy and liberal principles, an understanding of the world and of technology relating to the real damage that could potentially be caused by violent attack of one kind or another. The other is a reflection on the notion of threat and the nature of interconnectedness. This is a discourse of the imaginary, the playing field of terrorism (Oliveira Martins et al., 2022).

For terrorism nourishes a fundamental sense of insecurity that inhabits us all. Even though the attack is over, the target destroyed, damage done, people hurt or killed, it is essentially a reference to another, future attack, to an attack that has not yet taken place but is living in our imagination, an attack that is brewing in the hearts of every man and woman. The attacks of 11 September 2001 were catastrophic only in part because of what actually happened that day. They were also catastrophic because they fulfilled a collective fantasy of fear and destruction. We can see evidence of this fantasy in countless catastrophe films of the last decades. In this sense, the terrorist attack of the future is not really in the future at all. It has already taken place in our minds. The danger, the fear, the trepidation and the economic, social and moral costs are already being paid today.

In summary, the fundamental weakness in our 'defences' against terrorist violence is that it often builds purely upon a set of technological values. Yet, a terrorist attacker will not seek to disrupt the technical infrastructure with technical aims. Terrorist attack aims at a different pillar of technical infrastructure: its social, cultural and even ethical value. That value cannot be swept away by deploying more or stronger fortress solutions. The symbolic meaning can only be countered with the force of meaning.

Security and insecurity are thus implicitly related to human values. They are an expression of a certain understanding of human life, of individual and collective hopes and fears, of expectations about what might be lost and what is worth keeping, about what one is willing to sacrifice liberty for and, indeed, about what one is willing to fight or even die for. Security is a social, cultural, even ethical, concept. It does not primarily concern things alone but rather people who value things. Security is often associated with material and technical aspects of life because these tend, more and more in our age, to protect and embody the values of human life. Yet, they should not be confused with life itself.

To understand security and insecurity also presumes that one understands the socially and culturally determined values and motivations of those who would do harm. Sound, meaningful, effective and cost-efficient security research activities require research aimed at a thorough understanding of the social and cultural forces that:

(1) shape the values determining what is secure and insecure;
(2) motivate harm to what is of value;
(3) provide guidance in determining effective, appropriate and just responses to threat.

The primary weakness of the present specific programme on decision is that it essentially builds on an understanding of security as directed towards things. It must, in addition, be concerned with the significance, assumptions and consequences of the security of people.

The notion of 'security' is tied closely to the notion of threat, so our understanding of security depends on what we see as the main threats. As we know, the scenarios of threat and insecurity that both ordinary Europeans and European policy-makers confront have changed. Although the notion of 'terrorism' has a long tradition in European history, the fusion of terrorism and globalisation has created forms of transnational and supranational threats that defy the tried-and-tested State-based institutions designed to safeguard the modern nation-state. In one sense or another – and for better or worse – we have entered an era in which not only loyalties but also capabilities are no longer mainly aligned with any particular State, not even with intergovernmental agencies (Bellanova & de Goede, 2022).

As a consequence of this constellation of value and security, human knowledge and human behaviour as regards security are seen instrumentally as mere tools to be used in order to effect technological solutions to security problems. 'People' are regarded as a means to an end, instead of the end itself. Technological 'solutions' to security which do not seek to address the human at the heart of security and insecurity may end up defeating themselves or even the fundamental aims of the European project.

The Norwegian case shows the precariousness of the link between human life and the aims and end of security. Technology applied in security research which does not seek its finality in human value will ultimately have no value. It outlines a scenario of what can happen when security measures that, by design or neglect, become detached from the fundamental humanity at their roots risk becoming a source of insecurity instead. Among the oldest Western traditions is the notion that Europe is a project based on a set of shared values, that these values are the alpha and omega of provision of security. If, therefore, there is something called a 'security challenge', it is related, in one way or another, to the core idea of security as a set of values to which all material, technological, industrial and military means must ultimately return.

Security as knowledge

Security has undergone a fundamental shift in the last decades from an outward focus on a known enemy threatening the sovereign State to a general inward focus on a new constellation of threats that is at once globalised and localised, both ubiquitous and intensely individual. During the course of the

1980s and 1990s, the understanding of security shifted away from a logic of national security that opposed one State to other States. This logic, based on a range of conceptual oppositions – between self and other, the safe and the unsafe, the pure and the impure, good and evil, etc. – gradually began to wane. Instead, over the last thirty years, security as both concept and experience has undergone a shifting internal logic, in which security threats and the measures necessary to address them are more proximate, more common and more intimate. As a consequence, the politics of security has gradually shifted from being entirely about a foreign 'other' to being about us and, most significantly, about the other in us. Security politics increasingly concerns threats that do not respect borders and barriers. Rather, they are more ambient and more ubiquitous. Thus, globalised and localised security threats have changed their configuring of security from an optic whereby a border demarcates the end of security and the beginning of danger to an experience of the growing porosity of the security border. This shift has significant consequences for the way in which we understand a threat. Today, danger is increasingly perceived as residing among us, whether we speak of climate change, pandemics or data viruses, the danger is not a simple threat on the horizon, beyond the city walls or a well-guarded border. It is in some sense already here, already among us, already in us. It is thus easy to imagine that ubiquitous threats such as climate change, pandemics, cyber insecurity or food quality worries come to replace the classical geostrategic threats that characterised the Cold War, or that terrorism carried out by a state's own nationals is more menacing than the military threats that oppose one state to another.

Security and insecurity are gradually being internalised. It is no longer a question of shutting the threat out in order to assure security within what we might term prophylactic security, but rather of living with threat and the management of omnipresent danger (Bigo, 2006).

In a prophylactic configuration of security, the primary figure or symbol is the barrier. Security is understood as protection, shielding, refuge, a barrier against something 'other'. The prophylactic conception of security necessarily lends itself to a binary logic of threat, opposing security here to insecurity there, of us and them, friend and enemy, refuge and threat, and so on. Prophylactic security encapsulates the place or space of safety, dividing reality into an inside and an outside. The function of any security measure in this paradigm is to assure separation, that there is no leakage, contamination or corruption of the inside by the outside.

In this configuration, security measures take either the form of real separation actions – higher walls and thicker glass, surveillance measures which assure that the other remains where it belongs – or armed measures intended to force the 'other' to remain where it belongs. Non-physical and virtual prophylactic measures, while not playing out in space, nonetheless also apply a logic of othering to the danger or threats. Most consequential of these are the various forms of personal data-gathering, -sorting and -sharing practices that have come to dominate immigration policy in particular. The paradigms of classic war give considerable weight to this conception, and the now more or less discredited 'war on terror' has done much to revitalise and retool it.

More than ever before, security concerns us. As a consequence of the facts on the ground, the technologies that mediate the facts and the conceptual tools with which we connect our experience of the world and our embracing of or resistance against it, security has mutated into a reflexive enterprise. It has become self-ransacking in that we ourselves are accomplices in our own insecurity. At the level of high politics, this takes the form of the blurring of internal and external security matters. In fields dominated by information technology, such as global finance or communication, it is a question of becoming precariously dependent upon the very systems that threaten our stability.

Consequently, we can observe the concept of risk replacing the notion of threat in more and more contexts (Masys, 2022). The implication is that in today's 'security environment', even though we do not know what the danger is, we can respond to that ignorance by using risk as a kind of prosthesis of knowledge. Every unknown danger can be integrated into the calculus of how to respond as though it were a kind of known danger. This implementation of risk thinking is a response to the rise of non-conventional, non-national, non-contiguous threats, exactly those that have brought ambiguity to the interpretation of security threats.

This difference between the known and the unknown is not merely empirical (Nassim, 2007: 51–61). The unknown, in addition to being empirically unknown, is accompanied by an aesthetic, emotional and ethical effect of being unknown. The asymmetry of the known and the unknown lies in the shock of its potentially unexpected arrival. There is a near moral reaction or indignation when the unknown appears in a way that does not correspond to our preparations for it. It says something about us, our knowledge of ourselves and our surroundings and about our own moral character or disposition.

Indeed, instead of accounting for this strange meeting of pathos and fact, the social sciences deal with this phenomenon backwards. As Nassim Nicholas Taleb points out, the social sciences have feigned possession of tools capable of measuring uncertainty as though it were an empirical phenomenon since the beginnings of the conceptualisation of risk and risk analysis (2007: xvii–xx). The insurance and finance industries have brought this illusion to the highest levels: the uncertainty of loss is adequately calculated in order to entirely eliminate it from the equation of profit. Yet, in a real sense, what we do not know is far more historically consequential than what we do know. When what we do not know happens against all conceptualised likelihoods, its meaning is immense.

Clearly, this situation has important ethical consequences as well. For example, to take responsibility in any given situation implies relating to the unknown. To take responsibility in a strong ethical sense is to act in the absence of knowledge. Complete and integral knowledge makes responsibility meaningless. Knowledge sets aside the ethical imperative. Knowing, by contrast, and particularly in the realm of protecting from the non-perceived dangers of the unknown, requires no ethical insight. The transparent self-evidence of knowledge is factual and empirical, not normative, ethical or value-orientated. True responsibility takes the form of a kind of improvisation, of invention, of making something from nothing at all. Empirical or statistical knowledge about past occurrences can support our reflections but cannot tell us about what we should do.

In other words, the rise of risk in our time, and the expansion of the governance of dangers in place of a posture of protection against threats, is an ethical turn, a turn inwards towards the self. It seems clear that with the internalisation of danger in our time and the position of the social, cultural or political subject as the axis around which security and insecurity are experienced and pronounced, the constellation of ethical values is key. Yet, we lack a way to grasp the relation between security and the subject that it contributes to shaping or even generating.

Security and uncertainty

The increasing reflexivity of our insecurity fundamentally changes the equation of danger and protection that structures and justifies a range of social, political, economic and cultural institutions on both the national and international planes. More crucially, it disrupts a deeply entrenched understanding of how the self is constituted, and how the subject of politics understands itself and the horizon of reference and meaning available to it. Moreover, it reconfigures the very notion of what protection, danger and potential damage might be, how the vulnerable self, encapsulated in the vulnerable material borders of the body, meets the world of dangers. The decline of the prophylactic concept of security opens space for new insights into the self, new questions, uncertainties and insecurities.

This paradigm shift is not entirely complete. Despite this reflexive turn, the prophylactic impulse to deal with dangers by keeping them at bay remains in operation. We cling to the metaphysics of danger as a logic of presence-absence, whereby the aim of security measures is to remove threat and make absent the thing whose presence is endangering. At the same time, we remain haunted by the reality that danger is at hand in the very thought of its absence: fear arises as much from the thought of danger as it does from the presence of 'real' danger. This thought, perhaps even more than any material menace, is the primary cause of unease and insecurity.

In this sense, a certain degree of naiveté plays a role in the psychic management of insecurity. We can, for example, easily see ourselves as secure when we actually stand in imminent danger. Inversely, we can be convinced of our own insecurity while at the same time being in no danger at all. Security, in the shallowest sense, is inseparable from our own certainty of real and potential threats. Indeed, as the speed of politics and public expectations of political action in a media-driven public sphere increases, the old-fashioned distinction between the secure self, potentially threatened only by the contingent facts of a stable, objective world, and the objective or true source of threat becomes less tenable. The experience of 'threat', just like that of 'security', obeys the structures of an important and influential phenomenology. Threats are unlike others: they are not known, do not have force of presence and do not impact us as imminent damage or destruction might.

In other words, security and insecurity only 'happen' in the future. Security and insecurity are not experiences of the immediate present but of a possible destructive future. The contingency of insecurity, its status as possible but not inevitable, lies at the heart of its meaning and is key to its force. If a destructive event is certain and if we know of this unavoidability, then the destructive event is no longer a source of insecurity. It is already destruction, already the presence of the worst, already damage or death. Those who experience insecurity as certainty are, strictly speaking, not insecure because they are already dead. The only option for eliminating the insecurity of our imaginaries is the end of experience. This is not to downplay the 'experience' of death – if such a thing is understood as the end of biological life – but rather to say that the experience of the disaster and 'death' is displaced in time towards the present. For practical purposes, and notwithstanding post-death paranormal or spiritual activities that are beyond the scope of our reflection, insecurity is entirely played out before the event, but as the event. In other words, security is a singular experience of something that has not yet happened but which haunts our minds and shapes our actions with its inevitability. Obviously, the certainty of death cannot be experienced: the person who experiences death can no longer reflect upon the experience, nor relay it to others. It is this non-experience – and not death itself – that is the foundation of insecurity and the motivation for security measures of all kinds (Burgess, 2021).

Uncertainty thus becomes not only the basic epistemological support for experiences of and claims about security and insecurity. It is also its moral force, the source of its meaning, the support of the cultural, social and political differences in the way it is addressed and, to a large degree, the foundation for the political legitimacy of measures carried out in its name.

Security, in this sense, is a kind of prosthetic knowledge, knowledge of an unknown threat, knowledge of an unknown future. Security is knowledge of something about which, by any ordinary measures, we have no knowledge. An odd kind of knowledge, indeed! Security is knowledge that builds on everything except what epistemologists would call a sound basis for knowing. It is based on previous experience, traditions, culture, intuition, insight, wisdom, beliefs, superstition, etc. 'Politics' then becomes a discussion about what we don't know, about the unknown. It is about the unknown consequences of certain actions, unknown attitudes about what is 'best' for society, uncertain assumptions about the will of the people, etc. Were we to know with certainty what people wanted, what was possible, what the consequences of certain actions would be, then there would certainly be no role for politics.

Both classical epistemology and ethics maintain a fundamental and stable distinction between claims about what the world is and claims about what the world should be, between descriptive and normative claims. In addition to organising reality along the dividing line of the normative (to which we will return), this distinction also structures and supports the division of labour between academic fields and faculties. Much ink has been spent on this crucial question, and much more can be expected. It is impossible to do justice to this debate here other than to draw attention to the fact that it stems from the assertion that it is a matter of assertions. 'Knowledge' is reduced to assertions about 'knowledge' and, simultaneously, 'ethics' is reduced to assertions about 'ethics'. The question of the status, the reality or the being of knowledge and ethics is of particular interest. Is ethics, the theory of principles that govern behaviour, a kind of knowledge? Does knowledge itself possess the force of normativity? Behind these questions lies another set of postulates and a world of assumptions about what the world is, what its being entails and the divisibility of its being, not least being knowledge about the being of the world.

The core question for an ethics of security is: in what way can that which is not – that which is not yet – oblige us to certain kinds of actions? How can we foresee an ethics of future events that are formed and supported in the interstices of probability and supposition, whose ethos is couched in fear and an inability to effectively or successfully act (Burgess, 2011: 4–5)? I have argued that the basic premise of this distinction is a metaphysical insistence on the distinction between what is and what is not, even if 'what is not' actually exists in the form of a judgement about the future or the formulation of a normative claim. Yet, as we will see in a moment, risk thinking in our time transcends this notion. Risk analysis, management and communication are confronted – today more than ever before – with a future that lives itself out fully and powerfully in the present. More than ever before, value judgements involved in risk calculations not only reflect our past and characterise our present; they reach into our future, link to what we cannot yet know and what cannot yet guide us in our conduct. In other words, the status of knowledge about the world seems to give us indications about how we should act in the world.

I am not referring to certainty in normative statements (for example, what I should do if I acquire the knowledge that the dishes need to be washed). I am referring to the inherent certainty or uncertainty of knowledge itself, whose normative effects mobilise action. The force of not knowing something has itself enormous power, arguably more so than what we do know. This force of the unknown lies partly in the fact that we cannot plan for everything, that we must reconcile ourselves with the insecurity that lies in our inability to control events. There is always some degree of chance, of uncertainty in our future. We are aware that we always see 'through a glass darkly'. This is the very nature of consciousness. On the other hand, our lives are not governed by randomness, falling upon us in a purely accidental way, adding a layer of uncertainty or insecurity to everything we think or do.

The 'space' between these two kinds of normative claims, of necessity and randomness, is where ethics 'happens'. Ethics, from a certain point of view, is nothing other than making decisions in the absence of certainty. If there were certainty about our actions, if we actually knew without doubt what to do, then this could be many things, but it would not be called ethics. It might not even be part of human consciousness. Ethics lives in the world of inadequate knowledge and randomness. This is also the home of risk analysis.

Security as ethics

The relation between security and ethics is an old one. Particularly in the area of international relations, from the moment insecurity was formulated as a concern for the future with an implicit appeal to political or other action, it has been formulated in terms of implicit or explicit ethical claims. Indeed, one of the premises of realist international relations theory is the bracketing of ethical issues. The international arena is structured by networks of power in which value orientations are invisible. More recently, the maturing of one variant or another of liberal internationalism has brought an influx of works and debates about the ethics of international actors. Already in *Inside/Outside*, Walker critiqued this rapidly growing niche in IR theory, which called itself 'ethics and international relations' (Walker, 1993: 50). However, unlike Walker, who regards 'ethics' and 'international relations' as two autonomous discourses, too far afield from each other to have any conceptual communication, we consider ethical values and the international as inseparable (Burgess, 2011: 11–13).

The term 'ethics' has a broad range of meanings, which are the objects of innumerable historical and systematic debates (Steele, 2013). At the risk of overgeneralising, ethics, in the vast majority of philosophical perspectives, corresponds to one or another systematisation of substantial, stable, coherent, understandable, autonomous values of good and evil, virtue and vice, right and wrong, and so on. Different ethical theories set out different criteria and procedures for arriving at knowledge of what this value is, but all presume that it is a kind of knowledge, knowledge that is knowable by virtue of metaphysical assertions, deductive claims, consensus, political deliberation or tacit social or cultural processes. A variety of discourses of ethics are in play in such debates, far too many to canvass here. All such discourses of ethics share the aim of providing a stable platform for decision-making about human action, a system that is portable from one empirical setting to another and from one individual to another. The grandiose presumption of ethical theory understood in this conventional way is that ethics is knowledge, and that 'doing' ethics is a straightforward, empirically grounded process. Ethics is about discovering what is already out there, uncovering, exposing or casting light on the right, the good, the just, the appropriate in all its ideal, contextual or pragmatic diversity. Even though many ethical theories would take some kind of subjective moral faculty as a central support of ethical judgement, this subjectivity is, in the course of moral reasoning, inevitably recast as an object of ethical reasoning and argument. It becomes the crystallised anchoring point of a deduction based on observable facts and unwavering ideas.

The necessary assumption behind such discussions is a Cartesian subject of ethics whose premises are generally passed over in silence. The Cartesian subject – one of an endless range of the possible forms of the subject of ethics – is well known and well documented in other critiques of modernity, but seldom applied to a critique of philosophical ethics. It is rational, autonomous, sovereign, self-conscious, self-present, unified, stable and, above all, free. In short, the subject of ethics is – by nature or by principle – secure. When we take as our point of departure the assumption of a timeless, universal Cartesian subject of ethics (but also of politics, humanity, civilisation, etc.), we are making an assumption about the inviolability, the incorruptibility and unassailability of the subject of ethics. In short, we are making assumptions about its security. The traditional subject of ethics is one whose own security does not come into question.

The post-Cartesian subject of ethics, by contrast, is one guided and structured by insecurity. Thus, long before any observation or assertion can be made about the security of an individual, a group, a State, the planet or anything at all, the insecurity of the subject position from which such an observation or assertion is made is already in play. The security of the subject is already suspended. The insecurity of the subject, its fragility and vulnerability, the question or doubt about its security, is already active in any observation or predication. It is possible, even important, to develop the status of the subject in Western modern history subjectivity as less than self-evident; its position, stability and certainty are themselves subject to a certain kind of fragility.

To bring together this observation about the fragility of the subject of security and our insights about security as knowledge, a new conceptualisation of ethics itself is needed. A useable ethics must account for the reflexivity of security knowledge at the end of modernity without taking the status of the subject of ethics for granted.

'Ethics' is thus defined as the principle governing conduct in the absence of adequate knowledge of the future. This definition contains both a commonplace view about the situation of ethics in time and a provocation about the relation between ethical judgement and knowledge.

First, ethics is always about the future. The terms and conditions for action, for deciding on how to behave, are by necessity set out in reference to acts not yet carried out. Ethics is always future-orientated, organised around events that have not yet taken place, around facts that do not yet have the status of facts, relative to conditions that are not yet fulfilled and consequences that can only take the shape of potential.

Second, as a consequence of being about the future, the epistemological foundations of ethics in general and of security in particular are unlike any other. Ethics starts and ends in knowledge we do not have. Like security, it makes up a set of ad hoc principles not only about what has not yet happened but, more importantly, based on what has not yet happened. If security is 'knowledge' about the future, then assuring security is already a kind of ethics, already a way of deploying a certain set of ideas or principles in the face of the unknown. What is novel and crucial here is that the 'unknown' of the future and its way of being both unknown and unknowable is not some contingency, not some inconvenience that we can prepare for or hope to overcome. The unknownness of the future is the condition of security. Assuring the security of a future that is known (bracketing for a moment the fact that the future can by definition never be known) would simply not be security. As we cannot know what the empirical setting for future actions will be, nor what consequences our actions will have, inadequate, incomplete or imperfect knowledge is not the exception but rather the only available foundation for ethical judgement. If we supplement these insights with a more general understanding of security as both an experience of the compression or acceleration of time and a function of precaution in the face of an unknown and dangerous future, we arrive at a new understanding of the ethical subject of security.

By its very character, security does not organise knowledge as a function of certainty about imminent dangers. A threat that is 'imminent' – so imminent that it can be regarded as certain – is no longer within a logic of security (or insecurity). If the actualisation of a threat is utterly unavoidable, if its damage is on the order of necessity, it has – in the logic of security, based as it is on the modalities of fear and the practices of precaution – for all practical and conceptual purposes, already happened; there is no security-relevant difference between judgement of imminence and the disaster itself. This is because at such a point in the actualisation of threat, fear is absolutely justified and precaution is no longer a functional option. Fear that is factual, whereby the imagined catastrophe in fact corresponds to reality, is, strictly speaking, not fear. For fear depends, for its very coherence, on some minimum degree of unreality in order for the power of the imaginary to do its work. Precaution is equally incoherent and impracticable at the moment of imminence for the margin of time in which to exercise caution is reduced to immediacy. In other words, at the moment of imminence, in conceptual terms, the damage or destruction is already done. If the floodwaters are already rising, if the pandemic has arrived, if the bullet has already left the barrel of the gun, then we are in more or less severe peril, but we are no longer insecure (bracketing, for the sake of argument, the various knock-on-wood forms of insecurity, such as the economic insecurity caused by floodwaters, the immune system insecurity caused by pandemics or the insecurity of others caused by murder by bullet).

Insecurity and the ethics it supports thus obey a logic of contingency. They function in a frame of multiple futures. Security is a question of what options we have for saving ourselves, protecting ourselves, for preparing for what might come. It is a configuration of the present and future wherein the possibility of choice can lead to one or another varying future, differing results to a possible course of events. Insecurity is the space of choice, of the aleatory, of alterity, of a certain liberty. It is, in other words, the space of ethics. When danger is imminent, when there are no alternatives to the catastrophe, when the thought of options is absorbed into the careering locomotive of the necessary, then choice too disappears.

Insecurity is the experience of holding forth when we are unsure of the dangers, when the danger and its consequences still lie outside of the necessary. If we know what catastrophe awaits us, then the experience does not belong to insecurity. It is far more an experience of certainty, certainty of the kind that surely belongs to the order of the aesthetic, perhaps of the theological. It is for this reason that we conclude that security is itself ethics.

If we understand ethics as the principles governing behaviour in the absence of adequate knowledge, then surely security is an ethics. For security is simply an approach to the future that not by chance but by necessity is unknown and rife with dangers.

What we now describe as an 'ethics of security' does not correspond in its structure, concepts or content as a simple 'ethics of'. Indeed, the more general consequence of our reflection is that there is no sense in saying 'ethics of'. It cannot be a question of an ethics of security. We might understand by 'ethics of' that an autonomous set of principles for action or behaviour can be unproblematically brought to bear on a discrete object called security, such that the properties of the thing called security trigger the subjective principles in the *dispositif* called ethics, thus letting itself be governed by these principles. This is at best problematic because security itself is an ethical *dispositif*, a set of tools and arrangements that organise the future as an experience of the unknown, of unknown dangers, the very knowledge of which is an imposition of the choice with certainty with which the subject of security is necessarily made up.

Security is the moral, cognitive and aesthetic encapsulation of the horizon of danger that derails and re-rails the circuits of the self, the means, measures and logics by which the self sees itself, knows itself, values itself and takes measures in the world in order to advance and preserve what is of value to itself. This means something more than simply asking and adequately answering the questions 'Who am I?' or 'Who are we?' It means a continuous reorganising of both the question and the political meaning of the question.

Paradoxically, for risk analysis in the narrow sense of the term, ethics is not simply an alternative. By this, I do not mean that it would be advantageous to incorporate ethics into risk analysis; rather, that risk analysis is ethics from start to finish, if we define ethics, as I do, as making decisions under conditions of inadequate knowledge, decisions in which it is the incalculable, the entirely human, that takes responsibility.

This preoccupation with certainty naturally has consequences for the way that we study security: the kind of security research questions that are asked, by whom and for whom, and the kind of status the answers to such questions can actually have. Given the rise in risk studies as a sister field to security studies, it is unsurprising that security knowledge itself shifts towards an assessment of risk, which by definition reflects future realities.

As we know, the recent engagement of security studies with risk studies draws force from a scientific tradition growing out of the actuarial sciences. Security studies' reliance on science and technology and their easy adoption of the gadget fetishism of technological security management and less material techniques of governance are both odd and disquieting. The epistemological lineage of the natural sciences is organised by a straightforward logic of the epistemē, the opposition between the unknown and the known. Science derives its rationality, but also its normative force and legitimacy, from the primacy of the known or the immediately to be known. And yet, security is by definition excluded from this field. For security concerns precisely what we do not know. As soon as the unknown becomes known, it ceases to be a question of security.

The entire rationality of its politics revolves around one epistemological aberration: security is by nature a relation to what is unknowable. The moment the unknowable threat becomes known, it ceases to be a threat.

3

The invention of vulnerability

> A person is, among all else, a material thing,
> easily torn and not easily mended.
> McEwan (2016)

Security as spirit

Security comes from nothing more nor less, has no other origin or finality, than spirituality. In more everyday terms: nothing else matters. Spirit is the beginning and the end of security. From terrorists to tornados, from computer viruses to pandemic viruses, threats render us insecure by the transformation that lets danger find a path into that unique place in us that is the foyer of fear: human spirit. Security threats, to the extent they are transcendental, as I have argued in Chapter 2, are inherently spiritual. By this, I mean that they spring out of a sense of ourselves that is ecstatic, that is beyond us, surpasses or transcends us. Security is the discourse of a relation to our sense of selves, individual, societal, national, in religious, cultural or gender terms. It is the capture of the meaning of our lives and the form our lives take through our everyday activities. Security acquires meaning from the instant we seize our being, from the instant we understand ourselves as being in the world. Such being in the world, in the metaphysics of the West, expresses itself through a double experience.

On the one hand, it is existential in the sense that ascertaining that we exist, that we are, is only possible against the backdrop of our eventual non-existence, our destruction or death. Realising that we exist is a simultaneous realisation that the non-existence is possible. In purely material, biological terms, the character of the organic systems that make up the human body makes inevitable this possible non-existence. The biology of human life takes the form of a countdown to biological death. Our cells are programmed to age, to decay and decline. We hold enough basic knowledge of human life to know and understand to a certain degree that by affirming life, we affirm death as the termination of existence in the most concrete, material sense. Security is, in this sense, existential.

On the other hand, security is the thought of something that persists. In thinking of security, we attribute a kind of meaning to that which is, that which exists. We believe it has merit that something about this life should survive, is worth investing resources in, holds a perennial value. Any security measure is the expression of the meaning that surpasses the thing whose security is in question. The very notion that we invest ourselves or our resources to preserve something is a faraway call to preserve from the danger that threatens it in ways that can only be imagined. The reality of the future loss of life and limb or valued material objects is the spiritual existence of the thing and the spiritual experience of its being. Insecurity is the continuous authentification of the spiritual, of the existence of the Great Beyond, of the meaning that it transcends, of the sense that reigns from afar. Not insecurity cast by the Old Testament threat of a vindictive creator but rather insecurity as the ephemeral presence of the meaning of life. Even in a pragmatist vein, regarding the world with purely empirical eyes, from the side of the world, of things that are, that can threaten or be threatened, the objects that we most often associate with security, with being the cause of danger or its object, this experience originates in a place that is not ours (see Dupuy, 2015: 1–9).

No purely external action can assuage insecurity. No amount of locks and barriers, bombs and bullets, surveillance, control, intelligence or authority can extinguish the last external cause of insecurity if there is the least remaining ember of vulnerability in the heart of the observer. Far from the prophylactic guards with which nature has equipped itself, there is a core enabler of insecurity, that is, of humanity. The core insecurity is not itself the cause of insecurity. It does not suffice on its own to create the threat; it is not a threat unto itself, and yet, there is no threat before this thing. Its 'threat-ness', its need and ability to generate insecurity, paradoxically precedes, lies outside, while at the same time being intimately part of, it. It is what Kant called 'transcendentally external', something that is external without being external in space (Kant, 1998: 425–9).

The consequence of the metaphysical collapse caused by the shift from security as an experience of the other, of forces good and evil that are external to us, to an experience of security as an expression of the self is significant. An external danger is, of course, of a completely different order to an internal danger. Securitising for an external threat takes an entirely different quality of spirit to an internal one, a different moral tenor, a different form of courage, a different kind of defence.

The internalisation of security corresponds with the spiritualisation of security I am attempting to describe. Yet, it is more than a simple internalisation, more than simply moving the problem 'inside' – whatever this might actually mean for the nature of things, should we attempt to fill it with substance. Spirit was, of course, already 'inside', that is, tucked away in this non-spatial 'place' where spirits are supposed to live, in a paradoxical capacity that Kant uses pages to try to account for – the 'place' from which the moral experience of insecurity emanates, the reference, the orientation or the non-spatial coordinates that switch on the alarm bells that say, in our conventional thinking, 'danger'.

The internalisation of security is in effect the movement of a double insight. The first insight is that what is essential about the threat behind our insecurity was never spatially outside. As decades of critical security studies have shown, exteriority is the great ruse of the realist security policies. It is the narrative that insists that 'strategic' battles are won and lost by intervening in any number of external dangers, by the expansion of a certain kind of power through external means. The conflict, the realists insist, is 'out there', as is, therefore, the insecurity, and the ambition of re-established security. Thus, even where there is an external empirical event beyond the immediate reach of the subject of security, it is through the subjectivity of the subject that an empirical event becomes a security event. This first insight is linked to the discovery that insecurity, though it can be modulated by manipulating the external environment, is ultimately a function of 'internal' conditions, be they political, social, cultural, religious or other. The externality of threat depends to such an extent upon the internal subjectivity of the insecurity that the external/internal opposition is surpassed. This internalisation of insecurity is an extension of Beck's 1986 observation that the historical phase of late industrialisation corresponds with a similar internationalisation of ecological danger (Beck, 1992: 51–89). It is a shift from an understanding of external nature as the primary source of danger to the well-being of human society, to the insight that society has become the primary threat to itself, that the ecological by-products of industrial production have replaced the imagined dangers of exogenous nature.

The second insight is that the origin or the 'cause' of the insecurity that supports the security event is *not outside*. Insecurity is not perfectly exogenous. Insecurity 'without' is always prepared and supported by a certain insecurity 'within'. There is no externality that can be the entire cause of insecurity, of danger or of threat. The social, cultural, psychic or spiritual conditions of the observer are the fundament for an empirical fact or event becoming a source of danger. The precondition of any experience of danger is the pre-existence of that danger. In effect, any danger that is affirmed as danger has already been a danger, has already been affirmed, represented, suspected, intuited as dangerous. Danger is always already danger. It has no origin outside of danger, no extra-danger moment or quality. Danger, by its nature, is not dangerous unless it has already presented itself as dangerous. No fact or event that is completely unknown to be dangerous, but then presents itself as dangerous, can be the source of the experience of danger. What is perfectly, unmitigatedly harmless will never have access to the experience of danger.

To be clear, I am not suggesting that there are no events that are not harmful or destructive, far from it. I am referring rather to the possibility of experience of this harm, and, more directly, the experience of the possibility of this harm prior to it doing harm, potential harm, harm before harm, so to speak.

The perception according to which any security threat counts has merit, weight, credibility, etc., the proof that one is actually endangered and the indication of the degree to which one is endangered, is an image, an imagination of what could or would potentially happen, an imagined experience of the danger, the danger, in a sense, before the danger. This is, in the most concrete sense, what insecurity consists of. Insecurity is the experience of danger before the fact, the experience of danger that is coming, arriving but not yet entirely dangerous, danger-less danger, so to speak.

In this sense, danger also carries a certain amount of contingency. Any danger, or the insecurity that arises in relation to it, is to some extent based on the *wait*, on the fact that it has not yet come to pass, has not yet been realised. In other words, there is associated with it a moment of uncertainty, of contingency. The insecurity of insecurity has an order. The first order is a linear one, the relation to a direct threat, whether it be imminent or far off. Here, the insecurity is measured as a question of what will happen when it happens, when the danger presents itself and becomes a fact, of the degree of damage or of pain when what we know will happen happens. The second order is a geometric one. It corresponds to the insecurity created by the lack of certainty about whether what might come will come.

Around the end of the 1990s, the Norwegian public sphere could best be described as in a mood of crisis. On New Year's Eve 1991, the northwest coast of Norway was struck by the most dangerous weather system since measurements had begun in 1867. In the spring of 1995, eastern Norway was struck by a deadly flood. In addition, the transportation sector experienced several serious accidents. Among them, the MS Sleipner, a high-speed catamaran ferry which ran aground in bad weather off the southwest coast of Norway and sank in November 1999, killing sixteen passengers. In Åsta, Hedmark, a deadly train collision claimed the lives of nineteen passengers. These events, in addition to several other occurrences, put a focus on the potential for large and serious accidents related to Norway's late industrialisation and its technical and economic legacy. On top of these industrial accidents, concerns over the Y2K effect, the possible breakdown of crucial computer infrastructure at the turn of the millennium, drew considerable media attention to the possible vulnerabilities in society and social life. These events, as well as others, constituted what would be called by the Ministry of Justice at the end of the decade the 'new threat picture'.

This was the expression used in the communiqué that was initiated in 1999 to document and analyse these new vulnerabilities, to 'strengthen society's security and preparedness against crises and catastrophes' (JPD, 1999). As we will see, there was in this announcement, and the work of the commission that followed from it, a clear understanding of social phenomena and social need that could not be captured through the structure or values of the Cold War strategic discourses of threat. The commission would be responsibile for analysing this broadly cast concern was later given the name the 'Commission on Vulnerability', after the title of its final report, *A Vulnerable Society: Challenges for Security and Preparedness in Society* (NOU, 2000), which was submitted to the Minister of Justice a year later.

It is in the final report of the Commission on Vulnerability that we find the frequent use of the term 'societal security'. Even more importantly, we discover in relation to this newly forged concept an unprecedented reflection on what society is, what it means to threaten society, what it means to say that a society is security and what kinds of measures should be put into place in order to secure society. Through both the introduction of the concept of societal secure and the reflection about its meaning in society, the report became an essential milestone in Norwegian thinking on society and security. The report cleared space for a range of philosophical questions on Norwegian society by building upon considerable self-insight and uncharacteristic openness to self-critique. The Commission's final report still stands today as a primary reference for Norwegian thinking about societal security and an important point of orientation for the assessment of change in the relationship between the concepts of society and security, and the evolution in the concept through the following two decades. 'Societal security' and the concept of 'vulnerability' became the new signs of our generation.

Although the report *A Vulnerable Society* did launch the career of an influential concept, it is by no means a revolutionary document. The report's immediate impact was actually quite modest. Even though the leader of the Commission, former Prime Minister Kåre Willoch, would later regret how little the report's findings were attended to and how much the Commission on Vulnerability had got right about future threats to 'the Norwegian', the report still carries repercussions for security policy, and in particular societal security policy, in Norway (Tveita, 2008). The report first and foremost launched an important constellation of concepts, ideas, themes, terms and arguments, all of which were new in Norway, and for the most part in the world. As we will see, these continue to be misunderstood even as they are being instrumentalised to manufacture political gain. The concept of societal security has in this sense been a victim of its own success. We have arrived at the point where it is equally impossible to be 'against' societal security as it is to be against gravity. In Norway it has become an axis around which social politics can be formulated, an anchoring for formulating and debating societal values, for securing if not society then a discourse that keeps alive the question of what society is, or what it should be.

One expression of that politicisation can be observed in the way the Cold War's concept of security obstinately remained in public discourse, held fast like the lichens on a Norwegian fishing trawler. The bipolar security concept of the Cold War remains a relic that will not disappear, that clings to us or that we cling to with a tenacity that is not justified by its waning utility. At the same time, as the Commission on Vulnerability's report clears the way for new paths with its inventive take on societal security and preparedness, Minster of Justice Odd Einar Dørum, who mandated the Commission, turns his back to it and defaults to the old geostrategic security paradigm. In the announcement of the Commission's report, Dørum points out that: 'the Commission will work parallel with the commission analysing the Armed Forces' mission and ambitions, and will also cooperate with it'. 'The Commission's advice', he continues, 'will be important for the Government's further work with preparedness and measure in favour of society's vulnerability' (JPD, 1999). The Norwegian Armed Forces' Commission, named three months earlier and led by the leader of the Committee for Defense Policy at the time, Odd G. Andreassen, was to result in the publication of its own report in 2000, *A New Norwegian Armed Forces* (Andreassen et al., 2000).

The mandate of the Commission on Vulnerability

That two parallel analyses of 'societal security' should take place at the same time is not merely accidental. It is rather a sign of a paradigm shift and a certain competition for conceptual dominance. The naming of the National Armed Forces Commission, independently but simultaneously to the Vulnerability Commission suggests just such a tension. Whoever has control over the important political concept controls, at the same time, the most important public resources. In 1999, Norway's Armed Forces were faced with significant reorganisation. In a hierarchical organisation like the military, such a process was naturally painful. A new age of industrialisation and commercialisation of security driven and supported by the principles of New Public Management was bringing about a certain number of challenges to legitimacy in a land where both the public administration and the State enjoy widespread trust.

The Commission on Vulnerability is in many ways path-breaking as far as security thinking is concerned in modern, post-war Norway. As I will try to show in due course, this new thinking – let us call it the 'new bureaucratisation' – would come to leave a very strong impression on the modern understanding of both protection and preparedness. However, in many ways, the Commission also fell victim to this transformational moment in modern Norwegian history that it was essentially deeply tangled up with. Even though 1999 was a remarkable year in terms of insight into the degree to which Norwegian society was affected by international processes and a new threat complex, Norwegians continued to view 'security' as a different type of problem, one marked by Cold War metaphysics and realism's limitations, which I discussed in the previous chapter. The reverberations from the Cold War's traumatic splitting of the world into two segments, held apart through a strategy of mutual assured destruction, were still quite strong, the 'modern' political Norway having been reborn after the war, and Russia's geopolitical presence, primarily but not exclusively limited to a short, shared border, still the main focus of Norwegian geopolitical imaginary.

This tension between the new and the old becomes particularly clear in the Commission on Vulnerability's mandate and, to a lesser degree, in the mandate of the analysis carried out by the National Armed Forces Commission. In the announcement establishing the Commission on Vulnerability, the Minister of Justice underscores that 'the evolution in both security policy and society create new forms of risk for the security of our country' (JPD, 1999). The Commission's mandate appeals to two different types of problem and two different political discourses, connected to two different threat assessments, different mechanisms of governance and different economic resources. According to the Minister of Justice, the investigation on societal security would function as a kind of supplement to the one carried out by the Armed Forces Commission. It would, sure enough, map the 'force of resistance' against threats to 'our society', 'in addition to the security that can be created through military means' (JPD, 1999). In other words, the Minister's standpoint in 1999 was that societal security was a supplement to the security provided by the Armed Forces, a type of civil preparedness that in one way or another came in addition to that traditional kind of security thinking, which itself had deep and traumatic roots in the Cold War. What we will see, in part through our analysis of the Commission on Vulnerability's investigation, is that these parallel concepts of security, of what can and cannot threaten a country, about the relation between the 'social' Norway and the 'geopolitical' Norway, these two diverging visions of the country, society and the world, will converge in the course of the 2000s. They will be linked together with each other and develop a reciprocal dependency.

However, what can be seen is that the 'national and the international developmental traits of significance for the task of preparedness' would mark not only the 'new threat picture', that is, the dominant perception of the new dangers that appear through new types of weapon technologies, new types of dangerous criminal groups, challenges linked to global health, international migration and climate change. They were also to generate new questions about the toolbox that political authorities in Norway should have at their disposal. Security became increasingly a question of the changing relationship between *protection* and *preparedness*, about the ability of the National Armed Forces to protect the State and society's own inherent ability for preparedness relative to the new threats against society.

The tension between defensive military protection and societal preparedness is not absolute. It has, indeed, never been absolute. In this sense, the field of focus of the Commission on Vulnerability overlaps somewhat with that of the National Armed Forces' analysis. According to the Minister of Justice, the Commission was to provide an overview of the risk for 'extraordinary shock inflicted upon civil society in times of peace, security crises and war' (JPD, 1999). The Minister understood that war created not only security challenges but also societal challenges.

In this way, the ambivalence surrounding the relationship between the Armed Forces and the Commission on Vulnerability's investigation in 1999 was the expression of an altogether new historical context. This was basically the case for the whole conceptual history of civil preparedness, from the heights of the Cold War in the 1960s to the fall of the Berlin Wall. During the Cold War, most NATO members had some kind of national civil coordination in order to protect their populations against the nuclear threat and to prepare themselves for life after a nuclear attack. Such arrangements were based on coordinating and giving practical advice to citizens in the case of lines of communication being broken, the destruction of public institutions or the disabling of local or national governments. The arrangements were unique in that they focussed on the ability of the military connected to civil society and to an emphasis on technical and engineering tools that were available.

At the time, the concepts of civil preparedness and civil defence arrangements were unique in that they were used to call upon and assign responsibility for protection to the civil population itself. It was a kind of self-organisation and self-mobilisation in which, aside from a few low-level coordination officers, the entire population was to steer itself, to generate and incorporate its own legitimacy and the origin of its own governing power. Civil preparedness, such as it was practised at the end of the 1960s, constituted an early militarisation of the public sphere. It was the attachment of the unarmed public to one of the zones of responsibility of the military, namely, the defence of society. The population was assigned a number of tasks that would ordinarily fall to the military (Kincade, 1978). In Norway, civil preparedness as a concept of defence policy was introduced in 1949 as a result of the Defence Commission named in 1946 by the first post-war government and Prime Minister Einar Gerhardsen (Forsvarskommisjonen, 1949).

Three important elements should be noted in connection with the reorganisation of the relationship between the military and civil society. First, an attack using nuclear weapons would be so utterly destructive and comprehensive that the usual 'fronts' would disappear. Norms and rules for symmetrical war would be suspended. Second, the central societal institutions would be incapable of providing the necessary societal services. Third, the result of a nuclear attack would not be limited to military units or military personnel; civilian loss would be considerable. Mechanisms and arrangements that are usual for the military would no longer be valid.

In many ways, civil preparedness is the original expression for societal security, in the sense that it is society itself that to a greater or lesser degree must take responsibility for security. The logic is simple: if society stands on its own two feet, its own security will be more robust. If the link between individuals and groups in society is both stronger and more flexible, cemented through traditions, rituals and ways of being together, and is more organic, more prepared and willing to adopt new practices and members, it is also more secure. Civil preparedness is thereby the original preparedness. Of course, the original preparedness arrangements were not created from mere cultural or philosophical observations about the inherent robustness of societies but rather from the assumption that all infrastructure and publicly organised mechanisms of coordination would be obliterated in a nuclear conflict. Nonetheless, the trace of the nuclear threat from the Cold War's coldest time remains in the chemical, biological, radiological and nuclear (CBRN) threats that the mandate of the Commission on Vulnerability describes as 'risk, vulnerability, and preparedness on the civil side' (NOU, 2000).

Preparedness 'on the civil side' thus becomes expanded to simply 'preparedness' and 'preparedness systems', and the level for 'acceptable security for the civil population'. However, there is an essential difference between 'security for the civil population', such as when the Commission on Vulnerability received the mandate, and civil preparedness as it was understood during the Cold War. The difference lies in the conviction about who or what has the ability and responsibility to maintain that security. The Commission's mandate was formulated so that the recommendations on the authorities' prioritisation would be delivered to the authorities such that they could provide the needed security in the best possible manner. Society as a possible source of security has been forgotten, left behind in the twentieth century.

What is vulnerability?

It is not too trivial to say that the foundation of the Commission on Vulnerability, as well as the field of political tension it is played out in, is vulnerability. Vulnerability is, in many ways, an ideal political term in the sense that most political actors would have something to say about what it is and means, while at the same time, few would be willing to define it. A central challenge for the Commission on Vulnerability was therefore to clarify a concept that could make itself understood for all interested parties. The mandate of the Commission does not give any guidance about what vulnerability is, only indicating that it should be reduced: 'An expression for the problems a system has in functioning when it is exposed for an undesired event, as well as problems the system has with taking up its activity after an event has taken place' (NOU, 2000: 18). This definition is of a technical nature and is connected with an understanding of vulnerability as a technical challenge. That point of departure appeals, to some degree, to the original concept of civil preparedness assured by the population, supported by a variety of technical abilities themselves based on the modernisation of the quickly expanding industrialisation and professionalisation of engineering. As can be read in the Commission's report, the key ideas are the 'system' itself and the 'problems' the system can be exposed to when it is under extreme pressure. Vulnerability, in this constellation, refers to a system's ability to take care of itself under this extreme pressure. This kind of system thinking remained vital and was developed by the faculties of engineering and the early, first-generation ICT sciences that sought primarily to systematise an understanding of the likelihood that a link in any given technical system should fail.

By 'system', we understand a set of things that function together, an order, a logic that consists of several parts connected together, with reciprocal dependency such that when one or several components fail, the system becomes less functional in relation to its actual or original aims. At its most general level, a system consists of three elements: a structure, several components and a rule or logic according to which the relation between them is governed. The Commission on Vulnerability refers to physical, technical systems, highway and rail infrastructures, power grids, telephone networks, water supply, sewage, etc. In other words, it speaks of the mechanisms that, because they form the basis of Norway's well-being and further development, thereby become elements of vulnerability in the face of accidents, natural catastrophes or inimical actions. Preparedness in its traditional meaning refers to physical systems and material catastrophes. Vulnerability refers to the danger that these systems are damaged or destroyed to a sufficient degree that Norwegian society itself becomes threatened or damaged.

It is, thus, *physical* vulnerability that is the point of departure for the mandate of the Commission on Vulnerability. The Commission was charged with 'analysing the vulnerability situation and giving a principled assessment of the strengths and weaknesses in today's preparedness systems' (NOU, 2000: 17) These preparedness systems were and could be thought of as material, technological systems. There was, at that time, no tradition or concepts for thinking about security and preparedness as distinct ideas. Vulnerability was seen as vulnerability in the systems that took care of society. The mandate gives 'recommendations for measures for assuring an acceptable security for the civil population and critical societal functions in peace, crises, and war' (24), but security is not a part of, but rather dependent upon, the reduction of vulnerability of the physical systems that support society and hold it together. In this sense, the 'critical societal functions' contain something that is other than what services society itself. Among these tasks, the Commission was to evaluate the organisation of 'vulnerability-reducing work' (8).

'System' is understood here as a set of technical components bound together in a relation of interdependence. Failure of one component has consequences on how other components and systems function in their totality. The system's robustness or resistance is an expression of the degree to which individual components, the links between the components and the norms and rules that govern these things are impacted by crises or shocks, of whether the functions can be transferred to other parts of the system, whether new functions can replace older ones, whether unused elements can be retired or removed. In this sense, resistance of complex technical systems has long been a measure for the functionality of a system. Complex technical systems are made to be able to carry out a concrete set of tasks in a dependable, predictable and continuous way. Interruption is acceptable only as planned changes of components like, for example, an extension of reconfiguring with the aim of improving results to increase the speed, quality or quantity of the planned output. This is the basic understanding of resilience of a technical system.

Sociological research in the 1970s, most prominently Talcott Parsons, first brought the insight that society functions as a system (Parsons, 1977, 1991). It can, as well as other things, be understood as the assemblage of several components, unified through a structure and governed according to norms and rules. A society also has 'functions', as they are often described in the Norwegian literature on the security of society, even 'critical functions'. Society also has components, structures, networks, norms and rules that form the basis for 'normal' operations, processes and development over time.

In other words, there exists a certain ambivalence in the concept of 'system'. On the one hand, the traditional engineering sciences use the concept to describe technical, 'complex' systems. On the other hand, a parallel intellectual tradition evolved starting from the 1950s, represented by Talcott Parsons and later by Niklas Luhmann, that understands society and human organisations in general as systems (Luhmann, 1995; Parsons, 1991). Also, in this literature, the terms 'robustness' and 'resilience' are commonly used. Thus, even if the Commission on Vulnerability, in its investigation, refers to physical systems that can be exposed to threats during serious crisis events, its analysis is more concerned with several intermediary concepts, infrastructures, institutions, actors and practices that assure that the social is firmly bound to the physical and makes its physical predispositions into its social premises. Regarded in this way, terms like 'critical societal functions', 'societal values', 'societal preparedness' and, not least, 'societal security', all terms that appear frequently in both *A Vulnerable Society* and other associated scientific and political documents surrounding it, are deeply linked to the idea of a well-functioning system, one in which overlapping orders and types of 'solidarity' create what experts today call 'societal resilience'.

This strange ambivalence, this tension that opposes the human and the technical, is key to understanding societal security today. The leading hypothesis in this book is that this ambivalence is simply the unfortunate result of a misunderstanding or, worse, of a conflict of faculties, not even a logical short circuit or misinterpretation of facts. It is a necessity. It is the irreducible opposition between societal security understood as the security of those things that carry society on its shoulders and societal security understood as the security of society itself. It is the paradox that drives the debate about societal security today, and promises to give it meaning tomorrow. This book argues that the Commission on Vulnerability plays an inestimable role in the post-war history of Norway precisely because it advances the idea that society is something other than State, something other than the conglomerate of people that reside inside its border. It is something more, and something different. When, for example, the Commission's mandate from the Ministry of Justice specifies that

> A central question will be the prioritisation of future alignment of and tasks for the civil preparedness. The Commission will undertake a principled assessment whether, and eventually how, the work of preparedness in society should be changed as a consequence of the fundamental national and international processes of change.

the charge is not formulated and understood in terms of a purely technical or techno-political problem but rather as a combined social challenge:

> The Commission shall evaluate measures that can contribution to strengthening popular engagement, more voluntary engagement and greater prioritisation of the work of preparedness in the communes and private commerce.

> The Commission shall facilitate increased public consciousness, knowledge and debate on the problem of vulnerability in society. Security and vulnerability shall be weighed up against the desire for a more open society. (NOU, 2000: 17)

The mandate puts emphasis on society itself as an essential actor in the task of assuring societal security. Surprisingly, this goes well beyond dominant perspectives that, in the past and in more recent times, regard society as an inorganic, lifeless object, without any agency, action or influence in the matter of its own self-protection. The Commission was tasked with opening an organic dialogue with the people whose society was the object of security measures, creating a reciprocal relation between object and subject of security. The Commission's work was to join with the people, with their perceptions, preferences, needs, will, values and intentions.

This included assessment connected to society's growing vulnerability relative to potential interruption of important supplies of goods and services as a result of human error, technical breakdown, natural disasters, terrorism, sabotage or acts of war. The Commission was also tasked with collecting information and developing analyses about the risk of undesired or dramatic events as a consequence of new threats. Such threats, the Commission was wise in recognising, were presented as those that in the past were understood as external, foreign, exogenous and that must be dealt with as foreign phenomena, finding neither their origin nor their resolution within society. In other words, *A Vulnerable Society* is the first – and maybe the last – analysis that sees the security of society as fundamentally linked to society. It is the very first appearance in a public report of the difficulty of value-based decisions in a multicultural and thus multi-value society, an ambiguity that would continue to cling to expressions of societal security even until this day.

Societal values

Among the many innovative characteristics of *A Vulnerable Society* is the link it establishes between societal security and societal values. The concept of 'societal values' was, at the time of the report, not particularly new. It had shown up in a number of different management documents from the 1990s. There was, for example, a discourse about the responsibility of the police in relation to society's 'fundamental values' (NOU, 1994), 'societal values' and 'worldview' and the 'basic values of the Armed Forces' (NOU, 1995). However, when the Commission on Vulnerability formulated its vision for 'a safe and robust society that averts threats and overcomes crises', it was 'societal values' that are front and centre. As for the relationship between society's security and the basic values of society, the report is clear: in order to make society secure, the 'central societal values' must be secured. This innovation makes the Commission on Vulnerability unique. Whether one regards security from the standpoint of industry, focussing on occupational hazards and personal safety, or one is concerned with basic values from a political standpoint in relation to the nation-state in the wake of the Cold War, society as a societal phenomenon is essentially new.

At the same time as this new use of the concept represents an innovation in security thinking, it opens up a Pandora's box that has considerable political consequences. The political weight of the concept 'societal security' is formed on two levels. First, the idea that security can be applied to *values* was unheard of, a foreign idea in public policy thinking where concrete interests dominate and where values are taken more or less for granted as part of general common sense and political debate. On the other hand, if we first accept that there is something called 'value questions' in security policy, that society's core has something to do with values, then the question of *which* values we are talking about becomes unavoidable. Which values, and which ones are critical? How can they be secured?

In the academic field of axiology – the philosophical study of values – values are defined in several of ways:

(1) On the most concrete level, values are understood as the quantitative expression of an empirical measure. One speaks commonly of 'blood-alcohol level', for example, as a measure of inebriation, or of 'radiation value' in connection with atomic energy. These are levels, masses or lengths that, in one way or another, can be measured, calibrated and compared.

(2) In a similar, quantitative way, one also speaks of values that are simple economic measures. In this sense, a ring made of gold has a greater 'value' than a ring made of lead. This kind of economic notion of value as 'exchange value', that is, the possibility to be efficiently and completely exchanged for some other substance, presupposes a calibrating system or context, most often some sort of market, where the values in question can be converted according to a shared standard.

(3) One uses the term 'value' to express subjective preferences or priorities. If one prefers meat over fish, one can understand this preference as a value assessment.

(4) Finally, values can be understood as the implicit substance or content of a phenomenon, be it a thing, an experience, a memory or a feeling. This is value as 'intrinsic' value. It is in this sense we speak of 'human values', something that cannot be reduced to something else, cannot be converted to money or exchanged for something else. It is something that is in a sense distinct and independent from the one who holds it.

This short excursus is important because 'values', particularly in the discourse of political theory, tend to reveal themselves as quite difficult to define. Moreover, and more importantly, values and their discourse are a gold mine for political rhetoric. 'Societal values', which are so prevalent in the discourse of making societies secure, can be used to many ends in the political arena (some more useful than others). It is crucial to be attentive to the meanings and functions values are ascribed. Few concepts have the same political power and influence as 'values', and few concepts contribute more to advancing polemics in the place of policies. We can immediately observe this whenever politically orientated 'value' debates are performed, particularly in connection with security policy. What kinds of values do we want to promote with our security measures? Which values are we protecting? What are we willing to sacrifice for security? Where is the border between security and privacy? These difficult and often polemical questions acquire their force by mixing together in varying quantities the different components of the concept of 'value' outlined above. In both public debate and policy formulations, we often confuse values understood as implicit human properties and values understood as choices between viable political alternatives, advanced in the name of concrete political principles.

In the Commission on Vulnerability's report, the concept of 'societal values' is advanced as indispensable to the Commission's vision: 'Society shall be secured against threats against central societal values such as life, public health and welfare, environment, the democratic system and its legal institutions, national governance and sovereignty, the territorial integrity of the country, material and economic security and cultural values' (NOU, 2000: 8). According to such a summary, societal security includes a complex set of challenges and tasks. The broadest of the societal values comprises life itself. Obviously, for a society to be itself, it must have and support life. A society without living people who have living as their purpose can hardly be called a society. On the other hand, such a moral formulation is difficult to apply to the concrete elements of social life. It is, in a sense, so vague that one will have difficulty in giving tangible meaning to the tasks of society itself. If life and thereby vital values are the presupposition for the existence of any society, how can we conceive of a society as a variable whose calibration could somehow be the object of debate? At the same time, the biopolitical insight of our time relies on the affirmation that collective life is not equal to society, that the political formation of society is not reducible to the political governance of its population.

'Public health and social welfare' go nearly without saying in any European social democracy as primary constituents of society. But how fundamental are they? Public health is, of course, crucial to society and is among the first things to be weakened. Public values correspond to values in a political collective. They also correspond to certain political priorities, societal tasks, which must be carried out one after another, one before another, according to value calculation and implementation. Just how society chooses to manage these, through formal or informal institutions, does not carry a societal imprint in itself but unavoidably acquires one the moment the uncertainty it holds is inserted into political debate. Public health is crucial, and society is weakened when it is weakened. Health as a collective task, the protection against pandemics, the general transmission of sickness and other problems are central challenges, as are the problems connected to Norwegian society's relation to the environment, its place in the general and local ecosystem, etc. It can be observed that these practical matters are transferred as if automatically to the Norwegian debate about values, and thereby inserted into the question of societal security.

Such debates are decisive for liberal-democratic societies. It might even be said that they are the premises for a healthy, well-functioning, orderly society, and hence for societal security. Without open discussions about what is important and what is not, which priorities should be advanced and how they should be implemented, a democracy cannot guarantee inclusiveness, participation and stability over time. In other words, only when the content of value formulations is in some sense unstable, or even *insecure*, can society be and remain secure. A similar claim can be made about 'material and economic security' and 'structural values', all priorities for the work of the aforementioned Commission. Both priorities are, of course, frequently debated in open democratic societies. As in the discourses on the meaning of liberal values, it is not the values themselves that come under threat, are concretised, held tightly, protected from attack, from change or variation. It is, rather, the free agora, the space where disagreements can play themselves out, do their work, engage, negotiate, discuss and develop.

To secure society implies securing precisely this space, its potential for dispute, disagreement and dissent. It is the insecurity of the discourse of societal security that provides the guarantee of societal security itself. In a way, it is this ecology that is captured by the concept of an expression like 'democracy', which, in the Commission's eye, is the object of protection in the secure society. We will return to this complex question below.

The remaining element in the Commission on Vulnerability's mandate on societal security, for what it is in or about a society that is to be protected as part of the task of societal security, 'national governance', 'sovereignty', 'territorial integrity', is of a different character. These issues are rather to be related to traditional questions about national security and defence policy. In contrast to the various determinations of societal values proposed by the Commission, questions of national security are less open to discussion. As in all societies, they lie far closer to the realm of supposed *fact*, of what is taken for granted, through discourse of preservation of the national self through acts of individual and collective violence. Even though issues of national security obviously have their place in the discourse of what is and always will be, value assumptions lie right under the surface, should we only seek to scratch it.

Qualitative and quantitative risks to society

The matter of 'values' comes to play a part in the development and application of the most important operational concept in the Commission's report, as well as in the pursuit of security in general, namely, 'risk'. This concept, which I will analyse in detail below, functions as a connector between the likeliness that a certain danger will become reality and the impact or influence the encroaching danger can have. That influence depends upon a number of things, from the economic welfare of a society to the diversity of the political convictions of the given community. In this sense, 'risk' is an expression of values, of a perception or experience of what is important and what is not, of what should or should not be protected, of who deserves shelter and who does not. One particular syntagm, that occurs repeatedly in *A Vulnerable Society*, seeks to come to terms with the calculation of risk as a form of expression of values. Here, 'risk' is defined as an expression of 'danger for loss of important values as a consequence of undesired events' (NOU, 2000: 307). As for the question of which values, examples include 'life and health, environment, the economy and the carrying out of critical societal services' (18). The Commission, however, delimits its analysis of societal security to the risk of events that have 'meaning for society' and that 'threaten essential values' (20).

Thus, in terms of risk, the Commission makes a number of decisive strategic choices. It is clear in its argumentation and political direction that it considers as foundational the fact that risk is a qualitative and not a quantitative matter. Both in its early development in the 1970s and in its contemporary dominant form, risk science is for the most part practised as a *quantitative* science. Thus, when we describe risk as a link between the likelihood of an event and the influence the event might have, it is understood by most risk analysts as a mathematical measure, hence the impression that risk management is a primarily mathematical exercise, abstracted from all cultural, social and political constraints. The Commission on Vulnerability undertakes an exercise that is meaningful, and even to some extent radical, when it chooses an analytical direction that prioritises *interpretative* instead of quantitative methods.

Only in their purest economic form can political, social and cultural values be quantified. The Commission on Vulnerability answers the challenge of addressing and applying an analysis of risk by focussing on an understanding of societal values that presupposes a rich and multilayered conception of society. The themes taken up by the Commission can be characterised by this 'thick' understanding of culture, society and politics (Geertz, 1973).

Despite the fact that the Commission defines 'risk' as a question of values, it combines two quite different kinds of values into one concept of risk. On the one hand, it speaks of risk connected to what we have described above as 'subjective priorities and preferences', the danger to what we would rather hold on to, things like good and stable health, a clean environment, a stable economy and so-called 'critical societal services' (such as water and sewage systems, electricity, internet, fire departments and police). Life in society is understood in this sense as more valuable with these things in place than without them. They are therefore objects of security in the societal context. On the other hand, life itself is taken up in the understanding of a society at risk. Of course, life belongs to a different order and a different level of social belonging, what we earlier called an implicit or proper value. However, that does not mean that biological life does not also depend on the social context materially understood as an economic standpoint or a political orientation. Life is the very foundation, the presupposition, for any value and the point of departure for any risk assessment. Whatever one might think of societal security and risk, life itself is not an option that can be chosen away.

The concept of value is, thus, not only used in the Commission's report as an expression for a kind of cultural virtue. A more ordinary economic notion of societal value also finds its way into the report. Naturally enough, this occurs in the report's treatment of the danger for economic loss through one form or another of catastrophe, which would, in addition to material and human loss, bring economic loss. Companies and individuals are clearly in danger of losing money as a consequence of natural events and/or human actions, something discussed in the part of the report focussing on the extent to which the ICT sector and the national power supply are exposed to natural catastrophes. The risk is typically part of any economic planning conducted by any form of risk analysis or risk management.

Given this implicit assumption about the economic rationality of risk, the Commission's accomplishment is all the more formidable. It coherently and plausibly relates societal values as cultural, social and political matters and societal values as purely economic matters. The report points out how natural catastrophes like floods, storms and avalanches cause economic crises because they lead to a weakening or destruction of important infrastructures such as water sources or electricity supply (NOU, 2000: 37, 67, 76, 86, 281).

The normal and the extraordinary

Security measures are by nature extraordinary. This is because, paradoxically enough, expectations of security, be they personal, group-orientated, social, cultural or political, are expectations about what is normal, about what normality is and about what a rupture in that normality is imagined and projected as. How might we know that we have security? We would know that we have security if 'security' was not a theme, if it was not in question, not on our minds. If there was security in society, if security was actually to be found in some secure condition, it would not be conceptualised; it would fade into the background, become invisible, unthought, unspoken and unlived. Possible dangers, threats to security, etc. would remain beyond perception, beyond thought.

The thought of security is the measure of insecurity. We might even go so far as to say that the thought of security is a *cause* of insecurity – the 'secondary production of insecurity' we discussed above. This is, of course, a backwards way of saying that we can never be secure and know it. When a security event appears, the situation is understood as abnormal, as an interruption of the ordinary (secure) flow of things. The point of reference, the normal, the experience of a life without danger, of life un-endangered is, well, endangered. According to common sense, what is abnormal needs to be normalised, put in order, corrected, tidied up. Danger, threats, needs, crisis are the exceptions. Security is the rule.

Today as before, the language of 'extraordinary events' has become common in connection with security policy on all levels. This is a constantly recurring theme in *A Vulnerable Society*. Even the mandate of the Commission on Vulnerability is formulated as a question of the extraordinary:

> The Commission shall provide an overall description of the risk for extraordinary stresses on civil society in peacetime, in security crises and in war. This includes assessment connected to society's growing vulnerability to the interruption of important goods, supplies, and services as a consequence of human error, technical breakdown, natural catastrophes, terrorism, sabotage or acts of war. (NOU, 2000: 16)

What is remarkable in this sequence of the mandate is that the difference between the normal and the extraordinary is not fixed but rather varies from society to society, and from sector to sector within society at large. What is extraordinary for one person, group or sector is not the same for the next. Thereby, what is a security threat for one is not necessarily for the other. The question of who defines what is extraordinary is, of course, decisive. Because it must unavoidably be defined from a certain, fixed position – based on a given set of values and expectations, ambitions, culturally and socially determined fears and worries, resources, experiences and memories – the extraordinary quickly becomes a political question in the widest sense.

Clearly, most agree about when a major crisis has taken place. Everyone knows what a catastrophe is. At the same time, different groups and individuals in society are impacted in quite different ways, depending on physical situation, economic conditions, working situation, habits, customs, etc. One and the same pandemic illness, as we have so brutally witnessed of late, has widely differing danger effects depending on previous health condition, mobility, availability of health care, etc. Preparedness resources that are needed in large crises vary significantly in relation to levels of need in different contexts. This societal instability in the experience of extraordinary crises is significant. In terms of larger or smaller local crises, variations can be even greater. What constitutes a crisis for one local society can just as well not even be on the crisis radar for another. There are varying understandings of normality and abnormality, of the ordinary and the extraordinary.

Therefore, when the mandate for the Commission on Vulnerability defines the group's task as giving an 'overall description of the risk for extraordinary stresses on civil society in peacetime, in security crises and in war', much remains unsaid. The Commission's more or less politically inspired mandate is an invitation to political definitions of peace, war and security-motivated crisis. The latter is particularly interesting in that it can only be defined based on a political reference, a reference more or less governed by political interests, and yet neither the political foundation nor the political forces are commonly explicit.

The extraordinary is always extraordinary for someone and cannot be abstracted from a particular social context. An extraordinary measure always has an impact on the shared norms of society or the norms shared by particular groups within society. By their very nature, extraordinary measures set aside social norms and rules that might stand in the way of the security of society. Under certain circumstances, this can also imply that security authorities violate the limits of the law in order to re-establish security. Mobilisation of the army, military reserves or other security services is regarded as necessary for short periods until a punctual crisis is resolved. In this sense, the Commission on Vulnerability uses the forms of reaction to security crises as a way to delimit the concept of social security. The Commission will identify and give advice with the aim of reducing threats to societal security. These are, in part, characterised by the fact that society's usual civil security function is set aside in order to manage them. Society is threatened when society's everyday norms are suspended. The Commission understands vulnerability as a condition in which society lacks the ability to improvise, that is, to act in conflict with the same social norms and habits (NOU, 2000: 37). The ability to turn to extraordinary measures is precisely the characteristic of a 'robust' society. By contrast, a society that is 'dependent' upon 'stable access to goods and services', will most likely find it more difficult to be flexible and to take into use extraordinary measures.

Thus, crises are, nearly by definition, extraordinary situations. They are uncommon, unexpected. They occur suddenly and surprise a society that is more or less prepared for them. A society that is equipped to tackle extraordinary events is precisely one that can easily resort to extraordinary measures, a society that easily slides over into a position where ordinary ways of life are set aside or suspended, and measures requiring extraordinary ways of living are easily taken. The implications are considerable. Society can, in certain situations, disregard some of its norms as part of its measures for societal security. The risk is that the principles and values forming the basis for what the society is or sees itself as being can be, and often are, sacrificed. Society can, in certain situations, resort to measures that put into question society itself. Another expression for 'extraordinary measure' is, thus, 'state of emergency', an old idea with a tarnished political reputation.

The critical

The 'critical' is also a recurring theme in the descriptions, assessment and proposed arrangements about societal security. This is, of course, not a phenomenon limited to Norway. On the contrary, the critical presents itself as closely linked to, dependent upon, crisis. If crisis is a decision, the critical is a moment or place at which the decision must be made. This conceptual pair, the decision at a moment/place, is not only apparently universal across cultures; it is also universal across crises. On the one hand, societal security is meant to protect and care for society in the face of critical events, but, on the other hand, it is destined to maintain 'critical functions', that is, the functions that must be maintained within the 'critical' limits. In the first sense, it is a matter of the nature of crises, of a particular crisis, of the kind and nature of the decision that must be taken, of the nature of 'critical situations' (NOU, 2000: 9, 96), critical 'points' (62), critical 'dependency' (68), critical 'attitudes' (98), critical 'factors' (104), critical 'questions' (105) or critical 'variables' (217). In the second sense, objects or functions are often identified that can be regarded as necessary in order to maintain society as such, be it critical 'societal areas' (10, 119), critical 'societal services' (17), critical 'infrastructure' (20), critical 'operations' (39), critical 'deliveries' (78), critical 'ICT services' (79), critical 'sectors' (88), critical 'resources' (111) or critical 'goods' (112).

The critical is thought of as a relation to the extraordinary. The critical lies in our experiences but also in our imaginations and fantasies, on the border between the normal and the extraordinary. The critical is in itself a kind of borderland, a transition zone from what can be managed through usual means and thought through common ways of thinking, and what demands other means and ways of thinking (see Burgess, 2019).

Regarding the relationship between national security and societal security, the critical is also a transition, but this time of a different order. It is the transition between a 'normal' government, democratic norms and rules, existing institutions, rule of law, accountability and juridical coverage for policy carried out in the name of security. The critical thus also draws the line between the normal and the extraordinary, that is, the no man's land where norms, institutions and normal political processes are cancelled in order to manage a crisis. The critical is the situation where what we consider normal is itself threatened, where the normality of the normal is put under pressure, problematised or even loses its credibility. In other words, it is not only society that is threatened when there is a security threat to society; rather, it is the societal 'normal' itself that is exposed, be it the 'normal' social values, the 'normal' form of governance or, more importantly, the 'normal' scope of authority and legitimacy of the police and the surveillance agencies. The American 'Patriot Act', adopted one month after the attacks of 11 September 2001, and reauthorised several times (most recently in August 2019), is a clear example of the way in which an act of violence that deviates from the normal – in this case, in a spectacularly egregious way – leads to changes in the rule of law, its authority and legitimacy, all of which were its target. Society is thus targeted twice: once by the attack itself, then again by the damage it does to itself as a reaction in the name of security. The material and vital damage to society is doubled by the inability to grasp the degree to which it is the society, not its structure, not its individual citizens, that was threatened, attacked and sustained considerable damage. One state of emergency engenders another.

In this sense, what is 'critical' for one is not always critical for the other. What can be regarded as a societally critical function can vary considerably from one social group to another. What is critical for one group's welfare is not critical for another's, all depending on local values, traditions, local customs, traditions, interests, etc. It is easy to see how and how quickly cultural policy becomes security policy, how cultural values become securitised, used as pawns in political discussion about what is actually 'critical' for society, what is worth preserving, what is worth sacrificing, how much, and which costs are justified.

In short, the security of society, today as in previous expressions of societal security's fundamental idea, takes the shape of a political negotiation about society's basic values, about what is important and unimportant for social cohesion, well-being and longevity. As long ago advanced by Buzan et al., societal security is a question of who we are (1998: 119–24).

Asking the question of societal security

It is, of course, not by chance that when the breakdown of our key concept of 'societal security' first gets under way, the analysis is stopped in its tracks by an absence of definition or conceptualisation of the term. In spite of the fact that the report of the Commission on Vulnerability contains a lexicon of key terms of relevance for the discussion on societal security, the concept of 'societal security' itself is not mentioned as part of the list. This does not stop the discussion and the analysis from talking continuously about the concept in reference to other elements, but without defining it, nearly always in relation to closely related ideas and concepts – vulnerability, risk, societal values, the extraordinary and the normal, the critical, war and peace.

Nonetheless, a kind of frame is formed around the concept of societal security, a political frame, if only one of controversy and ambivalence, and its technological and operational footings. The framing also provides meaning and a measure of stability to the secondary concepts that draw meaning and political power from it. Based on these peripheral concepts, a direct portfolio of concepts has emerged with a seemingly robust ability to support even the most controversial political measures, suspension or dismantling of civil rights and legal protections, among others, all formulated and carried out in the name of protecting a society whose vulnerabilities have been superficially plumbed and whose authority and legitimacy are sometimes asserted fleetingly. In the Commission's report, we find calls for 'strengthening' societal security, an entire chapter on 'sector-wise measures for societal security' (NOU, 2000: 60–239).

The Commission on Vulnerability presents a well-versed conceptualisation of security in general, of the concept's scope and typical usage, but it does not seek to articulate the complex type of security that society itself makes claim to. This is in spite of the fact that the Commission's report appeals to social researchers to advance research on and insight into societal security. The report claims that 'society is more vulnerable than before' (6), which seems to imply that, in some sense, Norwegian society is more vulnerable than before, that some national, cultural particularities can be said to have increased vulnerability or lessened societal security. What is it that is more vulnerable than before? This is harder to assess. The invisible, enchanted societal self is in some way weakened, be it as a consequence of a threatening societal environment or because of a decline in the ability of societal institutions, material and immaterial, to support it. However, the suggested measures, particularly those in the long Part III of the report, are primarily material and technological in nature.

To be fair, the way the society has developed over the last few decades has likely contributed to the sense of a weakening of societal security. The report notes that Norwegian society has become more open, more transparent and more liberal. This comes with a cost. The encroaching neoliberal societal arrangements create an economic and cultural environment in which technological systems and mechanisms may be a source of ills, as the Beckian tradition of risk theory suggests, but are nonetheless indispensable to hold the train on the rails. The same goes for Norway, a society which is both very technologically advanced and enchanted by its organic bonding with nature, thus, paradoxically, more open to threats and more equipped to manage them. The liberal society that needs no enemies, it is said, is the origin of its own ills.

The concept of 'society' is thus used widely and generously in the report of the Commission on Vulnerability. The ambivalence of society, to which we will return in the next chapter, is somehow tacitly construed as the genius of societal security. Its enchanting, ubiquitous multifariousness is the magic elixir of societal security. The ambivalence of the notion of 'society', particularly visible in the Norwegian political discourse where it assumes multiple, overlapping and, at times, contradictory roles simultaneously, may very well be related to the significant level of societal resilience that can historically be observed in Norway, and which is acutely evident in the immediate aftermath of Oslo/Utøya. In other words, a link might be cautiously suggested between 'ambivalence' and 'complexity'. Versions of the inverse of this hypothesis – that complex societies require complex theories and methods of policing – have been carefully advanced within police science (Hollan, 2021): the notion that a complex, imbricated, complex, post-identity-politics self-understanding of society, particularly when coupled with a reflection on the ecological aspects of security and threat, may play a role in enhancing resilience in the face of events that would otherwise cause splintering (Preiser *et al.*, 2018; Rus *et al.*, 2018; Ungar, 2018).

The complex discourse enveloping society weaves together a range of unlikely theoretical components with which we close our analysis of the Commission on Vulnerability. Not only is society characterised by more complexity today, creating unforeseen interlinkages, whose origins and ends, depths and horizons remain invisible, but the Commission points out that, while society is perhaps more free than before, it is also exposed to more complex forms of danger: danger as complexity but also complexity as danger. Yet, 'society' is not only evolving in terms of its inner heterogeneity, with all the crises of security manageability that that implies, but it is also becoming something other. Its vectors lead towards a different kind of complexity, one that is ecstatic, beyond itself, other than itself, one which reaches its tentacles into new and different forms of the private, formerly non-social domains, a new civil society, a new global society, new sub-societies, all linked with each other technologically. It is for this reason that the Commission concludes with a warning that Norwegian society is no longer itself rapidly moving in directions that defy the traditional tracks of national governance – State, civil society and people. Perhaps this is why the Commission felt compelled to legitimise the semantic ambivalence of the notion of society, letting it encompass in this political document not only people, groups and institutions but also non-human resources that find their social identification by being implicated in the provision of societal security.

In retrospect, the reach of the report of the Commission on Vulnerability has been considerable, though much of its political force has faded in the intervening years. The concept of societal security is, as we will see, more confused and, following Oslo/Uyøya, increasingly bureaucratised. In spite of a comprehensive use of the term 'societal security', the report does not, cannot, penetrate far into its secrets. Indeed, it does not try to link the security of society to anything but the material frames in which societies live out their wildly complex lives, like a long line of policy research that will follow it. It regards society as little more than a shell, without its own resources and without a soul worthy of security.

Nonetheless, the Commission on Vulnerability remains a reference in as far as it is the first thorough reflection on the question of what it means to both threaten and protect a society. Is 'societal security' really about the security of society? The response made by the Commission on Vulnerability is ambiguous. Societal security is anything but societal. Indeed, according to the Commission, societal security is a property of the technical and bureaucratic system. As if predicting disenchantment, it sees societal security as something that can be threatened by concrete objects but also instrumentally managed. There is, moreover, a fundamental conviction that technical and bureaucratic measures have an important impact on society and its security.

4

Our coming security

> Nothing is more stable than driving into the abyss.
> Zeh (2004)

The evolution of vulnerability

As we have seen, the Commission on Vulnerability, whose report *A Vulnerable Society* was published in 2000, provided a far-reaching and prescient diagnosis of the material, social, political and, not least, value-determined reality into which Norway was entering at the turn of the millennium. The paradox that accompanied this transition was the practical consequence of the metaphysical coming of age of modern society, analysed in Chapter 2. On the one hand, the inward – or 'societal' – turn of the discourse of security at the close of the Cold War had led to exposing security and insecurity as particular properties of specific social and cultural values, identities, practices, etc. On the other hand, it had, from a longer historical point of view, led to a reshaping of the contours of an international system that aggregated, despite its explicit value-based principles, a relatively diverse group of national cultures. Was it simply that globalisation had caused a general homogenisation of Western national cultures and the multiple sub-cultures that made them up, or was it that the very Cold War notion of international security was already pre-programmed as a culture and value-homogenising function? The latter was clearly the case: the international system, which by necessity also propelled the creation of the system of international security, whose function was to preserve and protect the system confines, was never a *descriptive* concept. It was never an empirically informed idea meant to gather the diverse strands of peoples, States, nations and communities of the known world in order to generate an inclusive institutional body governed by a consensual set of values and interests. Rather, it was an idealistic, *proscriptive* concept, a child of the post-World War I Wilson principles, imposed, adopted and embraced in all their imperial glory (Acharya & Buzan, 2019; Duncombe & Dunne, 2018; Ikenberry, 2004, 2018). In other words, the historical framework and conditions in which *A Vulnerable Society* appeared announced, by their originality and specificity, a Norwegian *Sonderweg*, while at the same time reaffirming Norway's incorporation into the Western geopolitical modernisation process, and thereby its direct relevance to other countries, other regions, other societies of the international system.

Yet, based on the perspectives that I will outline in this chapter, the Norwegian experience of the societal turn coincided with a moment when Norwegians were doubling down on traditional security measures, as were most Western nations (even those that continued to be in denial).

By and large, as a spectator of the Cold War realist politics in which the US and Europe insisted on indulging, Norway had little more than a value-based, soft approach to international politics – exemplified by backchannel diplomacy. The most marked example was the series of negotiations that led to the Oslo Accords, signed in 1993, between Israel and the Palestine Liberation Organization (PLO). It advanced on the basis of intimate interactions, family relations, personal charisma and a conviction that insignificant States could play a role (Waage, 2002). Where societal approaches have made inroads through various mechanisms around the Western world, these advances often remain mostly limited to academic discussions. The realist imaginary embodied in Wilson's famous fourteen theses reveals a resilience of a different kind, the resilience of a security fantasy that organises reality around the assumption, discredited on countless levels, that danger always originates in an other. Thus, if Norway suffered a dreadful surprise on 22 July 2011, it did so to the degree that it too was partially implicated in the dominant narrative, materially and psychically unsubstantiated, of the realist, international system.

This system, along with the structures, sources and references that support it, regards vulnerability as a simple deficiency, as the negative horizon of security, as a linear security function: increased vulnerability means increased danger, and conversely. While the 2000 *A Vulnerable Society* certainly does not claim that vulnerability is a shield against security threats, it provides a far more nuanced and penetrating analysis of exposure to danger and disruption as a constituent of the social, cultural and political fabric. The Commission's recommendations outline the deep historical – but also new technological – links to the structural character of vulnerability: to the new digital background, the new material well-being and the new social and political relations that fix the foundations for dealing with the onset of crisis. The orientation of the report, its mapping of the ethos of the moment at which technological progress and innovation meet, generates its own vulnerability, in which the fragility of social systems becomes a by-product of social innovation, while setting the tone for a non-aligned analysis of the post-Cold War security landscape.

The immediate bureaucratic successor of *A Vulnerable Society* was a similarly commissioned study entitled *When the Accident Has Happened: On the Organisation of Operative Rescue and Preparedness Resources* (NOU,

2001). It was published by a new commission only one year after its predecessor, the Commission on Emergency Preparedness. Building largely on the previous one, the new report turns its attention to the aftermath of crises. Instead of seeking to clarify more deeply the causes of the crises of societal security, or what provides and does not provide security, what strengthens it and what weakens it, the report sets out to study societal security as a logic of 'recovery, restitution and rehabilitation'. It asks how operational rescue and preparedness resources should be organised in order to maximise resource use (NOU, 2001). Whereas the Commission on Vulnerability focussed on the social, material and technological circumstances of vulnerability, its conditions and determinants and its inscription in a constellation of values, the Commission on Emergency Preparedness chooses, less than one year later, to instead work on the *impact* of unforeseen crises, and on both the explicit and the less visible changes in forms of governance related to societal security. Instead of a concern for the *emergence* of security threats, it prioritises an analysis of the way such crises played out, what conditions constrained outcomes to specific paths and what kinds of policy lens could allow these to be rationally steered. It is concerned with the way external forces, and, among these, the forces of international politics and globalisation, contribute to the way emergencies are anticipated, prepared for and experienced, as well as how they should result in the modification of particular modes of steering and forms of governance (13). Some of these modifications – as the authors of the report repeatedly emphasise – are related to the reception of the 9/11 attacks in the US and to the vulnerability that this event generated as far away as Norway. The Emergency Preparedness report thus integrates an awareness of the immediacy of material vulnerability with the associative vulnerabilities and the impact of the importance of imaginary or associational threats.

It will then come as no surprise that the Commission on Emergency Preparedness had a clear focus on administrative preparedness, encompassing the extra-human components of crisis response, based on a clear mandate that made way for what was an increasingly familiar tone: 'Society needs an apparatus for rescue and preparedness that fills the requirements of functionality, quality and coordination' (8–9). This nearly continuously recurring theme of security as a well-functioning bureaucracy – before and after 9/11, before and after 7/22 – is voiced clearly here: 'The goal of this review is to accomplish the best performance possible in the area of rescue and performance, based on the best possible unified form of organisation and with a basis in a coordinated, overarching legal system' (9). Only the most functional, pragmatic and material aspects of social life belong to the vision of societal security promoted by the Commission. This premise is reflected both in the background text of the report and in the Commission's mandate, which affirms that it is functional solutions alone that are needed. Any immaterial, affective, subjective, intellectual, somatic, corporal, social, cultural or spiritual considerations are left aside in the report.

Society in all its states

However, less evident, and rarely noticed in the literature about societal security in general or Oslo/Utøya in particular, is the formal semantic quality of the assertion, one that will become everyday language in the political discourse of security, namely, that 'society' is the *subject* of security. As we will see through the analysis of all levels and all variations of the discourse, society is systematically attributed a subject position, and with it a form of collective identity, agency and qualities of subjectivity. Society is variously cast as backdrop and foreground, past and future, perpetrator and victim, actor and enabler, heroic and inept, security provider and hindrance to authentic forms of individually created security.

The force of ambivalence of 'society' in the Norwegian discourse is uncanny, improbable and remarkable. It invites a thorough semantic analysis that we can only partially satisfy here, but one that will represent a kind of running hypothesis, tested over and over again in these pages, that 'society', to a quite remarkable degree, can be semantically manipulated in order to preserve this ambivalence more or less acute, which, by the power of its uncertainty, does uncanny political work.

Society is the name of the indeterminate and diffuse collective encompassing 'us' together with the 'others', the imagined community, the greater thing to which we all belong, but mostly the subject who utters 'society', the higher meaning to which we tacitly appeal, the collective super-ego, our better angel, a semi-spiritual whole somewhere between heaven and earth, larger than life, deeper than what we feel, older than our age, yet utterly contemporary. It is the imaginary completeness the individual experiences a piece of, complicit in a meaningful project, idea or enterprise, without entirely grasping its meaning. It implicates the will that is only partly their own, the virtues that are only human and the vices they would rather attribute to others. Its centre lies somewhere associated with the idea of living together in an organised way, sharing customs, norms, traditions and values. All of these are more or less imagined, and projected on to others in the community and against those of adjacent communities that harbour their own shared laws, traditions and values.

Society refers simultaneously to the institutions, the organisations, the formal and less formal groups, of individuals, as well as to the principles and practices that characterise these and more or less define the rules of membership. It is the formal and informal bodies, in part rooted in traditions, in part linked to the democratically organised and sanctioned institutions of governance. They represent power, in various forms, power that is sanctioned to a greater or lesser degree by neighbouring democratic institutions that surround them, support them, legitimate and empower them, nourish their flourishing.

'Society' is also, among other things, the name of a subjectivity of *threat*, and a posture of *defence*. It's the name of the agency, in the form of both actors and organisations, that understands itself as being characterised by vulnerability, by a fundamental need to repel what is foreign, what is presumed to threaten it. It is the 'we' that defends the 'us', two entities which, paradoxically, despite appearances, are largely distinct from each other. Society does not precede security; on the contrary, it is constituted by its own insecurity.

Last but not least, society is the target, the entity that is threatened by threat, endangered by danger, made insecure by insecurity. It is the collective that imagines itself targeted by the forces of nature of vengeful serendipity or the force of evil of the vengeful terrorist. In all cases, its collective nature is a precondition for both insecurity and security. For better or worse, we are never insecure alone. Insecurity is a discourse of danger and demise, if it is not exchange with another individual experiencing fear on more or less the same level of intensity in the face of more or less the same imagined adversary; it is an internal discourse structured in relation to a threatening other that is mostly likely not less real than if the experience were shared with another or several.

It is for these reasons that the injunction 'we must do something' is hardly ever spoken from the place of 'we', just like the 'we' that experiences itself as threatened by one or another danger is hardly ever the 'we' that would, should the worst happen, actually fall victim. When it comes to security, language is, so to speak, at its worst.

The mandate for the Commission on Emergency Preparedness builds upon the observation that emergency agencies are organised in several forms and on several levels, with different institutional anchoring and different tasks and responsibilities, everything from volunteer organisations to private companies. The variety levels of organisations have several forms of reporting such that information flows are irregular and non-standard. The aim is to coordinate these, in particular, in view of the available resources of civil defence in peacetime. As we will see in more detail below, the changes in the civil defence sector, both in terms of finance and organisation and of military logic, all play a role in the new thrust towards preparedness understood less as an organically emerging, grassroots and individualised resource than as a unified, coordinated force. Even the mandate of the Commission on Emergency Preparedness never departs from the language of coordination, harmonisation and standardisation. The potential virtues of a multi-pronged or multi-level approach to preparedness and disaster management are never discussed, never even raised to be contradicted.

There is no firm assertion in official documents that the organic, heterogeneous approach is, in itself, inferior to the synthetic, streamlined, instrumentally governed and homogenised one. There is no criticism raised against standardisation or integrated governance or consolidated financial resource management in themselves. It is rather by virtue of their connection with or proximity to a certain technocratic New Public Management-inspired notion of efficiency that the drive for a unitary logic becomes the core ethos of societal security. Indeed, the very title of the Commission's mandate indicates 'a more effective preparedness'. The discourse wanders thereafter from 'organisational effectiveness' to 'rescue effectiveness' to 'resource effectiveness', from 'effective warning' to 'effective crisis leadership', 'effective traffic direction', 'effective oversight', 'effective leadership', to name only a few (NOU, 2001: 9–10).

The notion of standardisation in the name of efficiency becomes a ubiquitous fixture in policy-making for societal security through the subsequent years before Oslo/Utøya, culminating, but not ending with, the reactions to the attacks. As I will discuss below, the extraordinary resilience shown by a range of ordinary Norwegians is met with disinterest by official reactions, and attention is turned to either unifying the organisational apparatus, standardising support technologies or creating new higher-level bureaucratic units. The tendency is towards the general, the global, the universal. Yet, this tendency can only partially be explained by an impulse towards financial optimisation and the responsible and accountable use of public funding, where reduced bureaucracy is generally associated with reduced cost. In a number of cases, the contrary is proven to be the case: the condensation of low-level tasks and the absorption of low-level agencies and their administrative tasks lead to a disproportionate increase in high-level institutions.

In addition to an infusion of the now commonplace logic of 'rationalisation' in the preparation for, but also analysis of, crisis events, there is a shadowing impulse to standardise in the interest of homogenisation that is more complicated to explain. Perhaps for the last time in the Norwegian history of societal security, the Commission on Emergency Preparedness seeks to have it both ways. Or, perhaps, the body seeks to carry out its mandate by turning it on its head. In an environment in which the imperative to raise and standardise pretends to self-evidence, the Commission presents poignant documentation of the force, virtue, value and, above all, meaningfulness of the local, the particular, the determinate, the concrete, the proximate, the personal, the human. Thus, in the same moment the Commissioners advance the project of unification and coordination of the societal crisis governance, they recognise the value of the local or 'communal' level of crisis management in Norway. The 'commune' is the primary local level for the provision of everyday State-based administrative services, including police, fire protection, hospitals and primary health care.

The commons: security is always collective

In demographic terms, Norway is a highly dispersed country. The geographical make-up of the landscape, with enormously sparse land, small population centres separated by enormous distances and severe terrain, mountains and fjords, creates very local societal security needs and very local means of meeting them. More than most other industrialised countries, Norway is a country of local populations, of local identities. Even the massive nationalisation of telecommunication and media services that took place in the late 1960s when the Norwegian Broadcasting Company undertook the particularly challenging task of offering national (black-and-white) television coverage to essentially all Norwegians wavered between nurturing national unity and underscoring local particularity. Norway's uncommon national unity has not prevented a relatively heterogeneous society from maintaining a remarkable diversity of local cultures, customs and dialects. Cultural diversity, which, as elsewhere, has an intrinsic value and is a source of pride embedded in a spirit of national unity, in addition to the considerable geographical variegation, made Norway a laboratory for the virtue of local society.

A similar constellation of value-based belonging structures the institutional, but also the imaginary, organisation of the police and security forces in Norway. The classical assumption that organisational relations consist of other forces than the relations set out in the formal architectures of authority, responsibility, planning and tasking seems confirmed. One's position in an organisation is a complex interaction of experience, tradition, culture, values, knowledge, competence, etc., all qualities that are the properties of individuals with individual experience, customs, intuitions, moral character, properties that, while being to some degree captured by any organisation's organigram, also resist their formalisation and disrupt their unity exploding in them. Organisations are not only reflected in the constitutional structures that pretend earnestly or artificially to capture them; the very function of organisations, it can be said, depends on the fact that the components and practices of organisations exceed them, that the organisation is more and therefore other, both in essence and in practice, than what it is rationally and institutionally set out to be (see Kilduff, 1993; Knights, 1997).

No less can be said about the particular architecture of policing and security structures that essentially set the scene for the understandings of how the Oslo/Utøya security threats could and would unfold, whose expertise within the security organisation would have value, legitimacy and efficacy in the particular constellation of geographical, social, cultural and ethnographic components that determined the course of the events and the psychological, moral, institutional, legal and political processing of these events in the hours, days, weeks and months that followed (Christensen et al., 2015; Das & Robinson, 2001; Filstad & Gottschalk, 2010; Hansen, 2020).

A certain awareness of the challenge, but also the potential strength, of cultural diversity in organisations, of the overdetermination of local particularity in the deployment of necessarily generalised overarching particularly, is reflected in the report by the Commission on Emergency Preparedness, *When the Accident Has Happened*. It is conceived as a hybrid administration, anchored in local knowledge but serving a more general collective interest.

> The commune constitutes a foundation of the national planning system. There is at the same time an assumption that crises should be resolved on the lowest possible level. Most crises and catastrophes that occur will strike a commune. Based on their everyday responsibility communes will play several important roles in a crisis situation. The communes have therefore to a great degree carried out risk and vulnerability analyses to analyse the local risk picture and its consequences for possible events. Based on such analyses most communes have carried out preventive and damage reduction measures, among these preparatory planning in concrete areas, routines to assure the preparatory aspect of societal planning and crisis planning. (NOU, 2001: 46)

As with other local services, the responsibility for crisis preparation and management lies with local authorities, even if it should have, as in the case of the Utøya attacks, national consequences. The first contact point of the terrorist and the first point of intervention of police was the local Nordre Buskerud Police Department. Mobilisation of the national forces unit took place shortly after, though in a way that weakened the response. In the end, the local police force in charge, the so-called 'local incident officer', having more knowledge of the geographical context, roadways, population centres and coastal situation, essentially maintained leadership of the police operation when police protocol required that it be passed to the higher-level 'operations control officer', who also had direct liaison with the forces' troops who ultimately intervened and ended the stand-off. As the Oslo/Utøya events unfolded, events that were by any measure an organisational anomaly, completely unprecedented and unimagined, the operational control was shifted, through a series of chance occurrences and an unauthorised series of events, to a higher, communal level where authorities had less direct knowledge of the operation (Bye *et al.*, 2019). While this operational confusion is often diagnosed as a failure of organisational architecture, it might have easily been interpreted through an analysis based on one form or another of institutional adaptation.

In Norway, the 'commune' is the mid-level administrative unit, the intermediary between national-level policy and local, everyday experience. In most European countries, this three-level arrangement would not be adequate to transmit and mediate policy implementation from the national level to the local. The urge to align societal security policy, crisis management and general preparedness is not, at least from a pragmatic point of view, an approach appropriate for societies with strong grassroots cohesion, solidarity and culture. Thus, before returning to its mandated recommendation on the creation of a Directorate for Societal Security and Preparedness, the report documents and discusses the remarkable suite of local, grassroots agencies and units that play a crucial role in the provision of societal security. These include, in the public domain, local police; the fire brigade; emergency health services, including hospital and ambulance services; civil defence; local defence; reserves; the coastguard; the helicopter rescue service; a range of volunteer organisations such as the Norwegian Red Cross, the Ski Rescue Association, Norwegian People's Aid, Norwegian Rescue Dogs, Alpine Rescue Group, the Norwegian Aero Club, the Norwegian Caving Federation, the Norwegian Radio Relay League, the Aviation Traffic Service, the Petroleum Industry's Accident Preparedness Unit, among many others.

The performativity of institutions

Yet, such institutional structures have a life of their own. Far from structuring fixity, institutions structure movement. Their essence lies in the circulation that they permit. In their ideal form, they are media, the shape or form or even topology given to whatever value substance they instrumentally put into action. In their ideal form, institutions are input–output machines that simply transform input in terms of form, while leaving it unchanged in terms of substance. In other words, the function of institutions is to transmute value, to make it circulate between points of cultural interstices that reflect, to one degree or another, the social, cultural and thus political make-up of society. The points of transmutation involve, among other things, competences, strategic resources, legitimacy and operational authority. Taking institutional decisions implies organising the appropriate or necessary flows of information, legitimacy and authority from one position to another, and eventually on the executive position that processes information and value preferences, in order to then externalise the power, which is also conducted through the interstices of the institutional structure.

As will be discussed in Chapter 5, the 22 July Commission and other investigative bodies based much of their criticism on the claim that a variety of institutions failed to take the responsibility that they were thought to hold. Institutions have responsibility, it is claimed again and again in the government documents, and in order to improve our security in the future, this responsibility has to be assumed. What does it mean to say that an institution has responsibility? What does it say to deny it? Do institutions have a duty to their users? From where does it come? How is it implemented?

Institutions are notoriously difficult to define. And while this is not the place to enter into the fray of the debate around the question, it is enough to note that the most influential definitions tend to emerge from economic theories interested in studying the rational variables that determine how human conduct is governed (for example, Hodgson, 2006; North, 1990) Nonetheless, the deeper question of the relation between collective self-understanding and collective organisation, the relationship between individual morality and well-being and the shared structures that govern these take us back to early thinking about what society is in Rousseau's *The Social Contract* (1997 [1762]), Mill's *Utilitarianism* (2002 [1863]) and tensions between individual and common good set out in Kant's moral philosophies and re-actualised in, among others, Rawls's *Theory of Justice* (1971) and other liberal theories. Others, like Weber, whom I examined in the Introduction, saw institutions as components in the emergence of the modern bureaucratic State. Weber, who also understands institutions as a means of governing conduct, sees the particular form they took as public administrative structures to be a primary component of modernisation. In his *Basic Sociological Concepts*, he defines an 'institution' (*Anstalt*) as 'an organisation whose statutes can, within a given domain, be (relatively) successfully imposed on all whose action has specified particular characteristics', continuing, 'The prime instance of an "institution" is the state, along with all its auxiliary heterocephalous organisations – and the church, so long as its orders are rationally expressed as statutes' (Weber, 2019: 133–4).

These questions are addressed with an unexpected acuity by Ricœur in a set of otherwise unrelated lectures published in 1995 (2000). Whereas, for Rawls, justice is 'the first virtue of social institutions' (Rawls, 1971: 3), for Ricœur, institutions are the condition of justice. For Rawls, all the components of institutions, actors, structures, procedures are implicitly imbued with the moral substance of the whole. There is not a part of the institution that is not a carrier, in its own way and according to its own function, of the value of the institution as such. Institutions, according to Ricœur, are mediators of the moral substance attributed to the institution. They are neither its source nor its purpose or finality. 'Rights', he says, 'have need of the continual mediation of interpersonal forms of otherness and of institutional forms of association in order to become real powers to which correspond real rights' (Ricœur, 2000: 5). Institutions, past and present, make meaningful human social life. They are the mediation through which we can have a meaningful relation to others, the 'third part', as Ricœur describes it. We never have an immediate or unmediated relation to others. There is always an 'impersonal' mediation, most forceful being that of language (5). This is the work of the institution.

Yet, unlike what we might have learned to expect from a Weberian approach, the institution in Ricœur's analysis is far from instrumental. In the case of language as an institution, this moral substance takes the form of 'sincerity', the will to mean something, to communicate, to be understood, answered by the will to understand (Ricœur, 2000: 6). In terms of social and political relations, political institutions play a similar role. Political action and the means and modes of being together in a political community, large or small, are made meaningful by the political institutions that mediate them.

> This notion of a public space first expresses the condition of plurality resulting from the extension of inter-human relations to all those that the face-to-face relation of 'I' and 'you' leaves out as a third party. In turn, this condition of plurality characterises the will to live together of a historical community – a people, nation, region, class, and so forth – itself irreducible to interpersonal relations. (Ricœur, 2000: 8)

The *otherness* we experience with the other members of our community is neither self-evident nor spontaneous; it arises only as we are able to mediate our common ground through the third part, which is the collective institution. 'Without institutional mediation', says Ricœur, 'individuals are only the initial drafts of human persons'. Not only do we have conscious interest or aspiration to be together, to seek to realise collective goals, but this mediation through third-party institutions is the condition of being fully human (10).

Institutions are both the creators and purveyors of social meaning in the form of responsibility, but this creation only takes place through the mediation of individuals, from the interaction with each other through the medium of the institution. It does not emerge spontaneously from below, and it cannot be dictated unilaterally from above. Institutions, according to Ricœur's concept, are not intrinsically responsible; they are not carriers or crucibles of responsibility, nor do they transfer some kind of portable responsibility from the State to the citizen. They mediate or perhaps facilitate the imputation of responsibility through the mediation of citizens with and through the institutions.

Civilising preparedness: the three principles of responsibility

The Commission on Emergency Preparedness codified one of the central tools in the Norwegian tradition of crisis management policy-making: the tripartite principle for the distribution of responsibilities, which includes the principles of equality, proximity and responsibility. These principles have been a central feature of societal security thinking in Norway since 2001. I address the matter of institutional responsability from a variety of critical angles in what follows. For the moment, and in general terms, it is important to underscore the emergence of an imperative to 'redistribute' responsibility for the management of crisis, keeping in mind the criticism and warnings in the wake of Oslo/Utøya, where the public authorities were reproached of having instilled a system marked by the 'pulverisation' of responsibility, that is, the over-extensive distribution of responsibilities to actors, agencies and authorities, to the extent that an overview of the political, policy or perhaps ethical connections between the political, social or moral purposes of individual activities is lost. As I shall suggest in my concluding remarks, the question becomes a critical one in relation to the more fundamental or principled question of what a national policy for preparedness or anything else actually is and/or can be. What is 'responsibility' in a complex democratic system? How much connectivity is required in order to assure a coherent political course, in line with the explicit or implicit democratic rule? Is there not just one responsibility, namely, that to the people? To what degree can a diversity of responsibilities converge or even remain compatible?

The criticism of the 'pulverisation of responsibility' in the aftermath of Oslo/Utøya was, in all fairness, part of a discourse of efficiency. By 'responsibility', one essentially means 'coordination'. The response to Oslo/Utøya was not, at least according to popular perceptions, insufficiently coordinated. Communication between relevant actors was poor; interaction between different political levels was vague, with the result that the overall effort to move towards one goal, namely, to hinder or stop the malevolent plan of one man with a well-defined and executed plan familiar only to him, did not happen. The one single, brutally simple, operational responsibility perceived by the public and well exploited by and against the political class was to prevent the attack, or, at a minimum, to stop it before it should become excessively deadly or destructive. This unique responsibility cannot be operationalised by one person, one team, one agency or one service. It cannot be done at one time, in one place. It must be divided, dispensed, distributed, organisationally, chronologically and geographically. The oldest problem in organisational theory becomes a matter of life and death.

From a systems theoretical point of view, crisis management lends itself easily to a complexity analysis. A range of cross-fertilising historical processes of the kind evoked in Chapter 2 has led to a multiplication of different kinds of potential societal security events. Self-differentiating security epistemologies, far from simplifying, narrowing or in any way clarifying or sharpening our knowledge of security threats, their causes and consequences, have in a nearly linear way, provoking neither surprise nor consternation, systematically enriched the threat imaginary and actual security threats. In parallel, and not independent of this primary dynamic of complexity, is a significant institutional dynamic. The growth of the State's administrative apparatus naturally brings with it the problem of complexity. In the first order, there is any growing bureaucracy which is naturally increasingly complex: more citizens, more businesses, activities, commerce, circulation, generating a need for more agents of governance, each with its own clients and users. The expansion of bureaucracy is enhanced and intensified by an analogous epistemological shift bringing about an intensified relation to the differentiation, accumulation and technicity of knowledge. Like in any bureaucracy, these developments lead to a need for great numbers and greater differentiation: materially, quantitatively, qualitatively, ethically.

The deeper ethical question that lurks here relates to the degree to which the attribution of responsibility includes the responsibility and/or authorisation to attribute that responsibility in turn to another. Who can distribute responsibility? If my employer, through the authority bestowed by virtue of my work contract, gives me responsibility to a carry out a certain task, do I have the right or even the responsibility to attribute it to another? To distribute it to another, to a colleague, a friend or family member, by the power of a contract, informal or formal, established with that person? Is that person endowed with the right or responsibility to redistribute to another? Coming more directly to the problem of 'pulverisation', does the responsibility remain unchanged through the process of being re-attributed, re-dispensed? Is its meaning or its force reduced, watered down or 'pulverised'? If it is distributed to two individuals, is the responsibility reduced by half? If it is distributed to a thousand agents, is it in effect 'pulverised'? Or is responsibility commutative? When responsibility is given to multiple actors, does each attribution retain full responsibility?

Understandably, little attention is given to this complex knot of normativity and attribution. For better or worse, it becomes woven into a set of brutally simple principles that remain the core energy of the organisation and decision-making on preparedness and crisis management: the three principles mentioned above. Of these, the most prominent is clearly the 'Principle of Responsibility', and this plays the most wide-reaching role. It has a clarifying normative property, underscoring how and by what means and tools a given political priority should be operationalised. As we will see, this Principle returns repeatedly as the mainstay of societal security in Norway in the period after 2001.

> The term 'preparedness' in the mandate is a narrow concept of preparedness, and the Commission's mandate comprehends a smaller part of civil preparedness or what is called using a more contemporary term societal security. Preparedness for accidents and catastrophes falls within the mandate. Failure of water supply, electricity or important foods, falls outside of the mandate. (NOU, 2001: 11)

The prototype of the Principle of Responsibility appears for the first time, with the status of a 'principle', in the parliamentary communication *Main Guidelines for Civil Preparedness Activities and Development in the Period 1999–2002*, which itself arose out of an earlier discussion in the mid-1990s around the need to coordinate civil preparedness, a need voiced in a number of parliamentary discussions and debates (JBD, 1998). In order to strengthen coordination, the Ministry of Justice was empowered by Parliament with centralised governance of this task area and created for that purpose a Council for Civil Preparedness. The perceived need for this new unit ironically did not follow from the complexity problem we sketched above, though it became quickly implicated in it. The need for this bureaucratic adjustment was far more a result of the change in the relation between civil and military preparedness. Whereas the Principle of Responsibility in its mature form organises the relation between bureaucratic sectors in 'normal' times and those same sectors in times of crisis, the original form of the Principle, as it appears in the 1998 report, is concerned with organising the relation between military defence and civil defence in times of peace.

> There has been comprehensive change in civil preparedness in this period. This applies to both the traditional civil preparedness with regard to how best to exploit society's collective resource to the country's best advantage, and with regard to measures aimed at improving the capacity to deal with and prevent crisis situations regardless of their cause. (JBD, 1998: 3)

This development follows from reflection about the potential added value of the already existing, and, not least, well-structured and efficiently disciplined, civil defence corps, which already possessed the core competence, resources and, not least, experience to deal with non-military emergencies. As elsewhere in the world, the marriage between national defence and civil preparedness was an arranged one, based entirely on operational values and on the operational value added, and thereby reduced costs by tasking the units rigorously schooled in a military rationality to confront an entirely different 'enemy', i.e. non-military security threats to the civilian populations, in a more or less identical way.

This did not come without institutional frictions, since the Directorate for Civil Preparedness, tasked with focussing on the same non-military threats from a risk management and threat perception point of view, inevitably regarded the new horizon of insecurity and preparedness differently. This institutional gap became particularly relevant after significant flooding in Østlandet in the spring of 1995 when the need to direct crisis management resources for a regional disaster to the communal level was particularly acute. To a large degree as a consequence of budgetary needs, funds were funnelled from the civil defence corps to the local crisis management activities. As a result, the number of civil defence corps was reduced from fifty-four to forty, and 115 peacetime crisis response groups were established (3).

To be sure, the cause of a structural shift in the bureaucratic response to natural crises stemmed from the pragmatic administrative need to generate and find resources for actual crisis management activities. The practical bureaucratic advantage of this approach to meeting resource needs on a national basis is the proximity between the tasks and skill sets of civil defence corps and those of crisis response corps. The abilities and facilities of the civil defence corps, its work experience, institutional memory and organisational ethos, is already established through what amounts to a classical bureaucratic path of least resistance, where competence and responsibility are transferred from one area to another. The same goes for the transfer of the structure of responsibility: 'A main principle for civil preparedness is that the agency that has expert responsibility in peacetime shall also have responsibility for preparedness. A war or crisis shall thereby not create a new relations of responsibility than what existed before in the day-to-day situation' (51). There is, thus, a direct lineage to be found between the axis of crisis and normal politics bureaucracy and the axis of war and peace. The early militarisation of crisis response, far from being the result of some nefarious ideology of a bellicose society, is more a reflection of the banality and innocuousness of bureaucratic efficiency.

9/11: the view from Norway

The possibility that Norway can be the object of a terrorist attack in the course of the work of [this] committee became more real after the highjackings and attacks on the World Trade Center in New York and the Pentagon in Washington D.C. on September 11, 2001. The fight against terrorism and sabotage in peace time is assigned to the police, with the support of the Ministry of Defense, but if such actions nonetheless take place, the rescue services come into the picture, possibly also the Crisis Commission for Nuclear Accidents. Rescue and accident preparedness must be organised and dimensioned such that one also takes in consideration accidents, crises, and catastrophes caused by terrorist activities. The risk for vulnerability to a terrorist attack is evaluated continuously by central authorities, first and foremost the Police Security Service and the Defence Department. (NOU, 2001: 17)

The official report from the Commission on Vulnerability, published in April 2000, had a significant impact. This was perhaps due as much to the public esteem and notoriety enjoyed by the Commission's chairman, former Prime Minister Kåre Willoch, as it was to the thoroughness and insightfulness of the report's conclusions. The report was rigorous and thoughtful, demonstrating a kind of societal wisdom that went beyond ordinary technocratic investigations. Moreover, it was followed up by a comprehensive hearing and consultation process in order to increase its legitimacy and political impact. The public response to the hearing was overwhelming, with hundreds of written statements received. When it was finally entered into the public record, it was thus on solid footing. In order to follow up on the Commission's report and the hearing statement, hence completing its political cycle, the Ministry of Justice and Police, which was the ultimate addressee of the report, had planned an official report on the follow-up and measures taken in response to the Commission's work, to be published in April 2002. During the intervening period, the attacks of 11 September 2001 seized the attention of the world, and the ethos of any Western reflection on security. The faraway events reorientated the Norwegian conversation and the entire reflection of the vulnerability report, as well as the constellation of actors and practices involved in assuring security in Norway.

As elsewhere in the Western geopolitical community, the 9/11 attacks were immediately, for better or worse, inscribed in the logic and imaginary of the discourse of war and peace, with all the ambivalence and clumsiness they involve. This was also the case in Norway, though to a lesser degree because of the strong Bush II 'war against terror' discourse that was launched after the 11 September attacks than for the pragmatic, administrative reasons that emerged. The challenge for any Western government with an advanced awareness of an open and somewhat fluid concept like 'societal security' is to integrate the unexpected within it, but without erasing it in the process. How can one accommodate the monstrous 9/11, the murderous fury it brought against the most stolid forces of security the world has known, with the innocuous societal security ambitions of Norwegian society? Even if the required malice was there, such spectacular destruction could and would never be attained in the chilly Norwegian capital.

And yet, since the imagery of 9/11 unavoidably infiltrates every nook and cranny of the Western imagination, playing itself out as a tacit reference to the impossibly possible wherever there is reference to danger, security, harm, even good and evil, the Twin Towers immediately and understandably flash into view, and the spectre of an attack on its most dramatic level becomes imminent if not unavoidable. The earnest innocence of the report from the Commission on Vulnerability is shown to be illusory. According to the 2008 Ministry of Justice report *Societal Security: The Path Toward a Less Vulnerable Society*:

> The Commission on Vulnerability was formed and delivered its report in July 2000, in a favourable atmosphere for security policy. The terrorist events of September 11 show that the developments in a modern society require greater attention to which threats we can be considered to confront. For the government it is important that there is continuity in the effort to secure society and that measures to secure society will not be steered by events that take place, but build upon assessments of danger we may be confronted with. (JPD, 2008: 3)

It is for this very reason we must prepare not only for war and peacetime security challenges but also for the collapse of the fundamental distinction between the two, a threat in itself. At one level, 9/11 does not necessarily increase the threat level in Norway – though this will become central as part of a second-tier analysis – rather, it is a reminder of the unstable character of our own security analysis while not, at first glance, a disruption of our material welfare. There were no immediate material threats to the security of Norwegians on 9/11 – no disruptions of air traffic, no telephone or internet interruptions – and, least of all, to society, essentially no interruptions of everyday culture and common social relations. By contrast, the disruption comes in terms of the model of threat assessment, in the discourse of societal security. A sudden awareness emerges from the provincialism of the Norwegian approach to societal security, based primarily on low-grade, intimate natural disasters and accidents, local storms and floods, isolated avalanches and personally scaled industrial mishaps associated with the local, with its intimate values and tightly woven societal fabric, precious but with an inferiority complex for catastrophes. International terrorism and transnational criminality were, in 2001, only emerging issues for Norway. Not only were security imaginaries quite narrowly focussed but also security methodologies, both in the everyday practices of firemen and ambulance drivers and in the conceptual scope of the Norwegian research approach to insecurity. This was reflected in the persistence of the controversy over whether there was a meaningful difference between 'security' and 'safety', that is, whether the response to any and all security challenges is not one form or another of the device: 'be careful'. Against this backdrop, the Norwegian security landscape was impacted by events thousands of miles away.

> The terror attacks of September 1, 2001 show just how vulnerable modern society is and that peacetime events can have an equally large scope of damage

as wartime events. This change in the threat and risk picture, in which society must be able to meet a broad spectre of challenges in addition to the military threats, will have consequences for how the task of security that takes place in society is organised and prioritised. (7)

The 'vulnerability' observed refers, of course, to the exposure of the US World Trade Center and the Pentagon at the moment of the multiple attacks on 11 September 2001. The death and destruction endured in the US might well have been more normal, more a part of the imagined expectations of a wartime setting, had a US-led war actually been waged on US soil. It is true that such images of destitution are traditionally not observed in peacetime. Yet, a sharper – and less sympathetic – reading of the same text would have to account for the fact that, for Norwegians, the vulnerability was imagined. The Norwegian imaginary was, in some sense, vulnerable to an attack, not – or not only – on its citizens, its territory or its infrastructures but on its naive self-understanding as a cultural-spiritual entity enveloped in a blanket of societal non-violence. To a significant extent, this reading is also the truth. The investigative commission's report indeed uses the critical moment of 9/11, not only to analyse the facts and events but also to signal the intention to upgrade the quality of Norwegian risk assessment, to build a more rigorous and more scientific – and less 'naive' – approach to terrorist threat and to societal challenges in general. Based on 'the experiential material and analyses in the form of, among other things, statistics concerning accidents and serious events, calculations of likelihood, risk and vulnerability analyses, assessments of threat and of security policy' (3), the decade of completely avant-garde preparation and analysis in the area of vulnerability and societal security did not serve to prevent Oslo/Utøya, even while the report situates the 9/11 attacks in a unique evolution of tragic events that clearly raised the overall Norwegian popular and official consciousness, together with the MS Sleipner ferryboat crash, the train derailing at Åsta, a serious train transport fire in Lillestrøm, among others. All these small- to mid-scale accidents led Norwegian authorities to turn their attention to a new kind of security problem, at once nestled in a specific local context and subject to the communicative and imaginary forces of globalised security threats.

Thus, despite the complexities of its application to the Norwegian context, the local, even local-national, experience of 9/11 therefore acted as a significant driver of the evolution of societal security thinking in Norway. Actually, the Norwegian experience of the 9/11 attacks specifically impacted Norway on the geopolitical level. At least in terms of its world view, its understanding of itself in the world, Norway was thrust by these faraway attacks into a new kind of global dynamic, ushering in a responsibility it, of course, had always had, but had never had to assume so acutely.

The terrorist attacks of September 11, 2001, and the subsequent developments in the war against terror mark a time-shift. For the first time the NATO Alliance invoked Article 5 affirming that an attack on one ally is to be regarded as an attack on all. The UN affirmed through Security Council Resolution 1368 the United States's right to self-defence. (11)

By most regards and by a wide margin, Norway had been considered a beneficiary of the NATO Article 5 arrangement. With a short but significant shared border with Russia and a long and resource-rich west-facing Atlantic cost, it was considered a valuable member in an otherwise asymmetric alliance. Even so, its contribution to an alliance-led war on terror might generously be considered marginal: for a variety of reasons, it has certainly remained a low-value target for terrorism. With its highly homogenous social fabric and evenly distributed social goods, it was an unlikely – though not altogether impossible – home to radicalisation. Nonetheless, the historically minimal contribution of the Norwegian defence forces and Norwegian foreign policy turned, at least in a logistical sense and for a brief moment, towards the geopoliticisation of its own societal security. This intensification of externalisation of societal security resembles a movement which could be observed in many European States in the decade after 9/11. While everyday domestic security issues become increasingly guided by faraway threats and fears, the traditional external, geopolitical issues became internalised. This redistribution of the logic of danger naturally disrupts, at the same time, the distribution of tasks and the construction of the deployment of power in the State apparatus. Foreign policy becomes a domestic concern while internal politics are increasingly directed at issues of foreign borders.

This type of reconfiguration was no less evident in Norway where the problem of coordinating NATO Article 5 obligations after 9/11 was together with the new horizon of direct terrorist threat to the country. A double-sided policy approach was necessary, in Norway as elsewhere: active external contribution to a global war on terror and an even more active set of initiatives with the design of preparing Norway, its people and its infrastructure for the same style of attack that visited the US. Thus, although the overwhelming principal concern for Norwegian authorities was the possibility of an impending threat on Norwegian soil, on Norwegian citizens and on Norwegian institutions, the preparedness effort was coordinated by the Ministry of Foreign Affairs, which formed a national preparedness plan and set down a commission on preparedness whose task was to 'undertake a continuous assessment of the security policy, foreign policy and threat-oriented aspects of the situation' (17). In the wake of Oslo/Utøya, national preparedness was administratively shifted to the Ministry of Justice, which continued the coordination of information internally through a contact network between the different departments and agencies.

Beyond the basic high-level communication and coordination activities, mobile communication technologies were updated, in both the military and the civil sectors. The Ministry of Defence revised its preparedness procedures, security measures surrounding high-value installations and persons were enhanced and the Minster of Defence was granted authority to call up army reserves; the Minister of Justice was empowered to call in police reserves. Airport security was increased. The civil defence capabilities were strengthened, and security routines were sharpened around communication facilities, oil installations, water supply, health facilities. Decontamination equipment and training were provided (17–19). As in many other countries, both inside and outside the NATO alliance, the Norwegian societal security tidal change was powered by events that took place 6,000 miles away. Norwegian society became global overnight in the name of societal security.

Norway's learning curve in the months after 9/11 was steep. On this occasion, the methods, tools and procedures for dealing with societal security challenges were both enhanced and entirely reorientated. What was only months before the typical Norwegian societal security issue became transformed in a heartbeat. With this change came a new vision for societal security, for the way in which society could be threatened, what resources a society had to defend. It changed, in effect, Norway's very notion of a society. Henceforth, society was not a given, not an ambient reality on the background of which life played out, dangers appeared, adversaries were confronted, etc. Society was also in play, also part of the security equation, also dispensable.

> It cannot be excluded that Norway could be exposed to a terrorist attack that can strike suddenly and comprehensively. The society's security tasks concern, in contrast with the Cold War, a wide plurality of security challenges, which can present themselves either expectedly or unexpectedly. These challenges require a large and broad degree of flexibility in the work that is to be done in order to secure society. (29)

As elsewhere in the growing corpus of policy analyses of vulnerability, the report focusses on the vulnerability of technical systems which link in one way or another to the day-to-day function of the Norwegian welfare society. It concerns itself neither with the fundamental relation between the vulnerability of technical support and the vulnerability of society understood as a set of social relations, nor with the social determinations or social context and embedding of the technical systems whose vulnerability is their object.

Be that as it may, this paradoxical approach which consisted in safeguarding technical installations with the aim of protecting 'society' or 'societal values' runs deep and can be found not only in Norwegian public policy but at the EU level as well (Burgess, 2007). No matter how far policy formulations reach in order to touch and influence the actual human essence of the society, that path can only be described in technical, instrumental, even mechanical, terms.

> Societal security is used in this report to describe the ability of society as such to maintain important societal function and preserve the life, health and fundamental needs of citizens under different forms of stress. The concept of societal security is used broadly and covers security of a whole spectrum of challenges, from limited, natural events, to crisis situations that represent comprehensive danger to life, health, environment and material values, to security challenges that threaten the nation's sovereignty or existence. (JPD, 2008: 4)

Accepting, of course, the well-intended impulse to preserve and protect something called 'society', the constellation of elements that makes up that society is, in the formulation, remarkably disparate if not outright incongruous. Societal security refers to an 'ability', to a competence or capacity to maintain a certain number of societal 'functions'. Societal security, in this sense, is not a state of existence, as we would conventionally think of it, a static situation in which one is stably secure against one or another type of stable threat. Societal security is ultimately conservative: it takes the status quo as the default or baseline situation which it is the aim to maintain. Those qualities that would remain unchanged include a heterogeneous set of arrangements and experiences. Life is the least controversial of these, which is not to say that it is uncontroversial. What is the life to be preserved? What kind of life? On what terms? By the authorisation or the grace of whom? Also sheltered by societal security is the health of the members of society, a quality which, of course, contains its own politicisation. These qualities are engaged in a variety of discourses of threat, some intentional or human-made, others non-intentional, all of which can threaten life, health and environment, and, in addition, the 'material values' that demarcate and, in some sense, assure 'the nation's sovereignty or existence'.

In this formulation of societal security, life, well-being, a well-functioning society, material value and sovereignty thus all come under one umbrella. The resulting conglomerate is at once prickly to understand for citizens whose benefit it is the extension, though perhaps somewhat diffuse, objective of the bureaucracy it will give meaning to. Also, it is a challenging or even impossible mission from a point of view of administrative implementation. With criss-crossing competences, standards and cultures, but also rationalities and concrete understandings of concepts, concerted and coordinated effort seems a significant task. While we have already analysed the complex constellation of society in Chapters 2 and 3, we can underscore one key element that is particularly prominent in the post-9/11 thinking, namely, the condensation of societal identity and national sovereignty. If we, somewhat schematically in the tradition of Weber, consider society to be made up of individuals governed by structural forces, society can only be regarded as identical to nation in an entirely bureaucratic way, and even less to national sovereignty. While it is true that much is lost with the weakening or collapse of society, it is difficult to equate it with the violation of national sovereignty, in the way, for example, the 2001 societal security report does.

When is the nation under threat? When is society under threat? Regardless of where one situates oneself in the rich debates that played out in the 1990s around the essence or non-essence of the nation-state and what constituted it (Balakrishnan, 1996; Gellner, 1983; Hobsbawm, 1992; Hutchinson & Smith, 1994; Smith, 1991, 2003), the sovereignty of the nation and its national culture have been at odds with each other from the very origins of the term 'nation'. Indeed, as these debates evolved into the 2000s and 2010s, the question of national identity as a menace to national sovereignty has become actualised. The perceived threats from within the territorial borders of the State became politicised in a way that pitted them directly against the existence of the nation (Basaran, 2008; Bigo, 2001, 2002; Bigo *et al.*, 2007; collective, 2007; Walker, 1993). Whether one takes society, as Durkheim, to be a collection of the 'social facts' that transcends the existence and experience of individuals or whether one focusses on the individualisation of society through governing structures, a certain weakening or even obsolescence of the notion of national sovereignty precedes the rise of societal security as a political priority. The post-Cold War process described in Chapter 2 tells the story not of conflicting politics involving the opposition of one kind of security against another but rather of conflictual ontologies, an opposition of one reality against another. If one remains with the fundamentally realist ontology of realpolitik that, for better or worse, has suffered weakening but which is far from being left without influence, then threats mobilised and for some realised with Oslo/Utøya remain ephemeral caught in the geopolitics of distant evil. If, on the other hand, we accept the ontological premises of societal security, that sources of and conditions for the growth of insecurity stem from the human spirit, then we begin to understand the fundamental importance of the bureaucratic security measures taken in order to 'mend' the suffering of our world.

Part II

Making security sense of Oslo/Utøya

5

22 July 2011: event, meaning and affect

> I hate you so much that sometimes
> I can't think of anything else.
> Black (2019)

Live terror

Dagsrevyen is the centrepiece evening news programme of the Norwegian Broadcasting Company. It is the most viewed broadcast in Norway, with on average 20 per cent of the entire population watching on any given day (NRK, 2019; SSB, 2019). The programme went on the air as scheduled at 7 p.m., 22 July 2011, only three and a half hours after the explosion in the centre of Oslo. The opening vignette showed scenes of damage and destruction in the streets of Oslo, its iconic and idyllic landmarks, familiar in peacetime, either directly or indirectly, to most Norwegians. Windows were blown out in entire buildings; fire and smoke still appeared from broken fragmented walls and gaping window frames. Images of ambulances and emergency vehicles fill the frame; the voice-over begins. Norwegians, conscious and sensitised to the fact that their country spends more per gross national income on development than all but one of the Organisation for Economic Cooperation and Development (OECD) members, accustomed to seeing such scenes of devastation 'elsewhere' in regions in need of their care, turn up the sound on their televisions and think or even ask out loud, 'us?' (OECD, 2016). Ambulance personnel briskly traverse the frame with a victim on a gurney. As the voice-over begins, footage of a middle-aged, light-haired woman appears, her face completely bathed in her own blood, moving to safety with the help of a second woman holding her hand, cognisant, speaking as she moves out of the scene. The image would be petrifying coming from any distant war zone, and is utterly shocking to the eyes of this provincial nation, accustomed to its consensus politics, low-crime society and schooled in a 'culture of peace'. As the voice-over goes on to describe the damage, there are images of a ghostly, smoke-filled city, captured by the nervous, handheld camera of a running photographer. A nationally familiar female voice begins the voice-over as scenes of chaos pass one after another: 'Two are confirmed dead and several are missing after a powerful explosion in the government quarter in Oslo centre'. The news anchor continues the introduction as violent images flash on the screen, concluding with a frighteningly ambiguous command: 'police ask the public to leave Oslo centre' (NRK, 2011c).

As the frame shifts to the news studio, we at last see the emotion on the face of the news anchor: earnest, professional, clearly concerned. She greets the viewer against a screen-wide photograph of emergency workers walking in front of the cement ruins of well-known buildings. She continues: 'The situation in Oslo is very uncertain for police, and police ask people to stay away from the centre and avoid large gatherings of people'. Indeed, the situation was so unclear in many respects, the small fragments of confirmed information so new, that the only thing that was certain was uncertainty itself. Was the attack over? Were more people involved? Were there still phases to the attack that were yet unknown? As it happened, there were. The second, male, journalist in the studio continues: 'Just after what happened in the government quarter in Oslo centre, reports were received of a shooting at the AUF (Labour Party Youth Organisation) summer camp on Utøya island in Buskerud', where 650 young political activists, mostly teenagers, had been gathered for the annual summer event marked by political discussions, seminars and outdoor activities. Former Prime Minister and ecofeminist icon, Gro Harlem Brundtland, was scheduled to speak on the island earlier in the day. It was unclear whether she was still present. Prime Minister Jens Stoltenberg was scheduled to speak later in the afternoon (NRK, 2011c).

The broadcast moves to a live telephone report from a correspondent standing in Sundvollen, a holiday village located six kilometres from the ferry quay to Utøya. Against the background of an archive photograph of tents on a sunny day on the island and a file profile photograph, the reporter relays the sparse available information about an assailant dressed in police uniform carrying a Glock pistol. The reporter passes on an incorrect eyewitness report stating that shooting had begun at 5:30 p.m., one and a half hours earlier, and the similarly inaccurate information that five people had been shot, underscoring that police can, at present, neither confirm nor refute that anyone has been hurt, though they could indeed confirm that shots had been fired.

Thus, against a backdrop of uncertainty in Oslo about both what in fact had happened and what was continuing to happen, how many and who were hurt or killed, another chain of uncertainties on Utøya unfolded live on the most watched programme on national television. The explosion was located at the base of the Prime Minister's office. Had he or his staff been assassinated? Was the Minister of Justice, whose offices occupy the same building, alive or dead? Was there a link between the two events? In the absence of facts, spectators searched for references, what they knew, what they remembered, what was near, culture, family, friends.

All these questions were to remain unanswered for some time. At 8 p.m., one hour after the beginning of the news programme, the Prime Minister appeared on television from an undisclosed location, later revealed to be his official residence. The fact that he was obviously alive and well after the real possibility that he had been assassinated in the bomb attack on his office building was passed over in silence. The Prime Minister spoke to a sympathetic reporter, clearly moved, nervous, tense, perspiring and grave. Despite the extraordinary situation and uncanny ambiance, he had the presence of mind to firmly formulate a principle that would be repeated over the course of the next days and weeks, and which would become the hinge to the question of liberal approaches to illiberalism in many settings across the world. He affirmed that 'it is important to not let fear take the overhand; we want in times exactly like these to stand up for what we believe in, an open society, a society where political activity can take place in safety without threats, and where violence will not frighten us from completely normal activity' (NRK, 2011c).

As the programme nervously continues, reports are broadcast from eyewitnesses and hospital emergency rooms, response teams, fire personnel and police, details and data are offered, a continuously adjusted estimate of the number of the injured and killed, of the scope of damage, and the same summary update is made: things remain unclear, uncertain. It is as if uncertainty is the main headline of the four-hour broadcast. The strange dialectical logic of certainty–uncertainty cruelly sets itself in play: the more we know, the more we confront the limits of what we know, the more that which is 'beyond' knowledge plays a role: traditions, memories, cultural practices, history, mores, collective beliefs, spirituality, etc. Or, more precisely, the more we know, the more the scope and power of what must presumably be unknown grows. The details of the horrific attacks feed an economy of longing for knowledge. The continuous flow of detailed information does not generate more certainty and security. On the contrary, it engenders more uncertainty, more questions, more doubt, more suspicion and a more acute emotional need to know, need to be sure, need to be secure, to quench the thirst to know, need to connect with the past, with the known, etc.

This is the very ruse of instrumental knowledge, close kin to Hegel's nineteenth-century insight about the 'ruse of reason' (Hegel, 1991b). Naked facts, instrumental news, bureaucratically generated or managed information bytes do not reassure, do not give security, even less reduce risk and uncertainty. Factual, scientific knowledge, estranged from human, moral, cultural or even spiritual embedding, does not provide succour, does not give security. The instrumentalisation of knowledge and action, as replete with benefits as it might be, indispensable as it may present itself, can never bring the security that society seeks and for which it, in many senses, exists.

At the beginning of the broadcast and while it was still unclear what was happening on Utøya, the news anchors remained visibly moved. The headline was virtually: 'What we do not know'. The story of what is known unfolds over the course of the four hours' live, loosely programmed searching for answers, answers presenting themselves unsolicited, and increasingly unwelcome answers imposing themselves over the course of the evening and days that follow. Reports of death and destruction come live over the air. The news of the terrorist's arrest is announced live. The death toll on Utøya rises over the course of the news programme from two to over ninety, before being adjusted upwards again in real time, then down again in the aftermath. For a closely knit nation and a democratic make-up such that 'everyone knew someone', the stress is palpable.

Two specialists in terrorism appear in the first thirty minutes of the programme. The first is Helge Lurås, a well-known commentator who permits himself the cavalier speculation that the terror attack is the result of the Norwegian military 'adventure' in Afghanistan as a member of the NATO alliance. He ventures to add that, given that the bomb attack in the city centre and the shooting attack on Utøya were apparently taking place in a coordinated way, the perpetrator was likely a group, indicating the implication of larger-scale coordinated effort. In the intervening minutes, a spokesperson for the police department also connects the two events based on the observation that the summer camp taking place on Utøya was of a political nature and that the bomb was set off at the heart of the government quarter. The second specialist, Tore Bjørgo, is more circumspect, emphasising that the objective of terrorism is 'to create fear and to create a reaction such that society damages itself', adding that it is important now that society should not react in a way that terrorists want them to:

> The great task now, both for politicians and citizens, is to keep calm and not let terrorists decide what kind of society we are going to have. ... We are the ones who will decide how we want to live in this country and we must as far as possible preserve the way of life we wish to have. (NRK, 2011c)

The wisdom of the analysis, along with the moral responsibility it articulates, were acutely needed in the moment. Notwithstanding, we will see that its success depended on how the meaning of the formidable question it raised was interpreted and enacted: What was it, actually, that was under threat? What was 'our way of life'? What were the values we wished to preserve? What was our culture? What was it to be Norwegian (Burgess, 2001)?

Already before the start of the evening news programme, the general press corps was relaying information and communication harvested from social media feeds. Confusion reigned about everything from what had already happened, where it had happened, how many were dead or injured and who the perpetrator was. The number of victims was wrongly reported by both State officials and the press over the course of the next two days. At the end of the day, the official number of dead stood at ninety-two, though this would turn out to be overstated. The confusion was in part due to the fact that many of the victims on Utøya were still missing, either drowned or dispersed and simply not confirmed as alive. As we will see, this uncertainty was an object of criticism for the many reviews and investigations of the various authorities responsible for and involved in terrorist preparedness, starting with the report of the 22 July Commission, published one year later, and to which we will return in detail in Chapter 6. Naturally, the global press picked up the story. By the end of the day, all of the major news outlets had reported on events. World leaders had chimed in with their support and solidarity. At 9 a.m. the next morning, Anders Behring Breivik was charged for terrorist acts under the 'anti-terrorism' paragraph of the penal code of the Norwegian General Civil Law (JPD, 2006: §147a).

The press conference

The culmination of the first day of the attack also took place on the national news programme, which had already run continuously for over three hours, when Prime Minister Jens Stoltenberg stood together with Minister of Justice Knut Storberget to make brief statements and to answer questions. Visibly moved and in a shaky voice, the Prime Minister took the floor. The story he told again takes the form of a deeply human confrontation with uncertainty:

> Today, Norway has been struck by two shocking, bloody and cowardly attacks. We don't know who attacked us. Much is still unsure. But we know that many are dead and that many are injured. We are all shaken over the evil that struck us so brutally and so suddenly. (NRK, 2011c)

We do not know who our enemies are, what they want of us, how or to what degree they have hurt us. Perhaps most strikingly, and articulating a theme that will guide and structure the discourse around Oslo/Utøya for the rest of the decade and beyond, the question of 'why?' makes its appearance. Why would anyone want to hurt us? What have we done? Of what are we guilty in the eyes of the perpetrators in the eyes of God? In the discourse of forensic analysis, the question of 'why' is, of course, not relevant. Sorting out, documenting, analysing what actually, essentially, took place, what the 'facts' are, what the actual, factual circumstances were and are, the chain of events, the direction of the causality and the identity of the legal subjects to whom is ascribed legal responsibility for the attacks: these are the questions for first-line forensic analysis of the police. In short, first-order legal protocols require only an entirely depersonalised narrative of the episode, a series of actions and events that together form a juridical package of responsibility and, eventually, legally determined guilt that can be attributed to any legal subject, attached like an external legal appendage (Fraser, 1997). Determining this attachment represents another phase of the analysis and juridical procedure. Clearly, the 'suspect' can often be a key source of information in the forensic analysis.

The prioritisation of 'objective' forensic science is, of course, only one expression of Western 'scientism', which takes its most banal form in the simple valorisation of 'fact', 'evidence', 'proof', etc. over spiritual, moral, affective experience. This value hierarchy is in part supported and sustained by poorly supported assumptions about the unchanging and stable character of facts, and the fickle nature of the spiritual. As others have shown, one need not dig deep to discover that the contrary is far more likely to be the case (Daston & Galison, 2007; Daston & Park, 1998; Poovey, 1998). Even accepting the premises of classical forensic science, it might be more plausibly claimed, from a mere methodological standpoint, that spiritual, moral and affective experience, in so far as it is more fragile and fleeting, should be more urgently evaluated, archived, preserved, if such a thing is possible. Alternatively, if the analysis were to focus solely on the object of violence, the question of what is lost or damaged, a more powerful and substantial argument could be directed against forensic scientism, namely, that it disregards the expression of what violence has done to human spirit.

As it happens, we can observe a dynamic instability in this relationship between facts and spiritual life. In the days following the attack, there emerged a kind of spiritualisation, and then a subsequent de-spiritualisation, of the facts. The concrete, 'factual' events to which only few were unfortunate to have to bear witness or sacrifice their lives to became a general experience, a Norwegian experience, a Western experience, a human experience. 'We are all Norwegian' mirrors slogans like 'We are all Jews' or 'We are all Charlie Hebdo', which, albeit in a relatively harmless and superficial way, reflect this kind of experience of being part of the human family, collectively injured, collectively suffering and saddened. This is nothing other than a reflection of a spiritual shared experience.

Facts and values

The recourse to the dramatic characterisation chosen by the Prime Minister in a moment of personal and national shock ('cowardly', 'shocking', 'evil', 'brutal') is easily justifiable from a moral point of view. This is not our question. Far more crucial is the way in which the facts of the matter, 'terrorist' facts, are immediately and inevitably spiritualised as a function of the spiritual reaction of the objects of terror. They are torn away from their facticity from the moment they become established as facts. As the well-documented 1990s debate in political philosophy between 'facticity' and 'validity' revealed (at times against the good intentions of its participants), the empirical is at pains to remain empirical (see Habermas, 1996). The factual becomes human despite itself, as it morphs into human joy and pain, generates hope and inspires dread, all in the flash of the moment. This transformational power, and not the awareness of the instrumental facts of the matter and our potential to change what they might have been or perhaps in some future might be, is both an effect of the force of terrorism and of the power of healing. The same must be said about the not-yet-known facts, the uncertainty into which all Norwegians are suddenly cast, both in the late hours of 22 July but also in the uncertainty of the unforeseen future. Like the general experience of humanity evoked in naked facts of terror,

> this is an evening that demands much of all of us. The days that are coming will demand even more. We are prepared to meet this. Norway stands united in times of crisis. We mourn our dead. We suffer with the injured and we feel with their next of kin. This is about an attack on innocent civilians, on youngsters at a summer camp, on all of us. (NRK, 2011c)

An analogous appeal is made to a substance that both precedes and transcends the horrible facts of the attack, and the responsibility they demand of Norwegians and will continue to demand of much of us. What do facts demand? Nothing, of course, unless they are transformed or lifted to a plane of accountability, normativity, compassion, affectivity and action. All these qualities are in some sense evoked by the Prime Minister. Indeed, as the events and the reactions unfold over the next days, Norwegians and the Norwegian political class show themselves to be up to the challenge, as the Prime Minister had rightly predicted. They react to it in terms of their moral, cultural or spiritual experience, precisely on the terrain where it does the most damage by nature. For while the individual lives lost are tragically irreplaceable, the explicit and real target of terrorism is to weaken, damage or destroy the moral character of society: its values, its traditions, its historical substance, its forms of cultural practice, etc.

Against all scientific reason, the facts and values seem to be inseparable. Nonetheless, the factual and empirical, which hold the assurance and security of scientific indifference, is privileged by bureaucratic rationality, and thus the Prime Minister swerves back to the empirical – 'This is about an attack on innocent civilians, on youngsters at a summer camp' – before again collectivising, consolidating, spiritualising the violence as an attack 'on all of us'. The collective position and ethos continues as the Prime Minister delivers a 'message to those who have attacked us':

> It's a message from all of Norway. You will not destroy us. You will not destroy our democracy, our engagement for a better world. We are a little nation, but we are a proud nation. No one can bomb us into silence. No one will shoot us into silence. No one will ever scare us from being Norway. (NRK, 2011c)

The role of a political leader, representative of a sovereign State, is to send and receive political messages on behalf of the State. He or she possesses the political legitimacy to do so, representing the democratically determined general will of the people. All the same, the nature and content of the general will of a democratically determined people has long remained a mysterious political philosophy. The rights and obligations granted by the social contract have accompanied the long pedigree of the nation-state. In this sense, what it means to 'speak for Norway', either in war or peace, joy or sorrow, is unclear, though there is little doubt that Norway is spoken for, both through and around the person of the Prime Minister. The official bureaucracy, the enlightened public sphere, the political masses all participate, both in form and content, in the expression of 'the Norwegian'. Its institutions and authorities, by carrying on with business as usual, enact the Norwegian through the customs, traditions and values they embody.

Finally, in the closing sequence of what we can imagine was a speech hastily prepared under enormously trying circumstances, the Prime Minister again plays on the twin chords of Norwegian collective experience – the individual and the collective. 'This evening and tonight', he continued, 'we will take care of each other, give each other comfort, talk with each other, stand together. ... The most important thing this evening is to save human life, to show care, for all those who have been struck and their next of kin' (NRK, 2011c).

Surely only in Norway, where the imagined community is small – in fact, nearly five million people – would expressing such a sentiment be possible. Its plausibility stems from the presence in national, regional and local culture of traces of a folk culture, patterns of speech and behaviour, national customs whose pretence is to create comfort for those who understand the codes. It can be witnessed in the Norwegian popular culture, national manifestations, sports events and social life, even while being gradually displaced by globalising or Europeanising forms of professionalism, administrative and bureaucratic culture and New Public Management, all based on one form or another of the ideology of efficiency as homogenisation, accountability, inter-replicability and interoperability. This popular culture has also resisted, not without some effort, the marginal trend towards populism, which, compared to Trump's America or the various European new nationalisms, is difficult to take seriously. Norwegians can still, at least according to a certain imaginary, take care of each other, give each other comfort, talk with each other, stand together. And yet, for the Prime Minister, this imagined local imagery is linked to the equally, and necessarily, imagined collective agency of the Norwegian:

> Tomorrow we will show the world that Norwegian democracy becomes stronger when it counts. We will find those who are guilty and hold them responsible.
>
> ... We must never stop standing up for our values. We must show that our open society passes this test too. That the response to violence is even more democracy, even more humanity, but never naivety. We owe that to the victims and their next of kin. (NRK, 2011c)

According to the Prime Minister, the collective Norwegian implicitly knows and understands what is under threat when the Norwegian is under threat. It is something that transcends the hideous death and injury of individual Norwegians, transcends the horrific material destruction in Oslo. Norway as a society was targeted by the attacks, but the Prime Minister contributes to a discourse, as will many others in the days and weeks to come, that seeks to protect society, understood not as a collection of individuals but as a far richer, deeper, older collection of spiritual values and democratic customs.

The comments by the Prime Minister are, in this sense, remarkable, unique and admirable, perhaps even unheard of in the cultural politics of the post-9/11 era. They serve as the baseline for our analysis of the bureaucratisation of responses to terrorism, as the only visible path for the political apparatus whose task is to administratively embody the heart and soul of Norwegian society. The Prime Minister, together with others, expresses an idea of societal security that begins a journey moments after the attacks in Oslo and Utøya, from the preservation of the Norwegian as a spiritual matter to the preservation of the Norwegian as a bureaucratic matter.

At the same time, the Prime Minister has an understanding of society and the threats to it, which is in agreement with the attentive researcher Bjørgo, who appeared earlier on the same news programme with nearly no information to build his analysis on. Bjørgo had declined to speculate, in the absence of adequate information, on who the perpetrator might be, in contrast to Lurås, who spoke only moments before about Norway's military adventures in Afghanistan. He understood that by intimating that the attacks of the terrorist were perpetrated by some yet unidentified terror group, he was already doing the terrorists' work for them, already putting society itself into question, already weakening trust, damaging solidarity, supporting fear. Even while the dead were not counted, the alarmist attitude sought to move the battle into society, among Norwegians, among communities whose very foundation is trust in their own self-evidence.

Cracks in the discourse of collective spirit

Already the following day, 23 July 2011, the discourse had begun to bifurcate. On the one hand, the discourse of 'the Norwegian' and the societal security it implicitly generates, confident in its democratic principles, true to its spirit, loyal to its natural solidarity, its sense of community, human values, local network, care and familiarity. On the other hand, the discourse of the calculous and accountability, of expectations of performance, of quantified values, routinised safety and impersonal security.

The voice-over of *Dagsrevyen*, on a vignette of the Norwegian flag at half mast, begins 'Norway in grief', followed by a brief summary of the death toll – ninety-two at the time of broadcast, though still uncertain, the assailant, an ethnic Norwegian, was arrested, having surrendered freely. The fact that he was allowed to continue the rampage for one and a half hours is underscored. Then, a pivot to reactions from the world, a shot of a Norwegian Tour de France rider with a black armband and, finally, footage of the royal family greeting survivors and next of kin near Utøya. Several live interviews with reporters and witnesses tell two parallel stories of systematic police investigation, supported by determined statements by earnest political authorities, and of the experience of shock, injury and grief on the part of the survivors. Two Norways emerge from day zero. On the one hand, the principled, aloof, universal, responsible, just, rational, reliable, accountable and reasonable of the investigative, ethical, legal, administrative, bureaucratic Norway. On the other hand, the vulnerable, precarious, disorderly, emotional, yet noble and resilient, self-securing Norway (NRK, 2011c).

The two parallel tracks again become apparent in a live studio interview with the Prime Minister. Stoltenberg reports from the meeting of the government earlier that day where the primary outputs were a decision about further coordination between health personnel and first responders, the announcement of a national moment of silence the following day but, first and foremost, expressions of care and concern for the survivors, the next of kin, those still under treatment in hospital and those still waiting for news of the lost. The discourse of care, compassion and humanity is dominant. The anchor follows up by turning the discourse away from the object of the attack to its perpetrator and to the invisible presence of unknown danger: 'But is the threat situation, that is, the "terror" situation, clarified or not?' The anchor trips briefly but quite distinctly on the word 'terror', nearly unable to get it said on the air as though it were laden with taboo.

The concluding 'or not?' adds a slightly aggressive or at minimum indignant tone to the question, as though it were the 'real' question, once the humanitarian niceties are set aside. Nonetheless, the Prime Minister gently avoids a full-throated counter-discourse against the terrorist or terrorism itself, affirming instead that the police authorities have not recommended raising the national threat level, and that otherwise the police investigation is ongoing and there is no indication that anyone other than the one perpetrator was involved.

The anchor asks about his visit to Sundvollen near Utøya, where the survivors and next of kin were gathered. It was, the Prime Minister confirms, a very heavy and painful experience to meet people who have lost brothers, sisters, friends, sons and daughters. These cannot be consoled, he says, even if we do our best to express care and warmth. Still, the Prime Minister added:

> I also met many young people who were very clear that they would not be frightened into not being engaged or not being active. ... They said that the best way to honour the dead was to be more active, more engaged, and to show that they would not let themselves be frightened into silence by violence. (NRK, 2011c)

The Prime Minister thus steers the discourse gently but firmly back to the question of care, compassion and solidarity, drawing again on the red thread of human response, against the encouragement of the journalist to harden the discourse by reinserting it into one of threat and danger. Even while a kind of pressure towards analysis, conclusion, action or counteraction is stirring in many, represented to some degree by the news anchor in this scene, the Prime Minister holds tight to the discourse of compassion. Not only is compassion and care the discourse that he advances but he sees this as the political project advanced in an exemplary way by several members of the Labour Party Youth Organisation that survived the attacks of the day before. The best way to honour the victims, he says, is to fight for a certain set of societal values, rooted in the core value of open and democratic pluralism. There is not a hint of cynicism to be read in the Prime Minister's expression, but it is nonetheless to be remembered, as the news anchor points out, that he is officially leader of the party whose youth representatives were targeted, and that their claim to a certain set of societal values, clearly situated on a party political continuum, reflects upon his own.

In this way, the Prime Minister reveals what is ultimately the conservative character of societal security and the notion that providing security today means something largely different from what it meant during the years of the Cold War: security is a preoccupation not with the well-being of the State as a formal construction but with society as an organic, ethical substance. As we have already outlined from several angles, what is ultimately under threat in the post-Cold War era is not national sovereignty but societal values. Security is the security of society, of social norms and values, customs and traditions. Even while such societal values are under constant evolution, nourished by hybrid flows of multiple cultural inputs, constantly politicised and debated, it is this hybrid value set that is attacked when Norway is attacked.

The Prime Minister thus advances a kind of preservationist discourse, drawing on an impulse to protect society from being changed by the cataclysmic violence of the terrorist attacks, either by indulging in one form or another of vengeance or a law-and-order tightening of the civil liberties and expansion of police and surveillance powers. Ironically, what is commonly described as 'social conservatism' would be expected to militate towards severe or extraordinary response by the institutions of force and public order. The conservatism, advanced by the Prime Minister in the early phase of reactions, is a conservatism of another kind – let us call it 'societal conservatism'. The news anchor seems to be aware of this conservative thrust and gently challenges the political discourse of 'societal security' advanced by the Prime Minister by pressing him on the question of how he can argue that nothing should change after Norway experienced the worst violence in the post-war period. How can he talk about merely continuing the course when he himself knows or knows of so many of the lost and injured. The Prime Minster responds that it is not a question of simply continuing as before: 'this is not over', many are still unaccounted for, many are still in hospital, the investigation is ongoing. However, in the meantime:

> We as a nation must continue with warmth and compassion, and with the unity we display as a nation, in order to show care for the people who are struck. We must also as a nation, later, find a way to mark, to honour those who have lost their lives, because Norway has not experienced a worse violent attack since the war and one cannot simply remain indifferent to that. (NRK, 2011c)

The national news broadcast of the day after the attacks covers a wide range of aspects of the reaction to the violence. In all, thirty-four segments are presented in the one and a half-hour extended broadcast. There is a report from police headquarters, from the emergency personnel, a variety of live interviews and analyses in the studio, a report comparing the attack to the Oklahoma City bombing, images from the Oslo Cathedral, and other cities in Norway, reactions from Brussels, the US and from the sports world. The coverage is remarkably even-handed, balanced, self-confident, while at the same time capturing and expressing the deep pain and shock of the day. It is a remarkable journalistic moment, one that confirms, at least for a moment, the first naive predictions of the 1970s of how the new (televised) media would unify nations and peoples, even take over the role of print media in the evolution of European nation-building first theorised by Habermas, Smith, Andersen and others (Anderson, 2006; Habermas & Pensky, 2001; Smith, 1991, 1992).

Royal spirit

In the days and weeks after the attacks, it was natural for the royal family's reaction and their involvement in the care and comforting process to receive considerable news coverage. King Harald V, Queen Sonja and Crown Prince Haakon and his wife, the Crown Princess Mette-Marit, were particularly visible. Their activities and reactions were evoked in virtually all news reporting about the attacks, as one might expect to keep close track of a dear family member over the course of a day. The royal family took an active part in supporting victims and next of kin, speaking publicly on several occasions during the days and weeks of shock.

King Harald V made a live television appearance from the Royal Palace directly before the *Dagsrevyen* broadcast the day after the attacks, praising the police and emergency and health services, and volunteers, who made a 'heroic effort for all of us', then reflecting over the shared experience of shock and sorrow of all Norwegians, describing it as: 'An attack on the core of the Norwegian democracy. It is when our nation is put to the test that the strength, the unity and the courage of the Norwegian people becomes clear. Now, we will hold tightly to our values' (NRK, 2011a). In his brief speech, King Harald speaks of 'all', of 'us' and of 'we'. He goes farther than the Prime Minister in describing the horrific attacks as a shared experience, as an attack on society and on society's values. He speaks of taking care of each other, of strangers, who are not strangers. In terms of the questions that concern us, of the cultural-spiritual unity of the people, of informal forms of security, of trust in the face of uncertainty and the variability in the experience of danger, the King holds an entirely different status to the Prime Minister, Parliament, of any public officials. Norway, like the United Kingdom, Canada, Sweden, Denmark, Japan and others, is a constitutional monarchy, meaning that while the monarch holds sovereign power, that power is shared in the sense that he or she can only exercise it according to the provisions of the constitution, which sets out the executive powers and procedures. Nevertheless, the post of monarch is hereditary, based on the principle that his or her rights, obligations and, ultimately, constitutional powers are determined externally to their exercise within the framework of the democracy. The sovereignty is, and must be, external to the execution of sovereign power in order to preserve the source of legitimacy of the State and thereby to preserve itself as sovereign power. Actual governing is thus made possible by a kind of instantaneous suspension of the otherwise impermeable frontier between them. The monarch remains sovereign by virtue of transcending the political requirements of members of the government or the parliament, and the execution of the constitution remains possible by the chief of the government, drawing its mandate from the sacrosanct royal substance.

Unlike political representatives, the government and the parliament, the King, of course, possesses the ability and the competence to meaningfully evoke and utilise the shared national 'we'. The purely democratic 'we' is a mathematical abstraction; the regal 'we', by contrast, is a spiritual substance. It emerges and evolves, advances and withdraws in response to the spirit of the people embodied by the monarch. The character of that substance is implicitly and spontaneously 'known' and personified by the monarch, condensed into his or her actions, present in his or her thoughts. More than ever before, the King became, in the hours, days and months after the disaster, the 'father' of Norwegians, like all our fathers and mothers, unelected, yet implicitly virtuous and tacitly wise.

An equally essential and unique property of a constitutional monarchy is its embedding in history, both past and future, assuring a general historical and even ontological continuity. Within a certain metaphysical scope, the monarchy never begins and never ends. Its origin, that is, the origin of its sovereignty, is beyond the horizon of the past, beyond memory and has the status of myth. Its future, by contrast, is indeterminate in a different way. Again, with the scope of the world it both creates and sustains, a monarchy is never-ending. These two chronological end points are, of course, quickly debunked. As Benjamin eloquently showed in 'Critique of violence' (1921), any sovereign order is founded on an act of violence, and revolutions have brought the violent end to many monarchies (Benjamin, 1978). The key issue, however, is that both the beginning and the end of a monarchy are ontologically external to the monarchy; they belong to another 'world', another reality. It certainly cannot be realised within this world. This reality shift calls into question the nature of 'continuity', what it means and what is experienced when the state of political affairs, the distribution of power but, more importantly, the management of meaning, of sense and of value through time are stabilised and guaranteed by the presence of either a spiritual father or mother, or informal cultural-political processes that either dominate or accompany the republican, democratic processes.

Regal security

Something like a para-theological effect takes place when the presence of meaning in the manifest meaninglessness and absurdity of the 22 July attacks is created, even when it remains invisible or unplumbed, or simply analysed. The continuity that stems from the unconditioned historical transmission and retransmission of the regal spirit from generation to generation, without end, without any tangible conditions triggering revocation or suspension, also assures a certain trans-generational communication of meaning. Even if there are no words – and there were for many, indeed, clearly no words – and even though King Harald V had no words to explain the events and did not even attempt to conjure words of explanation, justification, clarification or even unequivocal condemnation, his words of comfort and recognition of the pain of others, along with his evoking of the communal 'we', signalled the spiritual interconnectedness that assures value and meaning, even though these might remain unarticulated, maybe forever.

This notion of a trans-historical spiritual substrate underlying the experience of the catastrophe will become more apparent in the following chapters, as we study more closely the maladroit and ultimately unsuccessful predisposition of security and preparedness authorities towards replacing 'regal security' with a mechanical, minimally cultural, marginally human and certainly history-less approach to the bureaucratisation of security and preparedness measures. It is important to remark, however, that this predisposition towards a mechanical, bureaucratic approach to security is the result neither of bad faith nor of incompetence but seems rather to lie at the root of the neoliberal self-understanding of democracy in general and security in particular.

'Regal security' should not be confused with authoritarianism, at least not in any simple way. On the contrary, it opens a set of questions about the sources of democratic legitimacy, which links it to the famous liberal-communitarian debate which left such a strong imprint on political philosophy in the 1980s, arguably launched by the publication of Rawls's *Theory of Justice* (1971). The origins of terms of the debate can be traced to early modern conceptions of the individual, formulated in terms of a 'liberal' model (Hobbes, Locke, later Rawls and Nozick) and a 'republican' (later 'republican-communitarian') model (MacIntyre, 2007; Nozick, 1993; Sandel, 1984; Taylor, 1992). The families of thought attached to these models are well travelled and will not be examined in depth here. According to the liberal view, the individual takes moral and political priority over the collective in order to arrive at the legitimacy of the State, the rights that emit from it and the responsibilities individuals have towards each other. 'Society' is understood as the aggregate of all individual distinctions. According to the republican view, it is linked with moral philosophy and virtue theory, foundations that transcend the individual and seek to articulate the meaning of life, the sense of society and the legitimacy of the State. The two models are obviously not symmetrically opposed to one another, and can only best be compared and contrasted on one level, namely, their respective concepts of 'the human'. For the republican-communitarian model, 'society' can be understood as a unity with a moral-cultural substrate. It is something more than or different to the sum of its individuals.

These positions, presented schematically here, naturally have consequences for the way that we understand the security of society. If, as is the explicit ambition of Norwegian leaders and security officials, the aim is to 'secure society', then the conception of society will be determinate. In a liberal security regime the security of society is derived from the security of the individual. Protecting society, preparing society for disaster, consists in preparing each and every individual such that when the hammer falls, the aggregate of the individuals will itself be protected. If we then add to the liberal equation the neoliberal fusion brought by Lippmann, Hayek, Friedman and others, we arrive at a power formula for neoliberal security, which has also been widely and insightfully studied by others (Friedman, 2009; Hayek, 2013; Lippmann, 1937). It involves an atomistic focus on the values, interests and experiences of the individual – which, despite its tangible, empirical aspect, can only function in social modelling as universal abstraction – and, furthermore, its integration with two additional discourses, that of value as an economic measure in the logic of late capitalism and that of the quantification (and later digitalisation) of value in the logic of instrumental rationality discussed earlier.

These classical models support a number of principles about what constitutes a society and will, of course, play a key role when it comes to understanding what it can and should mean to protect or prepare a society for threats to come. This is the core question with which the protagonists in this book constantly grapple, sometimes implicitly, sometimes in full view. Perhaps less expectedly, these models end up providing elements that will help us to understand the interpretations of core actors of the disaster that has already taken place. It is the understanding of what society is and what it would mean to destroy it, or, alternatively, to secure it, that guides and supports understandings of what happened on 22 July. It structures and guides perceptions about what was broken and lost, what societal structures were defective or ineffective, what societal promises were kept and which were betrayed. As we will see, it provides a strong guidance for the assessment and criticisms made of police and security services, and of the reproaches made to policy-makers who made political judgements about funding and overall organisation. The models also form the premises for appropriate expectations, but not only for the security 'services' 'provided' by the State, to borrow the neoliberal terminology, but, more importantly, yet more subtly, what expectations we have and appropriately should have for the social bonds, the social fabric, the informal organisation and the social contract, all of which quite powerfully precede and transcend the à la carte expectations of the 'service society'.

These expectations and the retrospective understandings to which they are linked cannot be accounted for using the categories and concepts, tools and procedures with which one attempted to account for them in the aftermath, analysis and ultimate political reactions. A living current of affective relations, flows of cultural memory, textures of belonging, trust and hope, moral conjectures, social expectations, flows of informal norms, spiritual connections and ineffable identities continue to give life to a societal reaction and relation in ways that the politics of remediation, riposte and reaction continue to operate unknowingly in parallel to. Not for lack of good will but for lack of a discourse that carries with adequate depth the human experiences to politically viable operationalisation. There are no words.

It is for this reason that the role of regal security is remarkable. For better or worse, the legitimacy of the crown does not stem from the formal democratic processes or an analytical logic of personal accountability to impersonal institutions; nor can it be threatened by them. It resists instrumentality, transcends the administrative mechanics of even the most perfunctory State apparatus and holds a charismatic, thus anti-democratic, and personal relationship with every one of its subjects. If there is any entity that resists bureaucratisation, it is a monarchy.

Democracy *på norsk*

When King Harald speaks of the 'impressions', the 'grief' and the 'feelings' of the 'nation', his speech is, on the one hand, based on the charismatic concentration of those sentiments on the person of the King, both his symbolic and regal functions, and, on the other hand, founded upon the King's royally and constitutionally sanctioned legitimacy to unite and mobilise the people through an apolitical register. Ironically, in engaging this moral responsibility, he echoes, to a large degree, the priorities advanced at the same time by the Prime Minister, but also emphasises, to an even greater degree than the Prime Minister, the collective, societal dimension of the attack and reactions to it. 'The actions that were carried out in Oslo and on Utøya were an attack on the Norwegian society that we value so dearly, and it is an attack on the core of the Norwegian democracy' (NRK, 2011a). The individual victims, the injured, the next of kin, the individual grievers, are set in the background as the discourse is opened to the collective level, to shared experience, to common values and universal experience. There is no difference between individuals, living or dead, more or less injured, lost or found, families, loved ones, unknown compatriots. We are all Norwegians in the King's sentiment. There is no internal differentiation in the way that 'we' cherish the shared societal values of Norwegian society. No one is included more or less, no one loves more nor less, no one is more or less loved.

Similarly to the Prime Minister's discourse, yet again reaching beyond it, the King calls upon Norwegians to remember their moral obligation to continue to be Norwegians: 'It is when Norwegian society is put to the test that the strength, unity and courage of the Norwegian people becomes clear. Now is when we stand by our values' (NRK, 2011a). The Norwegian 'we' is strongest and most distinct when put to the test, and this is a historic test. The unity and courage of 'the Norwegian' are naturally borne in the hearts of Norwegians. This is, in effect, one of the common traits envisaged by the King. The very notion of 'standing together', expressing our unity, is also a call to recognition of the actual heterogeneity of Norwegian society, the existence of different groups and cultures, who could, on one level, be concerned by the attacks and their aftermath in different ways, all of which nonetheless allow themselves to be unified. This unity lies beyond strength and courage in the values that are shared. In short, the primary values of Norwegian society transcend disunity and, indeed, support and drive forth this transcendence.

On the third day after the attacks in Oslo and Utøya, *Dagsrevyen* is shortened to one hour, and the discourses naturally become more complex and interwoven. The opening vignette features the Prime Minister, heavy with an emotional expression, perspiring, speaking to a gathering we later learn is a memorial service held that day, repeating a line that was often seen in social media and the press, that had originated with a member of the Labour Party Youth Organisation: 'If one man can show so much hate, think how much love we can all show together' (NRK, 2011b). The opening vignette switches to scenes of the rescue effort at Utøya two days earlier, and the voice-over articulates the concerned observation that one hour had passed from the moment that the police were notified until they arrested the perpetrator, that it is still unclear whether there were other collaborators involved, and revised statistics: ninety-two dead, thirty critically injured, six or seven still missing.

The main narrative of the broadcast then turns to the memorial service held earlier that day in Oslo Cathedral. Images of the royal family in tears, members of the political elite and grieving family members are shown, and extended video footage of the service is played, including yet another stirring speech by an emotionally moved Prime Minister. As he names examples of exemplary individuals, sobs echo through the church. The priest repeats: 'we are a people in grief'.

Reports from the other manifestations are followed by a report from Akershus Hospital, where one of the youths injured in the attack on Utøya had succumbed to her injuries and died. The focus of the broadcast then turns to growing criticism towards the local police station. The questions take primarily two forms: did the police adequately understand what was going on, and were the police adequately prepared to address the information that they received? A representative of the local police is interviewed and confirms that police arrived at the scene of the crime as soon as possible. As we will see, this controversy will continue to evolve over the coming year of investigation and impact the enquiry into the way the crisis was handled. The report presents an extended and detailed timeline of events as they unfolded, interposed with an interview with Buskerud Police Chief Sissel Hammer. Despite clear and objective responses from the Police Chief, the reconstruction of events distinctly puts into doubt the competence of the police, the procedures used and the decisions made. The critique of the time taken by police reappears in reports from the intensive care unit of Akershus, where speculative questions are asked about lives that might have been saved with more time, a theme that would become familiar in the days, weeks and months, and even years, that follow, and to which we will return in Chapter 6.

The Rose March and the Crown Prince's speech

Perhaps the most remarkable manifestation of the spiritual-cultural-democratic baseline ethos that I have tried to signal in certain parts of the official discourse, primarily in the discourse surrounding the Prime Minister, came from the unique public demonstration that took place in the evening of 25 July, the so-called Rose March. The demonstration quickly came to be known by that name because participants were encouraged to come carrying a rose, a logistic feat which, had it been centrally organised, would have doubtless been impossible, but which on a person-by-person basis produced an astonishing and moving manifestation. Estimates of the crowd ranged between 150,000 and 200,000 people, corresponding to about one third of the population of Oslo (Fuglehaug, 2011; Solberg et al., 2011). It was an extraordinary embodiment of solidarity and unity, which was thematised through songs, poems and speeches. The crowd was addressed by the Prime Minister and others, before the Crown Prince Haakon gave a speech that seemed to capture the mood of a nation.

The speech was the antidote to any kind of escalation or militarisation as a result of the attacks, vengeance or retribution. It focussed on unity and solidarity in a way that echoed the Prime Minister's statements in the preceding days and, most importantly, it emphasised the responsibility all Norwegians hold, to be clear about the fundamental societal values that are under threat and the response they should make to this threat, namely, through a reassertion of the values of openness and democracy. The speech was reproduced over the entire front page of the major national daily newspaper *Aftenposten*:

> This evening the streets are filled with love; we have chosen to answer cruelty with closeness; we have chosen to meet hate with unity; we have chosen to show what we stand for. ... Norway is a country in grief; we think of all those who have suffered loss, who are missing; of all those who made a historical

> effort to save life and to reestablish our security; and of our leaders who have been forced to face difficult trials in the last days; those who were on Utøya and in the Government Quarter were targets for terror, but it touched us all. ... After July 22 we can never again permit ourselves to think that our opinions and our attitudes are without meaning; we have to be present every day, armed in the fight for the free and open society we love so much. ... The Norway we want, no one will take from us; we are facing a choice. We cannot undo what has been done; but we can choose what it will do with us as a society and as individuals; we can choose that no one must stand alone; we can choose to stand together. ... It is up to each and every one of us now; it's up to you and it's up to me; together we have a job to do; it's a job that is done around the dinner table, in the cantina, in the clubs, among volunteers, by men and women, in the counties and in the cities. (Haakon, 2011)

The speech contains an appeal to unity, an appeal to meet hate with love, to feel and speak freely. It is a call to think about society and fellowship, about who Norwegians are and what they are, what it means, culturally, spiritually, to be a Norwegian. It derives an ethics from the spiritual unity it seeks to underscore: it sets out what 'the Norwegian' obliges Norwegians to do and, not least, what kind of actions and attitudes it is incompatible with. It might have come across as a series of clichés and banalities coming from a tall, impeccably dressed man. The presence of an intensely present crowd, spontaneously singing the Norwegian national anthem ('Yes, we love this land') and other well-known folk songs, gave body to the Crown Prince's message, performed in a way that was unique, particularly in an era of tough talk, militarisation and authoritarianism and against terror.

Following the speech of the Crown Prince, Prime Minister Jens Stoltenberg again took the stage with his societal discourse, perhaps for the last time in the course of the national grief process, when that discourse would stand unadulterated or even stand at all.

> Thousands and thousands of Norwegians in Oslo and over the whole country are doing the same thing this evening. They are conquering the streets, the market places, the public spaces, with the same stubborn message: 'we are heartbroken but we do not give up'. With torches and roses, we give the world notice: we do not let fear break us, and we do not let fear silence us. The sea of people before me and the warmth I feel from the country make me certain in my conviction: Evil can kill a person, but never conquer an entire people. ... There will be a Norway before and a Norway after 22 July 2011. But we will decide which Norway ... More openness, more democracy, resoluteness and strength – that is us, that is Norway. We will take back our security. Out of all of the pain we glimpse, paradoxically enough roots of something valuable. What we see this evening can be the greatest and most important march we have set out upon since World War II: A march for democracy, a march for unity, a march for tolerance. (Stoltenberg, 2011b)

From the *ethos* of collective responsibility to the instrumentality of accountability

Not unexpectedly, simultaneously with the discourse of unity, of 'the Norwegian' and of societal values, a discourse of accountability in a more or less narrow sense blossomed. During the three weeks between the attacks and the formal creation of the 22 July Commission, meant to review the events in their broad context, a number of critiques emerged targeting the actions of the police, emergency services, ambulance services, the Ministries of Defence and Justice, the Office of Public Works, local and national authorities, lawmakers, budget-makers and, not least, the government (Dragnes, 2011; Fuglehaug *et al.*, 2011).

It was noted that earlier security recommendations from a number of departments and ministries located in the government quarter had been in discussion about whether to close Grubbe Street, where the terrorist had parked the car bomb, for traffic. A decision had not yet been taken (Rustad & Bakkeli, 2011). It was also pointed out that it is in Norway far too easy to buy the kind of artificial fertiliser that the terrorist used to make the bomb that was detonated in the government quarter, and that more attention should have been paid to the fact that he had rented a small farm outside of Oslo but was not active in actually farming it (Skaug & Svelle, 2011). It was revealed that purchasing such a large amount of artificial fertiliser is illegal according to EU law, but legal in Norway (Hoel, 2011). Similarly, it was quickly disclosed that the terrorist was able to purchase the firearms he used in his attack online (Helgesen, 2011). It emerged that the terrorist's name was actually on a 'persons of interest' list of the Police Security Service (PSS) because he had purchased products for twelve euros from a Polish company identified as selling chemicals online. It was judged that there was no reason to proceed with any investigation. 'Even in a country like the former East Germany one could not have spotted him, simply because he has not broken the law,' the PSS director later said (Helljesen & Veum, 2011). There was criticism that police waited too long to finally send commando troops to the island (Winge, 2011). All of these issues were enveloped in the added realisation that a mass anti-terrorism exercise held in 2006 did not seem to have prepared Norway for what happened. During that exercise, large failures in coordination of the same type that happened on 22 July were observed and documented. With the wisdom of hindsight, it was repeatedly claimed that the experience gathered during the earlier exercise would have prevented or reduced the scope of the events of 2011 (Dragnes, 2011; Fuglehaug *et al.*, 2011; Mikkelsen *et al.*, 2011; Norsk telegrambyrå, 2011). Like all catastrophic events, those of 22 July seemed to be 'unthinkable'.

Yet, by far the most prominent and emotional critique raised against public authorities in the wake of the attacks concerned the time required for the police to arrive at Utøya. As we will see, this critique would lead to a more or less instrumentalised conclusion that since the terrorist could have been stopped earlier, more lives could have been saved. Since subsequent forensic analysis and reconstructions were able to pinpoint the precise time of death of each victim, highly speculative suppositions emerged, in part supported by the 22 July Commission report, that the closer a victim's death was to the conclusion of the shooting rampage, the more dependent it was on the efficiency and efficacy of the commandos in obtaining a ceasefire. As we will see, this linear, chronological, instrumental reasoning of life and death would tend to support and advance both a variable scale of responsibility of the public services for the deaths of individuals – the closer to the ceasefire, the more responsible – and a variation in the 'savability' of life itself – those who died later being forever regarded as more 'savable' than those who died earlier.

The threat to 'us' and the 22 July Commission

On 27 July, five days after the attacks, an extraordinary meeting was organised between all leaders of the political parties represented in the Norwegian Parliament and the Prime Minister. The meeting concluded with a live press conference featuring the Prime Minister backed by representatives from the collective political landscape. It was one more expression, which would prove to be among the very last, of unity and political solidarity. In the course of the press conference, the Prime Minister announced several initiatives agreed upon by the party leaders. The most important among these was the decision to name a '22 July Commission', whose task would be to 'find all the facts about the terrorist actions in the Government Quarter and the massacre on Utøya' (Salvesen, 2011).

A number of internal investigations had already begun within the different departments and agencies involved in both the emergency response and police aspects of the attacks. The outputs of some of these internal investigations are examined in this book. In opening the live press conference, the Prime Minister took pains to underscore the particularity of the commission being proposed:

> I wish to underscore that this is not an investigative commission, because we have very great respect for the work that personnel have now done and are doing, emergency services, police and many others, in different departments and activities of the public service. But it is important that we get a full review of what has happened: background, harvest, and learn from that. It will therefore not be the regulations for investigative commissions that will be applied.

We will create a set of regulations suited for this commission so that we get the review we want. (Zakariassen & Honningsøy, 2011)

In his remarks, the Prime Minister draws a line between two distinct types of commission, one of which does not yet exist.

The first type of commission is an ordinary investigative commission, for which there actually exists in the Norwegian State bureaucracy a set of regulations governing the use and work of investigative commissions. It takes the form of a proposed law, the Law on Public Investigative Commissions, which covers the rights and obligations of those being investigated, requirements to testify, transparency and rights of the persons impacted by the object of investigation, among other things (NOU, 2009). The proposed law is the output from a public commission, the Committee on Investigative Commissions.

The second type of commission, the kind that did not yet exist in any precedented or regulated form, would seek a larger overview of the events. It would be tasked with establishing the larger narrative, the broader reality and the background knowledge, an account of the experience and the expectations, all that which in totality made up the unified event of '22 July', the start of a modern myth. It is not a matter of establishing the micro-level relations of cause and effect, nor of identifying scapegoats, but to find out what actually happened. In line with the Prime Minister's multiple earlier statements in the immediate aftermath of the attack, he sees the report as one that will capture the societal picture of the events of that day. To that end, the commission, when it is named, will be given up to a year to do its work. Moreover, the commission will be independent of the many other investigations ongoing and still foreseen (Salvesen, 2011). In response to a question from the press, the Prime Minister responds: 'It is the scope of the matter that makes it special. Never in peacetime have we had such a large attack, and it's against the core of the Norwegian democracy' (Zakariassen & Honningsøy, 2011).

The questions to be asked, the foundation for the 'review' of the attacks, remained on the societal level, one of threats to democratic society, one which should not be reduced to individual victims, individual actors or individual components. It was a social reality that had been attacked. According to the Prime Minister, the conventional, bureaucratic investigative tools must be suspended in order to permit us to raise our gaze to the human-societal level.

Erna Solberg was interviewed after the press conference. Solberg was leader of the Liberal–Conservative government coalition that would take over after the defeat of the Stoltenberg II government in the October 2013 elections, and would be in turn replaced in 2021 by a new Labour Party government, led by Jonas Gahr Støre, including cabinet members who were survivors from Utøya. Solberg was interviewed after the same press conference. In her comments, she insisted that we should 'learn something' from the attacks, by which she meant something that was useful, operationalisable, applicable. The review should produce a certain type of knowledge. Not the type of overarching understanding of what has threatened Norwegian democracy but knowledge that can 'reveal holes or weaknesses in Norwegian preparedness, the conditions surrounding emergency communications, and similar things' (Salvesen, 2011). There is, of course, no question that such knowledge, detailed analysis, concrete data, insight into the mechanics of official procedures, personnel guidelines, etc. represent clear value-added contributions to the improvement of services and routines. It is not my aim to put into question the meaningfulness of such work. The aim here is to understand the way that security is understood in the wake of the attacks of 22 July, and how it evolves. What is security reality and what is security knowledge in era of terrorism?

The line between a spiritual, cultural, societal understanding of security and a bureaucratic one becomes increasingly indistinct, its blurring starting nearly immediately after the catastrophe. The results of the 27 July press conference show the degree to which differing security ontologies fall along party political and thus ideological lines. Considerable efforts at political restraint were made in the spirit of not making political gain out of the tragedy, but this press conference was to be the last manifestation of that restraint.

The 22 July Commission was appointed during a nationally televised press conference on 12 August 2011, three weeks after the 22 July attack. Its mandate and membership were set out in a speech by the Prime Minister, Jens Stoltenberg. The speech was simple and straightforward, bearing rhetorical traces of the many remarkable speeches and eulogies the Prime Minister had held during the preceding weeks. The tone was again unifying and non-partisan. It focussed on the collective dimension of the crisis, on solidarity and on the community and fellowship that form a deep component of the myth of the Norwegian people, whose shared values and societal cohesion had now been seriously threatened:

> Today it has been 3 weeks since Norway was struck by the bomb in Oslo and the shots fired on Utøya. That evening we were a country in shock. Without foothold, without knowledge about what awaited us. I am proud of the way the Norwegian people met this trial. We united around our fundamental values: democracy, openness, community. This has created a safe platform on which to meet the coming tests. ... It's about security and safety. Democracy depends on both. We will secure free discussion and our open and trusting society. At the same time we will make sure that people can walk the streets safely. A people in fear is not a free people. (Zakariassen & Honningsøy, 2011)

It is clear from the Prime Minister's brief address that the concern of the 22 July Commission and Norwegian political responses to the events involves not only the seventy-seven victims that were hit by 'the bomb in Oslo and the shots fired in Oslo' but also those that were not victims, or rather those that were victims in a non-physical way, essentially, all Norwegians. This is, of course, nothing new. It is a chapter out of the terrorist playbook and a general principle of asymmetric warfare. The 'targets' are not the actual target. The 'violence' is not the actual violence. In the logic of terrorism, the actual targets are those that 'survived', or, more precisely, that were not touched by the physical violence. The actual violence is not the kinetic violence that touched the seventy-seven arbitrary victims but rather the violence done to the social imaginary of surviving Norwegians. The target is something called 'Norway'. Consequently, the aim of this book is to ask the complex question: what is targeted when Norway is targeted? What is under threat when 'Norway' is under threat?

Thus began the 'rest' of the history of Norway. It is important to recall that the 22 July Commission was formed and carried out its work under extraordinary political conditions. It received its mandate and began its meetings at a moment when Norwegian society was deeply shaken and in a state of grief. The political situation and mood were unique in the post-World War II period. A number of essential cultural, social and political questions stood wide open. Thus, in addition to its party political and investigative functions, the formation of the Commission had a meta-political function: to demonstrate to the public sphere and the political class that the country's democratic institutions stood on stable ground, that they would continue to function, that the democratic principles that guided Norwegian politics, cultural ethos and the social democratic imaginary that had cemented the democratic culture would remain unshaken and that the voice of the reasoned and reasonable men and women of the 22 July Commission would get to the bottom of things. It aimed in part to reassure the public that political business as usual was possible and, indeed, the reality, that a well-prepared, sensible, systematic, cross-political study could be undertaken under the public gaze, that it could produce as its output a reason, an explanation and a meaning for the horrible events and a political confirmation of a certain continuity in the democratic public sphere. In other words, the 22 July Commission had as its mission not only an analysis of the events of 22 July, of the state of play of societal security, but also to somehow serve as the performative demonstration that society still existed.

The existence of society was, however, not the only thing that had to be confirmed. Still another component of the 22 July Commission's implicit tasks demanded even more. It took the form of an involuntary guarantor of the rationality of the Norwegian socio-political system. In essence, the very fact that there existed an investigative commission sanctioned by the State, charged with the task of generating a clear, well-grounded, coherent narrative of the events, also generated an important confirmation that the Norwegian society, government, culture, etc. were rational at their very core.

This was not the only function of the Commission. If Norwegian society was organised only of the rationality that the Commission was given the mission to affirm, it would be no society at all. Far more was at stake in the aftermath of the attacks and in the political rallying around a de-securitisation of the narratives of danger and loss. The meaning of Oslo/Utøya, the meaning of the collective project of assuring the security and well-being of an implicitly vulnerable society, was at its origin a question of the meaning of society itself: the silent, mystical, yet overwhelming and undeniable force of its presence the common ground of its existence, of its cohesiveness, its power and precariousness, the ambient fear of the loss of something, the shared will to preserve and protect it. This was the story that needed to be told but which, for a complex set of reasons I will attempt to make sense of in what follows, would never be told by the commission of experts.

6

The report of the 22 July Commission

> Stop making sense!
> Talking Heads (1984)

Security without society

While the concept of societal security is persistently present in varying forms and iterations, up and down its pages, the report of the 22 July Commission does not deal with societal security as such. There is no theory of societal security to be found, no synthesis of perspectives on society and security, nor any visible aspiration to apply some more or less controversial, more or less accepted, notion of societal security to the facts and circumstances of the run-up to and aftermath of the 22 July 2011 attacks. In many ways, the Commission is far more concerned with a kind of broad inductive construction of the societal security that should have, would have, could have been defined if a certain number (indeed, a very great number) of conditions had been met. Instead of taking the present and future societal security of Norway and its people as an objective for the documentation and analysis, instead of starting the reconstruction at the present moment, based on a harvesting of a more or less consensus-based perception and understanding of what the present status is and what present security needs and requirements are, it takes the present, or at least the present as of 22 July 2011, as granted and works backwards in a reconstruction of a kind of path dependency whose outcome is already known.

In line with its mandate, the 22 July Commission's approach is to document and analyse the chain of events that led to the attacks. Many of the events and actions in that chain remain, of course, unresolved and will likely never be resolved. Indeed, part of the approach of the Commission is to work in a contrafactual way, speculating, based on what is known, about what is not known, about what might have happened, could have happened and, ultimately, in a sometimes heart-breaking, and thus also ethically troubling, mode of investigation, what *should* have happened. Societal security is not explicitly thematised or made the object of the investigation. Norwegian society itself (following our introductory conceptualisation of 'society' as both protector and protected) is not definitively identified in terms of its role as security provider or security consumer, and the role of the society in assuring security remains unclear and indecisive. What is society? Which society are we talking about? Whose society? Society for whom? Rhetorically speaking, in a rock-solid social democracy like Norway, 'society' remains the fundamental anchoring point for a tacit understanding of a certain kind of security, security as an aspiration, a norm, a societal ambition, even a promise. In this sense, societal security is a project, an uncompleted undertaking, an enterprise in the making, one which the collective resources of the nation must participate in.

This ambient understanding and function of society as a provider of security fuels the drama of the report of the 22 July Commission. It is against the social democratic backdrop of society as a guarantor of security that the report concludes that Norwegian society failed, has let down its obligation to itself. This moral and very much moralising mood links to the deep *ethos* of the report. This background mood of bad conscience accompanies the report from start to finish.

Thus, 'society' in the 22 July Commission report nearly appears as a kind of riddle, a question mark, a misunderstood notion or even an unknown. A variety of understandings of 'society' emerge over the course of the report and it is assigned a number of different roles through the analysis. It has many functions, some overlapping, some contradictory, and many ways of being, of gathering us together, reprimanding some, rewarding others. As noted earlier, society appears at times as something under threat, something to be protected. Elsewhere, society is taken as the collective expression or symbol for an inherent vulnerability of all Norwegians. Elsewhere, it is an expression of the vulnerability of the State as a sovereign entity. Of course, from the national standpoint, there is nothing about 'the Norwegian' that is not worth preserving. (This is in part an expression of the melancholic ontological tautology: everything that is has implicit value by virtue of its very existence, etc.) Like most well-integrated nation-states, society in Norway is itself wrapped up in this logic in a very complex way, through the interlacing of people, organisations and institutions on the one hand, and by the long reach of history, tradition, heritage, etc. on the other hand. Society is the primary actor in the project of its own security. Society is, in many ways, a proxy, a stand-in, for its own security: it acts and is acted upon. By both acting and functioning as a society, it generates security, while at the same time accumulating the value which raises the spectre of the threat of its demise. Society is a security perpetuum mobile.

This composite, in part contradictory, understanding of society, inescapably linked to the circular economy of its own security, is used as the anchoring concept of the 22 July Commission report and the public policy throughout the decade that follows, aside from a brief summary reference to a handful of papers on the subject of risk and society, only vaguely specified and certainly undeveloped. It is used frequently in the report, with the most casual self-evidence, as something clearly desirable, an object of public policy, a cipher of communication across agencies and political levels, while at the same time remaining a mysterious, yet highly valued, condition. Seemingly, no one is in doubt about society's value, about the need to invest in it. It seems impossible to be 'against' it, and yet it seems equally impossible to determine what being 'for' it can mean. Its value is linked to the implicit goodness or well-being of the Welfare State, the implicit value to Norwegians of Norwegian democratic social values, traditions, norms, laws, rules, conventions, language, etc., all entirely decisive for maintaining the Norwegian-ness of Norway. This is part of the wonder – and danger – of the concept of societal security.

In any case, there is clear agreement that what defines us is under threat. This agreement is based on a representation of something that we are, an identity or a 'self', or societal 'we', and of an equally firm belief that this thing is in danger, can be weakened, distorted or displaced. 'Societal security' requires this idea, and therefore contributes to keeping it alive and well, in the midst of our everyday enterprise of being ourselves (see Wollebæk et al., 2011).

The inverse movement of the societal security perpetual motion machine is also energised in this way: somewhere in the core of our societal security lurks a danger. Since it is at the core of our security, it is essentially part of us. It is who we are; it belongs to the very function of being ourselves. It inhabits societal security as a kind of unavoidable, embedded irregularity substance of our well-being. As it happens, this incipient, inherent insecurity is essentially more part of the value function of society – arising from the experience of society as a value or, more concretely, as valuable – than from its societal or social character. The value system at the heart of any society is the secret generator of the dangers it faces. Value fundamentally generates insecurity (Burgess, 2010). Our challenge in this book, and in part the question posed by the 22 July Commission, is to understand how 'societal security' does this strange, even paradoxical, work that it does. What is its particularity? In what sense is it another social function, another variation on social welfare, human rights or human security? What sets it apart? What creates it? What strengthens or weakens it? In what way does it depend on other functions, on other sources or flows of power and influence in society? What is the structure and function of threats to society? In what way can a society be said to be under threat? What kind of measures are adapted to defend it? What does it mean to defend society? As we will see, 'societal security' for the 22 July Commission, as for other policy actors we can observe, builds on a tacit understanding – that society is never threatened as a whole, faced with the prospect of a total wipeout of everything that makes it what it is. Societal security, when it is threatened, is threatened in a specific, determinate way.

'Our' defence

As we will see, collective and collectivising forces are mobilised on many levels in the report of the 22 July Commission. This happens first and foremost by way of the raw, chilling facts of the attacks, the detailed review of the timeline of events that the report is extremely careful to reconstruct, despite a nearly unavoidable politicisation of the facts through their representation and analysis. In the 22 July Commission's representation, Norway collectively understands itself as a victim. Without expressing or implying any insensitivity towards the victims and their dependents, one understands that the investigation and the political analysis takes a position towards a kind of tacit reality that it was Norway that was struck, that Norway was victimised, that the Norwegian people now had to 'meet the coming tests'. The factual victims, the individuals who actually lost their lives or were badly injured, are obviously also victims, but in a different way. They are not the referents of the Prime Minister's speech, nor the addressees of the 22 July Commission report. Norway identifies with them, feels solidarity with them, but the self-identifying movement is a different one. The victims are 'identical' with Norway, and yet Norway as the name of a national identity in all of its plurality and heterogeneity is condensed into their lives – and deaths. Norwegians unite around the victims and identify themselves with them, paradoxically, not in the lived lives but in the loss of them. Their loss, their departure, their absence, anchors the fellowship, the particularly Norwegian community, a shared feeling that was not there before, one that was created in the instant of tragedy, in the moment of loss. Norway was emotionally and symbolically reconstructed, even recreated, through death, suffering and horror.

This dismal observation can nonetheless orientate our attention towards the nature of terrorism. As we know, it is not murder as such that is the aim of terrorism. Terrorism is far more characterised by the absence of instrumental logic. Terrorism is not structured as a simple means to an end. Terrorism understood in this way does not imply any particular intention. Or rather, the intention is that that there is no intention. The meaning of the violence and deaths generated by terrorism is that this cannot have any meaning, no abiding sense that one might hold on to for the purpose, for example, of casting moral judgement on the basis of simple moral values, such as good and evil. Terrorism urges upon us an original and unsettling concept of impersonal violence, violence as such, violence in itself. It is violence that is exercised without an object, without intentionality, without immediate or personal finality. In this way, among its many distasteful modes of being is its particular way of resisting moral judgement, of insisting implicitly, and at times even explicitly, on its own amorality. This does not, of course, in any way preclude us from judging it morally. This is necessarily, easily and often done, but terrorism does not lend itself to what might be called a moral conversation. As we have so often observed, a debate with an avowed terrorist about the moral standing of his/her deed is as good as impossible. Even the Clausewitzian vision of war as a rationalisation of violence for political means could not have prepared us for the indifference and inhumanity of the terrorist approaches to activism, in the name, of course, of a certain vision of humanity. For the ideal-type terrorist, there is nothing personal, nothing moral, nothing spiritual, nothing enchanted about the terrorist exercise. There are exceptions, but the ideal type tends towards a callous instrumentality. The case of 22 July might in some ways be described as a biopolitical one, that is, not one targeting individuals or even a number of individuals but, rather, one targeting a class of people distinguished by their political identities but also, speaking of the victims of Utøya, by their biological ages, their position in a certain generational logic.

Remarkably, as I will try to show, the particular Norwegian response, particular but not at all unique, evolved from a spiritually grounded, humanist ethos of compassion, empathy, solidarity into one of bureaucratic indifference to the spiritual tragedy and, more importantly, the spiritual force of the day. This renunciation of the spiritual solidarity at the core of a society's security is not to be misunderstood as the reproach of a specific Norwegian type of bureaucracy, even less as an attack on Norwegians themselves. It is meant to unpack the hypothesis that society cannot do otherwise. Society, seemingly as a function of being society, systematically, structurally, programatically reverses, or at best retranslates, the spiritual resources at the heart of the societal security. Terrorism undermines this spiritual substance, removes it from the horizon of moral judgement. The political translation of this effect is clear: terrorism is not evil. It is, in a sense, far worse: it is the detachment from moral judgement. It is this aspect of terrorism that renders it so very dangerous: of course, we can rebuild, yes, we can re-establish institutions, indeed, somehow, we can grieve the dead in the sign of one form or another of spirituality or religious belief. Terrorism blocks us from this path. It forces its nihilism upon us. Terrorism, as we know, is a message to the survivors, to the future, to the future without those who perished. It is a message in the form of a simple death knell, more like the notice of the future death of those still in life. It is a message that keeps on relaying its content, that keeps on hurting, scaring, causing suffering. Terrorism is obviously violence, but it is a vastly different kind of violence. Violence beyond violence. It is violence that injures and damages. Like many instances of violence, its injury and damage carry a symbolic dimension as well that permits them to touch those that were not physically touched by the attack, those who were not present but who belong to the community or the society that was struck and that remains struck. As much as this book sings the praises of community, of societal bonds, cultural fabric and moral solidarity, it is, ironically, community and societal cohesion that sharpens the knives of terrorism, where compassion and empathy guarantee the enduring violence of a terrorist attack. Oslo/Utøya was a borderline case. According to the perpetrator, the target was to not only to attack the 'cultural Marxism' represented by the participants at the youth camp on Utøya, but it was also to some degree a utilitarian campaign to destroy the lives of a certain group of innocents.

Thus, despite following a more or less well-travelled logic of terrorism, the Norwegian case stands somewhat alone: 'We have united around our fundamental values,' said the Prime Minister just before he announced the appointment of the 22 July Commission. These fundamental values – 'democracy, openness and community' – were, of course, not missing or in some way absent from the lives and minds of Norwegians. They were, however, far less conscious than they would become after the attacks. They were rediscovered in a new form of existence, a new reality. Suddenly, these run-of-the-mill political values were seen and experienced in their fullness. Norwegians rediscovered their fundamental values and, at the same time, discovered them to be threatened, or at least less than self-evident, less than given, rather in need of being asserted in the face of uncertainty. Society is supposed to be open and trusting at the same time, particularly in the face of the realisation that it is through openness and trust that it exposes itself to catastrophe.

Society and conceptual power

The concept of 'societal security' occupies a highly ambivalent position in the 22 July Commission report and, strangely enough, in debates concerning societal security following the Oslo/Utøya attacks. Since the political force of the 22 July Commission report revolves around the conceptual power it wields, this ambivalence plays an important role in shaping the political impact of the report. If, for example, we understand 'society' as an idea about a complex set of social relations that forms the basis for individual belonging and individual identity, then the political impact may prove to be insignificant. Societal security in this shape and form will concern the role of individuals in society and the challenge of protecting them. The neoliberal society of individuals emphasises security intertwined with close relationships but closely linked with the ability of each member of society to exercise its individual liberties, the ambitions of society being inseparable from the welfare of society at large. Society understood as a cohesive whole has little interest in societal security.

Another common form of ambivalence that finds its way to expression in the report is that of society as a unified actor, subject and object of security threats and security measures. In these terms, 'Norwegian society' is a condensed, unified, identified object which can be threatened and protected. Thus, Norwegian society is at times pointed to in the report of the 22 July Commission as a kind of entity that can in its totality be the object of a 'targeted attack' (NOU, 2012: 19). Such a use of this term 'society' represents a deviation from its function as a simple actor. The attack was indeed aimed at Norwegian society in the particular sense that the perpetrator intended it and the assailant did apparently believe he accomplished the task of attacking Norwegian society as a whole. Breivik had written in his manifesto that the greater European 'society' was under attack and that he himself was participating in a military campaign intended to come to its aid. He uses 'society' to refer to a set of collective values that is in play. From Breivik's point of view, his attack on Norwegian society is actually to be understood and carried out as a *defence* of a *different* Norwegian society. The attack can, of course, not be defended on these premises, but it is important to point out that the concept of society on which Breivik bases his thinking and violence is a different one to that which the 22 July Commission uses.

In a purely objective sense, the Oslo/Utøya attack on Norwegian society actually did lead to changes in the way society thought of itself, the way members of society behaved towards each other and towards society as a whole, as well as to the way central societal values were understood and practised. In political manifestations, in public debates and in public speeches, the basic principles of freedom, solidarity, liberalism, tolerance, etc. were continuously taken up as core references in political discourse. This alone constitutes a significant kind of reform, even if it is likely not what the Commission thought of as being its contribution to increasing Norway's societal security. The political discourse about freedom, openness and democracy also plays a significant part in the actual mandate of the 22 July Commission, although it is infrequently used in the Commission's report. According to its mandate, the Commission was to find out what can be learned from the attack 'in order to arm Norwegian society in the best possible way to be able to prevent and confront possible future attacks, while at the same time protecting central Norwegian societal values such as openness and democracy' (NOU, 2012: 38). Yet, while the same sequence that formulates the Commission's mandate and the values of 'openness and democracy' are named, the concept of 'societal security' is described as 'the ability of society and the authorities to ... discover ..., protect, ... and deal with threats to society's security' (NOU, 2012: 38). In other words, societal security is attributed an instrumental, organisational and even mechanical function. This underscores the mandate's somewhat ambiguous relation to the concept of societal security, the core concept for the report.

The ambivalent relationship between society and security, as it is presented by the 22 July Commission's analysis, also becomes clear in the report's structure and organisation. Six main areas of concern are identified in the report: anti-terrorism and surveillance, weapons and explosives, infrastructure, police actions, life-saving actions and crisis management. In the second part of the Commission's report, 'Threats, societal security and preparedness', the Commission further builds on a detailed analysis of the definition of terrorism given in Norwegian civil penal code. Terrorism is, namely, a punishable act when it goes with the intention of 'interrupting serious functions of fundamental importance for society, for example, legislative or executive authorities, energy supply, secure supply of food or water, banking and monetary institutions, or sanitary preparedness and disease protection' (NOU, 2006). The 22 July Commission thereby identifies a basis for interpreting 'society' as something other than a collection of individuals and groups linked together through one form or another of social fellowship. As we have seen earlier, the law, just like the security authorities, struggles to identify and conceptualise those dimensions that either create or challenge society's security, where society is understood as a unity equipped with solidarity, belonging and considerable resilience.

The social function of terrorism

The 22 July Commission report goes quite far, compared to other more spontaneous analyses of the terror attacks in the US and Europe in the course of the twentieth century, in taking an explicit position relative to the relation between violence and society. It formulates a series of claims about the link between malevolent acts of all types and the way that these are taken up, dealt with and transformed in society itself, how society reacts to such acts and how acts of terror are impacted or structured by society's value-based make-up.

As we have seen, the Police Security Service (PST), the National Security Authority (NSM), the Directorate for Societal Security and Preparedness (DSB) and other authorities use the expression 'society' to paint a threat picture that excludes individual people as subjects from the security equation.

The 22 July Commission treats this problem, in Chapter 5 of the report, 'Responsibility and organisation', by clarifying and delimiting the concept of society in relation to security. Nonetheless, the hard-won conceptual clarification is both brief and somewhat meagre. Section 5.2, 'Central concepts', is comprised of around two pages of text (NOU, 2012: 68–70). The brief documentation, analysis and reflection about 'societal security' and other central concepts provides a strong basis for claiming that the Commission finds the clarification of the central concepts either uninteresting or irrelevant. This might be seen as problematic, even though the discussion in the report takes its point of departure in the explicit observation that the concept is not 'precise'. Had the multivalence of the concept been a more central object for analysis, the picture painted by the Commission might well have been a different one and might have attracted more attention and analysis instead of less.

As a conceptual foundation for discussion and use of the term 'societal security', the Commission's report builds upon two documents: the Justice Ministry's follow-up on the Commission on Vulnerability's report that we have earlier discussed at length, *Societal Security: The Path to a Less Vulnerable Society* (JPD, 2008), and the Parliamentary communication *On the Tsunami Catastrophe in South Asia and Centralised Crisis Management* (JPD, 2003). We have already seen how the Parliamentary communication *Societal Security* links together the protection of 'the life, health and fundamental needs of citizens' in addition to the 'critical societal functions', and how this formulation clears the way for the integration of social values, moral attitudes, cultural, religious and political traditions. Although there seems to be openness to the idea that societal values do not merely function as an object of protection but also as a resource that can care for different sectors of society, these characteristics are not given any particular attention. It is not human beings – as either resource or vulnerability – that are the focus of the report but rather society itself, abstracted from its very members, understood as a technological entity, as an assemblage of technologies or as an internally technical organisation and administration, or even in relation to the formal structures that frame the bureaucracy. Society's informal, human side has no place here.

This understanding of people and society constitutes a conceptual decision with deep political consequences. There was never any doubt that the bomb attack in Oslo and the shootings on Utøya were criminal acts that could have been investigated and prosecuted within the confines of the criminal justice system, deriving its legitimacy in an ordinary way from the Norwegian criminal law. There is, in other words, a *normal* legal procedure that is used according to well-known and well-travelled patterns. Norwegian civil penal law takes its point of departure in the fact that a criminal act has been committed by a legal subject, a rational, autonomous individual, and that the victim or victims are also individuals (NOU, 2006). Yet, as we know, it is precisely that presupposition that was problematised through the psychiatric evaluation made in advance of the trial of the terrorist.

What, in effect, marks any act of terrorism is that its consequences, both material and immaterial, have impacts that surpass the individuals that are immediately touched by them. In other words, terrorism, by its very essence, never limits itself to the individual level. A terrorist act is always collectivising. It always appeals to a collective that is both larger than the act itself and larger than the actual victims of the act itself.

This link between those people who are actually touched, killed or injured, either physically or psychically, and those who experience the event at a distance in a mediated way is, of course, a complex one, difficult to disentangle. It is often characterised by popular political, social and cultural norms and expectations, which together form and constitute the group. The distance between criminality that touches individual, identifiable persons and terrorism that mobilises symbolic values, collective experiences, common traditions, feelings, etc. first and foremost opens up a political space and eventually opens serious questions and ethical paradoxes about who we are, what a society is and how individuals, groups, associations and clubs weave themselves together to form an enduring collectivity. This unity is formed and re-formed continuously through the impulses of political presuppositions and assumptions, as well as through society's self-insight and self-understanding. In this way, the influence of terrorism can leave its mark on society's own political and social property.

For the Prime Minister of Norway on 12 August 2011, that collectivity was, first and foremost, Norway. It was, according to what was said that day, 'Norway' that was hit by the bomb in Oslo and the shots fired on Utøya. Even though the Prime Minister should not in any way be reproached for appearing insensitive to the individuals who were killed or injured, his message took aim at how Norway, understood as a collective unit, could and should manage the crisis. That is his political frame of reference and political point of orientation. It is not about individual people in Norway but about 'a land in shock', 'the Norwegian people' and a strong common 'we' that has the experience of being exposed to a particularly dreadful experience (Stoltenberg, 2011a). Even though the victims are individuals, it is important for the Prime Minister to emphasise how 'we' as a nation can and must continue. Even though nothing explicitly or apparently justifies the Prime Minister to transfer the sorrow and suffering of the victims to the national level, it is precisely what he does, together with several others, by claiming that it is the 'we' that suffers, the 'we' that grieves over the injuries caused by the attacks three weeks earlier.

On what grounds does the Prime Minister presume to do this? When is a justification motivated and when is it arbitrary? When is a justification justified? In order to understand the premises and motivation for the Prime Minister's description of suffering and grief, his transfer of the damage and death from individual victims to the Norwegian public sphere, we need to develop a discourse of multiplicity and individuality. The political dynamic that makes it possible to appeal to the continuity between the individual and the imagined community is security itself. This bridge or transition from the many to the one is what in fact provides security, not merely by giving safety and assurance to the masses but by the feeling of belonging that gives the experience of collectivity its meaning.

By the same token, as a 'lonely wolf', the reality of the terrorist also builds upon an imagined community, unified through a fantasy about a shared threat. Ironically enough, Breivik's self-proclaimed crusade had as its objective to defend and protect Norway, to preserve his country against a certain 'we' thought, through a complex delusion, to be a threat to Norway and Norwegian culture, Europe and European values, and the Norwegian and European way of life. His mission was, in this sense, patriotic. But what makes the terrorist's perspective unique is the loneliness of the 'we'. Is Breivik in effect a part of a collective, one that is under threat, one that once was unified and now has become something else?

This unpleasant irony does not make the main point less valid: terrorist violence, no less than the grief that springs from the wake of terrorist action, finds its legitimacy in collectivity. Exactly like fear, violence is collectivising. It is only first-order violence that kills, maims and destroys through its physical reach. The psychosocial effects are transferable; they are steered and regulated through society's way of structuring its social values, through political action and through the cultural disposition of the people. Breivik's own sociopathy does not make his experience of insecurity less authentic. The social structure of authenticity is not less valid or true when it leads to catastrophe.

When managing insecurity, uncertainty and vulnerability, society stands at the centre as a mobilising force. It is unclear whether we find the consequences of this idea revolting or inspiring. Collectivity gives societal security a moral weight, a meaning, a destiny that has no need for justification, either political or juridical. It is, of course, also society that stands in the centre of the 22 July Commission's mandate from the Norwegian government, both as a point of departure for deciding what is worthy of being protected and as a tool for security against future attacks.

The 22 July Commission's mandate

The formal mandate of the 22 July Commission sets out its aims in the following way:

> The purpose of the Commission's work is to undertake a review and evaluation in order to learn from the events such that Norwegian society will be as prepared as possible to prevent and confront eventual future attacks while at the same time preserving central values in Norwegian society such as openness and democracy. (NOU, 2012: 38)

The mandate thus sets out not one but three parallel functions and three different tasks.

The *first* function of the Commission is to document and analyse what happened on 22 July 2011. The Commission will, in this sense, serve as a kind of public archive, function as a kind of primary source for public actors that need to know what the situation actually, factually, was, how the different pieces of the event fit together and what actually happened. It will carry out the crucial task of deciding what documentation is relevant, what is not, what should be collected and collated, what should be registered and archived, according to what criteria and categories. The 22 July Commission serves as a kind of purposeful, living documentation. It is itself an event. In this sense, it carries with it the dilemma that all archivists are forced to live with: the tension between content, material, documentation, etc. on the one hand, and the choice, delimitation and control of the content on the other. The 22 July Commission's report is, in this sense, not only the authorised, legitimate archive for Oslo/Utøya but the unfolding of power. This applies not only for what was included in the report but also for the way in which what was included in the report was made to be meaningful. The power of selection is political power, discursive power, power over history, over memory and over national heritage.

The *second* function of the Commission concerns the way that the mandate is to be carried out. This applies not only to the content of the mandate but also to how the content is to be implemented, through whom and what it is to be put into practice, and in relation to whom it will be made into practical action. These first two functions – content and implementation – are charged with contributing to making society as a whole as well equipped as possible to 'prevent and confront eventual future attacks'. The different tasks related to documentation, analysis and archiving are to be carried out with the purpose of increasing society's ability to protect itself against future attacks similar to those which took place on 22 July 2011. Although in the early phase of the Commission's work, it is not yet specified what specifically will be investigated, it is already clear that the results of the investigation will be used to 'equip' society for preventing future attacks.

A number of gaping assumptions stand behind this formulation of the mandate. It assumes that, first and foremost, society is not already equipped, even well equipped, to prevent attacks of multiple types. Secondly, it presupposes that the 22 July Commission, a group of prominent personalities selected not primarily on scientific merit but rather on the basis of their distinction in relevant areas of public policy, culture and society, is capable of instructing society, the addressee of the report, on how it can be better equipped. This also assumes that the Commission in some way stands outside of the society which it will study and instruct, occupies a kind of alternative position with society or is somehow extra-societal. The hypothesis and main argument in this book is that exactly the opposite is the case. Society is the best 'equipped' to preserve itself and this was precisely what functioned best during the attacks on Utøya and in the government quarter. Society is the solution, not the problem.

The *third* function that is expressed in the 22 July Commission's mandate involves a new type of protection. This time, it concerns how and to what degree different security measures lead to secondary security. It is commonplace that increased police presence in the form of more surveillance, and more armament, sharpened vigilance, etc., leads on one level to increased security as a direct consequence of more security measures and resources being implemented, but it leads, at the same time, to new forms of insecurity on the imaginary plane, in the form of unease, worry or fear about the invisible threats that the material security measures explicitly or implicitly refer to. The imaginary force of the supposed security threat comes into play in at least two ways. On the one hand, security measures are taken in relation to security threats; they are intentional in the strong sense of the word: the target and object; they prepare for an object, one thought together with the function of the measure. They are, from a certain functional point of view, inseparable. On the other hand, the presence, and indeed the preparation for any given security, invokes, in individuals not even directly associated with the event, fear and trepidation for its concrete realisation.

The central precondition for all of these functions is, again, that a certain experience or understanding of the very notion of 'societal security'. It builds on an understanding of security as 'averting danger' to society. As I have suggested, and will develop further, this is only one among many ways of understanding the term. It assumes that its object, in this case, society itself, is clearly, discretely identifiable and identified, that it is a stable, known object, that there is a consensus around its scope and limits. Most importantly, it assumes that it is autonomous, that if there is a threat to it, this threat is exogenous. In this perspective, societal security and well-being are conditions that can be attained by maintaining what already is, most commonly by averting what threats touch it from outside through external actors or forces that might potentially endanger it, be it pandemic disease, tsunamis or terrorists. Security measures are, in this sense, barrier technologies which hold at bay that which is undesirable.

As we have seen before and I will focus on at length in the analysis below, this understanding of both security and society stems from a significant misrepresentation and misunderstanding of society's capacity and possibility to create and maintain its own security. In its report, the 22 July Commission essentially reproaches society over and over again, in myriad forms, for having failed when, in reality, it was society that proved to be the most effective security response during the attacks. Moreover, the report's criticism is misleading: it is precisely the social values – openness and democracy, among others – that prove to have been the best and strongest measures against terrorism. Society, the terror attacks showed, is not simply a passive, innocent, vulnerable entity – though it is that too. Rather, it is a key actor in the preservation of its own security.

Society as an accountable actor

The 22 July Commission uses the term 'societal security' in several different ways and attributes to it several in part contradictory or at least incompatible definitions along the way. Even though the 22 July Commission report avoids analysing the multiple oppositions and crossing definitions, it is everywhere clear that societal security is the central axis around which everything turns. More than most concepts explored in the 22 July Commission report, the most central of concepts, 'societal security', is oddly taken for granted as unproblematic, transparent, non-political, etc. Society is nonchalantly regarded as an ambient experience of what is and has been, and, by all measures, will remain so, as self-evident as the air we breathe. The Commission does not seem to be interested in reflecting on what society – an idea so deeply implicated in its mandate – actually is, what it might mean to threaten it, what functions it performs, what its scope and reach are, what makes it function as it functions and, of course, how it might be protected.

In fairness, this indifference should not be laid entirely at the feet of the Commission. While this is not the place to develop the argument, at first glance, we can observe a chronic indifference on the part of most public agencies charged with the well-being of society, to what society is, most notably, when it is in political or existential play. Society is like a blind spot for anyone interested in formulating claims about the security of society. Yet, in the case of the 22 July Commission, this blind spot is all the more remarkable given that society played an extraordinary role in the events surrounding the 22 July attacks. The role of society was notable during the terrible events but also in the wake of the attacks, and in the days and weeks after them. And yet, as we have emphasised above, the societal dimensions of the process of working through the shock of the attacks, as well as the range of experiences of grief and loss involved, are more or less disregarded. In general terms, the complexity of society and the complex role it plays in the experience of security and insecurity on multiple levels and in multiple aspects would suggest that it might take on far greater importance than what one actually finds.

In the complex of meanings that emerges from the basic constellation of society and security, the meaning of 'society' is paramount, and yet remains ambiguous. While there are many branches to this ambiguity, its primary uncertainty stems from the contradiction between society understood as actor and society understood as acted upon. The logic of the opposition is straightforward. On the one hand, there is the understanding of society that positions it as the central actor in a range of functions, as a perceiving, thinking, active, reactive, autonomous entity capable of participating actively in its own security, among other things. On the other hand, it is often understood as the *passive* recipient of security measures, of that which is under threat, that which is to be protected and preserved. Clearly, one can imagine any number of configurations where these overlap and interrelate. Indeed, this is the case, in more or less explicit ways, in the 22 July Commission report.

The *first understanding* of society as an actor forms the basis for the report's grisly introductory provocation: 'How could our society let this happen?' (NOU, 2012: 13). Society is thus a responsible and not least accountable actor. This summary enunciation, accompanied by an entire package of concepts and discourses, sets the tone for the report. It positions the undefined 'society' as directly responsible for the actions and failures that led to the attacks. The breathtaking simplicity of the claim at once ascribes responsibility for the attacks without any reference to any morally accountable individuals, least of all, the one individual that without any ambiguity and with the full force of the legal adjudication is taken to have responsibility for the attacks.

We will return to both the ethics and legality of responsibility for terror attacks in Chapter 8. Keeping, for the moment, our focus on the question of society and of society's agency in general, and in relation to specific terrorist attacks in particular, this statement stands in contrast to the findings of the earlier Commission on Vulnerability, among others, whose report takes an entirely different approach to society, regarding it as the best equipped to take care of itself (NOU, 2000). Even though both documents show interest for the different types of societal existence, and the different types of agency and passivity that are possible within them, 'society' for the 22 July Commission is most often, but by far not always, taken to be an extension of an arm of the public authorities, responsible for both the good and the bad that might take place under their specific purview, while the Commission on Vulnerability understands 'society' as the answer to a certain kind of question about what kind of collective organisation of human beings is actually worth protecting.

In the 22 July Commission report, there is clear recognition that society has a presence, that it indeed does exist and that it represents something substantial. It remains mostly undefined and indeterminate while at the same time being ascribed key properties of agency, most notably, responsibility for or complicity in the attacks that took place, including responsibility for seeing to it that such an event should not happen *again*. This is, of course, an uncommonly strong position, a vast onus that gives bitter insight into how the 22 July Commission understands its own ethical-legal responsibility. In other words, where the Commission on Vulnerability of 2000 ascribes to society a proper value characterised by an implicit vulnerability, the 22 July Commission regards society as a set of bureaucratic practices, security routines and technological tools, the collection of which expresses a responsibility for protecting something else, something external to it, something which is, strictly speaking, not society and, above all, something that is not capable of protecting itself. The two-dimensional, paradoxical vision of society differs dramatically from the ethical, cultural, social and spiritually rich version set out a decade before.

What are the implications of this difference in vision for the claim that society has 'let this happen'? The 22 July Commission expresses itself with indignation about the fact that society – an undefined, more or less abstract, maybe even imaginary entity – has done or not done what it ostensibly should have done to protect the government quarter with its societal ways and means. Should 'society' have taken better care of the youths on Utøya? Does this mean that society should have taken better care of Anders Behring Breivik in his growing up and moral education? In other words, from the very outset, 'society' is considered responsible for preventing or protecting from terrorist attacks in general, and the Oslo/Utøya attacks of 22 July in particular.

Which society? Well, this society, our society. Even if the 'we' of 'our society' remains unspecified and the roles of protector and protected sometimes overlap, there is a distinct understanding that it is not a question of *just any* society. This assignment of responsibility of 'we' is neither emanating from just any society nor directing its accusation at any society. Even while any thinkable referent 'we' might plausibly consist of is included in the accusation (from the society of humans, to European society, to the society of police officers, to name just a few), it invokes a category of responsibility that does not apply to other societies than the Norwegian one, even while the average Swede in the streets of Stockholm is, in any material terms, just as 'responsible' as the average Norwegian in the streets of Bergen, or even a Norwegian software developer based in Singapore. The society that is ascribed responsibility is not society as such, not 'the social' or 'the societal'. It is not about European society, or occidental society, or the global society, or even the cosmic society, if such a thing can be thought or expressed. It is about something about 'this' society, our society, something implicit or inscribed in our society, the Norwegian society. Society, in the view of the 22 July Commission, takes on the bitter obligation, a social contract with entirely new terms, a new form of spontaneous accountability, one that did not exist before the attacks.

What, then, does it mean to say that a society holds responsibility for such a thing? The idea that a given society holds a certain responsibility, a responsibility that other societies do not have, must in some sense stem from the principle that it possesses special qualities, special capabilities and thereby special responsibility to prevent security threats. That Norwegian society should have 'failed', an idea that later figures strongly in the conclusion of the report in the form of the idea that the 'authorities' have failed, must mean that the implicit values in society, its properties, its identity, etc., have failed, not merely the political components that make up what the Commission designates as 'society', its form and substance. This platform permits the 22 July Commission to execute its mandate as one of comparing and coordinating the 'expectations' about security that were created by public authorities with the efforts that 'society' and the 'authorities' actually managed to mobilise and deploy, from the unthinkable disruption of the Norwegian post-war peace to an architecture of accountability that reconstructs the dominoes that fell in a chain of cause and effect that transforms the unthinkable into the inevitable. 'Did the system and the crews function as expected?' the report asks (NOU, 2012: 13). It seems clear that the bureaucratic apparatus, with its detailed guidelines, mandates and instructions, can be held responsible for the correspondence between task and performance. But can society itself? Can a society be held responsible for something other than being itself? When, and under what circumstances, is there a collective responsibility?

Society as *ethos*

The *second understanding* of society as an actor is of a different type than the first. It is the image of society as a complete entity that acts and takes decisions. Despite the report's focus on public authorities and the accountability of the institutions that act in the name of the collective, this version of 'society' refers to something greater and different from the policy measures taken in relation to societal security. From this perspective, societal security is understood as entirely collectivised to the extent of being conglomerated, melted together into one homogeneous, but nonetheless active, mass. Thus, when the 22 July Commission discusses society's 'failure' during the 22 July attacks, the matter becomes more complex. This unified entity that is understood as society is composed of a kind of national ethos, culture and social elements, traditions, history, politics, ethics, psychology, etc. Thus, assessing it in terms of decisions made, tactics, unified leadership strategy, in the field is complicated indeed. Societal security is no longer simply a matter of leadership, tactics, strategy, etc. 'on the ground' but rather corresponds to a much broader matter of putting into question, even deeply problematising, the entire notion of social responsibility, fellowship and belonging.

In other words, a somewhat tormented concept of societal security emerges as a kind of toolkit for those authorities responsible for security. Society is ascribed a narrow, instrumental meaning. 'Society', in this sense, comes increasingly to be identified with those public authorities who, in 'normal' times, or under 'non-extraordinary' circumstances, are said to have responsibility for the security of society. However, on the other hand, when 'society' is turned to identify with a certain conception of the public sphere, unrelated to official institutions and their tasks, societal security naturally assumes another meaning altogether. Both of these meanings operate in the report of the 22 July Commission, sometimes distinctly, sometimes weaved in and out of each other.

As we saw earlier, the one meaning of society comprises authorities with executive responsibility for society. The other functions with a far more plastic notion of society. Society remains essentially undefined or, to be generous, taken for granted as that entity that is in danger. In the 22 July Commission report, society is not only a construction; the main foundation of its construction is danger itself. Society understands itself as being under threat. It renders itself visible as that which is in danger, as what might be lost, damaged, deformed or destroyed. Society, in this way, appears in the form of a kind of negative image, like a negative-light photograph: what is darkened by the spectre of its destruction becomes the thing itself. We become sensitised to something at the moment it is potentially lost. This negativity of society (which is not to be understood in any qualitative or moral sense but rather as its presence in its potential absence) makes itself frequently felt in the pages of the 22 July Commission report. The Commission remains consistently mute about what society is in its very substance, while offering descriptions of the failure of the security that should have been provided for (is this the idea?) that actually achieve to make sense of the existence of society.

The 22 July Commission report is, first and foremost, concerned with the authorities responsible for security and preparedness, their organisation, routines, tools and actual activities. It is not interested in the different social groups that might be implicated, their organisation, the interpersonal relations and structures, traditions, informal systems, etc.; indeed, it is not interested in just about anything one might expect to reflect on when one is concerned with 'society'. This society – the society of social relations, cultural values, ties of filiation, traditions, beliefs, memories, experiences, troubles and fears, hopes and disappointments – is not the society that would have, ideally, according to the report, 'discovered and prevented plans or protected itself against threats' (NOU, 2012: 15), tasks which, of course, ordinarily are not the responsibility of the citizen on the street.

This choice of terms, or perhaps the omission of certain words, explains to a large degree why 'societal security' in the usage of the 22 July Commission has so little to do with society. Nonetheless, such terms reveal how 'society' is understood in the report. The concept covers active measures, the discovery of certain threats, their prevention, the hindrance of inimical forces, etc. It concerns what falls under the realm of what we earlier called 'prophylactic security', that is, security whose primary aim is to hold security threats at bay, with little attention to their human or social meaning or the human component of the societal situation coming under threat. This definition of security stands in stark contrast to a posture that accepts that certain situations of danger are unavoidable or that the price for avoiding these in relation to the political, military or policing-based options of securitisation is untenable.

It is worth noting that 'security' is not understood by the 22 July Commission as a state or condition. On the contrary, it appears as a kind of activity, as an action or as a kind of ongoing work. Formulations such as 'security work' or 'work with security' appear frequently in the report and in the political discourse and debates surrounding the events of 22 July 2011. 'Security work' or 'work with security' tend to serve as a condensation of 'security' itself. The perception of being safe, of the absence of fear or even of the objective absence of danger slide quickly into a way of thinking about security that presumes it to be an ongoing and continuous activity, something that can never be completed, a kind of activity without end, where security measures are not the exception but rather the continuous rule.

This can partially explain the privilege given by the 22 July Commission report to the role of the authorities in creating security for 'society' compared to a reflection on society's participation in the production of its own security. In reality, this is quite unusual when one thinks about the degree to which *society* can or should be the key to *societal* security. Among the 'relevant aspects of the chain of events', as the mandate to the 22 July Commission formulated it, neither society nor society's ability to generate its own security are enough to protect its own core values and care for the citizens and residents that are thought to inherently possess them. On the contrary, the 'tragedy of 22 July', according to the 22 July Commission, reveals the need for 'many types of changes', among them, changes in 'society's attitude' (15). Societal security is for the 22 July Commission a project of changing society for the sake of its own security benefit. 'Societal attitudes' eventually emerge in the report as some of the most tangible incarnations of society at large. To the degree that the effort to change attitudes leads to an engagement in actual societal matters, concerns, fears, assumptions, etc., it has the chance of providing an antidote to the near structural exclusion of society's scope and breadth in most of the report.

Society as system

A long and noble tradition with social theory, from Parsons to Luhmann and beyond, starts from the premise that society is a *system* (Luhmann, 1995; Parsons, 1977, 1991). In this tradition, as mentioned above, society is understood to be an organised gathering of distinct elements connected together in a network of distinct functions, identities and ways of being. For Parsons, such elements are related to the capacity for meaningful action; for Luhmann, the elements are constituted in relation to each other, often through self-referential networks of communication. All the elements are unique, but all have something in common. The relationship between the different elements constitutes a structure, a logic and a rationality. It is this structure, this logic, that gives meaning to the social system. It is this structure that allows 'society' to appear as meaningful both to its members and to those who experience it from the outside. It is this structure that assures that 'society' has a social meaning, a social being, also when it comes to the global system of societies in which it is necessarily embedded. It is also this structure that coordinates and harmonises the sense of the society for its members, beyond what individual members would be able to perceive or experience. To return again to Anderson's concept of the nation as an 'imagined community', society is in its own distinct way always an 'imagined' community.

In this context, the now fashionable notion of 'resilience' directs us to an understanding of a social system as an entity that is malleable enough, in particular at the level of culturally bound sub-groups, to remain unchanged under pressure, to preserve its societal characteristics, to maintain a substance that is recognisable for all, with the same 'societal functions' – a critical term of the 22 July Commission, to which we will return – carrying out, organically, the same functions that led it to participate integrally in the societal system that bears the signs that let it be recognised as continuous with what it was before (210–11, 48). When the 22 July Commission wonders 'would the outcome have been essentially different under marginally changed conditions?', the question is directed towards the 'resilience in society's systems' (14). It is against this backdrop – that is, of society continuing as a system – that the Commission enquires whether the system functioned 'as intended', even while it is unclear to whose intention such an idea might refer or to what agency it would have to appeal or to what measure it would submit in order to fulfil such an intention.

Thus in general a key question that recurs throughout the Commission's report, both explicitly and implicitly, is: what can be expected of society? What can and should be expected of a society in a crisis situation, or in 'ordinary times' for that matter? And what does it mean to say and presume such a thing? How can we as members of a society expect something that cannot be anticipated at all, namely, the most serious terror attack on Norwegian soil ever? Should we have expected this, and should we have expected that the authorities had expected this? Should the authorities have expected that we had not expected it and nonetheless reacted in an expected way? Is it, moreover, possible to 'prepare society's ability to manage the next crisis' (14)? In other words, can society 'learn'? And if it can, what does such a learning process look like? How would it take place? The answer to this question leads us back to the Commission's somewhat unique understanding of what a society is and what kind of system it represents.

Early in the report, the 22 July Commission defines society as 'the sum of individual persons that take decisions and carry out actions' (NOU, 2012: 14). That definition is remarkable for several reasons. First and foremost, it represents society as an aggregate of individuals, 'individual persons', as being completely atomised, autonomous and independent. Following this defition, the 22 July Commission's concept of society is thus not based on social relations of any kind. On the contrary, it regards the social as a constellation of contingently related particles. The components in this social system live and experience each other without influence or impact. The individual's capacity to act is individualised and internal, not collective. Will, intention, design are somehow conceived and experienced individually and expressed in relation to other particles that are themselves conceived in the same way. They are not understood intersubjectively as a relation to other thinking, feeling, experiencing individuals, as psychic, moral and social subjects endowed with the capacities and experiences similar to our own. Rather, in the society of the 22 July Commission report, 'members' of society relate to others across a space of two-dimensional objects, as though they existed only on paper. To read the report of the 22 July Commission, one is left with the impression of a world of lonely individuals, to say the least, a world without community or solidarity, without cooperation or collaboration beyond the most instrumental and mechanical. Society, in this bureaucratic vision, has no texture or depth, only lateral links, no collective depth, only cumulative extension. While it is not at all my claim that Norwegian society in actuality corresponds to this representation, we are invited to confront the fundamentally analytical question of why such a representation dominates the definitive analysis of the events of 22 July 2011.

Security and responsibility

If 'societal security' is not central to the reasoning and world view of the 22 July Commission's report, concepts like 'steering', 'organisation' and 'administrative responsibility' do indeed dominate the discourse. 'Responsibility for the security of society', the report confirms, 'rests on all levels of management, both central and regional' (68). As generalising as this may sound, such a characterisation tends to summarise the report's relation to society as an object for administration, management and regulation. Society is not an actor with agency in relation to its own security but rather an object for securitisation through the official actors that are, by definition, excluded from the question of societal security.

The concept of responsibility is key to this dilemma. 'Responsibility' is, of course, an essential concept in the logic of administration. As we pointed out in Chapter 4, responsibility for Weber is what ties together the different segments in the bureaucratic structure, which in turn guarantees the function of administrative processes, administrative authority, regulation and political legitimacy. Formally speaking, it is bureaucrats who do the work of caring for this relation between the bureaucratic infrastructure and the responsibility it is meant to carry.

It is important to note that from the point of view of management, responsibility is not a moral concept. Indeed, it does not appeal to moral judgement of individual, free human beings and their free choice in relation to different questions representing different value standpoints or value positions. Responsibility is instead a *logical* link that connects together different processes that are nonetheless dependent upon one another so administration can function and fulfil its objectives. It is equally true to say that administrative responsibility includes human tasks and decisions in relation to such objectives. Nonetheless, and this contrasts with common notions of moral responsibility, the decisions are given and programmed in advance. The choices that are made from the position of administration will never surprise anyone. Of course, surprises are the worst result for an administrator. Administrative responsibility thus has little to do with actual human properties that might possibly need or even provide security or protection for human beings in the form of anything unforeseen. When the 22 July Commission report points to the situation of responsibility, a situation that functions or did not function as it was meant to, it is by no means referring to moral responsibility, to people, their moral judgement and the way they behave during a crisis. It is far more referring to how the system's *mechanisms* function. Of course, it belongs to the mandate of the 22 July Commission that it should not take a position in terms of criminal liability or legal responsibility (NOU, 2012: 38). Responsibility in the 22 July Commission report is a technical concept. It is the wires, bolts and hinges that hold together a moving machine (see Seibel, 2015).

The 22 July Commission thereby attaches itself to the scientific and operational differentiation between three 'principles' that are meant to regulate the way that security and preparedness work should relate to unknown dangers and risks. As we saw in Chapter 4, these principles were developed in the governmental study *When the Accident Has Happened*, published nearly simultaneously with the attacks of September 2001, though just too late to be directly influenced by them (NOU, 2001).

In addition to the 'principle of equality', the 'principle of proximity' and the 'principle of cooperation', the 'principle of responsibility' holds a central position as the key reference for authorities concerned with the security of society. As is the case for any principle, it does not fall to the principle of responsibility to clarify what is meant by 'responsibility', what actions are responsibly required or not. Principles do not define 'themselves'. The principle does determine, in this case, who has responsibility. The principle of responsibility in this version concretely ascribes the responsibility for individual elements of a larger and more complex system of tasks and objectives. Rather than focussing on the content of the principle, it functions as a kind of code for distribution of responsibility and, not least, dispensation from responsibility. According to the 22 July Commission, 'the agency that has responsibility for one field of expertise in a normal situation also has responsibility for managing extraordinary events in that area' (NOU, 2012: 23). The report points to some of these concrete areas of responsibility that are themselves specified by a variety of segments implicated in the administration of security in Norway in different arenas, for example, government cabinet members, the National Security Authority, the PST, the Intelligence Service or the Coordination and Advisory Committee for the Intelligence, Surveillance and Security Service, among others (72).

'Responsibility' is actually a rather frequent, even dominating, concept in the report of the 22 July Commission. This appears to be the consequence of the fact that the Commission understands its critical task to be to repair a bureaucratic apparatus that has either fallen apart or urgently needs adjustment and upgrading, an essential moment in the report's handling of the events of 22 July 2011. A mapping of the events takes its point of departure in a mapping of the responsibilities. In other words, this means assessing whether the actions that should have been taken were in fact taken. Any mapping of responsibility thus implies an examination of the link between individuals, institutions, agencies and objectives. The criteria for the form and content of the assessment of the question of responsibility is predetermined. The criterion is set before the facts, indeed, before any fact, while its execution remains independent of any fact. Though the adequacy of the actions relative to the criteria obviously depends on what happened, on the facts of the case, the criteria themselves are immobile, a priori fixed, unchanged by the actual state of the world. The fixity of the criteria for proper execution of responsibility also implies a certain need to interpret actions taken on the ground, intentions and understandings, and a judgement about the correctness and adequacy of the concrete actions that were carried out. It becomes quickly evident that even for the most concrete and accountable administrative action, there can be a significant gap between understanding and result.

'Responsibility', as it appears in the 22 July Commission report, corresponds to or specifies the points of intervention where corrective measures are possible and appropriate. When 'responsibility' is discussed in the report, possible failures exposed and potential political handling are underscored that might lead to changing present governing mechanisms. In general, wherever 'responsibility' is identified, one can also find a link in the system where control or power can be exerted, and where, as a consequence, political adjustments in relations of power can be made.

Thus we see that 'responsibility' has a curious double meaning in the 22 July Commission report. On the one hand, responsibility stands for accountability. It means that we account for our actions relative to others, for what happens in relation to others. It is an admission, a kind of surrender, to the reality that we are dependent upon others, upon the gaze and the implicit or explicit judgement of others relative to the norms to which they hold, the values they are prone to and the more formal regulations or laws to which they submit. This is essentially how the 22 July Commission report understands 'responsibility': it is the name of a link in a system, a link that does not necessarily correspond to an individual person but that can be an entity or an entire institution.

On the other hand, and almost paradoxically, 'responsibility' connotes a kind of *independence*. If we are responsible, if we are 'taking' our responsibility, it essentially means that we are left alone to our own resources, moral or otherwise. If we are responsible, then we must depend on our own knowledge, experiences, memories, tradition, culture, religious beliefs, values, priorities and so forth. Thereafter, responsibility becomes a far more human matter than a formal or bureaucratic one. It becomes a process of judgement where moral uncertainty and ambiguous position-taking are far more the rule than the exception, where internal, implicit, inherent processes and moral intuition play a dominant role, opening at the same time a far greater role for social, cultural, emotional or even spiritual influences. It is this side of the experience of responsibility that fades to nothingness in the report of the 22 July Commission. Responsibility is never described in situ, in relation to the social, political, cultural reality in general, nor, more importantly, in relation to the socially, politically and culturally determined events of 22 July 2011. In the 22 July Commission report, responsibility is never expressed as a question of human values, of human experience, of lived life, past, present or future. It is never described or interpreted in relation to the ethical or value-based settings where it alone can be assessed. Responsibility is understood and handled as if it were not at all a question of human beings.

7

There is no alternative to security

> Reason has always existed, but not always in rational form.
> Marx (1844)

The work of societal security

At around the same time as the 22 July Commission was set up to carry out its investigation of Oslo/Utøya with the instruction to 'put the facts on the table, unvarnished and honest' (Stoltenberg, 2011a), the Ministry of Justice and Police set about formulating its own report with the same objective, the same audience and yet far less public attention, titled simply *Societal Security*. This white paper grew out of a policy initiative that had already been in the planning before Oslo/Utøya, but which took on new political meaning and scope by being published after the attacks (JPD, 2012). The report was originally intended as part of the cycle of reports aimed at shaping national policy on societal security in its pre-22 July meaning. As noted in Chapter 3, 'societal security' in the years before 11 September 2001 referred primarily to the low-grade, sub-national security concerns of everyday life for Norwegian industry and citizens such as security and preparedness for local events, prevention of accidents with fire and electricity, health and safety of industrial workers, product and consumer safety, etc. After the creation of the Directorate for Societal Security and Preparedness (DSB) in 2003, it published the first of what would be an annual report on the state of societal security in Norway. A new report was planned for 2012 when the Oslo/Utøya events made necessary a considerable widening of its scope. The white paper *Societal Security* was delivered to Parliament only two months before the 22 July Commission report was to be presented to the general public. *Societal Security* is thus both a general review and an update of policy approaches to societal security in Norway, covering a range of activities and services in the areas of crisis management, communication, search and rescue, information technology as well as evolving forms of cooperation between traditional law enforcement agencies, the military and international organisations. Most of these changes are relevant to the Oslo/Utøya events, and although they could just as well have stood alone as upgrades, they are overshadowed by an initial chapter dedicated to a review, from a policy perspective, of the attacks. By the same token, the policy issues provoked by the attacks become a bundle of red threads running through the paper, starting with the re-baptising of the Ministry of Justice and Police to the Ministry of Justice and Preparedness.

Although the *Societal Security* white paper does not coin the term 'societal security work', as it had already appeared in a range of official documents, white papers, reports and analyses, it certainly mainstreams and institutionalises the concept more decisively than several well-crafted, and undoubtedly relevant, documents preceding it. As in other similar declarations, white papers, resolutions, etc., the 'work of societal security' is a standard reference to which many policies and activities inevitably return. It is among the handful of key terms in Norwegian politics that play a crucial role in organising the logic of societal security, determining the rationality of the politically tailored security division of labour and the type and level of outcomes to be expected, and, finally, the political responsibility for the entire chain of conceptual command, linking actors to means and goals. What is, indeed, the 'work' of societal security? Repeatedly in policy documents, the expression indicates a strengthening of what is already being done on behalf of society's security. Importantly, despite the world-shaking events of 22 July, the work of societal security is primarily the same, in terms of its value orientations, political priorities and ethical imperatives, as before the attacks.

And yet, the somewhat clumsy concept of societal security 'work' also plays a role in determining and delimiting, or at least corroborating, what must be called the *ethos* of security in Norwegian society and in the Norwegian self-understanding as a complex of values, codes and norms, and belonging. As much as one of the explicit aims of this book is to uncover and analyse the logic of societal security in the Norwegian tradition, its tacit aim is to trace the contours of societal security, its interface to both the traditional and modern Norwegian value set, the ambivalence between its cultural traditions and ambitious longing for modernity and the deeper historical Norwegian roots of security itself.

Here lies perhaps the most significant political difference between the 2012 *Societal Security* white paper, issued by the Ministry of Justice, and the independently prepared report of the 22 July Commission, published just after it. Whereas the 22 July Commission report gives itself free rein to take issue with the political bases of decision-making, the Ministry's report limits itself, in line with its traditional tools and methods, to concerns for operational matters and to the relationship between existing and even traditional political values and responsibilities, and the tools at its disposal. It does so, however, with a far richer and perhaps even more culturally conservative sub-structure. As I will try to outline below, the Ministry of Justice's white paper *Societal Security* reaches deeper into the shared Scandinavian value set, finding there the stable principles of mutual trust between State and citizens confronted by the shock of terrorism.

From security to preparedness

This makes the decision taken by the government to rename and retool the long-standing Ministry of Justice and Police all the more surprising. Indeed, the body's internal organisation was reviewed in order to establish the 'Ministry of Justice and Preparedness', along with an increased budget, with the aim of 'assuring that Norway can meet the challenges to risk and vulnerability that society faces' (OPM, 2011). This change of concept manages to shift the purview of societal security 'work', expanding it to encompass domestic policing and fighting criminality as well as security and preparedness, thus generating a need to engage with the rich politics of the unknown that is to be found there.

There is an observable tendency in a variety of Western governments to upgrade the functions of domestic law and order with the aim of dealing with clearly specified, juridically defined events and actors through enhanced or special powers. Addressing criminal acts require the well-ordered application of principles of law enforcement and criminal justice. By contrast, matters of security and preparedness are not defined in advance, not codified as such. They are 'defined' according to need and political exigence. They are meant to apply to *exceptional* actions, micro states of exception, the start of the withdrawal of democracy, the beginning – in the worst of cases – of a weakening of accountability.

As decades of research in security theory have demonstrated, declaring something a security threat under appropriate conditions of legitimacy and communication instantaneously increases the power of the declaring actor, generates a dependency on the agent of security, etc. (Balzacq, 2010). 'Security and preparedness' is the name of a transformation of politics of events. It corresponds to a shift from known events and types of events in known, concrete, given settings to identifiable citizens under the purview of investigative and executive law enforcement agents with clearly defined and delimited tasks within a distinct scope of legal authority. 'Security and preparedness' shifts not only the object of action, its origins and ends, but also what we might call its metaphysics, that is, its more general situation in reality as a function of time and space. Rebaptising the Ministry in terms of security and preparedness reorientates political priorities by reorientating time, and the course of events in time. It introduces a shift in the presence of the future, in the proximity of dangers that have not yet become a reality but which will quickly, and perceivably, become so on the horizon of an imagined future. It is not just a matter of becoming aware of the increasing number of nefarious things that might come, the increasing number and diversity of objects of security, the product of a range of technological, social, economic, cultural, even spiritual processes. It is also a transformation of time itself. Einstein might never have imagined, in the general theory of relativity, that time is not only warped by gravitation but also by danger.

Like time, danger is a phenomenon, in the narrow, philosophical sense of the word: it is a thing that becomes present by way of experience, experience that widens the strictly empirical sense-based notion of experience. It is not limited to the purely empirical information that is delivered to the brain by one or several of the five senses. Rather, it is the experience of a broader sensory apparatus that might be called awareness. Like time in Einstein's theory, time in the phenomenology of danger is equally variable, malleable. It races towards us, recedes, hesitates, bumps and hiccups as a function of the perils that it carries in its current. The experience of time thus maps distinctly on to a phenomenology of danger. Whereas a philosopher like Kant regards time as the transcendental precondition and backdrop of any experience of the world, a solid given, a foundation of perception and cognition, other philosophers after him have understood time as a component of experience, not a precondition of experience but rather something that is produced in and through experience. Nowhere is this more evident in our time than through the mediatised experience of threat and danger. Decades are flattened by the spectre of past dangers and the future is precipitated by the projection of memories onto the miraculously present catastrophes of the future. Time is distorted by danger.

This reorientation, even in its least accountable forms, can save life and property. The crucial shift in the Ministry's shift from crime to security is that political control needs to be rethought and recaptured to ensure that the freedoms granted to government agencies in the name of authority do not end up weakening society. Thus, where, on the one hand, the explicit purpose of the change in name and mission of the Norwegian Ministry of Justice is to 'clarify' and 'strengthen' the Ministry's 'responsibility for society's security and preparedness', its political scope actually becomes more ambiguous to the degree that it becomes enlarged and empowered. As a consequence, the object of its power becomes more ambiguous, determined by increasingly unidentified and unclarified threats. Even more critically, the expansion of powers in relation to the unknown is not only thwarted by the diminishing level of certainty required to mobilise the political powers of the State, but it is this uncertainty that comes to form the very core of the deployment of power, both in terms of its scope and its reach.

The notion of uncertainty is implicit in both the concepts of security and preparedness. The novelty of the exercise of renaming the Ministry of Justice has greater consequences than what appear at first glance. If the stroke of a pen can reconceptualise a fundamental security-giving bureaucratic structure, the basic imagined exposure to danger is equally destabilised.

But uncertainty no longer functions as a chance misfortune of intelligence-gathering, an accidental or contingent glitch in a thorough system otherwise operating on the basis of stable knowledge and foreseeable consequences. On the contrary, the political nourishment of security governance is uncertainty itself. It is the *lack* of knowledge or inadequate knowledge that drives the politics and mobilises the forces of order. Furthermore, the knowledge that is always uncertain does not simply concern the undetermined future, innocent and promising. The future that is the concern of security governance in the age of uncertainty is a dangerous one. It is not merely a matter of the unknown but of unknown threats. As in many governments across the world, the spectre of a threatening future orientates the legitimacy of the Ministry of Justice towards unspecified, and thus ungoverned, situations. Whereas the traditional role of the Norwegian Ministry of Justice, like that of analogous ministries in Anglo-European States, is to assure justice in the prosecution of criminal law, the shift of security and preparedness is to a sharply more political orientation, and with it an optic of governance and control through tacit political powers.

Prevention or preparedness?

Thus, the addition of the term 'preparedness' to the name of the Ministry of Justice and Police is not merely politics. It links the Norwegian understanding of crisis management to an international cloud of reference, with the political expediences and risks this entails. Following the model of the US Department of Homeland Security and the discourse of homeland security in the EU, the Stoltenberg government accepts the wide-ranging assumption that 'justice' should not, or does not, simply refer to the handling of criminality in Norway; in other words, that its responsibility is not solely to formulate and clarify policy to prevent crime and/or to be in charge of policing as a measure to prevent or reduce crime and, where this not possible, to administer the publicly governed punishment that is attuned to the task of responding in a just way to crimes against the national law. Beyond the role of organising the legitimate and just governance of public police forces and the well-regulated public prosecution of accused criminals, the new Ministry of Justice and Preparedness, both in name and in substance, takes an entirely new orientation, one that echoes a global movement and tendency.

'Prevention' – as in 'crime prevention', 'accident prevention', 'disease prevention', etc. – is an instrumental, prophylactic posture. It builds on an essential distinction between danger and what is endangered. It understands a threat or peril as something other, some fundamentally different, heterogeneous, from what is threatened. As a consequence, the task of prevention is most commonly regarded as one of keeping the dangerous thing 'out there' from becoming part of the safety and security that 'we' are. The logic of prevention can (though does not always) overlap with a fortress logic, one that affirms that preventing crime means reinforcing the locks on our doors, or that preventing accidents means keeping materials or activities that tend to cause accidents away from where 'we' are, from what 'we' are doing, or that preventing disease means nose-and-mouth masks and quarantines. It can often mean taking a technical and technological approach to preventing unwanted events, building walls and windows, locks and hinders, surveilling the others who might be threatening to us, making lists, categorising human beings through registers and databases of those that fall into groups of 'others' who might be threatening to us. Prevention builds upon a distinct, even rarified, self-image, an idea that given what or who 'we' are, only something foreign can do us harm, only something heterogeneous to our nature can corrupt the essence of what we are, put into question that existence, etc. In short, prevention puts the spotlight on the other and on the dangers it provokes in part by virtue of it being other, incompatible with 'us'.

Prevention is an ontology, a way of structuring and organising reality itself. It is a way of lining up things that exist in the world, in society, in our communities, in our lives, such that some of them appear to put into question the existence of that world. Of course, if prevention is to be about threats to things in the world, it must first make a range of silent assumptions about the world – and about threats. The logic of prevention – in order to do its work, in order to mobilise and legitimate the activities of agencies and individuals, political processes and psychological operations – must make enormous assumptions about what the world is, and in particular what a threat to that world is. Most importantly, it assumes a world that is without danger in order to make sense of a world in danger. This world without danger, a world of safety and security, is a strange, implausible, maybe even unthinkable thing. It is a world where everything that is has somehow always been, and will always continue to be, a world where all is as it should be, not in the sense of harmony but in the sense of an untouched, uniform, homogenous, selfsame and autonomous well-being. It is a world, finally, where the existence is identical to security, where to be is to be secure and thus where security is hardly even a concept. Prevention assumes that this ideal situation is also the 'normal' situation, the way things normally or naturally are. Consequently, insecurity is experienced as abnormal, as exceptional or as a divergence. Insecurity is a situation to be corrected, to be eliminated, terminated, eradicated or removed.

In terms of operations or practice, the logic of prevention implies that security actors – those agents, agencies or institutions tasked with keeping 'us' secure – play an instrumental role. In the practice of prevention, the agent is neither us nor them, neither good nor bad, neither secure nor insecure. Agency in general plays, rather, a purely instrumental role, assuring, in an essentially disinterested way, that there is no mix of the two essential components of the security equation: we and danger. These two terms form the naked axis of the discourse of prevention. Security, in the discourse of prevention, has only two components. It operates on a binary kind of logic, which repeats in any number of terms, from safe and unsafe, to dirty and clean, hot and cold, pure and impure – the list of conceptual options is endless. It is organised around essentially one governing rule.

By contrast, the reorientation towards 'preparedness' introduces a fundamental change in the way we understand ourselves in the world, the way we see ourselves in relation to dangers, to our survival, to our existence, etc. The logic of preparedness, by re-tasking the provision of security, brings the danger home, relocates, or rather rediscovers, it, not out beyond the horizon but at our doorstep. The logic of preparedness shifts this axis of danger in two fundamental ways. First, preparedness does not build upon the assumption that dangers lie somewhere out on the horizon. It does not seek to form a strategy or practice of stopping the danger from becoming a reality, from threat being realised. Preparedness is far more the posture that the undesirable thing is somehow on its way, somehow coming, that it bears a certain inevitability. Preparedness is the complex admission that certain dangers cannot be stopped or deflected.

And yet, secondly, this sense of inevitability of danger or threat at the heart of the notion of preparedness goes deeper. Beyond being a danger that is somehow on the way, the danger, which is the object of practices of preparedness, is a danger that is, in a certain sense, already present, already threatening in a potential kind of way, something which is inseparable from who we are, what we are. In the logic of preparedness, it is society itself that is intimately implicated in the threat and, by extension, in the work of countering the threat.

What does it mean to counter a threat according to the logic of preparedness? In contrast to the logic of prevention, which would call for stopping the danger, the logic of preparedness asks which measures will make us secure given its inevitability. It means turning towards the society, the institutions, the groups where the danger already exists as a kind of imminent or potential danger. We can see that this means understanding society in a new and unusual way, not only as the thing that is to be secured but also, in some sense, as the source of the insecurity and, lastly, in some sense again, as an effective provider of the needed security.

Conundrums of cooperation

The 22 July Commission's analysis of the Oslo/Utøya attacks points to a lack of coordination between key elements in the policing and crisis management apparatus (NOU, 2012: 66–78). Disturbing tales of missed calls, unseen messages and misunderstood signs flooded the media in the days and weeks after the events. Scandal-seekers had ripe material to draw on. According to accounts, a police cruiser drove a dozen kilometres immediately behind the terrorist's vehicle on the way to Utøya without knowing who the driver was; a misplaced Post-it note led to a lack of information about the assailant's whereabouts; an overloaded emergency response telephone line led to delays in response; the inaccessibility of a police helicopter hindered efforts to reach the island in good time. Awareness of all these weaknesses in the overall crisis response system contributed to a response by official crisis management agencies and organisations that was not up to muster as far as expectations for the public sphere were concerned, creating popular political pressure on officials to make fundamental changes, whether or not necessary, from any other point of view than popular perception.

At first glance, the primary weakness seemed to be in coordination and cooperation. The very public blunders by the police in their attempt to reach Utøya were primarily attributed to lack of cooperation. The elements of the crisis response system that worked optimally were in first reports often overlooked or marginalised. Coming to terms with the fascination with prevention, with the idea that the entire attack could have been prevented, is demanding: if only different decisions had been made, different paths taken; if only one organisation or another had possessed or used different equipment; if only different methods had been applied; if only different constellations of resources had been dispatched at different times to different places; if only different policies had been enacted based on different premises in different areas if only one post-it note had been moved – all entirely displacing the question of the role played by people in society as actors and objects of security. The question of avoidability, which we have seen plays a central role in the conclusions of the 22 July Commission report, simply displaced the question of what societal security actually is to a discourse of fault and misconduct, of procedural right and wrong, of organisational performance and of bureaucratic virtue and vice.

Thus, in a retroactive, popularised, politicised assessment of what threatens Norway and Norwegian society, the blunders and missteps of highly trained, serious and conscientious professionals of public security came to set the tone and the agenda for a decade to come, shoving into oblivion the human event, from victims to volunteers to the extended Norwegian societal collective. The force of experience, both tragic and hopeful, the solidarity, ideological pillar of Norwegian post-war social democracy, the absolutely unique forms of fear and unease, which emerge out of deep moral and cultural traditions, the experience of loss and redemption, of care for strangers and support for others, of mistrust and suspicion, action and complacence, patience and uncompromising stubbornness, of memory and ambition, inspiration and courage, cowardice and egoism – experiences that constitute the force and impact of societal security in any setting, and provide the elements of analysis and understanding of the Norwegian experience of catastrophe – all these were and continue to be relegated to the scrapheap of history in favour of technical debates about radio bandwidth, post-it notes and the structure of State bureaucracy. The aim of preventing undesirable events, of rendering them impossible – rather than admissible and manageable – was the first-generation response to the catastrophe.

Both the roots of this reaction and its conceptual support rest solidly on well-formulated policy positions that go back to the Commission on Vulnerability's report from 2000, then continued in the many societal security reports that would follow. The dominant doctrine for 'work' towards assuring societal security through public agencies was the white paper *Societal Security: Cooperation and Coordination* (Norwegian Parliament, 2007), As its title indicates, the white paper drew attention to the importance of cooperation in ensuring societal security. The events of 22 July 2011 demonstrated for many that this insight needed to be dramatically strengthened and mainstreamed in the official agencies responsible for societal security (Bjørgum, 2010).

Thus, after announcing the major political message of the newly empowered Ministry of Justice and Preparedness, the 2012 *Societal Security* white paper turns quickly to a retooling of the organisational principles behind 'national societal security and preparedness' (JPD, 2008). These principles, as pointed out earlier, were set out in the 2002 white paper *Societal security: The Path to a Less Vulnerable Society*, the report that resulted from the original 2000 report, *A Vulnerable Society*, and underscored in the official response to the recommendations after debate in Parliament (NOU, 2000; Stortinget, 2012a). They establish the decade-long foundation for societal security policy based on three pillars: the principle of responsibility, the principle of equality and the principle of proximity (NOU, 2012: 70). However, whereas the 2008 follow-up white paper on societal security, *Societal Security: Cooperation and Coordination*, introduces the concept of cooperation, it gives official force to a principle of societal security in the next generation of policy formulation that will not only make it more visible in policy-making and practice but essentially revolve around it. While the original three concepts have functioned adequately, it argues, they communicate poorly the need for good cooperation 'between the different responsible actors' and 'the need to see all of society's resources in context'. For this reason, *Societal Security* announces that the government will henceforth build 'cooperation' into its efforts as a supporting element together with existing principles (JPD, 2012: 39).

The 'principle of cooperation' is defined in the form of a paradox. It 'requires that authorities, agencies or departments have an independent responsibility to ensure the best possible coordination with relevant actors'

(JPD, 2012: 39). It is noted that the principle of coordination is already applied, for example, in the area of life-saving services at sea, where public authorities are dependent upon the private-level and volunteer services available at local levels. The ambition linked to introducing the principle in the area of societal security is to establish a kind of global, automatic coordination, regardless of sector or level and independent of what kind of crisis one is dealing with.

In the sphere of social relations, however, cooperation is a more complex and layered matter than first meets the eye. The white paper's newly formulated ambition to impose cooperation as a fourth fundamental principle in an effort to ensure societal security gives a hint of this complexity. For if cooperation is the principle, what authority is the subject of the principle? From which position, from which point of view, is the general principle to be exercised?

We recall briefly the other three principles applicable to societal security. The principle of responsibility holds that the actor or agency that is responsible for a given area under normal operations is also responsible for that area under extraordinary or crisis operations. The principle of equality extends the principle of responsibility, holding that an actor or agency should, as much as possible, remain itself during normal and extraordinary or crisis situations. In essence, an organisation should not fundamentally convert itself in order to deal with an emergency. The principle of proximity requires that an extraordinary situation or crisis should be dealt with on the lowest possible organisational level.

Together with these three original principles, the principle of cooperation requires that cooperation be an 'independent' responsibility. It asserts that each entity, organisation, agency or actor in the societal security system should be independently responsible for assuring that cooperation with other such entities takes place. The decision to cooperate and the implementation of cooperative measures is thus to be taken independently, non-cooperatively. The principle of responsibility requires that the implementation of the principle of cooperation takes place in a non-cooperative fashion, as a function of the responsible authority of each individual component, individually responsible, at the lowest possible level, for dealing with societal security issues that might arise. The content of the cooperation, i.e. the aim or effort towards which the cooperating parties are to cooperate, is uncertain. Equally uncertain is the question of which entity, in its independent responsibility to cooperate, will set out the terms of the cooperation, which organisation will determine the content of the cooperation, its overall objectives and intermediary objectives. Nor can it be determined beforehand, in conformity with the principles of responsibility and equality, which means and methods, tools and procedures are to be applied or prioritised. It goes nearly without saying that if there are two entities, agencies or organisations, it is because they have two functions, two sets of values, two sorts of competence, two missions, two bylaws, etc. Asking them to cooperate in terms of the pre-existing hierarchy is already a task of cooperation: cooperation before cooperation.

Against this background, Oslo/Utøya is not simply an ironic and unfortunate accident of the Norwegian societal security environment or of this particular attempt at policy formulation. On the contrary, it lies at the very heart of organisational logic in the provision of security for and by society. To put it in a nutshell, security is not an organisational matter. Security cannot be generated through the hierarchically governed organisation of human beings. On the contrary, from a psychosocial point of view, the notion of cooperation in the provision of security would have been both conceptually coherent and practically implementable. Cooperation in non-coordinated, social spaces takes place spontaneously, individually, either through the implicit or intimate practical understanding between humans or through spontaneous non-formal agreements between parties with tacitly harmonised means and explicitly shared aims.

In short, the societal-level operations that take place between unspecified members of society, informal groups and communities, or intimate circles, have the ability to more or less organically and automatically realise the ambitions and goals apparently envisaged by the principle of cooperation. By contrast, where cooperation is the most problematic from a conceptual point of view and the most difficult in practical terms is the situation where it is mandated, required or made the necessary object of a principle formally codified in law.

Complexity and coordination

The primary challenge to this new phase of cooperation in preparedness and societal security is repeatedly legitimated as a problem of complexity. The complexity challenge refers to both the perception of inherent and increasing complexity of society and to the complexity of the constellation of security threats to be faced by society. This double complexity becomes a leitmotif in the white paper. It also provides an opening for a better understanding of what society actually is in the eyes of the Norwegian societal security actors and agencies: 'The increasing degree of complexity in society and dependencies across sectors means a great need for collaboration across the different areas of responsibility, both as far as they concern the work of preventive preparedness and crisis management' (JPD, 2012: 40).

'Complexity', here, refers to a more common notion that components of a system are connected through multiple entanglements, linkages and heterogeneous flows. In societal terms, the components that make up society, its individuals, groups, organisations and institutions communicate and interact in many ways and on a range of levels. The history of any society is from a certain point of view the history of its increasing complexity. The *Societal Security* white paper sees society as multiple, divided, diversified, with poor technical connectivity between the components that make it up. Connectivity, like complexity, is here understood as a simple matter of linearised connections, after the metaphor of the closed cabled system. If all the cables are plugged together, the system is interconnected and inter-operable. Yet, basic complexity theory tells us that with the increase in countable connections, of plugs and cables, the complexity, the meaning-giving, unforeseeable, un-chartable interconnectivity of thought even in the most technologically heavy system, is impossible to understand, let alone control, in its totality. Complexity theory has grown in popularity in recent decades due to some degree to its reverberations with the subset-networked society represented by social media and other internet-based practices of connectivity. While internet connectivity represents only a shadow of the notion of connectivity understood in complexity theory, it is an analogy and model for a new reflection on both how to analyse crisis management challenges and, not least, how to understand crises themselves as complex systems (Christensen *et al.*, 2016).

For the *Societal Security* white paper, complexity is closely linked to the notion of cooperation and the newly introduced 'principle of cooperation'. 'Complexity' skates on the surface of the actual problems of complexity in crisis management, and asks, rather, how continuity of responsibility for crisis management across these different areas can be assured. 'Complexity' is essentially applied as a governance concept, a way of understanding how best to create and maintain ties of legitimacy, recognition, information in managing crisis preparation activities and actual operational activities. These are activities that by their nature are transversal governance institutions. There is a recognition of the complex nature of crises, and, at the same time, a general assumption that the institutions and actors traditionally charged with non-complex crises, those that are traditionally localised geographically, isolated within distinct systems and engaging discretely identifiable individuals, have no role to play. This set of assumptions is echoed in the mobilisation of the 'principle of cooperation' as a way of better linking the actors and responsible agents already existing without disrupting the basic organisational, administrative and also governance structures in which they are situated.

> The principle of responsibility [that responsibility for managing crises belongs to the actor that also has non-crisis responsibility for the area] does not imply any changes in basic responsibilities. The principle of responsibility is continued as the primary principle for the distribution of responsibility between the different actors in society's collective preparedness. (JPD, 2012: 40)

We have, of course, run across the 'societal double genitive' before. It is, in a sense, the crux of the argument of this book. To refresh it in brief, the double construction contains two assertions, or perhaps two questions: is it society that is the object of collective preparedness? In other words, is it society that should be taken as the object of preparedness, as the object of concern, the target of preparedness operations – and thus the object of policy, operational initiatives, political action, etc.? In short, is it society that is to be secured? Or, inversely, is it society itself that is the subject, the operator, the actor, the security-giver in the society–security equation?

The ambivalence – one might even say a necessary ambivalence – between the two positions is further enriched and complicated by an additional conceptual shift in the way that society itself is presented and manipulated as an extraordinary kind of security actor, not an individual actor, less again an institutionalised authority or agency, but rather a kind of generalised ability to respond to security needs and mobilise security measures.

The aim of these instructions is to advance a global and coordinated work towards societal security and preparedness, which will contribute to increasing society's ability to prevent crises and undesirable events, and increase the ability to manage crises (41).

The *Societal Security* white paper reaffirms the sideways logic of societal security in Norway after 22 July 2011. It contains a sub-narrative that indicates the shape of the core structure of security as a bureaucratic problem, and the bureaucratic tools available to address security concerns in a way that is more or less detached from society as an empirically distinct object of security as well as society's actual function as a source of strength, solidarity and security. The bureaucratisation of danger treads the relatively narrow path between society understood as an object of security and society understood as a subject of security. But it ultimately tends far more towards a 'societal security machine', a mechanism that involves real people only as operators and technicians in a collective process that exists in a space outside of security. The only real people involved in the real provision of security are those who are exempted from it.

The nationality of risk

The unique function of security bureaucracy as the means and logic of a security *dispositif* is, in some ways, extended through the retooling of risk itself as a logic of the national, motivated and organised by a modality of national belonging, which can be observed and unpacked through the *Societal Security* white paper's reflection on 'national risk assessment'.

In Norway, as in essentially all of Scandinavia, and a number of small to mid-sized nation-states, coordination of risk management takes places on the national level. Laws and regulations are national. They are conceived and formulated on a national level, most commonly through national legislative norms and procedures and in terms of national values, national policies and priorities, and adjudicated and implemented through national institutions. They are unified, generalised and advance a notion that 'the national' is the primary scale – with some variation – for the assessment of risk. The objects of risk are understood to be of national interest and national remit even when they are only indirectly connected to individual actors.

A number of cultural predispositions support and nourish this notion of a strong national continuity in the face of risk and danger. The first, and most basic, is the idea of an imagined cultural community, an implicit cultural homogeneity that expresses the notion that risk to one person is a risk to another, that the risk to one group is a risk to another, that one regional claim to risk is another regional claim to risk. The second, slightly more complex idea is implicit in the Norwegian bureaucratic approach to risk and revolves around a vertical continuity.

The idea of a vertical continuity is not to be confused with simple transversal solidarity – which one might be led to expect from the type of deeply engrained social democracy that has set the tone for the social and economic policy in Norway and much of Scandinavia since the end of World War II. It is far more a reference to an imaginary sameness, uniformity and fundamental equality – understood not as a social-cultural-economic principle, supported by the basic tenets of democracy and human rights – but rather as an implicit biopolitical fact of equivalence among citizens, by virtue of being citizens and by, in some sense, also the motivation or even cause of citizenship. Thus, citizenship in Norway and other Scandinavian settings also resists a strongly quantitative notion of democracy – i.e. a land is democratic and thus egalitarian to the degree that the plebiscite is distributed according to a logic of mathematical equality, relying instead on a far more ethnically orientated notion of democratic equivalence. We are equal by *ethnos*, not by a virtue of democratic ratio.

Either risk to Norway concerns all nationals on more or less equal footing, thus requiring a culturally, socially and economically blind actor, finding relevant only properties of the risk environment that partake in a shared experience of danger, threat and vulnerability, or risk to Norway is atomised, particular to certain individuals, specific groups, certain regions, etc, building a one-size-fits-all risk assessment.

There are good reasons to approach risk management in this way. Within this 'national risk picture', the division of labour falls along the lines of the individual departments of State bureaucracy. These departments have responsibility for 'sectors', which are naturally defined by their legally constituted mandates and governed by Parliament. Responsibility is mandated bureaucratically. Each administrative unit is accountable for a portion of the national risk picture, generated through information-gathering and analyses carried out by the analysis component of the bureaucracy, most notably and comprehensively by the DSB. Since 2011, the DSB has been mandated with the task of producing an annual national risk analysis, building on input from the PST, the National Intelligence Service (*E-tjenesten*) and the NSM, each of which has its own sector of responsibility and each of which maintains and overviews its part of the national risk analysis. In this way, the nationally formulated, analysed, composed and disseminated risk analysis is de-constituted according to the bureaucratic structure, then reconstituted through a process by which the functions, processes, personal and professional norms are harmonised. The aim is 'to establish a better and more comprehensive common basis of reference for cross-sectorial planning and cross-sectoral exercises' (42).

The *Societal Security* white paper makes a point of underscoring that the DSB national risk analysis is directed at *large* events, those that require 'extraordinary effort on the part of authorities', and hence limits itself to 'worst-case scenarios': 'events that are relatively unlikely but which nonetheless can occur and which Norwegian authorities should therefore be prepared for. By concentrating on large undesirable events with cross-sectoral consequences the risk analysis will contribute to increased awareness of the reciprocal dependencies between infrastructure, societal functions and preparedness actors' (42).

The granularity of risk is a challenge to any authority responsible for identifying and managing it: risk never occurs, is never perceived nor managed, in isolation. It always manifests itself as part of a system, and hence is structured by the parameters of the system, motivated, supported, governed by that very system. The danger at hand is never objective but enabled and shaped parasitically by the collective and particular values whose expression and livelihood it threatens. By the same token, it can never be entirely abstracted from the system, the whole that makes up its environment. If it is truly a risk to the system, it is only in so far as it is intrinsic to it. If it were a contingent or occasional danger, it would not be one at all. The system is the system by virtue of the risk that lives in it. Like Shylock's pound of flesh, there is no taking only the evil from the body, as the body depends on its own bodily make-up for all it is and has.

Managing risk is thus a highly charged political affair, one in which the struggle for values can end up causing the suffering or even destruction of the entire body politic. At what level of risk is intervention in the value ecosystem necessary? Whose risk? Risk to what or to whom? What is the scope and what are the constraints of the management? Under whose authority is risk managed? With what means of detection? With what means of prevention? Certainly, these questions can and should be asked in settings where power is applied in and through a discourse of risk management. They apply to many cases beyond the Norwegian one, but are particularly interesting here, to the degree that, in Norway, the collectivity whose security is in question is particularly closely knitted.

Moreover, risk is always a risk to another: another individual, another group, another sector, another region. Self-risk management is incompatible with the understanding of danger as another, as external, as heterogeneous, as something that disturbs the safety, security, well-being and integrity of and about the self. Risk management – in Norway or elsewhere – is carried out on behalf of a community of others, a community that is, as a consequence of the logic of risk, external to its management. The logic of management is a logic of othering, only seldom a logic of compassion or empathy, integration or assimilation. The discourse of mastery, the governmentality at the heart of all sciences of management, holds danger at bay not by a counter-tactics that would serve to inoculate the danger implicit in the risk. The discourse of risk management is, like most discourses of security, a reinforcement and repetition of what already is, what the society or the body politic already consists of. Risk management is the management of another, on behalf of another, in view of danger that is external or other. It is the management of another, which, however, is foreign but not quite foreign enough, cannot be simply ejected, or exiled, beyond the confines of the system in which it circulates. Indeed, risk management is the management of otherness, the management of the heterodoxy that often structures and enables identity itself. The risk manager manages the other. This epitomises the relationship between identity and security, between who we are and what threatens us. We are formed by what we fear, by what threatens us. We are confronted continuously by the exertion of control on a system of resources and practices which itself generates danger – in the traditional logic of 'reflexive risk', as developed by Beck and others (Beck, 1999; Beck et al., 1994).

The leitmotif of coordination is an intensified perception of the increased complexity in security problems, not only in terms of technological complexity but also in terms of societal complexity, multi-ethnic, multi-religious, multilingual, transcultural and transnational. The risk management system envisaged in *Societal Security* interprets this rise in complexity, and the increased interdependencies across the sectors of societal management, as the expression of a need for rearticulating and, above all, clarifying the responsibilities of public authorities and encouraging collaboration between different areas of responsibility and both preparedness and crisis management. Both differentiation of tasks and strengthened interweaving of activities are called for through the introduction of the 'principle of cooperation', a fourth principle added to those formulated previously, together with the principles of responsibility, equality and proximity. It forms the backbone of the report. According to the principle, the basic relations of responsibility among public authorities will remain unchanged (JPD, 2012: 40).

As a consequence, 'national risk analysis' will have to, as a function, be comprehensively formulated, fragmented then reconstituted. Risk management will be both holistic and a set of well-coordinated elements. Each department will have responsibility for its own risk management, while, at the same time, the major national risk management institutions (the Politic Security Service, the Electronic Investigation Service and the National Security Authority) will each, from its individual risk management perspective, values, resources and tasks, develop its own risk assessment, covering the individual risks associated with its areas of special responsibility. The key to this system of fragmented holism is a 'harmonisation' process whereby the different areas of risk will be compared with each other in order to establish a better and more general reference point for cross-sector planning and exercises (42).

What is an attack on society?

It goes without saying that the Oslo/Utøya attacks cast a long shadow under which the concept of societal security in decades to come will find its meaning and the context in which reflection and policy on preparedness and danger will be perceived and formulated. This includes not only the heightened awareness of Norway's exposure to terrorism and political violence, and the politicisation of religion and minorities which, despite heartening pronouncements about fighting terrorism by strengthening liberal democracy, has more or less continuously devolved – as elsewhere in the world – into increased government authority, enhanced surveillance of all citizens and a broad empowerment of the police. It also includes a kind of anti-liberal contagion linked to non-nefarious societal security issues. Where efforts are rightly made to retain all threats to Norwegian society under the umbrella of one unique concept of societal security, the logics of fear and dissuasion that characterise anti-terrorism measures cannot help but undergo a 'function creep' towards natural disasters and infrastructural events.

The discourse of security touches all of society. Indeed, society itself is, from a certain point of view, inseparable from a certain concept of security.

A society is obviously not a fixed entity. It is moving and changing, pushing and pulling, strained and stretched by political, cultural and social pressures from within and from without. As society is never 'all in'. It is a discourse of inclusion that is inseparable from a discourse of exclusion. Society is an ongoing debate about what society is, a permanent reformulating of the question 'what is a society such that "we" are a society?' It is a dynamic of power and struggle, of seeking one's interests in conflict with the interests of others. The terrorist Breivik, if anything, considers himself noble, a patriot, engaged in a just war for the benefit of a certain vision society, a vision shared by very few but – let us be clear – by more than Breivik himself. Society takes the form of a question.

Against this background, the white paper *Societal Security* notes that 'the attacks on 22 July 2011 put society's preparedness to the test'. A central aim of the white paper is, then, to better understand 'how [society's] preparedness for this kind of event has functioned and to identify what can be learned from it and necessary measures' that can be taken in order to improve it (JPD, 2012: 8). We recall that a similar task was given to the 22 July Commission: 'to review and evaluate the events in order to learn from them with the aim of making Norwegian society as well-equipped as possible to prevent or face future attacks while at the same time protecting central values in Norwegian society, such as openness and liberty' (Stoltenberg, 2011a). Thus, the parliamentary resolution of 11 November 2011 solemnly declared: 'In order to assure that Norway can meet the challenges of risk and vulnerability society confronts, the responsibility of the Ministry of Justice and Police for society's security and preparedness functions in peace will be clarified and strengthened' (Stortinget, 2012b: 57). The ambivalence about the meaning and function, quality and character of society is here as glaring as anywhere in the struggle to formulate meaningful policy about how to assure the security of society. For what is the society that is being referred to here? What do we understand when we read that society's preparedness was put to the test? What does a society prepare when it prepares for a terrorist attack? How does a society prepare for it? We understand what a military unit prepares for when it prepares for an attack from an enemy unit. We see clearly what a sovereign nation prepares for when it prepares for an attack from a foreign power. We can quickly understand what an individual does in order to prepare for the attack of an aggressor on the open street, but when is a society prepared for an attack?

If asked whether an army was harmed after the attack of an enemy force, we would conventionally count fatalities and casualties, assess the loss of material resources like food, medicine, perhaps fuel and ammunition and, of course, terrain that might have been lost during the battle. When we ask whether the individual was harmed after a mugging on the street, we might also look for physical injuries, then psychological damage, perhaps material loss, money stolen, etc. What do we ask when we assess the harm done to a society?

We would start by asking what a society is in the first place. On this point, there are, of course, many points of view. Most would agree that a society consists of a set of shared values – though many would disagree on what those values actually are. Some would say that a society is a certain contract between individuals, a tacit agreement to respect a number of fixed or moveable norms. Others would say that society is a natural bond between groups and individuals; others still would associate society with social institutions and formalised groups. This is not the place to solve the question of what a society is. We can, however, suggest that regardless of how we define a society, a threat to it and, in the worst of cases, its damage or destruction, is of a very special kind, unlike the damage or destruction of a military unit or an individual on the street. To damage, injure or destroy a society would be to destroy some or all of the shared values that make it up, to destroy the contract between individuals, to crack the social bonds or disrupt the institutions.

The Oslo/Utøya attacks resulted in a terrible, unacceptable loss of life and injury, in many cases, permanent, unrepairable injury. This cannot and should not be passed over. Yet, if we are to measure the well-being of Norwegian society by any of the indices mentioned above – values, social bonds, social contracts, institutions – then Norwegian society, despite the loss of cherished individuals, was unscathed, or nearly unscathed. In short, as a society, Norway was prepared. I underscore 'nearly' unscathed. Norwegian society has changed slightly; it has been scarred (Rafoss, 2015; Syse, 2018; Wollebæk et al., 2012). Notwithstanding, this change has not been at the immediate hands of the terrorist. Rather, it has been Norwegian society, driven by the fear and the prospect of another attack resembling that of Oslo/Utøya, that has taken political decisions to change itself, marginally reducing civil liberties, encouraging a discourse of migration based on the notion of the foreigner as a threat, building traces of suspicion into the social-administrative ecosystem. This has, of course, taken place elsewhere as well as in Norway. It is the sign of our times; the logic of the other as a threat has taken hold all around the world. It flows from an inability or unwillingness to understand security as a relation of society to itself, as a relation of members of society to each other and to society as a whole. It is caught in the logic of insecurity as a function of the other, and security as the prophylactic exercise of keeping the dangerous other at bay.

In Norway, this effect has been only marginal. This is due to the unusual robustness of Norwegian society. By this we mean by virtue of its uncommonly strong social ties, its cultural homogeneity, the high level of transparency in its public institutions, the exceptionally high level of trust in government and its strong democratic tradition. It is not complicated to understand that these are the qualities that make a society secure. It is equally simple to document that prophylactic measures for securing society have far more ambivalent effects: where security-added value might be gained by hardening the relationship between the police and the general public (through, for example, impersonal rules, inflexible procedures, increased reliance on hard technologies at the expense of human relations, information- or data-based instead of human-based governance, etc.), such a decision comes at the cost of weakened social relations, diminished trust, reduced transparency and social fragmentation. Terrorism is effective only when the society (unwillingly, of course) collaborates.

Critical infrastructure as a proxy for society

Obviously, this way of understanding societal security rests upon a distinct understanding of society itself. We cannot open a discussion on the very long debate on conceptualising society, a debate that has essentially carried on since the very invention of the social sciences around the turn of the twentieth century, the primary object of the social sciences being to some degree a continuous re-posing of the question of what society is. Despite this, the contours of a notion of society as it plays out in the provision of societal security can be sketched (Wagner, 1994).

It is sometimes said that a society is a 'community of values'. To this it should be quickly added that while a society may be said to be constituted by the assemblage of individuals and groups who understand themselves as sharing values, these values are both imagined and contested. They are imagined in the sense that, stemming from the moral, spiritual and perhaps aesthetic predispositions of individuals, they are concretised in many different ways and communicated in many more. They are contested in the sense that extrapolating values from the level of the individual to the level of the social community implies a vast field of dispute and debate. Indeed, the ambiguity of imagined values lies at the heart of the democratic ethos. Thus, society can be understood as a community of individuals holding shared values whose substance is under continuous democratic negotiation.

By its very character, this negotiation resists termination, resists being finalised. This is, of course, fortunate: the end of the discussion about what a society is, about what kind of values make up its bulwark, would be the end of society itself. A collectivity without this negotiation would resemble a dystopian collection of alienated entities, spinning on their own axes of self-referential identity, independent of one another, disinterested and, paradoxically, ultimately threatened by the other. What would a more static, stable conception of society imply? It would be a society that could be totalised as a finite body, regulated by a distinct definition, an invariable set of members, unambiguous criteria of inclusion – and exclusion – rigid rules or laws about the socially permissible conduct of one member towards another and, perhaps most importantly, determined by a distinct actor who necessarily transcends the thing it defines. The timeless challenge of institutionalising the management and good governance of societies understood as dynamic, evolving hybrids lies in the fact that institutions are far less supple than human relations. Even the most dynamic of institutions are an instrumentalisation of the human social agility it seeks to respond to.

The governance of society cannot, by its very character, involve the direct intervention into social relations. Societal governance implies the erection of the institutions, both material and immaterial, that shadow the dynamics of a fluid, organic society, influencing it, by persuasion or coercion, as need may be, never directly, only tangentially touching the substance of the society it seeks to govern. Complex State apparatuses can only increase the granularity of this interaction, tweaking the degree of intrusiveness, letting themselves be felt but never directly steering. The State is not the society but, in a sense, shadows it through the multiple fingers of its institutional influence. This indirect influence is one of the many expressions of governmentality (Dean, 2013; Foucault, 1991; Lemke, 2011).

Still another way of shadowing society in order to serve it or govern it is through what is today called 'critical infrastructure'. This is the material (though sometimes also immaterial) support of society's ordinary (critical) functions. Critical infrastructure helps to make the societal functions, the democratic processes described above, tick. As the Commission on Vulnerability clarified in 2000, it is the nuts and bolts, the processes and procedures, the technologies and devices, that assist the functions of society. What makes critical infrastructure, and the discourse that surrounds it, so unique and politically valent is its *double character*. Critical infrastructure is, on the one hand, intimately associated with society and societal functions, indeed, to the point of it being critical to it, and, on the other hand, it must be rigorously distinct from it. To put it bluntly, critical infrastructure must both be part of society and not part of it at the same time. It must mirror the critical needs for society while at the same time remaining abstracted from society, thus, enmeshed but distinct, involved while indifferent (Burgess, 2007).

This paradox is particularly important when the security of society is associated with the security of society's critical infrastructure. The critical infrastructure that supports the critical functions of society essentially mirrors those functions as support, while at the same time being distinct from them. Critical infrastructure, like social institutions, functions as a kind of proxy or stand-in for the critical societal functions they support. Intervention into social relations in the name of their security is not only impracticable, it is conceptually incoherent: a critical infrastructure or social institution that intervened into social relations would no longer be an institution or a critical infrastructure; rather, it would become part of the social relation, part of society. Thus, the function of critical infrastructure is to reflect as closely as possible the needs of society without disturbing it. Clearly, maintaining the security of critical infrastructure will benefit the security of society.

This is also the way the 2012 *Societal Security* white paper sees the matter. It affirms that as societies become more complex and interdependent, it becomes increasingly important to formulate new requirements for 'preventing and handling undesired events'. For this reason, it is:

> particularly important to work to reduce vulnerability in critical infrastructure and critical societal functions in order to be able to maintain ordinary operations. ... A complicating factor is that several infrastructures are connected together across national borders and the task of securing critical infrastructure for this reason also has a trans-national factor. (JPD, 2012: 9)

How can we assure that the increasing complexity of modern society does not leave it more vulnerable to undesirable events? I set aside, for the moment, the claim that complexity brings insecurity. A significant literature around the concept of resilience would contradict this idea, claiming that increased societal complexity increases the resilience of society, since any shock to the overall societal system can be compensated for in the short and long term by other paths of social activity, which in the system's architecture leads to a reconnection, with sometimes productive mutations, of the originally disrupted function (Chandler, 2013; Reid, 2013).

What is particularly important about the conceptualisation of the *Societal Security* white paper, and essentially all Norwegian public policy orientated towards societal security, is that it conflates critical infrastructure with society itself. On the one hand, a blow to critical infrastructure is taken to mean a blow to society; on the other hand, the effective protection of critical infrastructure corresponds to the protection of society itself. Policy formulations such as the *Societal Security* white paper treat critical infrastructure as a proxy for society. When critical infrastructure is protected, society is protected. When critical infrastructure is in 'operation', then so is society. Yet, in the end, how critical is the infrastructure?

It does a disservice to Norwegian society at large, given the considerable societal robustness displayed in the aftermath of Oslo/Utøya, to claim, by name or insinuation, that one infrastructure or another is 'critical'.

Our stipulation would be that so-called critical infrastructure is far from critical to the well-being of society, that a significant discussion could be opened about what is critical and what is not critical to the Norwegian societal well-being, that what goes under the name critical infrastructures might better be referred to as critical middle-class conveniences. In this way, the reflection on critical infrastructure and critical societal structures meets a certain reflection about the paradox of neoliberal society, whereby the normal is only maintainable through a constant state of emergency (JPD, 2012: 11).

Autonomy and complexity of critical societal functions

We have already seen how in the Norwegian government report *When Security Is Most Important*, the question of societal security could be translated into the question of critical infrastructure (NOU, 2006). I have tried to show in the previous chapter how critical infrastructure is understood as a material support for the values that shape the society that is ostensibly under threat, even while these particular societal values – the values that make this society different from any other – are distinct and, therefore, distinctly threatened. Values are notoriously difficult to articulate and once they are articulated, they are particularly difficult to obtain consensus about. This is, of course, not necessarily a bane. It is the contentiousness of values, the discussion or debate about what values are and what makes one a priority in relation to the other, that lies at their heart. Equally tendentious, however, is the way in which material supports in general, or, in this case, critical infrastructures, can be understood and used as means to deploy society's values and to implement social policy. This is the challenge of policy action in general: how can objective, finite, material things and actions further principles? As we have seen, the bridge concept developed and applied to span the distance between societal values and material infrastructures is 'critical societal functions'. Yet, as we saw, even the identification of the societal functions that are critical to preserving key societal values and, in effect, preserving society itself, such as its members understand it, is a difficult task. In the *Societal Security* white paper, the challenge of implementation becomes the main challenge.

In the six intervening years since the 2006 government report, the clear focus of infrastructure protection in Norway became, as in many places, the information systems on which everyday life was significantly dependent. It relaunched the question of critical infrastructure and critical societal functions, in terms of implementation and complexity, and in terms of a specific type of critical infrastructure, which was information technology. 'Experiences from events in the last years have illustrated the breadth and complexity in the work of societal security. It has become more difficult to maintain an overview of the dependencies in play across sectors, activities and infrastructures' (JPD, 2012: 52).

The 2012 white paper takes pains to outline the work that has been accomplished in strengthening critical infrastructure in Norway after the attacks of 22 July 2011. One crucial property of critical infrastructure that is repeatedly underscored is 'systematisation', both in relation to what is regarded as taking responsibility for following up analyses of the terrorist attack, its antecedents and the premises, but also in installing societal security measures in what is widely assumed to be the future paths of security needs. As we have seen before, the repeated anchoring points and central references for societal security are the 'critical infrastructure' and 'critical societal functions'. The first is regarded as the primary source of societal security and its most important vulnerability; the maintenance of the second is considered to be its ultimate goal. As pointed out in Chapter 2, the criticality of critical infrastructure is ambiguous, and highly politicised. In the 2012 white paper, it is directly and indirectly described in relation to a multi-pronged system of policy, political authorities and bureaucratic values.

> The government will strengthen and secure critical infrastructure and critical societal functions. Several processes are already in motion in this work. Both regulations for preventive object security, which is part of the Security Law and administered by the Norwegian Security Authority (NSM), the Directorate for Societal Security and Preparedness (DSB)'s task of developing a model for identifying what are critical infrastructure and critical societal functions, and the European programme for protection of critical infrastructure (the EPCIP Directive) are meant to contribute to identifying and protecting critical infrastructure. These processes should be seen as closely related. (6)

Both critical infrastructure and the critical societal functions they purport to protect are in the opening pages of the white paper described as closely interrelated, imbricated and integrated. On the technical level, in the Norwegian context, the individual modes of critical infrastructure are closely related in their actual functions and the function of their interrelated technologies. On the administrative and bureaucratic levels, where their smooth operation and management depend on inter-communication and interaction, they are equally close-knit. And in the international sphere, where Norwegian national laws and directives require close coordination and harmonisation with European directives and laws, they are tightly bound. Critical infrastructure protection and the assurance of critical societal functions seem clearly to be matters of interrelation and complexity, the good functioning of one depending on the good functioning of the other, and the effectiveness of one individual element dependent upon the coherence of the whole.

A core tenet of complexity theory is, in this sense, played out in the way that the criticality is conceived and made into a core political priority: complexity means complex interdependence, heterogeneous interdependence. Without entering deeply into the cavernous contours of complexity theory, we can glimpse the challenge of its central hypothesis: widely – sometimes absolutely – dissimilar components, in inner essence or their outward manifestation, tend to hold together – physically, conceptually, morally – through an ineffable force. In short, the cohesiveness of a system can be simply incoherent; belonging can be nothing more than a paradox of exclusion.

A parallel and equally mysterious conundrum arises when we shift the level and focus of the analysis to the human beings involved. Societal security, as I have discussed above, is, on the one hand, the expression of something to be gained or lost by a society, something it has and risks losing. It is also, as I have underscored, something that a society *performs*, something it does, creates, assures, imposes, etc. It is having and doing. Nonetheless, this conundrum in the societal perspective is also regulated by a type of complexity and similarly lends itself to analysis by the theory of complexity.

It is, thus, all the more puzzling and intriguing that there is declared and enacted in the Norwegian approach to societal security a turn to autonomy, as a consequence of the *principle of responsibility*:

> An important aim of further work is to clarify that individual activities have autonomous responsibility for identifying what is critical infrastructure and critical societal functions. Those departments with responsibility of such structures and functions shall develop and determine goal and result indicators based on their own defined national goals. In addition, the departments shall have responsibility for coordinating measures between relevant departments and organisations. Finally, the Ministry of Justice and Preparedness shall through its coordinator role follow up if it is discovered that there is no correlation between established goals and the work of the individual department in that area. In this way the Ministry of Justice and Preparedness will also develop an integrated picture of risk and vulnerability across sectors and areas of responsibility. (52)

The intention of these well-deliberated security arrangements embodies and expresses another basic paradox of complexity. The aims of the collective whole – in this case, society at large – presupposes the autonomy of aims of the individual elements – in this case, the individual sub-departments – whose objectives can possibly be partially, but never entirely, aligned with the aims of the collectivity of which they are part. The principle of responsibility at the centre of the new societal security policy foresees a distribution of responsibility through the bureaucracy, according to a clear precept. The white paper formulates the principle of authority as the notion that 'the authority, organisation or agency that has daily responsibility for an area also has responsibility for necessary preparatory actions and for the operational services in crises and catastrophes' (JPD, 2008: 10; JPD, 2012: 39). Realisation of collective names presupposes the realisation of the sub-aims, themselves autonomous, self-sufficient, individually justifying, individually legitimate. In order to serve the needs and interests of society, such naming processes must serve the needs and interests of a component of society, although these are by nature (and by definition) unlike each other. Society is not the same as one of its components, as it is more than each of its components. That is what makes it the enveloping society that it is. The paradox comes alive through a variety of illustrations, many provided by the white paper itself. For example, the hurricane Dagmar that struck the part of western Norway known as Vestlandet in 2011 was countered by a range of operational resources assembled from all over the country. In short, in the name of a political or perhaps cultural community that did not correspond directly with their pragmatic, financial, administrative or operational interests, certain other agencies from other parts of the country, not directly concerned by the storm, became involved. The collective is formed and survives by virtue of components that are not identical to it, do not share its needs or resources. These societal collaborators share a belonging through their sameness indifference, because they are prepared from calamities that will never strike them and because they are struck by calamities for which they are not prepared.

At the same time, this paradox of complexity opens into a moral paradox of its own. The ethical question that is generated by this observation is dramatic: does the call for responsibility – itself fruit, among other things, of the principle of responsibility, a central pillar, as we have seen, of the new societal security policy – constitute a simple call to moral and social autonomy, to isolation, disintegration, disaggregation, to dismantling of societal ties, social integration, human ties, shared values, shared claims, etc.?

What is critical about a 'critical societal function'?

This dilemma of the distribution of resources links to a simple operational – but also cultural-moral – dilemma of its own: preparedness is always directed to something that has not yet happened. It is necessarily incomplete, virtual; it is always a speculation about the future, a suspicion about danger, about an unreality – and a dangerous one. We can never be completely prepared. Indeed, being completely prepared would represent a kind of dystopia of full-out danger being completely present and us being complete at its level in terms of precaution, a hyperwar, endless danger matched by endless defence, catastrophe all the time. In some sense, the unexpected resources provided by a close ally, a close friend or a compatriot are indispensable. The distribution of response to danger is a distribution of the danger itself, the preparedness itself being the presence of danger in reverse. Perfect preparedness does not give reassurance; it makes the danger perfectly present.

Only some objects can be perfectly protected. Only part of the ensemble of precious things that make us what we are can be retained. Only certain parts of our society are critical to society. Others can get lost without society being impacted, without notice, without harm. How to choose? What is critical and what is non-critical? What are the infrastructures that are indispensable for society to remain itself? What are the functions we need in order to be a society? Not unexpectedly, the new Ministry of Justice and Preparedness was charged with the very delicate task of identifying the necessary functions, 'a detailed plan for strengthening and developing the robustness of critical infrastructure and societal functions' (JPD, 2012: 52). This kind of formulation is common to the history of societal thinking in Norway and elsewhere. What is critical? What do we *really* need? What will permit us to continue in our existence, continue to be who and what we are despite crisis or catastrophe? This is the question commonly asked. I have critiqued elsewhere the notion and logic of the 'critical', of the criticality of 'the critical', of what makes 'the critical' critical, etc. The usage of the concept of 'critical societal function', however, raises another kind of 'critical' problem, with a different set of stakes and a different kind of responsibility to us and to our authorities.

> The aim of [this plan] is to draw attention to the particularly challenging vulnerability and develop, where necessary, a plan of action to prepare resistance and capacity to reconstruct critical functional abilities if an undesirable event should require it. The plan should be measured against the on-going work in all sectors to identify buildings, systems and installations in relation to regulations on object security. (52)

The starting point of this shift towards critical societal functions is by many measures prudent: a clear picture of those 'functions, activities and deliverables' which are most important to secure (52). Once these are identified, the work of societal security will be lighter, and the protection of these critical functions easier. It will also, as the white paper claims, form the basis for planning and rioritizing preventive and preparatory measures and will contribute to securing 'robust solutions and continuity in governance and societal functions' (52). As a follow-up to the conclusions of the 2000 Commission on Vulnerability, the task of developing a model for a standardised assessment model of critical societal functions was assigned to the DSB, which established a research and policy unit to this end and began documentation and analysis in earnest. Its first conclusions were collected in the 2006 government report *When Security Is Most Important: Protection of Critical Infrastructure and Critical Societal Functions* (NOU, 2006). When the DSB began its now annual analysis and report on the Norwegian 'national risk picture' in 2014, this standardised and significantly evolved model, to which we return below, featured prominently, its most significant feature being the inclusion of human experience into the analysis.

In the 2012 white paper, a somewhat more two-dimensional analysis must suffice. The 'critical societal functions' in question are fully conceptualised in collaboration with the relevant technical expertise; this expertise takes a marked form, based on a particular conceptualisation of societal functions and in terms of 'delivering critical societal efforts' – the white paper names, in particular, health, water, food, energy, financial services and communication (JPD, 2012: 52). It does not read 'critical societal functions' to refer to the cultural, social, political, economic, moral, religious, even mnemonic and value functions that make a society what it is. Nor does it regard 'critical societal functions' as what are critical to a society's existence and flourishing, and, when threatened, threaten in kind to lead to the collapse of the society. Instead of these, roughly speaking, 'immaterial' functions, the technologically bound approach to societal security that has held forth in Norway all the way from its first expressions in the 1950s until the emergence of the notion of the social character of society in the work of the DSB in its risk assessment model, 'critical societal functions' are limited to 'critical technological functions' which society in its present form enjoy.

Thus, the failure of the Norwegian banking system will not in itself lead to the collapse of Norwegian society. Rather, it would lead to inconveniences and hardships that, indeed, would pressure and test the bonds and institutions, formal and informal, that make Norwegian society what it is; it might damage some social ties, damage certain relations, marginalise some members of society, introduce certain situations or properties that are at odds with traditional Norwegian society. It might, for example, introduce financial inequalities, raising tensions and discontent, or bringing hardships, exploitation or labour disputes. All of these things would then stretch and try the strength of society. They would put to the test what we might actually call the critical functions of a society. Thus, the question at the heart of the societal debate, the question of societal security, is whether the critical societal functions can and will have the resilience to withstand the failure of the critical societal technological functions, primarily technical infrastructures. This is the question that, in general, remains unasked and unanswered. Instead, the question that is asked – and answered – in the 2012 white paper, as in its antecedents, concerns only the degree of vulnerability of the critical infrastructures that support society (i.e. critical societal functions), not society itself. The vulnerability of the critical infrastructures of Norway, Europe or its neighbours is *cast as entirely independent of society and its human members* (Burgess, 2007).

Throughout the presentation of this societal security world, the question of responsibility – and, in particular, overarching responsibility – remains the strongest and most far-reaching concern. Neither ordinary members of society nor societal groups come into play. Society's members – arguably its strongest resource, everywhere present, always contemporary to themselves – are evoked neither as actors or objects. Only that which can be systematised, which can contribute to a 'systematic follow-up' or be brought into a bureaucratic chain of responsibility is considered as relevant and viable to the governance of societal security. The aim is that each entity in the chain of responsibility can become more deeply aware of the potential vulnerabilities, such that this awareness can contribute to better planning and preparedness.

8

Giving and taking responsibility for terrorism

> To pretend, I actually do the thing:
> I have therefore only pretended to pretend.
> Derrida (2004)

Terrorism and responsibility

Who is responsible for terrorism? The question proves to be more difficult to answer than one might think. What, after all, does it mean to take responsibility for a terrorist act? Is it somehow different from taking responsibility for other acts of violence, or for any act in general? Does extraordinary violence engage extraordinary responsibility? Does the 'terror' implied in the violence intensify the responsibility? Does it transform or shift it? Is there a threshold beyond which violent crime becomes extra-criminal? Alternatively, what does it mean to assign responsibility for a terrorist act? What does it mean to disavow responsibility for a terrorist act? Where does responsibility begin, and where does it end?

If someone is capable of committing the, by all accounts, extraordinary terrorist act that was perpetrated at Oslo/Utøya, is he or she not manifestly too ill to be held responsible for it? How could someone with their wits about them do such a thing? Does common sense not tell us that any person who violently murders seventy-seven people is patently ill? Is this not the act of a broken person, a defective moral judgement, a pathological deficit of empathy and a damaged sense of proper measure for political action? While in Chapter 4 we examined the common understandings that lead us to attribute responsibility to institutions of the modern State, we now turn to the notion of responsibility as the expression of individual moral accountability.

We commonly use the term 'responsibility' to frame and address a wide number of daily tasks and activities, obligations and duties. Children learn the word early. It is used frequently in the home, in work settings, in organisations, in traffic on streets and motorways and in countless social contexts. At first glance, the term 'responsibility' has a relatively simple and applicable use. We take responsibility, we have responsibility, we assign responsibility, we disavow responsibility, we impose responsibility and we deny responsibility. Where does this responsibility come from? And where is it going? When is it legitimate and when is it illegitimate? Who has it and under what circumstances can the one who has it give it away?

As an academic terminology, on the other hand, the concept of responsibility is part of a complex hierarchy of ideas and relations that engage everything from legally binding contracts to religious convictions. Philosophers and lawyers often use the term to organise the relationship between individual and collective political and social responsibility, professional duty, legal obligation, innocence and guilt. It is used as a tool for discussing matters of virtue, ethics, morality, proactive and retroactive obligations, among many other things. A long and rich tradition in Western moral philosophy has shaped the way we think about responsibility today and provided a vocabulary for articulating it along a variety of axes. These range from questions of chronology, responsibility for future events and consequences of past actions, questions of liberty to choose certain acts as opposed to the necessity of acting. They involve matters of competence, and whether the capacity to act in accordance with one's responsibility has a bearing on that responsibility. There are debates about accountability and attribution of responsibility, about whether responsibility can be assigned, transferred or exchanged. There are debates about the role of virtue and intuition in accepting or rejecting responsibility, while some historical analyses raise the question of collective responsibility in relation to political justice.

In short, responsibility is a difficult idea, composite, complex and deeply human. It becomes even more difficult, complex and human when we ask the question of responsibility for terrorism, a phenomenon that by definition touches our most sensitive nerve, the deepest sensibility of human experience. Nothing grips us like terrorism. Terrorism sends our understanding of responsibility into a tailspin. It blinds us, confuses us, misguides us. Notwithstanding, there are few concepts in our universe of ideas that have such deep roots in the modern ethos, and in the modern self-understanding of humans equipped with autonomous, rational, moral faculties of judgement.

Still, by necessity or chance, and through a special kind of creation and contortion of the components of what surely must count as responsibility, a series of popular political events become instrumental to the historically inscribed and still evolving understanding of Oslo/Utøya. In the process of coming to terms with the responsibility surrounding the attacks, unavoidable detours have been made, new elements have been introduced, old elements discarded, all in the name of reducing, through a quite considerable set of discursive, argumentative, psycho-therapeutic and psychosocial detours, the complex moral, metaphysical, legal question of responsibilities to a manageable form. What else would we expect? An act of terrorism is not one act among others, and 'taking' responsibility for such an act is not one placement of responsibility among others. Should the applicable concept of responsibility be a simple extension of what we apply to others? On the one hand, an act of terrorism comes from a dark and enchanted place that is difficult for us to understand. An act of terror that is inspired by anger, hate, suffering, sadness, humiliation and madness is not an act that submits easily to legal or even moral reasoning. It connects to forces that run at a deeper and certainly more mysterious level. It calls for explanations of the unexplainable, reasonable approaches to the unreasonable, reconciliation and forgiveness that stretches well beyond run-of-the-mill secularised Judaeo-Christian expressions of grace. It is the darkness of these unseen forces that nourish the terror that it causes.

Responsibility as accountability

What can we count on in times of crisis? Who can we count on? The conceptual translation of responsibility understood as a moral assessment, itself understood as an instrumental, even actuarial, one, has deep roots in both language and in the evolution of neoliberalism in modern society. Its observation and analysis have been the object of eloquent analysis from Weber to Gauchet. In rough terms, an instrumental approach to responsibility relies on the reduction of a given moral duty or obligation to a universally applicable, readable and assessable set of criteria. Being universal, such criteria are thus non-contextual, impersonal, portable and fluidly comparable. Being accountable means formulating tasks and activities in such a way that they can be according to rules and norms that can be correlated or compared with previous iterations of the same tasks and with analogous tasks carried out by others.

The modern origin for this distinction between 'instrumental' rationality and 'value' rationality is, of course, attributable to Weber, who, as we saw earlier, was also a central inspiration for the notion of enchantment at the core of this book. In the widely cited conceptual introduction to his 1920 *Economy and Society*, Weber describes four types of social action, action that is determined by:

(1) purposive rationality: through expectations of the behaviour of external objects and other people, and employing these expectations as a 'condition' or 'means' for one's own rational ends, as sought after and considered objectives;
(2) value rationality: through conscious belief in the unconditional and intrinsic value – whether this is understood as ethical, aesthetic, religious or however construed – of a specific form of particular comportment purely for itself, unrelated to its outcome;

(3) affect, especially emotion: through actual emotions and feelings;
(4) tradition: through ingrained habituation. (Weber, 2019 [1921]: 161)

Instrumental ('purposive') rationality, in Weber's vision of it, contains, among many curious assumptions, that of action as a kind of translation of the rationality into an impact on the world. On the one hand, action in the instrumental or purposive rational mode is a vision of this 'through-put', of the unmitigated and undisturbed flow from the rational intellect to the world, the transparency or invisibility of the material world, understood as a potential instrument for reason and thus simultaneously for its own insignificance and erasure (Nozick, 1993: 133–81). On the other hand, it builds upon a blanket assumption of the use of other members of society towards one's own ends. This means it assumes not only a kind of seamless communication with and between these members but also that the will of the actor, once effectively communicated, will lead to the subjection of others to the will of the actor, that their own will is an extension or subset of the actor's. Ironically, it is this mode of social action which, though it may appear to be the least probable, is in essence what has come to implant itself in our time in the form of certain neoliberal forms of efficiency and governmentality. It is one of a variety of models based on New Public Management according to which accountability is increasingly construed as 'countability' and, thereby, 'accountability'.

The instrumental mode of action proper to neoliberal social and economic thought cannot automatically valorise moral or spiritual reflection. Weber indicates as much in his analysis of the social components of modern economies that the preferred type of economic social action is instrumental. 'Rational economic action' requires instrumental rationality in this orientation, that is, deliberate planning, principally disqualifying moral judgement, spiritual insight, intuition, courage, affect, etc. (Weber, 2004: 12–13).

If 22 July 2011 was the longest day in modern Norwegian history, the period from the nomination of the 22 July Commission, mandated with the task of analysing the event, on 12 August 2011, one month after the attacks, until the ceremonial delivery of its report to the Prime Minister on 13 August of the following year was, to be sure, the longest year. Yet, what is most striking about this long year of waiting for the assigning of responsibility for the death and destruction of Oslo/Utøya is that it was in effect no wait at all. By this, I mean that, while the 22 July Commission retreated into the silence of a year-long sequestering, protected from the gaze and influence of an increasingly politically charged public sphere, a new form of politics emerged and took on a vigorous life. A significant spectrum of explicitly political reconfiguration took place in the space opened by the sequestering of the apolitical, presumptively scientific or at best non-partisan procedures of analysis. This was ostensibly used to find out 'what really happened', politics happening, instead, in the space between what was marginally possible and what was necessary to happen (see Burgess & Helland, 2003). These two bookends of possibility, the limits that commonly form the frame for any dialogue, be it contentious or not, as well as the political force that correlates with the temperature of contentiousness, are themselves made possible, as we know, by the wait for rationality. It is only because there is a silent, invisible guarantee of the space of dissent, disagreement, accord, etc., in short, of politics.

In this way, the one-year wait for the Commission's report opened in remarkable ways a space of political change, spiritual searching and cultural upheaval, a year of soul-searching during which the best and worst of mundane party politics could take place. Also, it was a long year during which the cultural norms and historical assumptions of the Norwegian self-understanding would be rattled to their core. It was a year during which the uncommonly stable and institutionalised Norwegian normal was made abnormal, as it became destabilised by the most remarkable of dramas surrounding the trial of the terrorist, a 'Norwegian' among Norwegians and also a mass murderer. It was a year during which an essentially unchallenged and innocent judicial system, with deep roots in enlightened criminal justice and liberal rehabilitation practices, was called upon to rise to the challenge of passing judgement on a killer who wore his Norwegian patriotism on his sleeve and who had carried out the most heinous acts in the name of protecting his homeland. It was a defendant who not only consciously linked his actions to both political and religious discourses but, as we will see, also insisted on being judged in those terms. It was a year of political shake-up, resignation and restructuring, of self-evaluation and reconfiguration, new institutions, new people.

It was also a year for an evolving discourse of terrorism, a revolution in the understanding of threat, what the threat to Norway actually was, how Norwegians had got it wrong and how it could be recalibrated. Party political adjustments were continuous throughout the year. There were new political cards dealt, to be reshuffled according to the rules of a new political game. That game bears only partial resemblance to the delirious well-being of the Norwegian post-petroleum age, one in which well-being and a sense of gratitude-filled exceptionalism competes across multiple domains of daily life. The economic growth unleashed by the discovery of oil, the waves of wealth rolling across nearly every aspect of everyday life. Like a national heartbeat, the 22 July Commission, slowly but steadily doing its work, was presumably sheltered from the monstrous question of justice and accountability. It was shielded from the cosmetic political shake-ups designed to stabilise the political boat, and calming the seas so that the catastrophe could quietly be reduced to something psychologically, philosophically and legally manageable, withdrawing before politicised judgements, and seemingly sinking into an aloofness to the politics of threat, risk and insecurity.

Taking responsibility

'Taking responsibility' in the English language does not, of course, refer to 'taking' anything at all. Rather, it refers to recognising and assuming the responsibility that has already been given and taken. When I take responsibility, I place myself on the inside of logic of some axiom of responsibility that is already true, already the case, but which I have up until now held myself aloof from, denied the factual basis for or rejected the legal or moral premises for. 'Taking responsibility' is recognising and affirming that one had already had it. Already? If one already held or possessed responsibility, for how long has this responsibility been held? When was one first given the responsibility that one now 'takes'? At the moment of the attack? At the commencement of that eternity which will be the aftermath of the attacks? Were those responsible for the attack responsible for it *before* it took place?

Responsibility for an event cannot not exist before the event exists. The responsibility is singular, pointed, present at the moment of the act. I am responsible for the act as it presents itself to me, no longer as a horizon of possibility lying in the future, no longer as a memory with now immediate presence, but where its consequences, material and immaterial, are multiplied and expanded into the future. The moment after the point zero of the event, its immediate destruction is gone. It is transformed into an after-event, the implanting and rapidly expanding system, streaming through the question of who was responsible, itself transformed in a flash of timelessness from the question of who will have been responsible.

In the conventional discourse, responsibility is never responsibility for an actual act. It refers to a potential act, an object of intention to an act that has not happened but which could happen, one that exists or is happening in the form of the *possibility* of its happening. The responsibility is what exists before the event. Responsibility is not invented at the moment of the event, nor is it even produced by the event. Indeed, the responsibility for the event cannot in any way be regarded as a consequence of the event. It must be created in advance. How, after all, could one be responsible for something that had not happened yet, for a future event, a future event whose empirical qualities could not yet be known? The responsibility for an event can, logically speaking, be attributed only to an event that is at least partially unknown. The element of uncertainty, of indeterminacy, is therefore a primary antecedent for responsibility. Thus, the strange conundrum of responsibility: I am fully responsible only for that which I could not with certainty have known was going to take place. I can only have responsibility for an event whose origins and course are indeterminate, cannot be measured or addressed in an exhaustively responsible way. I cannot be said to hold responsibility for events into the course of which I cannot intervene, cannot possibly have adequate knowledge to appropriately influence or prevent. In short, I am responsible only for that for which I cannot be held responsible.

The trivial counter-example is, of course, clear. What if it were the case that I had full certainty of the coming event, possessed not only full knowledge of how it would take place but, furthermore, had full control and the ability to stop the event from taking place? Can one be held responsible for an event that was unavoidable? Far from being in a position of responsibility to prevent the event, I would then be its cause. Is it, after all, not the factual knowledge of a coming or even past event that forms the basis for responsibility? Is it not knowing the future that creates the conditions for responsibility? On the contrary, it is from the position of uncertainty that responsibility is held and exercised. It is only in the face of what cannot be known and what is nonetheless possible, situated on one end or another of a continuum of likelihood, more or less improbable, imaginable and imagined, but not necessary. There is never a causal chain between a given set of facts and the responsibility for these facts evolving into something unexpected and undesirable, something catastrophic. From the known to the unexpected: if this path can be fully grasped, it is, of course, no longer unexpected. Then, it becomes a path from the known to the known, and by following this path, responsibility for preventing its outcome dissolves.

In the Norwegian language, however, taking responsibility has a different tenor. In modern Norwegian, for a person in a position 'of responsibility', the expression 'I take responsibility' is often a euphemism for 'I resign my position of responsibility in the political system', with one notable exception, namely, when Prime Minister Stoltenberg proclaimed during the political shake-down following the publication of the 22 July Commission's report: 'I take responsibility and I will not resign'. It fell to him, the original protagonist of the enchanted approach to national tragedy, to understand and act upon the call for responsibility in a way that reached beyond his immediate present.

During the days immediately following the presentation of the report of the 22 July Commission, on 13 August 2012, public officials nearly needed to stand in line in order to have their chance to 'take responsibility' for their part in the official handling of the events. All those who speak in the public debate seem now to regard the notion of responsibility with a special set of eyes, regarding intervention as a way of 'taking responsibility', as though the political currency shifts from the responsibility as a politically costly good, so politically harmful that discursive and sometimes institutional measures had to be taken in order to remain unharmed by it.

The Prime Minister had, we have seen, affirmed that he '[had] responsibility for everything that functioned and didn't function on 22 July', and that he held 'the highest responsibility for the police, the preparedness agencies, and for the safety of citizens. After 22 July, this responsibility implied that I took responsibility for ordering this [the 22 July Commission] report' (Færaas & Rosa, 2012).

Yet, while the Prime Minister tried to clarify his responsibility, the Minister for Innovation, Rigmor Aasrund, followed up on the evening debate radio programme *Dagsnytt 18* by assuming responsibility for 'further developing responsibility'. At approximately the same time, the Director of the Norwegian Police, Øystein Mæland, affirmed that he 'could feel the heavy responsibility for what went wrong in the police' (NRK, 2012). In a published opinion piece, the leader of the Christian Democrat party, Knut Arild Hareid, criticised the government for 'disavowing its responsibility' (Hareide, 2012). Erna Solberg, leader of the opposition Conservative Party was particularly sharp in her criticism of the degree to which the Prime Minister carried his responsibility in relation to the PST (Kristiansen & Lode, 2012). Finally, it was reported that the leader of the Constitutional Oversight Committee, Anders Anundsen, affirmed that his Committee would address the report of the 22 July Committee by seeking to 'look for responsibility' (Sandvik, 2012).

Political commentators were equally fixated on the question of responsibility. Magne Lerø pointed out in the weekly paper *Ledelse* that all actors are to be measured according to the same standards and claimed that the concept of 'responsibility' had acquired a new definition as a consequence of the 22 July experience, going as far as to say that 'responsibility' had become 'gibberish' (Brekke & Auestad, 2012). Marie Simonsen, a prominent commentator in *Dagbladet*, attempted to answer the question of who holds responsibility for something by claiming that 'someone must take responsibility that 22 July does not change Norwegian society' (Simonsen, 2012). In *Nationen*, Kato Nykvist commented that the 22 July hearings were an exercise in the agencies and ministries pushing responsibility between each other (Nykvist, 2012). The political scientist Trond Nordby wrote about what the notion of responsibility meant in the Norwegian parliamentary form of government and asked whether politicians should not rather be faced with letters of impeachment (Nordby, 2012). Drude Beer claimed, also in *Nationen*, that the Prime Minister, the Minister of Justice, the Police Chief and the other responsible persons should each assume their part of the responsibility. In addition, she affirmed that guilt follows from responsibility and that it was only Police Chief Mæland who had up until then taken that upon himself. She wrote that responsibility must be brought out into the light of day, based on the findings of the 22 July Commission. Magnus Thue commented in *Minerva*, affirming that the Commission's report must now be the beginning of a debate about responsibility (Thue, 2012). The editor of *Aftenposten*, Per Anders Madsen, commented that '22 July exposed an enormous split between wishes and abilities, between plans and results, in everything having to do with security and protection', then asked whether the Prime Minister actually can take responsibility for the future without bearing the responsibility for the past (Madsen, 2012). Others again were even stronger in their positions with respect to the question of how responsibility should be understood and distributed as a consequence of the 22 July Commission report. These comments are for the most part directed towards the Prime Minister but also touch the Minister of Justice, Knut Storberget, who, as we will see shortly, was forced to resign as a consequence of 'taking' responsibility (Sandvik & Krekling, 2012). As late as April 2012, the Norwegian State itself had considered suing its own police force in order to assign responsibility for the attacks (Bakke Foss & Johansen, 2013).

Assigning and denying responsibility

One did not have to wait long after the shining warmth of the parade of roses before the discourse of Oslo/Utøya became infused with the discourse of responsibility and its neoliberal first-cousin accountability. Responsibility became the central element in the public debate surrounding the attacks and their follow-up, described by one journalist as 'high season for placement of responsibility' (Lerø, 2012).

The immediate political follow-up to the terror attacks consisted of two immediate and short-term forms: a shift in the government make-up and, more subtly, a change in the prestige of certain government posts relative to others. The other immediate consequences involved a set of reflections and revisions around the national budget as part of its normal consultation and adoption process. There was a widely held perception in a range of departments and agencies that Oslo/Utøya and the conclusions of the 22 July Commission should have wider implications for the way that societal security was understood and assured on several levels of the State apparatus. This perception becomes clear in the proposals made in the run-up to the parliamentary debate.

From a certain point of view, societal security can be defined by those who implement the policies that stem from it. The various ministries, departments and agencies that perform societal security, that present themselves as societal security actors by bearing the legitimacy of making societal security policy, are, from a certain point of view, the performative meaning of the notion.

As we noted, the 22 July Commission was named just over three weeks after the 22 July attacks. The mandate given to the Commission underscores that it is not part of the Commission's remit to 'take a position with regard to criminal responsibility or any other legal responsibility in connection with the events' (NOU, 2012: 38). Political, moral or any other types of responsibility were not mentioned.

The question of any responsibility outside the remit of the criminal justice system was quickly taken over by the political discourse. The exclusion from the 22 July Commission's mandate was quickly filled by the public debate on responsibility for the attacks. The Minister of Justice, Knut Storberget, and the Minister of Defense, Grete Faremo, both addressed Parliament on 10 November, nearly four months after the attacks. The Minister of Justice, Knut Storberget, confirmed that 'the framework for the Police Security Service's responsibility is derived from the Police Law and includes serious criminal action that threaten the security of society and the fundamental societal institutions', and that 'the Chief of Police is responsible for the Police's handling of all types of events in his/her police district, among these crises'. 'The municipalities have, in the period following 22 July, had responsibility for the psychosocial follow-up of those impacted' (Norwegian Parliament, 2011).

The Minister of Defense, addressing Parliament in the same session, confirmed that 'both the Armed Forces and the Police's roles are to protect democracy and to create security and safety for the residents of Norway, each within its respective area of responsibility' (Norwegian Parliament, 2011). She followed up by reminding the parliamentarians that the Armed Forces had 'primary responsibility for managing terrorist attacks that are considered to be armed attacks in line with the *United Nations Charter*, Paragraph 51 [on the inherent or collective right to armed self-defence]' (UN, 1946). She affirmed that the 22 July attacks were clearly a serious criminal act and that responsibility for such matters lay with the police. 'The Armed Forces', she said, 'have an autonomous responsibility to secure military targets, even in times of peace'. Finally, she reminded the parliamentarians that the Home Reserve Force today has 'territorial responsibility and among other things carries out missions such as military maintenance and the securing of important objects and infrastructure' (Norwegian Parliament, 2011).

The characteristics of responsibility invoked by the Minister of Defense in order to support her formal lack of it in relation to Oslo/Utøya, as well as in relation to the events and associations potentially or actually leading to it, and to the nefarious consequences that would follow it and indeed had not yet finished following it, would be mirrored in multiple policy formulations and, to some degree, in the future report of the 22 July Commission.

The Minister's assertion of the division of the world into objects for which she, in her capacity as Minister of Defense, is responsible, already a significant division of responsibility between the responsibility which she might be considered to hold as a moral subject, guided by the moral faculties set out and transmitted through the European tradition of Natural Law or, as the case may be, by a moral submission to an Abrahamic God, institutionalised through the framework of the Norwegian national Lutheran Church, and the responsibility she is recognised as bearing as an embodiment of the State and the Ministry of Defence, with all the political and geopolitical obligations and privileges that invokes, themselves deriving from a certain concretisation of occidental modernity and the institutions of legitimacy and sovereign power that sustain and advance it, reflects the way that two fundamental prosperities impose themselves while, at the same time, complementing each other.

First, responsibility is divided and distributed. Responsibility is never global or universal. In order to function as responsibility, as the implicit or automatic assignment of moral, legal or political obligation, responsibility must be limited. It must be limited to certain actors, moral, legal or political subjects of responsibility, and it must be limited to certain objects of responsibility, those things that fall within a given and finite scope of moral obligation. Second, this limited scope and reach of responsibility is articulated relative to other scopes and reaches of other responsibilities, invoking in parallel fashion the subjects and objects of other responsibilities. As a consequence of this necessary relation between two fields of responsibility, the field of one is dependent on the other. In concrete terms, what the Minister of Defense affirms is the responsibility of the police is both based on what she considers to be her own and has an impact on shaping that responsibility.

Thus, decrying that the Home Reserve Force (HRF) has a 'territorial responsibility' implies not only that it is charged with the responsibility of defending the national territory but also that it is resolved to take responsibility for upholding the respect for the responsibilities of other actors defending other areas of responsibility. The HRF has a responsibility to not interfere, not intervene, least of all not intercede in police matters. An integral part of the responsibility of the HRF is to let the police do its work, protect the responsibility of the other. Thus, when, for example, the responsibility of the HRF to concern itself with 'military maintenance and the securing of important objects and infrastructure' is announced, the responsibility becomes all the more complex when the exercise of the responsibility requires agreeing to forge agreement on what maintenance has to maintain and what the importance of 'important objects' should be understood to be. In the ultimate analysis, the responsibility for delimiting responsibility, for determining, asserting and taking responsibility for maintaining the autonomy of what is not the responsibility of a given moral, legal or political actor, is a core component of taking responsibility at all.

Political responsibility as *auto-da-fé*

The common procedure for 'taking responsibility' in a modern social democracy like Norway is the review of the public institutions in which the public puts its trust. The technique of ordering a more or less transparent review of the institutional mechanisms intended to implement the politically formed policies of those who 'hold responsibility' is a common exercise. If the institutions of the State are meant to be a seamless conduit for carrying out the wisdom of the people, as expressed by the political leader, then their instruments, procedures, functions should both be unfettered by political clutter and unhindered by inefficiency.

Reaffirming the 'responsibility' of public institutions takes place in an entirely different way to that of political leaders. Political leaders exercise their responsibility by loyally embodying the moral and spiritual investiture given to them by the people, not only through the mechanism of the popular election but also through the projection of confidence, belief and support, in the everyday – and extraordinary – governing of the country. This responsibility is embodied in part through the charisma that political leaders hold, charisma which is, so to speak, only borrowed. The enchantment of power is both fragile and fickle, while at the same time indispensably robust when it comes to confronting crisis. Public institutions, by contrast, embody their responsibility in nearly an inverse configuration. Public institutions best fulfil their purpose when they are devoid of enchantment. There can be no charm in political institutions. The measure of their success is their tediousness, the paucity of imagination and the absolute predictability of their output relative to their input.

The viable methods for reviewing the responsibility of political leadership and public institutions are likewise fundamentally distinct. The affirmation of the political responsibility is generated, nourished or weakened through public discourse, through unrefereed, formally unfettered, ungoverned, extra-political debate, whose outcome is unpredictable, sometimes scandalous. This unpredictability is the hallmark of its enchantment, and the source of its political gravitas. The reassertion of the correct responsibility of the public institution can only take place by docking the institution to the enchantment of an external charismatic personality: an elder statesperson, or a celebrity, whose authenticity, like that of the political leader, cannot be reduced to any formal source but is derived from his or her notoriety in the spiritual ecosystem of national politics.

On 11 November 2011, still months before the publication of the 22 July Commission's report on Oslo/Utøya, Knut Storberget, Minister of Justice and Police, took the rostrum before the Norwegian Parliament and prepared to give his last speech as a member of the Stoltenberg II government. A career politician and lawyer, Knut Storberget was appointed Minister of Justice and Police in 2005, in the first Stoltenberg government, and remained until his resignation on 11 November 2011, in the wake of criticism of the police's reaction to Oslo/Utøya.

Shortly after his briefing of the Norwegian Parliament on 11 November 2011, discussed above, Storberget resigned. It had been reported earlier that the move had been in the works for some time but had, ironically, been delayed by the events surrounding Oslo/Utøya. He served as Minister of Justice for six years, a relatively long time, all things given (Wernersen & Kongsrud, 2011). The function of Minister of Justice was assumed by Grete Faremo, who stood beside Storberget before Parliament only hours earlier. Faremo, it is probably no accident, would prove to be a far more law-and-order Minister of Justice, spearheading a reform of the Ministry of Justice and leading a rebranding to the Ministry of Justice 'and Preparedness'.

Though there was never any link made by either Storberget or the Prime Minister to the events of 22 July as a cause for the recognition, this did not hinder Tine Skei Grande, leader of the agriculture industry-orientated Left Party, to congratulate the former Minister of Justice for 'taking responsibility':

> I think it's a great gesture. I think it is magnanimous of him to take responsibility. Even if he did not carry the responsibility alone, it's great, in line with European tradition, which is that when such things happen, those who have responsibility take responsibility. I think it gives him credit as a politician. (Ertesvåg et al., 2011)

In the case of Minister of Justice Storberget, the taking and giving of responsibility was autonomous, preceding him and his actions, and outliving his actions in the imaginary of able politicians.

Responsibility in the wake of the release of the 22 July Commission report would also spell the end of the brief tenure of Øystein Mæland as Chief of the National Police. Mæland, who was both politically active in the Norwegian Labour Party since his youth and a highly regarded psychiatrist and civil servant, became Chief of the Norwegian National Police only three weeks before the Oslo/Utøya attacks. Essentially, all of the structural elements of national police preparedness were the responsibility of Mæland's predecessor Ingelin Killengreen, in particular, internal governance, coordination and, not least, a largely dated ICT system. The former Director of National Police was quite severely criticised, casting a long, dark shadow over her tenure (Johansen et al., 2012). This, however, did not shield Mæland from having to shoulder his 'responsibility', 'take' it and resign, even if it was patently unreasonable to hold him responsible for the organisational and technological deficiencies of the National Police, having been its director for only a matter of days.

The political question that his superior, the Minister of Justice, faced was less whether he was the right man for leading the National Police in general than whether he was the right man for the task of 'cleaning up' after his predecessor. The political relations between the actors were complex, as is often the case in the bubble-like Norwegian political milieu. Mæland had held a variety of political posts in Labour Party governments and bureaucracy, including a period as State Secretary under Faremo, the Minister of Justice now responsible for making the decision of his eventual firing. Indeed, in the course of events, the Minister of Justice chose to recuse herself of the decision, implying that her responsibility as a close colleague or friend to Mæland in her view risked interfering with her responsibility as Minister of Justice and primary politician responsible for implementing the conclusions of the 22 July Commission report (Tjernshaugen, 2012).

The responsibility that Mæland himself 'took' was that of his office and the actions of the previous holder of that office. 'I have been ready to accept responsibility for leading the work of improving the Norwegian Police, and felt strong support from the country's police chiefs today.' Predictably, the opposition leader, Siv Jensen, agreed: 'I think it is crucial for confidence in the government that somebody takes responsibility and resigns. The 22 July Commission's report is crushing in relation to leadership' (Sætre et al., 2012). Jensen's position was predictable not from any personal or moral background but because it reflects her own responsibility, an organisational and political one, to her own constituents in the Progress Party.

In the formal hierarchy of sovereign responsibilities, the Prime Minister holds the ultimate responsibility. The reality is otherwise, more complex, imbricated, multi-dimensioned. It nonetheless came as some surprise to many that the Minister of Justice was the first of the high-level government officials required to take his hat and go. As noted, in nearly all Norwegian public discourse, we understand that taking responsibility means what we might relate to the euphemism 'falling on one's sword': responsibility as self-destruction and with it the cancellation of any possibility of making policy-based changes through leadership, delegation, example or discourse that would actually contribute to improving a situation or solving a problem. To 'take responsibility' in this Norwegian euphemism is precisely to renounce responsibility, or at best to attribute it to some structural morality that inhabits the position itself, not the position-holder.

We see that 'responsibility' has a curious double meaning in the 22 July Commission report. On the one hand, responsibility stands for accountability.

It means that we account for our actions relative to others, for what happens in relation to others. It is an admission, a kind of surrender, to the reality that we are dependent upon others, upon the gaze and the implicit or explicit judgement of others relative to the norms to which they hold, the values they are prone to and the more formal regulations or laws to which they submit. This is essentially how the 22 July Commission report understands 'responsibility': it is the name of a link in a system, a link that does not necessarily correspond to an individual person but that can be an entity or an entire institution.

On the other hand, and almost paradoxically, 'responsibility' connotes a kind of independence. If we are responsible, if we are 'taking' our responsibility, it essentially means that we are left alone to our own resources, moral or otherwise. If we are responsible, we must depend on our own knowledge, experiences, memories, tradition, culture, religious beliefs, values, priorities and so forth. Thereafter, responsibility becomes a far more human matter than a formal or bureaucratic one. It becomes a process of judgement where moral uncertainty and ambiguous position-taking are far more the rule than the exception, where the internal, implicit, inherent processes and moral intuition play a far more dominant role, opening at the same time for a far greater role for social, cultural, emotional or even spiritual influences. It is this side of the experience of responsibility that fades to nothingness in the report of the 22 July Commission. Responsibility is never described *in situ*, in relation to the social, political, cultural reality in general nor, more importantly, in relation to the socially, politically and culturally determined events of 22 July 2011. Responsibility is never expressed as a question of human values, of human experience, of lived life, past, present or future. It is never described or interpreted in relation to the ethical or value-based settings where it alone can be assessed. Responsibility is understood and handled as if it were not at all a question of human beings. This makes the Prime Minister's official response to the report before Parliament in August 2012 all the more remarkable.

Responsibility as the incarnation of values

Having received the 22 July Commission report, it now fell to the government and the Prime Minister to draw the political consequences of the strong claims about what 'could have been', a political challenge that under normal circumstances would be considered logically incoherent and morally absurd. These defects did not hinder the popular political locomotive from rolling forward. Stoltenberg began his presentation to Parliament by pointing out that the 22 July Commission had already given relatively concrete suggestions on changes to be made. Citing the report he recalled:

> The tragedy of 22 July revealed the need for many kinds of changes: in planning and regulations, in the disposition of competence and resources, in organisational culture, prioritisation and focus, indeed even society's attitude. Some of these changes will be able to be adopted by the authorities. These are the most simple changes to accomplish provided there is political will. Other and more fundamental changes – in attitudes, leadership and culture – must be developed over time. (NOU, 2012: 15)

The Prime Minister notes that the most important recommendations actually do not involve spending more money but rather in changing attitudes and cultures about risk, implementation, cooperation, the use of ICT and 'result-oriented leadership'. It is not about money – that would be an easy solution – but rather about attitudes and culture, about leadership, those qualities we need in order to 'understand dangers in a safe society' (Stortinget, 2012a). The responsibility for these things, he says, belongs to leaders at all levels. In order to implement the new plan across the board, we must 'call upon the best in the history and administration's history and culture: duty, responsibility, loyalty and integrity' (Stortinget, 2012a).

In these introductory remarks, the Prime Minister takes an uncommonly sharp turn away from the logic and rhetoric of the Commission's report, and the tendency that had become dominant in the year that had elapsed since the attack. That orientation towards technocratic and technological responses to the perceived security situation that was revealed by Oslo/Utøya, but also, as I have tried to show, produced by it, had become the dominant one, even before the publication of the report in August 2012. In a strong reminder of the human response he called for in the days and weeks after the attack, the Prime Minister again takes as a point of departure the humane, principled, moral, even spiritual approach to managing security based on the values of duty, responsibility, loyalty and integrity – not mentioning at all, for the moment, the infrastructural, organisational or other equipment needs, but noting instead that 'the least demanding is to grant money, adopt plans' (Stortinget, 2012a).

The Prime Minister, in his speech, identifies a number of areas where he proposes to mobilise these principles, before turning to the question of responsibility.

> A central question in the debate that has come in the wake of the Commission's proposal is about responsibility. What does it mean to have responsibility? And what does it mean to take responsibility?
>
> It is the authorities that have responsibility for preparedness. I have therefore repeatedly affirmed that I have the highest responsibility. For preparedness,

for the emergency services, for the military, for the health services. I have the highest responsibility for what went wrong and for what went right in the handling of 22 July.

I and the government take responsibility after 22 July. First, we took responsibility for finding out. We named the commission with the message to work independently of the Government, Parliament and the Administration. The result is a report that inspires general confidence. We have received a common understanding of the reality.

And then we take responsibility for acting. We will use the knowledge we have gotten to create increased safety. We will reduce the risk for attack and we will reduce the consequences if something should nonetheless happen.

The fact that the Prime Minister has the highest responsibility does not free others from their responsibility. Following our state customs the individual Minister has the constitutional responsibility in his or her area, in line with the laws and allocations the Parliament has given. (Stortinget, 2012a)

Responsibility exists within a certain distribution of responsibility itself determined by the constitutionally determined organisation of State functions. Responsibility is enabled and applied in a relational system in accordance with the function it holds and the role it plays. Responsibility neither has an absolute origin nor a finality that would absorb all the other components of the system. Responsibility relies on customs, non-juridical norms and guidelines that are self-validating and self-mobilising. Customary responsibility is the cultural interface that adapts the sterile legal concepts of universally applicable rights and duties to cultural particularities of the people, particularities which themselves evolve as a function of changing demographics, social, economic development and technological evolution.

The members of the political opposition parties who were part of the Control and Constitutional Committee of the Parliament were not convinced by the Prime Minister's conceptualisation. According to the Committee's resolution,

the Prime Minister was not clear about what responsibility implies or what responsibility the Prime Minister has for the system failure that was revealed after the 22 July events. These members believe the Prime Minister through his statement has contributed to unclarity about what political and constitutional responsibility implies. (Stortinget, 2012b)

The same committee resolved, with a vote along party lines, to advance a vote of no confidence. A key element in the vote, held on 5 March 2013, was the simple fact, repeated by the opposition, that the Prime Minister had not apologised for the Government's failures during the attack. The vote in Parliament was unsuccessful along party lines (Melgård, 2013).

A remarkable exception to this usage is the reaction of Prime Minister Stoltenberg to the release of the report of the 22 July Commission, when he announced: 'I take responsibility and I will not resign'. Asked by a reporter whether he had considered resigning after the massive criticism that came out in the report, he answered:

> I have the highest responsibility, that includes how the police carries out its tasks. I take that very seriously. After 22 July I have taken responsibility by reviewing the report which is now on the table, which can learn from and thereafter take action.
>
> ... I have taken responsibility for having gotten the facts, for us learning and acting. (Gjerde *et al.*, 2012)

One prominent commentator described the inversion of the Norwegian concept of responsibility in the following way:

> yesterday Jens Stoltenberg turned the very definition of responsibility upside down: He insisted that to take responsibility was to make sure that action would now be taken, not by resigning as a way of taking responsibility for what happened.
>
> The Prime Minister is thus inviting a difficult discussion. For it can be interpreted as saying that responsibility is something one takes for what has not yet happened, while resetting responsibility for what actually happened. (Stanghelle, 2012)

When at last the 22 July Commission released its report on 16 August 2012, a little more than a year after the attacks, the Commission's criticism of the political leadership, for which the Prime Minister had nominal responsibility, was severe.

Two strands of political responsibility emerge in the Prime Minister's self-assessment. The first stems from the official, formal response to the Norwegian Parliament, in which he welcomed the damning conclusions of the report as well as the 'unpleasantness' of the cause. After a brief review of the main findings, the Prime Minister turns to the matter of 'responsibility': 'A central question in the debate that has followed in the wake of the Commission's report has to do with responsibility. What does it mean to have responsibility? And what does it mean to take responsibility?' (Stoltenberg, 2012a). The Prime Minister proceeded to lay out his understanding of responsibility, the same one that supported his conclusion that him taking responsibility did not mean him resigning his post. He reaffirmed that he and the government had the 'highest responsibility' for preparedness, for emergency services, for the military and for the health services, as well as for 'what went wrong' and 'what went right' on 22 July.

This responsibility, he affirms, involves the 'responsibility to know', thus, the formation of the 22 July Commission, and the 'responsibility to act', that is, to use the knowledge gained to improve things. The Prime Minister reviews the 'principle of proximity' and the 'principle of responsibility', discussed at length in Chapter 7, concluding his parenthesis by reminding the Parliament, 'it is the perpetrator who has responsibility for his deeds. And him alone. We must never forget that' (Stoltenberg, 2012a).

Responsibility is a condition of obligation that not only stems from the event but also frames it. Responsibility precedes and follows the act, and, of course, intensely inhabits it. Even before the thought of the attacks touched the life of any Norwegian, implicated or not in civil security, crisis management, risk and resilience, even before the attacks became a reality for these individuals, they were carrying responsibility, to a greater or lesser degree, for it. If we understand the pending attack, if our present is connected to its future, then, to a small or large degree, it is already happening as part of our psychic or imaginary relation to the world: the world is defined as the reality in which a given catastrophe is thinkable, imaginable, possible. The tentacles of terror are not wrapped around the compact kernel of the present; they are reaching through time: from a far-off distant future to the imaginary relics of our past, those capable to nurture and give empirical body to our worst fears.

The criss-crossing squabbling about who bears responsibility and what political or moral consequences that responsibility implies might at first glance seem confused, cynical or perhaps opportunistic. At closer examination, it appears far more like the witness of a complex flow of the responsibility idea to a concrete thing, from knowledge to act, from fantasy to reality.

Responsibility is the enabling condition of the event. It precedes and succeeds the event. Its reality imposes itself long before and long after the thing for which responsibility is taken or given. If there were neither responsibility that preceded the disaster nor residual responsibility, borne out through guilt and anger, materialised through one form or another of adjudication, there would be nothing that could be considered an event.

The terrorist as responsible actor: the trial

Responsibility is, of course, embodied, in a specific and concrete way, in the institution of law. According to the rule of law, legal responsibility is a core pillar in the function and the legitimacy of the State. Ideally, legal responsibility will take over the role of providing a codified and institutionalised embodiment of it. Ideally, legal responsibility would build upon the same moral infrastructure and come to the same conclusions as moral responsibility, but institutionalising them within the political legitimacy of the State. To the degree the State embodies the moral substance of its citizens, it will transform moral responsibility seamlessly into legal, then political, responsibility. This is, of course, in an ideal world. As the trial of Anders Behring Breivik shows, the overlap between moral responsibility of the individual terrorist and the legal responsibility that it is the trial's function to assign him is far from ideal (Østli, 2013).

The shift from the extended jostling over political responsibility for the 22 July attacks to the personal, moral and legal responsibility of the terrorist was seamless, nearly as though the two realms of responsibility had little or nothing to do with each other.

The trial of Anders Behring Breivik began formally on 16 April 2012. He had been charged nine months earlier in the Oslo District Court under the 'terrorism' provisions of the General Civil Penal Code for 'destroying basic functions of society' and 'creating serious fear in the population' (Ministry of Justice and the Police, 2006). Structural preparations for the trial had been ongoing for months, including a complete remodelling of part of the Oslo District Courthouse with a new court room, spectator galleries for televised simultaneous broadcast and facilities for the 170 news organisations expected from around the world. Though the trial was scheduled to go on for ten weeks, the drama of the opening session would not be surpassed, including the long, methodical reading of the criminal charge in its entirety, including chilling, detailed descriptions of the manner of death of each of the seventy-seven victims. Actually, even before that can happen, the terrorist draws forth the question of responsibility. Before the first word is said, he pivots the entire scene and the scratching at the foundations of law, State and moral responsibility which interests us here: 'I do not recognise the Norwegian court or law because you have received your mandate from parties that support multiculturalism' (cited in Seierstad, 2015: 438). The terrorist's exclamation becomes clearer on day 2 of the trial when he is allowed to read out his testimony in which he presents himself as a kind of freedom fighter, a patriot in the struggle to defend Norway and ethnic Norwegians from the onslaught of immigrants brought about by the failed policies of multiculturalism. Instead of a democracy, Norway had been taken over by a 'cultural marxist dictator' (in Seierstad, 2015: 448–74). 'I acted out of necessity on behalf of my people, my religion, my city and my country. I demand therefore to be acquitted of these charges' (Seierstad, 2015: 438).

Breivik, thus, indeed considers himself as responsible, as having taken responsibility for initiating this single 'battle' in the war against cultural Marxism, against the enemies of the authentic Norwegian people that he nobly represents. He is, in this sense, responsible for an act of resistance of an act of war in defence of his people, not in the criminal sense of having been the author of a crime, characterised by the convergence of moral and legal responsibility.

The political editor of *Aftenposten* newspaper summarised the day this way:

> We are faced with a study in evil. A warped idea that became a bestial act. That's why there is almost something logical about the fact that Anders Behring Breivik doesn't recognise the Oslo District Court. He won't stand for the judge as is the custom in Norwegian courts. And if he recognises his acts, he does not accept his culpability. Behring Breivik takes no responsibility for the tragedy he has caused. He prefers to hold others responsible. It is as confusingly turned on its head as is possible. (Stanghelle, 2012)

Furthermore, even before the proceedings could begin, at the moment the court was declared to be in session, another crisis of responsibility, of a different nature, before a different set of criteria, was in play: the responsibility of the terrorist in relation to his own mental competence.

A further nuance in the question can be set out, to be returned to later. If we are to recognise, at any level, the foundations of responsibility claimed by the terrorist, that is, not only those that are attributed to him, which, not surprisingly, differ considerably from the those that he claimed, the terrorist decries the responsibility of 'Christianity' and 'negationists' in causing the current cultural crisis to which the attacks are meant as a response. He imagines the responsibility of every Muslim to carry out Jihad. He is convinced of his noble mission, regards it as a historical necessity and sees a clear responsibility that falls to the terrorist's collaborators to fulfil the project he has started, to respond to the 'responsibility of the West' (Breivik, 2011: 52, 53, 153, 446, to name only a few examples).

Modern States are guided by a principle of rule of law that relates doubly to the concept of responsibility. On the one hand, as the sovereign source of the authority of law, it requires a certain responsibility of all citizens. Citizenship is an enactment of, among other things, the acknowledgement of the authority of law and thereby the obligation to adhere to the law, and to accept the constitutionally grounded consequences of the not adhering. On the other hand, the sovereignty of the State which underwrites the rule of law that organises the responsibility of citizens is continuously dependent upon the acknowledgement of the citizens and of other States. The recognition on the part of the citizens of their responsibility as subjects of the rule of law is a necessary, though not sufficient, condition of the rule of law.

The terrorist, as we mentioned, refused to recognise the legitimacy of the Oslo District Court, that is, embodying the rule of law in Norway, on the grounds that the State sovereignty on which it was mandated was not legitimate. The terrorist declared himself a revolutionary freedom fighter.

He was a State unto himself, auto-sovereign, whose responsibility seemed to be clear to him and flowed directly from a classical self-understanding of the flow of sovereign power: natural law (or God) – the sovereign State governor – the sovereign, rational, moral, autonomous individual.

He not only bombed and massacred innocent individuals. In the words of the Norwegian jurist Hans Petter Graver, Breivik put a 'bomb under the rule of law':

> Behring Breivik launched his own individual war. He detonated a bomb and undertook an armed attack on defenceless children and youth. In our eyes he isn't a traitor or a soldier, but a mass murderer. However he didn't just blow up the government quarter, he also put a bomb under the rule of law. His case threatens to blow up the requirements for equality before the law, respect for the integrity of the accused, fair trial and the guarantee of no punishment without legal conviction. The intention of his actions was to reshape our democracy and our rule of law in order to prepare them for battle in what he sees as a crucial defensive war. (Graver, 2012: 289)

It is one of the characteristics of contemporary terrorism that perpetrators do not regard themselves as acting in an ordinary, intersubjective way, as one autonomous, sovereign, political actor to another. If we understand the modern political subject, theoretically grounded in a model of subjectivity inherited from Descartes and a model of political value inherited from Kant, then that subject is *intersubjective*: it anchors its rational qualities, capacity for judgement, moral values, etc. in the complex relation to other subjects, and is founded on the recognition that they provide. To be a political subject is to derive one's moral and political autonomy from a relation to others who, by the same token, exchange their recognition for one's own. The investment in the viable, legitimate, appropriate rational aims and claims that one supports, to a greater or lesser degree, those of the other.

A civil war, in theoretical terms, erupts at the moment this structure of reciprocal recognition is broken, by one or several parties to a confrontational issue. By withdrawing the recognition of the (other) party, the succeeding party withdraws recognition of the legality or, most often, illegality of its actions. From the point of view of the political body against which a civil war is claimed, the war is always illegal. From the point of view of the party that demands succession, it is always both legal and indispensable. Where the Norwegian State regards Breivik as a murderer, he regards himself as a patriot, preparing a battle, as Graver puts it, against the rule of law itself. The cause that he defended was built around a confrontation not with the State but with the 'State-ness' of the State. This means that from his position as political subject, his crime is not a personal crime, nor is it an assault against a State, for he is a citizen of that State, which he defends with disconcerting jingoism. His attack is against the legitimacy of the State, a legitimacy which – paradoxically – he is obligated to recognise in order to launch his crusade of correcting the wrongs done by the political bodies that make it up.

At the moment of his arrest by the special forces unit, the terrorist clarifies that the action was a coup d'état:

> It's not you I'm out after. I see you as my brothers. ... This has a political aim. The country is being invaded by foreigners. This is a coup d'état. This is the start of hell. Its going to be worse. The third cell is not yet triggered. (Recounted in Seierstad, 2015: 354–55)

In the onsite interrogation that took place shortly after by Norwegian criminal police, the terrorist insisted on speaking of the attack in terms of 'we'. When asked 'who are we?', he responded:

> This was not murder, this was political execution. Knights Templar Europe gave me permission to execute category A, B and C traitors. I believe, I believed, we believed that Knights Templar is the highest military and political authority in Norway.
>
> ... My responsibility is to save Norway. I take full responsibility for this here, and I am proud of the operation. ... In Norway I am the highest leader of our organisation, I am the commander here. I am also a judge. I am sovereign here in Norway. The international Knights Templar cannot micro-manage the Norwegian commander. (378)

Several hours earlier, Breivik had turned himself in by telephone to the Søndre Buskerud Police Department, declaring: 'I am commander in the Norwegian Resistance Movement ... Knights Templar Europe ... the anti-communist resistance movement against Islamisation of Europe and Norway ... given that the operation is completed, it is acceptable to surrender to Delta [special forces unit]' (350).

The claims of sovereignty, of sovereign force and, not least, of sovereign right as a 'judge' are linked in complex and controversial ways to the claim of executing an attack as part of a 'resistance movement', itself loosely justified as part of a 'European civil war'. On the one hand, to put the matter far too simply, all civil wars are illegal, and yet, some civil wars have historically led to the formation of legitimate States. On the other hand, no civil war is illegal because all civil wars find their genesis in the legitimacy of the State, the very State whose foundation also carries the legal substance of the illegality declared over civil insurrection. In short, from the point of view of the civil warrior, it is the law that is illegal, that is, illegally or illegitimately grounded (Butcher, 2017; Findley & Young, 2012; Kalyvas, 2004; Stanton, 2016).

What interests us here is the question of the responsibility that Breivik takes upon himself as 'commander' in what turns out to be an invented or fantasised – a question we will return to shortly – militant, revolutionary body, exercising its legitimate right to defend Norway and Europe against what it regards as threats to it. As it happens, the terrorist, as gifted as he might have been in the logistical organisation of his murderous rampage, was not capable of the philosophical argument required in order to make a convincing case for the revolutionary legitimacy of his cause, and the question of his political or ideological responsibility, to my knowledge only mentioned in this preliminary interrogation, quickly dissolves, for better or for worse, into the forensic-psychiatric question of his responsibility relative to his own faculty to understand the world around him.

Counting on insanity: being held accountable to reason

The Norwegian legal expression that corresponds to the English 'criminally insane' is (*'strafferettslig utilregnelig'*). The word *'tilregnelig'* – linked to the term *'regne'* ('to calculate') (*'regnskap'*, 'accounting', etc.) – is taken to mean 'accountable' in the sense of 'responsible', dependable, normal, even wise. Someone who is *'tilregnelig'* is someone we can count on to make good decisions, someone with a good reputation, who possess the thinking skills, experience and, most importantly, the moral character to be left with the responsibility for a matter. It refers to someone who is normal, who will not produce any surprises.

In English, 'insane' refers to the quality of someone who suffers from mental illness, often measured in terms of the degree of distortion in one's awareness or understanding of reality. The term 'criminally insane' supplements the assessment of mental illness with the consequences that 'insanity' will have for the discourse of law and concrete legal applications. It implies that the person suffering from mental illness is or should be dispensated from legal accountability or responsibility for acts committed or alleged. (The term 'insane' has popular currency but is uncommon in medical diagnoses. Likewise, 'criminally insane' is increasingly uncommon in legal discourse.)

In the discourse of Norwegian criminal law, *'tilregnelig'* becomes a condensation of a medical judgement and a moral one. Whereas the medicalised term 'insane' denotes a general set of conditions of mental illness, a certain class of *medical* symptoms, which is mobilised in order to draw conclusions about the responsibility of the actor relative to a certain action and possible consequences for the assessment of guilt or innocence in juridical terms, the notion of '*tilregnelig*' condenses the medical condition of mental illness and moral responsibility without recourse to the mediation of the court. In the English language conceptual cluster, there is a two-step establishment of responsibility, whereas in the Norwegian one, responsibility is ascribed as part of a medical condition adjudicated by medical experts (see Gröning et al., 2019; Skålevåg, 2016: in particular, 180–201). This medicalisation of law displaces the position of legal responsibility from within the institutions of the rule of law to the institutions of care. Responsibility becomes a therapeutic concept, and the ascribing and disavowing of responsibility, guilt or innocence are regarded as analeptic functions.

The trial of Anders Behring Breivik began on 16 April 2012, nine months after the attack and four months before the 22 July Commission would present its report. On 28 July, well before the trial began, and only two weeks after the actual attack, the Oslo District Court appointed two court psychiatrists to evaluate the mental health of the terrorist and to make a determination as to whether he was '*strafferettslig tilregnelig*'. The appointment of two recognised and experienced psychiatrists was carried out in accordance with the Norwegian legal provisions on criminal procedure on the request of the Oslo District Police. The facts of the case were not in question: Breivik had already confessed to carrying out attacks, describing in considerable detail the planning and execution of the actions during the interrogation. He had, however, not admitted criminal culpability on the grounds, as we noted, that he did not recognise the authority of the court. The primary question that remained was whether he was of right mind when he carried out the attacks and thus accountable and punishable. Were he determined to be 'criminally sane' at the moment of attacks, he would surely have received the hardest punishment foreseen under Norwegian law: twenty-one years' imprisonment. Were he, on the other hand, determined to be criminally insane, he would be released to mandatory psychiatric treatment. The task of the court-appointed psychiatric team was to determine whether Breivik was accountable for his actions. Four months later, on 29 November, Synne Sørheim and Torgeir Husby submitted their 243-page report to the court (Sørheim & Husby, 2011). After thirty-five hours of interviews, the authors diagnosed Breivik as a paranoid schizophrenic, concluding that he was psychotic at the moment of the attacks. Following court protocol, the report was submitted to the court's Forensic Commission, which, despite some internal disagreement about the report's conclusions, approved it for submission to the judge of the Oslo District Court as evidence in the trial.

The news of the findings of the reports created considerable public debate. If Breivik was criminally insane, and therefore not accountable for his deeds, then he could not be held responsible. He would, in effect, not be considered to be a terrorist and judged according to the norms and criteria of criminal justice but rather as an individual suffering from a mental illness, in need of treatment. Pushback came along several lines and from several sources. First and foremost, there was considerable dissent in the forensic-psychiatric community about the ways that the psychiatric definitions were applied in the case of Breivik. Not least, the Forensic Psychiatric Commission, whose official task it was to validate the psychiatric report before it was to be submitted to the court, was itself divided, with a large majority voting that the quality of the psychiatric examination and analysis was not adequately assured. Accusations of conflict of interest emerged out of the insular community of psychiatric experts in Norway (Grøndahl, 2011; Sætre & Moland, 2011). Others were critical of the methods used by the assessment team, in particular, that interviews were not carried out in appropriate conditions (Johansen & Bakke Foss, 2011). Still others claimed that it did not adequately measure the importance of the political dimension of his actions (Haugen, 2012).

The survivors, families and victims were equally upset that the terrorist would possibly not be held responsible for his actions, and that he would not be formally punished. They, in turn, pressed their council to contest the report and request that the court name a new expert committee to re-evaluate Breivik's responsibility for the attacks (Seierstad, 2015: 430).

Finally, the terrorist Breivik, who had read the report in its entirety, was unpleased. He felt that the authors of the report were trying to ridicule him, by calling the compendium of texts he distributed online the day of the attacks 'banal, infantile and pathetically egocentric', and motivated by his 'grandiose delusions of his own exceptional meaning'. As the conclusions of the report became public, he began to receive correspondence from admirers in Europe who pointed out that if he were judged criminally insane, the effort would have been for nought. Taking their point, Breivik insisted to his court appointed defender, who had been preparing the case based on the hypothesis of insanity, to change strategy, complaining that the problem with psychiatry was that it did not take into consideration religion or ideology, and even proclaiming: 'if it were up to the psychiatrists, all priests would be checked into the madhouse because they have heard the call of God' (429). Ironically, the court in its judgement would raise similar concerns about the apolitical character of the assessment.

As part of their procedure, the judges in the case, led by Wenche Elizabeth Arntzen, personally reviewed the psychiatric report, noting a number of lacunae, weaknesses and errors, sufficient in Arntzen's judgement to warrant an additional assessment (Ekroll & Melgård, 2012). In light of the controversy and the multiple levels of opposition to the conclusions of the report, the court chose to request another psychiatric assessment of the accused.

On 13 January, two new expert psychiatrists were named by the court to re-evaluate Breivik. The new report, authored by court psychiatrists Terje Tørrissen and Agnar Aspaas, was submitted to the court on 10 April 2012, six days before the trial began. The report concluded that while Breivik suffered from 'antisocial personality disorder', he was not psychotic during the attacks or while under observation (Tørrissen & Aspaas, 2012). Both reports became part of the court record as the trial began. But the court ruled that the second report, declaring Breivik competent to stand trial was adopted by the court as the juridically juridical assessment on the basis of which the sentencing was made.

As a consequence, the question of the criminal responsibility remained a loosely tethered, blunt object, like the violent effects of the terrorism he authored. It is not overstating the matter to conclude that psychiatric science was not only of little help but indeed led to a kind of unresolvable ambiguity, the uncertainty of responsibility increasing as a function of the scientific ambitions to capture it.

After thought

> The past is never dead. It's not even past.
> Faulkner (2012)

Remembering to forget

On every 22 July since Oslo/Utøya, a number of events, serene and melancholic, poignant and bitter, have marked the passing of another milestone, another anniversary of the attack. The day is typically filled with several memorial services, an ecumenical service in the National Cathedral attended by former and current prime ministers and the royal family, followed by a service on Utøya attended by political and civic leaders. At noon, church bells around the country ring seventy-seven times to commemorate the lives lost.

The tenth anniversary remembrance stretched over three whole days. It began on 20 July with a democracy workshop for young people at the new facilities on Utøya. 21 July then followed with a conference and panel debate at the new 22 July Centre in Oslo centre, followed by a forum of international leaders and experts at the University of Oslo in the afternoon. 22 July began with a ceremony at the government quarter, followed by a religious service in Oslo Cathedral, then a ceremony at Utøya where the Crown Prince and others spoke, followed by a reading of the names of the murdered on the Utøya quay, followed by a reception at Oslo City Hall. Leaders and members of all political parties were involved in all aspects of the memorial, which was televised nationally from end to end. The day ended with a nationally televised memorial concert.

Even those of us softened by the bias of a close sentimental relationship to Norway and Norwegians would have to agree that the televised memorial programme, like its predecessor transmitted with much more haste on 21 August 2011, was uncommonly thoughtful and sensitive. This kind of montage of political and academic discourse, everyman's debate, the voices of children and a cultural manifestation with deep historical, aesthetic references is a formula that is experienced strongly by Norwegians as truth-telling. Its form, along with its sensitivity to production quality, the unpretentious tone, the style of the speech, the timber of the music, were impactful. Together, these modes of truth-telling offer a meaningful and important alternative to the massive and prolonged security rationality that equates truth with freezing the facts. These regular cultural manifestations temporarily mute the numbing nihilism of the State's self-serving, self-effacing and ultimately clumsy self-destructive security discourse. Cultural manifestations like this remind us that the meaning of violence isn't factual, isn't technical, isn't even utterable.

In the Norwegian language, such an organised event is called a 'marking' (*markering*). It is a moment of public or private notice or emphasis given to a meaningful event, past or present, a programme or ceremony that serves to strengthen the attention of those who attend, an intensification of thought, a calling forth of something that is present but also absent, something whose presence can be magnified without any pretence of recreating or re-establishing that presence, of bringing back in any physical or tactical sense the thing that is memorialised. A 'marking' is a conjuring, a mystical, magical, enchanted moment, in which essentially none of the means, methods and messages of security governance are present.

A 'marking' is, of course, a kind of writing. We place a mark in a notebook, on an electronic document, on a piece of cloth, on a wall or on a mountain trail. So what are we communicating by writing on the object of the marking? And to whom is it addressed? To the person, the thing, the event that is not present in any ordinary sense, but one that is being *conjured*. We place a mark in order to call forth that being and to fix a relation to it, to link or to associate with it. A marking is enchanted writing. It is magical communication to the dead, who are clearly not dead. It is an exchange with the meaning of the event, a meaning that we need in order to give meaning to our own existence, our own presence, whether we like it or not, after the loss.

Indeed, to paraphrase Faulkner, not only are the departed not gone, they are powerfully present, intervening in the lives of survivors in many-faceted ways. This includes both the survivors of those who perished, family, friends and loved ones for whom they are acutely, sharply present, not only for the immediate survivors, who escaped death by a narrow margin, but also for those who simply survived the day, and mark it in their own ways.

In the course of this long decade, Norwegians have found it particularly arduous to learn how to remember. At first glance, the things that seemed to belong to the past – the events, the facts, the names – now all seem to remember themselves. On closer examination, it is not difficult to understand that the past also changes us.

Twentieth-century popular psychology has given us the term 'closure', a kind of cosmology that directs us to seek a certain narrative rationally fused with psychosomatic healing through a method of freezing the sense of past events. It is the declaration of the finality of a past event, its definitive sense and the therapeutic conclusion of its (generally conceived negative) impact. We speak of closure in a relationship, the moment of a decisive break after which emotional association is suspended. We evoke the closure brought when 'justice' is 'done' in a legal proceeding, most commonly hinged on the idea that a traumatic event can somehow put an end to its own effects.

Collecting all available information, analysing all aspects and angles, providing plausible accounts to those involved, transparency, clarity, rationality and, in the case of criminal acts, the full and proportional application of the instruments of the criminal justice system: all these things together – so goes the pop psychological argument – will permit us to close the case, seal the files, definitively draw a line between the painful past and the fresh new future that is to be lived in its wake. The closure of the past 'episode', its finiteness, is understood as a kind of precondition for 'moving on', for continuing to live humanely in the future, that is, in the same world in which the traumatic events took place, to inhabit a reality with those events, to be part of the same system of human cause and effect, the same chain of events that makes up our history.

The political career of memories

On the other hand, it is trivial to say that the past is present, that it shapes experience, thought and emotion. Yet, as universally, imposingly present as the past might be in human life, it seems never to dampen the seemingly endless need for memorials, artificially conceived reminders of the past. Unlike the life of memory, which is *infinite*, memorials play a role of channelling, constraining or *delimiting* the past. Memorials are by their very nature *never* about the past writ large but rather about a particular past. They give meaning through the semiotics of reference to a singular object in a way that is foreign to non-mediated experiences of the past. Even though memorials are symbolic in themselves, they are already the product of interpretation and of meaning shaped and determined by others (Barry *et al.*, 2004; Edkins, 2003).

A gut-wrenching process of the memorialisation began in the wake of Oslo/Utøya and, at the time of this writing, is not yet complete (Heath-Kelly, 2020; Talsnes, 2020). Already at the end of 2011, the Norwegian government determined that two official national memorials would be erected in memory of the events, one in the government quarter in Oslo, the other near Utøya. An international competition was organised to select the designs. It was to be judged by a committee made up of members of the Utøya support group, representatives of AUF, experts named by the government and by the Norwegian public arts funding organisation KORO. In 2014, the jury selected *Memory Wound*, and two other works by the Swedish artist Jonas Dahlberg. *Memory Wound* consisted of a 3.5-metre cut through the uninhabited island of Sørbråten, close to Utøya. The selection was met with enormous international enthusiasm. However, local disagreement about the memorial quickly took hold and became both widespread and highly publicised (Harelius & Haynal, 2021). In June 2017, the memorial was cancelled, and the decision made to erect a memorial on the Utøya quay instead. A new architect was chosen for the contract. The other two works to be placed in the government quarter, *Dialogue for the Future*, a temporary memorial, and *Time and Movement* were cancelled together with *Memory Wound* (Heath-Kelly, 2019). However, as a result of the controversy and the international reception of *Memory Wound*, the memorial has become highly recognisable, even though it was never constructed. The high-resolution, computer-generated image that became briefly known around the world, and which is featured on the cover of this book, already gave it a memorialising effect, making it into a virtual memorial (Hjorth, 2019).

The new memorial design features seventy-seven small brass columns, one for each of the victims who perished on 22 July 2011. The design was also met with controversy. Protests began from the first announcements of the construction. These came primarily from neighbours of Utøya who objected to the fact that they would be reminded on a daily basis of the attacks since they were required to drive by or even see it directly from their homes. As one of the neighbours who had helped to save the lives of some victims who escaped the island by swimming put it, 'Both my grandchildren and I have been awarded a medal of honour from the King. But from AUF and the Ministry we get a cemetery right outside our door' (Svendsen *et al.*, 2020). In other words, the memorial was, in the eyes of many neighbours, too memorial-like. Neighbours sued the communal government, effectively stopping construction. The lawsuit was eventually struck down and construction began in August 2020. It was again stopped in November when local neighbours protested that the construction risked causing psychological harm to them. This suit was also struck down and building continued.

The memorial debates did not end there. Already in 2011, the Norwegian sculptor Nico Widerborg took the task of designing a memorial for all Norwegian municipalities. However, as the funding was anonymously provided for Widerbog, criticism arose over the lack of democracy in the process. Another memorial again, *The Clearing*, was erected on the island. It consisted of a large metallic ring, hung from surrounding pine trees, embedded with the names of all deceased victims. It has remained more or less undisputed. *Iron Roses*, another memorial, was erected outside Oslo Cathedral in

2019, making reference to the sea of roses that appeared outside the church in the days after the attacks. Moreover, the temporary national memorial has been placed in the government quarter, close to the high-rise building that was bombed at Oslo/Utøya, and *Terra Incognita* was successfully unveiled in Trondheim centre, adorned by texts written by local children.

To the debate around the memorialisation of Oslo/Utøya must be added the equally excruciating debate on the question of what should be done with Utøya itself. The question concerned whether it should be abandoned by AUF altogether or, if not, how it should be preserved, either as a protected reserve, renovated or completely rebuilt. The national debate and negotiations began in the immediate aftermath of the attacks, continuing for several years. The centre of the controversy was the café building where thirteen of the victims were murdered. According to an early plan, it was to be demolished in order to erase any trace of the violence. However, many of the families of victims and survivors felt that destroying the building would pulverise the memories as well. The decision was then reversed and followed by a series of different plans for making Utøya a useable site, a kind of village, with a memorial function, an educational centre and a place for reflection on the future of democracy. After countless rounds of patient consultation and negotiation (Frydnes, 2021), the decision was made to artfully encapsulate the café building and the remnants of the murders that took place there in a new building, and surround it with new buildings forming a historical and educational centre (Skafjeld & Brønseth, 2015).

Finally, still another set of memorial controversies is ongoing surrounding the future of the government quarter and the architectural and artistic treasures it contains. The debate is equally far-flung, raising important questions about what can and should be preserved, transformed or destroyed. These debates together form a kind of materialisation of the memory-political question of what should be remembered, revised or forgotten (Heath-Kelly, 2015).

We are the bureaucracy

In the aftermath of Oslo/Utøya, the centre-left government coalition led by Jens Stoltenberg, in power at the moment of Oslo/Utøya, was replaced in 2013 by a centre-right government, which remained in power until 2021, when the political pendulum then swung back to a centre-left government. After leaving the government, Prime Minister Jens Stoltenberg became Secretary General of NATO, where he remains today.

More or less all of the ministers and department leaders with any association with the security and preparedness apparatus in play at Oslo/Utøya have been replaced by other politicians and bureaucrats whose primary qualification is – in addition, of course, to holding the same basic education, career aspirations and life experience – to not have held the post they now hold in the relevant position of the bureaucracy. Other major bureaucratic changes include the renaming of the Ministry for Justice and Police to the Ministry for Justice and Preparedness in 2012, and the disbanding, in 2017, of the Directorate for Emergency Communication, its responsibilities for emergency communication moving to the DSB.

As for policy measures in response to Oslo/Utøya, already in his statement to Parliament in response to the report of the 22 July Commission, the Prime Minister evoked a number of measures already taken to address its conclusions. These measures, in part initiated before the appearance of the report, include improvement of helicopter facilities, a new civilian situation centre, an increase in emergency telephone capacities, clarification of the requirements necessary for the military to assist the police in emergency situations, a review of the PST, an upgraded alarm system, proposals for revision of legal definitions relative to terrorism, the establishment of a security centre to advise in the reconstruction of the government quarter, training, procedures, guidelines for ICT and improvements in the coordination of health services.

As noted, about a year after the Parliamentary handling of the 22 July Commission's investigation, the left-centre government fell to a right-centre government; Jens Stoltenberg was replaced by Erna Solberg as Prime Minister. The government proved resilient and was renewed, with changes, in 2018. It expanded the roster of measures taken, some already discussed in these pages, in the fields of:

- *Culture, attitude and leadership*, including the creation of a unit for crisis management and preparedness in the administration and a reorganisation of the PST and the emergency rescue services in the Ministry of Justice and Preparedness, in addition to measures for sensibilisation, eduction and leadership;
- *Prevention*, including a plan of action against radicalisation, training, research on extremism, improved collaboration between PST and electronic surveillance services, a new law for prosecuting terrorists, a new weapon law, limiting access to weapons;
- *Crisis management*, including new procedures for collaboration in emergency services, a strengthening of the existing police situation centre, and PST's operations centre, and the opening of a civil situation centre;
- *Communication*, comprising infrastructure upgrades, increased access, improved technical capacities, better transparency;
- *Collaboration*, including the establishment of a counter-terrorism centre, a reorganisation of the emergency rescue services, three new intervention helicopters and sixteen new rescue helicopters;

- *Police staffing and methods*, including a considerable increase in numbers of police, new standards for police response time, strengthened surveillance practices, armoured vehicles, new more liberal rules for arming police;
- *ICT*, including a new commission on 'digital vulnerability'.

These measures come in addition to the major proposal of a new 'security law' (commented above), a new building regulation, a new national CBRN strategy, a new ministerial strategy for societal security, new methods for government supervision, new management of security-relevant exercises, the identification of fourteen 'critical societal functions' and corresponding governance policies including a new programme for linking societal security to military security, a new parliamentary resolution on risk, a training programme for emergency fire and rescue crews, a new report and law proposal for accountability for those accused of extreme crimes.

Dozens of regulations, hundreds of instructions, thousands of guidelines have played Hamlet's ghost for addressing terror over the last ten years, leaving the gnawing impression that everything was addressed except for the essence of insecurity.

The commission, as we have seen, is the preferred tool of stable bureaucracies. A commission for the review of Norway's unusually liberal weapon law was named several months before Oslo/Utøya, although its report was completed under the long shadow of the attack (it affirms that the law's important principles were fixed before the attack (NOU, 2011: 11)). The report suggests, among other things, throwing out the present law and replacing it with one that better preserves 'Norwegian weapon culture', while adapting to future categories of weapons and the new weapon landscape that comes with them. New forms of terrorism and the challenges underscored by Oslo/Utøya led the Commission to suggest stricter control on paths to acquiring weapons (NOU, 2011: 84).

A commission on policing delivered its report in 2013, recommending the concentration of more resources for both local police work and for adapting to new and evolving police tasks, in addition to an overall 'quality reform' (NOU, 2013a: 9). A commission was appointed in 2013 to review the civil defence regime. Its report was delivered the same year with recommendations on coordination and collaboration of the increasingly siloed security resources against the background of overlapping tasks and demands (NOU, 2013b). In 2014, a commission reviewing criteria for legal accountability, the Rieber-Mohn-led Commission, proposed solutions to the definitional conundrums surrounding legal definitions of psychological competence and accountability that sprung out of the Breivik trial (NOU, 2014). A 2015 commission on digital vulnerability took up the discourse of 'vulnerability', coined by the Willoch Commission in 2000, applying to digital matters

(NOU, 2015). A new commission emergency collaboration was named and published its report in 2016 (NOU, 2016). A commission on police weapons came in 2017 (NOU, 2017) and on ICT in 2018 (NOU, 2018). Finally, the most notable and, above all, the most desperate commission named in the wake of Oslo/Utøya was the one charged with assessing the conditions for a state of emergency legal framework and evaluating under what conditions civil rights can and should be suspended (NOU, 2019).

Knowing nothing, being everything

In association with the ten-year anniversary of Oslo/Utøya, researchers from the Norwegian Center for Research on Extremism (C-REX) (itself an institution created as the result of one of the many policy measures enacted as a follow-up of the report of the 22 July Commission) carried out a transversal survey of Norwegians, with the aim of mapping how Norwegians perceived and understood the attacks ten years after.

On the question of who the target of the attacks was, the results converged: 60 per cent of those surveyed responded that it was democracy itself, while 55 per cent responded that the Labour Party was attacked and 40 per cent responded that it was multicultural Norway that was attacked (Bugge Solheim & Jupskås, 2021: 115). These robust numbers confirm the narrative promoted and sustained, in particular by the Prime Minister, that this was an attack on democratic values and that Norwegians succeeded in rising to this challenge. It is notable that this understanding has varied little over the ten intervening years. What the authors call the 'narrative' of social democratic values, analysed in detail in the article, is a strong and stable one.

However, if there is convergence around the understood 'causes' of Oslo/Utøya, Norwegians are quite divided about its impact. Over a quarter of Norwegians believe that the Labour Party, which was the target of the attack both in the government quarter and on Utøya, has sought to benefit politically from it. From a certain point of view, we do not require the survey to tell us who or what the target of the attack was. The survey was carried out with uncommonly sophisticated methods and scientific precautions. Yet, while answering certain kinds of questions with quantitative precision, it also does us the service of opening up, nearly as a by-product of its scientific pretence, a space of mystery, of enchantment.

On the one hand, to ask individuals – unqualified and unprepared, unknown, unfamiliar, far away in space and time, beyond the reach of shared experienced though certainly connected through a kind of shared imaginary – is already itself an act of magic in the best sense of the term. We are all such informants: we express ourselves about our own understanding, about how we see the events we have not seen, hear the sounds we have heard, feel the pain and the joy of others. This is what the transformation into a science of insecurity does, indeed, what it must do. It shows that there is a transfer, an imaginary, a relationship that is created, a relationship with the scientist, of course, but a relationship with something new. The experience of Oslo/Utøya is created by the incitement to say what Oslo/Utøya was, precisely what the researchers incite us to do. While this is true of any past event, the effect is multiplied a thousand-fold by the infrastructure of scientific pretence, the alienating effect of being the object of method and the end of theory.

On the other hand, such individuals, earnest and honest, willing respondents to such an investigation, are ironically chosen not because they have knowledge of the event but rather because they do not have knowledge. Their qualification is their lack of qualification. Their testimony is the experience of not knowing, of not attending, their knowledge of uncertainty, the witness of cluelessness. The theory of science tells us that in scientific investigation – human, social and natural alike – perfect observation is impossible. For the enchantment theory of security, this non-knowledge is everything. Discovering its topology is golden. These respondents, aggregated experts, are the source of true knowledge about security. Only being nobody and knowing nothing can give us insight into the nature of the insecurity we feel and the faint clue we harbour about the terms and conditions of the security that might be available to us.

Time and politicisation

The responses of the results of the C-REX survey on understandings of Oslo/Utøya ten years on do not converge on another key point. As the authors point out, the results also reveal considerable disagreement on the question of what they call political 'behaviour' in the aftermath of the attack. The authors underscore that the divergence in opinions is particularly notable in relation to reactions to the controversial statement 'The Labour Party has exploited July 22 for political gain': 'While a significant minority (31%) disagree completely with this argument and many others disagree somewhat (15%) or a little (10%), as many as 30% agree to a greater or lesser extent' (Bugge Solheim & Jupskås, 2021: 116).

This finding aligns with an increasingly polemic reflection that evolved over the long decade since Oslo/Utøya of a cynical instrumentalisation of the attack. The reproach was most often laid at the feet of the Labour Party and intensified as the September 2021 parliamentary elections approached. Party leaders were criticised for appearing either as the actual mortal victims of the attack – all but two of the victims on Utøya were members of the organisation, and several of the victims in the government quarter were employees of the Labour Party majority government – or as the secondary victims by symbolic association of the attacks.

In 2018, the Norwegian filmmaker Erik Poppe released a dramatisation of the attack on Utøya titled *Utøya 22 July* (Poppe, 2018). It was a unique film in that it was created in close dialogue with forty of the Utøya survivors. What is more, it was cinematographically remarkable in that it was filmed with one single take, mirroring the seventy-two real-life minutes of the attack. It was highly anticipated, and indeed well received. It was nominated for the Golden Bear at the Berlin International Film Festival, won the award for best cinematography at the European Cinema Awards and two Amanda awards at the Norwegian International Film Festival.

On the eve of the film's release in Norway, populist politician and Progressive Party Minister of Justice Sylvie Listhaug commented on her official Facebook page, in relation to a parliamentary debate about stripping Norwegian foreign terrorist fighters of their citizenship, that: '[The Labour Party] believes that the rights of terrorists are more important than national security' (Svaar, 2018). Labour Party leader Jonas Gahr Støre responded immediately: 'I have two challenges for [Listhaug]: first she should see the film, then she should be ashamed of herself' (Torset *et al.*, 2018). This in turn provoked a reaction from the Conservative Minister of Education and Integration Jan Tore Sanner: 'It should be possible to discuss this concrete matter, namely what means we have for stopping terrorists without Jonas Gahre Støre drawing the 22 July Card' (Torset, 2018), thereby introducing into the public discourse a term that would travel well, especially in conspiracy-driven, right-leaning fora. It would provide the title for a moody and sharp-edged book from 2021 titled *The Utøya Card* (Vallen, 2021), which reconstructs the evolving difficulty, or perhaps impossibility, of holding sensible political debate around Oslo/Utøya at all.

On the one hand, the book suggests that the Labour Party is accused of seeking political advantage from Oslo/Utøya and, on the other hand, that members of the AUF have difficulty in participating in political debate on even ground. As time passes, the terrain has become rougher. Both survivors and Labour Party politicians have regularly received death threats (Strand & Haga, 2018). Research has also shown the degree to which continuity can be found between the way that populist politics in Norway before 22 July 2011 nourished the terrorist's discourse connecting cultural politics and the threat of the other (Berntzen & Sandberg, 2014; Wiggen, 2012).

The Progress Party has explicitly mobilised against what it terms 'sneaking Islamisation', a terminology easily associated with the American-born language of the 'great conversion theory'. This 'theory', which features surprisingly sharp paranoia for a mainstream talking point and complete disregard for the demographic mechanisms of the evolution of populations, decries the perceived threat of the integral replacement of the caucasian segment of the US population – which is, incidentally, neither indigenous nor majority – by 'foreigners'.

Indeed, in the months between just prior to the memorial services of 22 July 2021 and the parliamentary elections that took place only two months later, the surge of cultural energy that we described earlier as characterising the mood of Norwegians had dissolved, dissipated or, perhaps, revealed itself to be false. The need to see convergence in the debate gradually faded. As has been widely noted, the discursive approach taken by the Prime Minister immediately after the attacks was to cast it as an attack on Norway, on Norwegian social democracy, on a certain Norwegian cultural way of life. For many, and there are signs that they are increasing in numbers, unity of purpose and culture presupposes a unified, singular understanding of what happened (Brenna, 2021; Jakobsen, 2021; Lenz, 2018; Notaker, 2021).

The continued rights and responsibilities of the terrorist

As part of the recent population survey cited above, respondents were asked whether Oslo/Utøya was the work of a 'crazy person' or purely 'ideological': they essentially answered 'yes' to both (90 per cent and 80 per cent, respectively). As the researchers point out, this can be taken to mean that Norwegians do not accept that the two alternatives are mutually exclusive as was the definitive presumption of the Norwegian courts as part of determining whether the terrorist was to be held accountable or not for his deeds (Bugge Solheim & Jupskås, 2021: 114).

In the years since his detention, Breivik has taken clear responsibility for his own well-being, availing himself of the rights and principles that he knows protect him and to which he, as a mass murderer, has access to. He has made comprehensive use of the liberal, rights-based legal system that sentenced him to 'preventive detention' for a period of twenty-one years, the most severe punishment available in Norway. In March 2016, Breivik sued the Norwegian government on two points. The first was for the 'inhuman and undignified living conditions' inflicted upon him in the terms of his imprisonment. These were claimed to violate the terms of the European Charter of Human Rights. Skien prison was, as a consequence, required to improve the conditions of incarceration on several points, and to pay Breivik's legal costs. The second was a claim to the violation of his privacy. This part of the suit was rejected.

Breivik's sentence of twenty-one years' preventive detention provides for a minimum incarceration of ten years, after which he has the right to request release on parole one time per year. On 18 January 2022, the handling of the first such request began.

After his client greeted the court with the traditional Nazi salute, wearing right extremist markings on his clothes and bag, and showing ideological posters to photographers, the court-appointed attorney commented to the press that the scene was, as before, carefully planned. The terrorist's one-hour statement to the court was a general presentation of his extreme views, a more targeted justification for the political nature of what he had done at Oslo/Utøya and an appeal to be let free on parole. His arguments were described by the prosecutor as 'totally unrealistic and not anchored in reality' (Foss, 2022b). A court-appointed psychiatrist who had examined Breivik before the hearing presented her conclusions that Breivik remained a high risk (Foss, 2022a; Hanssen, 2022).

Finally, in the ten years and more that have elapsed since the trial, the incongruous ambiguity surrounding the sanitary and legal status of the mass murderer has not been clarified. Following his conviction, he was imprisoned in an isolated suite in a high-security block of Skien prison, close to Oslo. In March 2022, he was transferred to Ringerike prison, located on the banks of Tyrifjorden, ten kilometres away and in plain view of Utøya, and under the same security conditions.

In the ten years since his incarceration, Breivik has received only three visitors, a military chaplain every two weeks, the writer and historian Matthias Gardell and his mother Wenche Behring Breivik, who visited him several times and maintained telephone and letter correspondence with him until her death by cancer in 2013. One week before she passed, she visited the terrorist one last time 'in order to say goodbye'. During that meeting, the terrorist was permitted to enter the visitors room and physically hold his mother in his arms and bid her farewell.

In the end

This book's argument is a metaphysical one, but it's a metaphysics made for children: the past is called past because it cannot be changed, cannot be 'avoided'. If there is one clear, material, concrete or real thing one can say about the past, it is unchangeable. All other definitions of the past are variable, contingent, dependent, relational, perspectival. Everything can be avoided, everything can be changed, done differently, thought differently, lived differently – except the past.

On 13 August 2012, just over a year after Oslo/Utøya, a half-black front page of the daily *Aftenposten* announced three bullet-pointed results of the report of the 22 July Commission. A sombre Commission leader, Alexandr Bech Gjørv, appears against the black background, equally ghostly in her gaze, the eyes of someone who has been to the precipice and has seen what would, could and should have been. The headline screams:

22 July Commission
- The bomb attack could have been avoided
- The police could have been on Utøya sooner
- Many lives could have been saved.

Epistemologically speaking, these claims have the same truth value as 'Napoleon could have been victorious at Waterloo'. They are exercises in counter-factual history. Their claims are absolutely valid and without any value added whatsoever, like the Asimovian tale of the chimpanzee locked in a room with a typewriter who, given a long enough passage of time – thousands or millions of years – will have typed all of Shakespeare's works, the *Bible*, the genome sequencing, the theory of general relativity, etc. Everything is possible.

Counter-factual historical claims are meta-stories not about what should have happened but about the infinite variety of things that could have happened. How to tell the story of what is unresolved? From the moment Jens Stoltenberg unilaterally declared before the Norwegian Parliament that the report of the 22 July Commission was henceforth the 'shared narrative' of Oslo/Utøya (Stortinget, 2012d), the absurdity of the commons has only become more acute and more poignant (see Kvinnsland, 2014).

Of all the ways one can make empirically untrue claims – to say that it is Thursday when it is Wednesday, that I am sipping coffee in Oslo when I am sleeping in my bed in Paris, that it is raining when the streets are dry – the one exemplified by the 22 July Commission, but practised even more effectively by many others, is that the past should have been different, should have been something it wasn't. On those grounds, the 22 July Commission points a condemning finger of guilt at individuals inside and outside the security apparatus, accusing them of being responsible for death and destruction based on a past that the Commission can imagine could have been different. This without any certainty that it would have been different.

All ambitions to truth aside, the actual truth value of the 22 July Commission's claims is of little interest. The function of the Commission, like all commissions of its kind, is not to provide truth, neither about the past nor the future. This Commission and its report, as many have pointed out, was *performative*. It played a therapeutic, political role. That role was to stabilise the security problem created by Oslo/Utøya, not to solve one of which it was a result, to manage security expectations and fears on the basis of something that happened.

The 22 July Commission also did its part in *creating* security threats, not only in the obvious imaginary sense, by setting aflame the insecurities of a generation of Norwegians by scrupulously documenting everything they might potentially consider being afraid of, but also by actually distracting the entire bureaucracy by inciting it to address, plan for, equip and supply, train and prepare, for an event that has *already happened*, and which, given its overwhelming uniqueness and complete dependence on being *unthinkable*, will never happen again.

More importantly, as any security 'expert' will confirm, the Commission's report is also a guidebook for how future terrorists can avoid improved routines, upgraded equipment, hardened infrastructure, sharpened training. In practical terms, the 22 July Commission report is an anti-guidebook on how to attack Norway. For this reason, it was not given a secret classification in order to avoid this challenge. Had it not been totally public, it would have been impossible for it to play out its soul-cleansing performative function.

This is poor consolation. Security cannot be thought because the thought of security is the solicitation of insecurity. It is the admission that insecurity is an option. And if insecurity can be envisaged, it is already too late – we are already lost. To riff on Carl Schmitt: 'Whoever says "security" is lying'. Only those who never ask themselves the question of security will ever have a chance at security.

The equation is simple and brutal: we cannot prepare for the unthinkable and yet only the unthinkable can hurt us. What is already thought, already possible, has already attacked us in our imagination. Its damage is already done; we have already suffered its pains in the form of the anxieties that shape what is real to us. 'I anguish, therefore I am' is the Cartesian formula for the new millennium.

While it is true that the 22 July Commission's report, like its numerous sister commission reports made in its image, does not do nothing, it has little or no consequences for the security of Norwegians. This is not its fault. It does, however, carry a stunning message about the disenchantment of terrorism. It does its best to remove the transcendental horror, the fear, the anguish and the sadness from all sides of the story, replacing them with mechanical, procedural, technocratic, organisational solutions to the deepest challenges of our spiritual beings.

And yet, this is the only coherent claim that can be made: only the poorest, least imaginative, most sterile form of hindsight can assume the almighty position of affirming, with self-certainty, that there exists a reality in which Oslo/Utøya would not have happened. The metaphysical or theological scandal that this hubris implies is redoubled by the claim that that world is, in fact, the world in which Oslo/Utøya would not have happened.

Only the most naive, history-less, politically obsessed thinker can take the position that all harm necessarily engages responsibility, and that the absence of harm implies the absence of responsibility. This idea, that the normal state of the universe is one organised by a kind of logical perfection in moral judgement, characterised by emotional indifference and spiritual ambivalence, is untenable.

Among the many treasures of the Norwegian language is one that may give us comfort in the face of the aporia of terrorism and the force of the unthinkable: *etterpåklokskap* (hindsight). It's an idea that appears in one form or another in virtually all Western languages, referring to the ability to see more clearly looking backwards in time. Clothed in the Norwegian language, it means in literal terms 'wisdom after the fact'. What the term hauntingly reminds us, in the charm of its literalness, is that all wisdom is indeed retrospective. Hegel said it in a bit more of an inspired way in the last pages of his *Philosophy of History*: 'the Owl of Minerva flies at twilight'. In other words, it is at the end of the world that we at last can have full knowledge of it (Hegel, 1991b).

Blame for the frustrating and profoundly human insight that knowledge always comes too late is by no means the fault of the 22 July Commission or other similar investigative commissions whose political mission it is to right the national ship, as it sails perilously close to the precipice of not being in full control, through full knowledge and full understanding. For better or worse, the unfortunate, unofficial activity of party politics consists of continuing the project of reassuring us that everything is going to be fine. The sober, respectable, predictable, inoffensive members of a carefully curated committee, tasked with creating a sensible report, not too long, not too difficult, words that will clarify, codify and comfort, carefully shaping the thought of Oslo/Utøya into something credible, manageable and, above all, remembnerable, have accomplished with honour their task. The resulting report fits into an A4 format that slips neatly into the sober, faux-leather briefcase of a humble and discrete bureaucrat.

Be that as it may, people are not duped. Even while wanting to be comforted by reassurances that the world is indeed what it seems, and exists for our benefit, that anything standing in the way of this is simply an anomaly that can be corrected through the even-handed work of a well-ordered investigative commission, even so, there is a splinter in the mind of every human, certainly every Norwegian, that something is not right. It is not the thinkable that can hurt us, it is the unthinkable.

The 22 July Commission report is just such a tidy and discreet book-length document, an easy day's read. Yet, where the words and sentences that make up the Commission's report have a beginning, a middle and an end, discrete and clear, just like the measures they prescribe that hold a kind of manageable wholeness and completion, Oslo/Utøya has no beginning, middle or end. Just ask its survivors. It has no past deep enough to be called its origin. It has no middle because for anyone who had any experience at all of it, it is happening *right now*, as I type these words, it lies in my own fingers, it is in the hands and bodies and lives and relations of everyone who was touched by it. And the insecurity caused by Oslo/Utøya has no end.

Every day of our lives is hardened and made heavier by the unbearable lightness of disenchantment, a nearly imperceptable force that seeks to make secure a life that goes beyond its very reach. Paradoxically, its finite force comes from within our infinite selves, pretending to protect us from threats that are themselves endless.

Alas, the only life this force can protect is the life made in its own bounded image, already disenchanted.

Still, the sprouts of enchanted life will push up again through the heavy soil of time, carrying with them both wonderment and danger.

References

9/11 Commission (2004) *The 9/11 Commission Report: Final Report of the National Commission on Terrorist Attacks upon the United States* (New York City: W.W. Norton & Company).

Aakvaag, Helene Flood, Siri Thoresen, Tore Wentzel-Larsen, Grete Dyb & Ole Kristian Hjemdal (2014) 'Shame and guilt in the aftermath of terror: The Utøya Island study', *Journal of Traumatic Stress*, 27(5): 618–21.

Acharya, Amitav & Barry Buzan (2019) *The Making of Global International Relations* (Cambridge: Cambridge University Press).

Ahmed, Akbar (2005) *After Terror: Promoting Dialogue among Civilizations* (Cambridge: Polity).

Anderson, Benedict R. (2006) *Imagined Communities: Reflections on the Origin and Spread of Nationalism* (London/New York: Verso).

Anderson, Eric, Mark Burgess & Alva Couch (2002) *Selected Papers in Network and System Administration* (New York: Wiley).

Andreassen, Odd G., Elisabeth Aspaker, Tron Erik Hovind, Svein Erik Lysgaard, Anders Mjelde, Ann-Kristin Olsen, Bård Vegar Solhjell, Sunde Stensønes, Tamnes Hjalmar Inge, Rolf Skjelland, Espen Heløe, Gunnar Stenersen, Espen Leirud & Atle Tangen (2000) *Et nytt forsvar [A New Defence]* (Oslo: Statens forvaltningstjeneste).

Andrews, Molly, Catarina Kinnvall & Kristen Monroe (2015) 'Narratives of (in) security: Nationhood, culture, religion, and gender. Introduction to the special issue', *Political Psychology*, 36(2): 141–9.

Bakke Foss, Andreas (2022a) 'Har vurdert Breivik minst syv ganger siden 2011: Dette mener hun er risikoen for vold dersom terroristen løslates på prøve [Has evaluated Breivik seven times since 2011: This is what she believes is the risk if the terrorist is released]', *Aftenposten*, 14 January.

Bakke Foss, Andreas (2022b) 'Aktor etter Breiviks forklaring: – Totalt urealistisk og ikke forankret i virkeligheten [Prosecutor after Breivik's statement: Totally unrealistic and not anchored in reality]', *Aftenposten*, 18 January.

Bakke Foss, Andreas & Per Anders Johansen (2013) 'Politiets Utøya-aksjon kan havne i retten [The police's Utøya operation can end up in court]', *Aftenposten*, 5 April.

Balakrishnan, Gopal (1996) *Mapping the Nation* (London: Verso).

Baldwin, David A. (1997) 'The concept of security', *Review of International Studies*, 23(1): 5–26.

Balzacq, Thierry (ed.) (2010) *On Securitization: The Design and Evolution of Security Problems* (London: Routledge).

Bangstad, Sindre (2014) *Anders Breivik and the Rise of Islamophobia* (London: Zed Books).
Bangstad, Sindre (2016) 'Norwegian right-wing discourses: Extremism post-Utøya', in *Fear of Muslims? Boundaries of Religious Freedom: Regulating Religion in Diverse Societies*, edited by Pratt, Douglas & Rachel Woodlock (Munich: Springer): 231–50.
Barry, John, Brian Baxter & Richard Dunphy (2004) *Europe, Globalization and Sustainable Development* (London: Routledge).
Basaran, Tugba (2008) 'Security, law, borders: Spaces of exclusion', *International Political Sociology*, 2(4): 339–54.
Beck, Ulrich (1992 [1986]) *Risk Society: Towards a New Modernity* (London: SAGE).
Beck, Ulrich (1999) *World Risk Society* (Cambridge: Blackwell).
Beck, Ulrich, Anthony Giddens & Scott Lash (1994) *Reflexive Modernization: Politics, Tradition and Aesthetics in the Modern Social Order* (Stanford: Stanford University Press).
Beetham, David (1987) *Bureaucracy* (Minneapolis: University of Minnesota Press).
Bellanova, Rocco & Marieke de Goede (2022) 'The algorithmic regulation of security: An infrastructural perspective', *Regulation & Governance*, 16(1): 102–18.
Benjamin, Walter (1968) 'The work of art in the age of mechanical reproduction', in *Illuminations: Essays and Reflections*, edited by Arendt, Hannah (New York: Harcourt Brace Jovanavich): 217–51.
Benjamin, Walter (1978) 'Critique of violence', in *Reflections*, edited by Demetz, Paul (New York: Harcourt Brace Jovanavich): 277–300.
Beres, Louis Rene (2019) *Terrorism and Global Security: The Nuclear Threat* (London: Routledge).
Berlant, Lauren Gail (2011) *Cruel Optimism* (Durham: Duke University Press).
Berman, Paul (2004) *Terror and Liberalism* (New York: W.W. Norton & Company).
Berntzen, Lars Erik & Sveinung Sandberg (2014) 'The collective nature of lone wolf terrorism: Anders Behring Breivik and the anti-Islamic social movement', *Terrorism and Political Violence*, 26(5): 759–79.
Bigo, Didier (2001) 'The Möbius ribbon of internal and external security(ies)', in *Identities, Borders, Orders: Rethinking International Relations Theory*, edited by Lapid, Yosef, David Jacobson & Mathias Albert (Minneapolis: University of Minnesota Press): 91–116.
Bigo, Didier (2002) 'Border regimes, police cooperation and security in an enlarged Europe', in *Europe Unbound: Enlarging and Reshaping the Boundaries of the European Union*, edited by Zielonka, Jan (London: Routledge): 213–39.
Bigo, Didier (2002) 'Security and immigration: Toward a critique of the governmentality of unease', *Alternatives*, 27: 63–92.
Bigo, Didier (2006) 'Internal and external aspects of security', *European Security*, 15: 385–404.
Bigo, Didier & Julien Jeandesboz (2010) *The EU and the European Security Industry: Questioning the 'Public–Private' Dialogue* (Brussels: CEPS).
Bigo, Didier, Laurent Bonelli, Dario Chi & Christian Olsson (2007) 'Mapping the field of the EU internal security agencies', in *The Field of the EU Internal Security Agencies*, edited by Bigo, Didier (Paris: L'Harmattan): 5–66.
Bigo, Didier, Philippe Bonditti, Julien Jeandesboz & Francesco Ragazzi (2008) *Security Technologies and Society: A State of the Art on Security, Technology, Borders and Mobility* (Paris: Centre d'étude des conflits).

Bjørgum, Lena (2010) *Samordning og samvirke for samfunnssikkerhet. En studie av prosessen rundt St.meld. 22 (2007–2008) 'Samfunnssikkerhet, Samvirke og Samordning'* [Coordination and Collaboration for Societal Security: A Study of the Process surrounding Parliamentary Resolution 22 (2007–2008) 'Societal Security, Collaboration and Coordination'] (Bergen: Universitetet i Bergen).

Black, Holly (2019) *The Wicked King: Folk of the Air* (New York: Little, Brown and Company).

Borchgrevink, Aage Storm (2013) *A Norwegian Tragedy: Anders Behring Breivik and the Massacre on Utøya* (London: Polity).

Breivik, Anders Behring (2011) 2083: A European Declaration of Independence, Internet Archive.

Brekke, Anders & Gunn Evy Auestad (2012) ' "Ansvar" har blitt et svadabegrep ["Responsibility" has become gibberish]', *www.nrk.no*, 14 August.

Brenna, Tonja (2021) *22. juli og alle dagene etterpå [22 July and All the Days that Followed]* (Oslo: Adlibris).

Bromark, Stian (2014) *Massacre in Norway: The 2011 Terror Attacks on Oslo and the Utøya Youth Camp* (Lincoln: Potomac Books).

Brown, Wendy (2015) *Undoing the Demos: Neoliberalism's Stealth Revolution* (Brooklyn: Zone Books).

Bubandt, Nils (2005) 'Vernacular security: The politics of feeling safe in global, national and local worlds', *Security Dialogue*, 36(3): 275–96.

Bugge Solheim, Øyvind & Anders Ravik Jupskås (2021) 'Consensus or conflict? A survey analysis of how Norwegians interpret the July 22, 2011 attacks a decade later', *Perspectives on Terrorism*, 15(3): 109–31.

Burgess, J. Peter (2000) 'Maktens begrep, begrepets makt [The concept of power, the power of the concept]', in *Maktens strateger [The Strategists of Power]*, edited by Neumann, Iver B. & Inger-Johanna Sand (Oslo: Pax Forlag): 167–90.

Burgess, J. Peter (2001) 'Learning to be Norwegian: Nation-building as cultural pedagogy from Aasen to Slagstad', in *Culture and Rationality: European Frameworks of Norwegian Identity* (Kristiansand: Norwegian Academic Press): 39–67.

Burgess, J. Peter (2007) 'Social values and material threat: The European programme for critical infrastructures protection', *International Journal of Critical Infrastructures*, 3(3/4): 471–86.

Burgess, J. Peter (2008) *Human Values and Security Technologies* (Oslo: International Peace Research Institute).

Burgess, J. Peter (2009a) *Cultural Values in Risk Assessment* (Brussels: CHALLENGE/Centre for European Policy Studies).

Burgess, J. Peter (2009b) 'There is no European security, only European securities', *Cooperation and Conflict*, 44(3): 309–28.

Burgess, J. Peter (2010) 'The value of security', in *Europe's 21st Century Challenge: Delivering Liberty*, edited by Bigo, Dider, Sergio Carrera, Elspeth Guild & R.B.J. Walker (London: Ashgate): 251–62.

Burgess, J. Peter (2011) *The Ethical Subject of Security: Geopolitical Reason and the Threat against Europe* (London: Routledge).

Burgess, J. Peter (2012) *The Societal Impact of Security Research* (Oslo: PRIO).

Burgess, J. Peter (2014) *The Future of Security Research for the Social Sciences and Humanities* (Strasbourg: European Science Foundation).

Burgess, J. Peter (2015) 'An ethics of security', in *Transformations of Security Studies: Dialogues, Diversity and Discipline*, edited by Schlag, Gabi, Julian Junk & Christopher Daase (London: Routledge): 94–108.

Burgess, J. Peter (2019) 'The insecurity of critique', *Security Dialogue*, 50(1): 95–111.
Burgess, J. Peter (2020) 'Epilogue: Security without society?', in *Nordic Societal Security*, edited by Rinhard, Mark (London: Routledge): 235–50.
Burgess, J. Peter (2021) 'Security and temporality: Heidegger's fears', *New Perspectives*, 29(2): 128–43.
Burgess, J. Peter & Frode Helland (2003) 'Som det egentlig var? Det egne og det andre i 1800-tallets kulturhistoriografi [As it actually was? The selfsame and the other in nineteenth-century cultural historiography]', in *Kulturforskning [Cultural Research]*, edited by Hodne, Bjarne & Randi Sæbøe (Oslo: Universitetsforlaget): 19–28.
Burke, Edmnud (2008) *A Philosophical Enquiry into the Origin of our Ideas of the Sublime and Beautiful* (London: Oxford University Press).
Burns, Alan, John McDermid & John Dobson (1992) 'On the meaning of safety and security', *The Computer Journal*, 35(1): 3–15.
Butcher, Charity (2017) 'Civil war and terrorism: A call for further theory building', in *Oxford Research Encyclopaedia of Politics*, edited by Thompson, William R. (Oxford: Oxford University Press).
Butler, Judith (2004) *Precarious Life: The Power of Mourning and Violence* (London: Verso).
Butler, Judith (2009) *Frames of War: When Is Life Grievable?* (London: Verso).
Buzan, Barry, Morten Kelstrup, Pierre Lemaitre, Elizabeta Tromer & Ole Wæver (1990) *The European Security Order Recast: Scenarios for the Post-Cold War Era* (London/New York: Pinter).
Buzan, Barry, Ole Waever & Jaap de Wilde (1998) *Security: A New Framework for Analysis* (Boulder: Lynne Rienner).
Bye, Rolf J., Petter Almklov, Stian Antonsen, Ole Magnus Nyheim, Asbjørn Lein Aalberg & Stig Ole Johnsen (2019) 'The institutional context of crisis: A study of the police response during the 22 July terror attacks in Norway', *Safety Science*, 111: 67–79.
CASE Collective (2006) 'Critical approaches to security in Europe: A networked manifesto', *Security Dialogue*, 37(4): 443–87.
CASE Collective (2007) 'Europe, knowledge, politics engaging with the limits: The CASE Collective responds', *Security Dialogue*, 38: 559–76.
Carle, Robert (2013) 'Anders Breivik and the death of free speech in Norway', *Society*, 50(4): 395–401.
Center for Research on Extremism (2022) 'Bibliography on Norwegian and international research on July 22', University of Oslo. Available at: www.sv.uio.no/c-rex/english/groups/bibliographies/22july/ [Accessed 3 October 2023].
Cerulo, Karen A. (2008) *Never Saw It Coming: Cultural Challenges to Envisioning the Worst* (Chicago: University of Chicago Press).
Chalk, Peter (1995) 'The liberal democratic response to terrorism', *Terrorism and Political Violence*, 7(4): 10–44.
Chalk, Peter (1998) 'The response to terrorism as a threat to liberal democracy', *Australian Journal of Politics & History*, 44(3): 373–88.
Chandler, David (2013) 'Resilience and the autotelic subject: Toward a critique of the societalization of security', *International Political Sociology*, 7(2): 210–26.
Christensen, Dag Arne & Jacob Aars (2017) 'The 22 July terrorist attacks in Norway: Impact on public attitudes towards counterterrorist authorities', *Scandinavian Political Studies*, 40(3): 312–29.

Christensen, Tom, Per Lægreid & Lise H. Rykkja (2015) 'The challenges of coordination in national security management: The case of the terrorist attack in Norway', *International Review of Administrative Sciences*, 81(2): 352–72.

Christensen, Tom, Per Lægreid & Lise H. Rykkja (2016) 'Organizing for crisis management: Building governance capacity and legitimacy', *Public Administration Review*, 76(6): 887–97.

Coaffee, Jon & David Murakami Wood (2006) 'Security is coming home: Rethinking scale and constructing resilience in the global urban response to terrorist risk', *International Relations*, 20(4): 503–17.

Cockayne, James & Emily Speers Mears (2009) *Beyond Market Forces: Regulating the Global Security Industry* (New York: International Peace Institute).

Connolly, William E. (1991) 'Liberalism and difference', in *Identity/Difference: Democratic Negotiations of Political Paradox* (Ithica: Cornell University Press): 64–94.

Coombs, Kate (2010) *The Runaway Dragon* (New York: Farrar Straus Giroux).

Cooper, Melinda (2004) 'Insecure times, tough decisions: The nomos of neoliberalism', *Alternatives: Global, Local, Political*, 29(5): 515–33.

Culcasi, Karen & Mahmut Gokmen (2011) 'The face of danger', *Aether: The Journal of Media Geography*, 8: 82–96.

D'abashi, Hamid (2012) *Corpus Anarchicum: Political Protext, Suicidal Violence, and the Making of the Posthuman Body* (London: Palgrave).

Dalby, Simon (2002) 'Contesting an essential concept: Reading the dilemmas in contemporary security discourse', in *Critical Security Studies*, edited by Krause, Keith & Michael Williams (London: Routledge): 3–31.

Dalby, Simon (2009) *World Politics, Security and Culture: Critical Connections* (London: Routledge).

Das, Dilip K. & Amanda L. Robinson (2001) 'The police in Norway: A profile', *Policing: An International Journal of Police Strategies & Management*, 24(3): 330–46.

Daston, Lorraine & Katharine Park (1998) *Wonders and the Order of Nature, 1150–1750* (New York/Cambridge: Zone Books).

Daston, Lorraine & Peter Galison (2007) *Objectivity* (London: Zone Books).

Dean, Mitchell (2010) 'Power at the heart of the present: Exception, risk and sovereignty', *European Journal of Cultural Studies*, 13(4): 459–75.

Dean, Mitchell (2013) *The Signature of Power: Sovereignty, Governmentality and Biopolitics* (London: SAGE).

Demarest, Heidi B. & Erica D. Borghard (2018) *US National Security Reform: Reassessing the National Security Act of 1947* (London: Routledge).

Der Derian, James (1987) *On Diplomacy: A Genealogy of Western Estrangement* (Oxford/New York: Blackwell).

Der Derian, James (1993) 'The value of security', in *The Political Subject of Violence*, edited by Campbell, David & Michael Dillon (Manchester: Manchester University Press): 94–112.

Der Derian, James (2001) *Virtuous War: Mapping the Military-Industrial-Media-Entertainment Network* (Boulder/Oxford: Westview Press).

Derrida, Jacques (2004) *Dissemination* (London: Bloomsbury).

Det kongelige Justis- og politidepartementet (2003) St.meld. nr. 37 (2004–2005) Flodbølgekatastrofen I Sør-Asia og sentral krisehåndtering *[On the Tsunami Catastrophe in South Asia and Central Crisis Management]* (Oslo: Stortinget).

Dillon, Michael (1996) *Politics of Security: Towards a Political Philosophy of Continental Thought* (London: Routledge).

Dillon, Michael & Julian Reid (2009) *The Liberal Way of War: Killing to Make Life Live* (London: Routledge).
Doran, Robert (2015) *The Theory of the Sublime from Longinus to Kant* (Cambridge: Cambridge University Press).
Døving, Cora Alexa (2020) '"Love your folk": The role of "conspiracy talk" in communicating nationalism', in *Religion and Neo-Nationalism in Europe*, edited by Höhne, Florian & Torstein Meirels (Baden-Baden: Nomos): 189–202.
Dragnes, Kjell (2011) 'Oppsplittet beredskap [Divided preparedness]', *Aftenposten*, 11 August.
Duncombe, Constance & Tim Dunne (2018) 'After liberal world order', *International Affairs*, 94(1): 25–42.
Dunne, Tim (2009) 'Liberalism, international terrorism, and democratic wars', *International Relations*, 23(1): 107–14.
Dupuy, Jean-Pierre (2015) *A Short Treatise on the Metaphysics of Tsunamis* (East Lansing: Michigan State University Press).
Dyb, Grete, Tine K. Jensen, Egil Nygaard, Øivind Ekeberg, Trond H. Diseths, Tore Wentzel-Larsen & Siri Thoresen (2014) 'Post-traumatic stress reactions in survivors of the 2011 massacre on Utøya Island, Norway', *The British Journal of Psychiatry*, 204(5): 361–7.
Eckert, Julia M. (2008) *The Social Life of Anti-Terrorism Laws: The War on Terror and the Classifications of the Dangerous Other* (Berlin: Transcript Verlag).
Edkins, Jenny (2003) *Trauma and the Memory of Politics* (Cambridge: Cambridge University Press).
Ekroll, Henning Car & Marie Melgård (2012) 'Dommerne plukket psykiatrirapporten fra hverandre [The judges dismantled the psychiatric report]', *Aftenposten*, 24 August.
Englund, Liselotte (2012) *The Bomb Attack in Oslo and the Shootings at Utøya, Norway, 2011: Experiences of Communication and Media Management*, Kamedo Report No. 97 (Stockholm: National Board of Health and Welfare).
Eriksson, Johan & Giampiero Giacomello (2006) 'The information revolution, security, and international relations: (Ir)relevant theory?', *Revue internationale de science politique/International Political Science Review*, 27(3): 221–44.
Ertesvåg, Frank, Ole N. Olsen, Marianne Vikås, Andreas Nielsen, Terje Helsigneng, Julie Lundgren & Sindre Murttnes (2011) 'Justisminister Storberget går av [Minister of Justice Storberget resigns]', *Verdens Gang (VG)*. Available at: www.vg.no/nyheter/innenriks/i/npQ1B/justisminister-storberget-gaar-av [Accessed 6 January 2023].
Færaas, Arild & Ida de Rosa (2012) 'Stoltenberg om 22.juli-rapporten: Vi har fått det vi ba om [Stoltenberg on the July 22 Commission report: We got what we asked for]', *Aftenposten*, 13 August.
Faulkner, William (2012) *Requiem for a Nun* (London: Vintage).
Filkuková, Petra, Gertrud Sofie Hafstad & Tine K. Jensen (2016) 'Who can I trust? Extended fear during and after the Utøya terrorist attack', *Psychological Trauma: Theory, Research, Practice, and Policy*, 8(4): 512–19.
Filstad, Cathrine & Petter Gottschalk (2010) 'Collectivism versus individualism in police cultures', *International Journal of Human Resources Development and Management*, 10(2): 117–35.
Findley, Michael G. & Joseph K. Young (2012) 'Terrorism and civil war: A spatial and temporal approach to a conceptual problem', *Perspectives on Politics*, 10(2): 285–305.
Forsvarskommisjonen (1949) *Innstilling fra Forsvarskommisjonen av 1946 [Opinion of the Defense Commission of 1946]* (Oslo: Forsvarsdepartement).

Foucault, Michel (1991) 'Governmentality', in *The Foucault Effect: Studies in Governmentality with Two Lectures by and an Interview with Michel Foucault*, edited by Burchell, Graham, Colin Gordon & Peter Miller (London: Harvester Wheatsheaf): 87–104.
Foucault, Michel (2002) *The Order of Things: An Archaeology of the Human Sciences* (London: Routledge).
Foucault, Michel (2010) *The Birth of Biopolitics: Lectures at the Collège de France, 1978–1979* (New York: Picador).
Franzen, Jonathan (2010) *The Corrections* (London: Harper).
Fraser, Nancy (1997) *Justice Interruptus: Critical Reflections on the 'Postsocialist' Condition* (New York: Routledge).
Freud, Sigmund (1953) 'Mourning and melancholy', in *The Standard Edition of the Complete Psychological Works of Sigmund Freud*, Volume XIV, edited by Strachey, James (London: The Hogarth Press): 243–58.
Friedman, Milton (2009) *Capitalism and Freedom* (Chicago: University of Chicago Press).
Frydnes, Jørgen Watne (2021) Ingen mann er en øy [No Man Is an Island] (Oslo: Res publica).
Fuglehaug, Wenche (2011) 'Kvelden Norge viste samhold og styrke [The evening Norway showed unity and strength]', *Aftenposten*, 26 July.
Fuglehaug, Wench, Per Anders Johansen, Cato Guhnfeldt & Lars Andreas Elingsgard Øverli (2019) 'Terrorøvelser avslørte beredskapsmangler [Terror exercises revealed lapses in preparedness]', *Aftenposten*, 27 July.
Galtung, Johan (1990) 'Cultural violence', *Journal of Peace Research*, 27(3): 291–305.
Geertz, Clifford (1973) 'Thick description', in *The Interpretation of Cultures: Selected Essays* (New York: Basic Books): 3–30.
Gellner, Ernest (1983) *Nations and Nationalism* (Oxford: Blackwell).
Ghervas, Stella (2021) *Conquering Peace: From the Enlightenment to the European Union* (Cambridge: Harvard University Press).
Gjerde, Robert, Karen Tjernshaugen & Gunnar Kagge (2012) 'Sier han tar ansvar, men går ikke av [Says he takes responsibility but does not resign]', *Aftenposten*, 14 August.
Goodman, Michael & Jesper Falkheimer (2014) 'Crisis communication and terrorism: The Norway attacks on 22 July 2011', *Corporate Communications: An International Journal*, 19(1): 52–63.
Graeber, David (2016) *The Utopia of Rules: On Technology, Stupidity, and the Secret Joys of Bureaucracy* (London: Melville House).
Graver, Hans Petter (2012) 'Bomben under rettstaten [The bomb under the rule of law]', in *22.juli. Forstå – forklare – forebygge [22 July: Understand – Explain – Prevent]*, edited by Østerud, Svein (Oslo: Abtrakt Forlag): 289–306.
Grøndahl, Pål (2011) 'En forvirret debat [A confused debate]', *Aftenposten*, 6 December.
Gröning, Linda, Unn Kristin Haukvik & Karl Heinrik Melle (2019) 'Criminal insanity, psychosis and impaired reality testing in Norwegian law', *Bergen Journal of Criminal Law & Criminal Justice*, 7(1): 27–59.
Gros, Frédéric (2008) 'Désastre humanitaire et sécurité humaine. Le troisième âge de la sécurité [Humanitarian disaster and human security: The third age of security]', *Esprit*, 3: 51–66.
Gros, Frédéric (2012) *Le principe sécurité [The Principle of Security]* (Paris: Éditions Gallimard).

Grosz, Elizabeth (2020) *Volatile Bodies: Toward a Corporeal Feminism* (London: Routledge).
Haakon, H.K.H. (2011) 'Kronprinsens appell på Rådhusplassen [The Crown Prince's appeal on City Hall Square]', *Aftenposten*, 25 July.
Habermas, Jürgen (1996) *Between Facts and Norms: Contributions to a Discourse Theory of Law and Democracy* (Cambridge: MIT Press).
Habermas, Jürgen (2001) *The Postnational Constellation: Political Essays* (Cambridge, Mass.: MIT Press).
Halliwell, Stephen (2012) *Between Ecstasy and Truth: Interpretations of Greek Poetics from Homer to Longinus* (Oxford: Oxford University Press).
Hansen, Lene (2006) *Security as Practice: Discourse Analysis and the Bosnian War* (London: Routledge).
Hansen, Stig Jarle (2020) 'Striving for the impossible? Policing and territoriality in the age of the war on terror', *Journal of Human Security*, 16(2): 9–18.
Hanssen, Inge D. (2022) 'Psykiateren avkler Breivik fullstendig [The psychiatrist completely exposes Breivik]', *Aftenposten*, 19 January.
Hareide, Knut Arild (2012) 'Terrorberedskapen sviktet [Terrorism preparedness failed]', *NRK Ytring*. Available at: www.nrk.no/ytring/beredskapen-sviktet-1.8281241 [Accessed 6 January 2023].
Harelius, E. Johanna & Kaitlyn Haynal (2021) 'The politics of a Memory Wound: Norwegian exceptionalism and the trauma of July 22, 2011', *American Behavioral Scientist*, 65(13): 1787–804.
Haugen, Jørgen (2012) 'Psykiaterne redder Norge [The psychiatrists save Norway]', *Aftenposten*, 3 January.
Hayek, Friedrich August (2013) *The Constitution of Liberty* (London: Routledge).
Hayes, Ben (2006) *Arming Big Brother: The EU's Security Research Programme* (Amsterdam: Transnational Institute).
Heath-Kelly, Charlotte (2015) 'Picasso at the bombsite: Whither resilient place?', *Politics*, 35(1): 72–7.
Heath-Kelly, Charlotte (2019) 'Memory Wound: Architectural controversies in Norway after the 22 July attacks', *Ethnologie française*, 49(1): 119–29.
Heath-Kelly, Charlotte (2020) 'Memory loss: Post-terrorist sites in Norway', *The Architectural Review*, 10 January.
Heath-Kelly, Charlotte, Lee Jarvis & Christopher Baker-Beall (2014) 'Editors' introduction: Critical terrorism studies: Practice, limits and experience', *Critical Studies on Terrorism*, 7(1): 1–10.
Hegel, Georg Wilhelm Friedrich (1991a) *Elements of the Philosophy of Right* (Cambridge: Cambridge University Press).
Hegel, Georg Wilhelm Friedrich (1991b) *Lectures on the Philosophy of World History* (Oxford: Oxford University Press).
Helgesen, Ole K. (2011) 'Den halvautomatiske våpentypen som ble brukt på Utøya kan kjøpes helt lovlig på finn.no [The semi-automatic type of weapon used on Utøya can be purchased legally on finn.no]', *ABC Nyheter*. Available at: www.abcnyheter.no/nyheter/2011/07/26/134795/vapentypen-brukt-pa-utoya-selges-pa-finn.no [Accessed 4 April 2022].
Helljesen, Vilde & Eirik Veum (2011) PST ble informert i mars [PSS was informed in March], *nrk.no*. Available at: www.nrk.no/norge/pst-ble-informert-i-mars-1.7726734 [Accessed 4 April 2022].
Helsingeng, Terje, Julie Lundgren & Sincre Murtnes (2011) 'Justisminister Storberget går av [Minister of Justice Storberget resigns]', *Verdens Gang (VG)*. Available at:

www.vg.no/nyheter/innenriks/i/npQ1B/justisminister-storberget-gaar-av [Accessed 6 January 2023].

Hemmingby, Cato & Tore Bjørgo (2016) *The Dynamics of a Terrorist Targeting Process: Anders B. Breivik and the 22 July Attacks in Norway* (London: Palgrave).

Hjorth, Ingeborg (2019) 'Minnested mellom virkelighet og virtualitet [Memory Wound: Memorial between reality and virutality]', *Norsk Medietidsskrift*, 106(3): 1–19.

Hobsbawm, Eric J. (1992) *Nations and Nationalism since 1780: Programme, Myth, Reality* (Cambridge: Cambridge University Press).

Hodgson, Geoffrey M. (2006) 'What are institutions?', *Journal of Economic Issues*, 40(1): 1–25.

Hoel, Yasmin Sunde (2011) 'Det er dessverre altfor lett å lage så kraftige bomber som dette [Unfortunately it is much too easy to make powerful bombs like that one]', *Aftenposten*. Available at: www.aftenposten.no/norge/i/pL3B1/--Det-er-dessverre-altfor-lett-a-lage-sa-kraftige-bomber-som-dette [Accessed 4 April 2022].

Hollan, Brian T. (2021) *Policing for the 21st Century: A Complexity Theory-Based Approach* (Annapolis: Naval Postgraduate School).

Hutchinson, John & Anthony D. Smith (1994) *Nationalism* (Oxford: Oxford University Press).

Huysmans, Jef (1998) 'Security! What do you mean? From concept to thick signifier', *European Journal of International Relations*, 4(2): 226–55.

Ikenberry, John G. (2004) 'Liberalism and empire: Logics of order in the American unipolar age', *Review of International Studies*, 30: 609–30.

Ikenberry, John G. (2018) 'The end of liberal international order?', *International Affairs*, 94(1): 7–23.

Jakobsen, Siw Ellen (2021) 'Vi bør bli enige om hva som skjedde den 22.juli, mener tidligere AUF-leder [We should come to an agreement about what happened on 22 July, says former AUF leader]', *forskning.no*. Available at: https://forskning.no/terrorisme/vi-bor-bli-enige-om-hva-som-skjedde-den-22-juli-mener-tidligere-auf-leder/1869990 [Accessed 6 January 2023].

Jakobsson, Niklas & Svein Blom (2014) 'Did the 2011 terror attacks in Norway change citizens' attitudes toward immigrants?', *International Journal of Public Opinion Research*, 26(4): 475–86.

Jay, Martin (1992) '"The aesthetic ideology" as ideology; or, what does it mean to aestheticize politics?', *Cultural Critique*, 21: 41–61.

Jayakumar, Shashi (2019) *Terrorism, Radicalisation and Countering Violent Extremism: Practical Considerations & Concerns* (London: Palgrave Pivot).

JBD (Justis- og beredskapsdepartementet) (1998) *Hovedretningslinjer for det sivile beredskaps virksomhet og utvikling i tiden 1999–2002 [Main Guidelines for the Activities and Development of Civil Emergency Response in the Period 1999–2002]* (Oslo: Stortinget).

Johansen, Per Anders & Andreas Bakke Foss (2011) 'Eksperter tviler på grunnlaget for diagnosen [Experts in doubt about the basis for the diagnosis]', *Aftenposten*, 5 December.

Johansen, Per Anders, Andreas Bakke Foss & Håkon Letvik (2012) 'Valgte den billigste løsningen [Chose the cheapest solution]', *Aftenposten*, 16 August.

Jore, Sissel H. (2019) 'A means or an obstacle to achieving security?', in *Standardization and Risk Governance: A Multi-Disciplinary Approach*, edited by

Olsen, Odd E., Kirsten Juhl, Preben H. Lindøe & Ole Andreas Engen (London: Routledge): 150–65.
JPD (Justis- og politidepartementet) (1999) 'Dørum etablerer sårbarhetsutvalg ledet av Kåre Willoch [Dørum establishes vulnerability commission led by Kåre Willoch]', press release, 3 September (Oslo: Justis- og politidepartementet).
JPD (Justis- og politidepartementet) (2002) *Samfunnssikkerhet. Veien til et mindre sårbart samfunn [Societal Security: The Path to a Less Vulnerable Society]* (Oslo: Justis- og politidepartementet).
JPD (Justis- og politidepartementet) (2006) *General Civil Penal Code* (Oslo: Justis- og politidepartementet).
JPD (Justis- og politidepartementet) (2012) *Samfunnssikkerhet [Societal Security]* (Oslo: Justis- og beredskapsdepartementet).
Kalsnes, Bente, Arne H. Krumsvik & Tanja Storsul (2014) 'Social media as a political backchannel: Twitter use during televised election debates in Norway', *Aslib Journal of Information Management*, 66(3): 313–28.
Kalvig, Anne (2016) 'Death in times of secularization and sacralization: The mediating and re-mediating of the Utøya tragedy in the Norwegian public sphere', in *Mediating and Remediating Death: Studies in Death, Materiality and the Origin of Time*, edited by Christiansen, Dorothe Refslund & Kristen Sandvik (London: Routledge): 23–42.
Kalyvas, Stathis N. (2004) 'The paradox of terrorism in civil war', *The Journal of Ethics*, 8(1): 97–138.
Kant, Immanuel (1998) *Critique of Pure Reason* (Cambridge: Cambridge University Press).
Kant, Immanuel (2007) *Critique of Judgement* (Oxford: Oxford University Press).
Kilduff, Martin (1993) 'Deconstructing organizations', *Academy of Management Review*, 18(1): 13–31.
Kincade, William H. (1978) 'Repeating history: The civil defense debate renewed', *International Security*: 2(3): 99–120.
Knights, David (1997) 'Organization theory in the age of deconstruction: Dualism, gender and postmodernism revisited', *Organization Studies*, 18(1): 1–19.
Krause, Keith & Michael C. Williams (eds.) (1997) *Critical Security Studies: Concepts and Cases* (London: Routledge).
Kristiansen, Bjørn S. & Veslemøy Lode (2012) 'Ansvar er ikke bare å si at man tar ansvar [Responsibility is not just saying that one takes responsibility]', *Dagbladet*. Available at: www.dagbladet.no/nyheter/ansvar-er-ikke-bare-a-si-at-man-tar-ansvar/63124106 [Accessed 5 January 2023].
Kuhn, Thomas (1994) *The Structure of Scientific Revolution* (Chicago: University of Chicago Press).
Kvinnsland, Elisabeth (2014) *Fortellingen om 22. juli: Kan 22. juli rapporten betraktes som en helhetlig fortelling eller består den av konkurrerende fortellinger? [The Story of 22 July: Can the 22 July Report Be Seen as a Comprehensive Story or Are There Competing Stories?]* (Stavanger: University of Stavanger).
Lacy, Mark J. (2014) *Security, Technology and Global Politics: Thinking with Virilio* (Abingdon: Routledge).
Lægreid, Per & Synnøve Serigstad (2006) 'Framing the field of homeland security: The case of Norway', *Journal of Management Studies*, 43(6): 1395–413.

Lango, Peter, Lise H. Rykkja & Per Lægreid (2011) 'Organizing for internal security and safety in Norway', in *Risk Management Trends*, edited by Nota, Giancarlo (London: IntechOpen).

Latour, Bruno (1987) *Science in Action: How to Follow Scientists and Engineers through Society* (Milton Keynes: Open University Press).

Laval, Christian (2019) *Foucault, Bourdieu et la question néolibérale [Foucault, Bourdieu and the Neoliberal Question]* (Paris: Éditions de la découverte).

Lefort, Claude (1986) *The Political Forms of Modern Society: Bureaucracy, Democracy, Totalitarianism* (Cambridge: MIT Press).

Lemke, Thomas (2011) *Foucault, Governmentality, and Critique: Cultural Politics & the Promise of Democracy* (Boulder: Paradigm Publishers).

Lenz, Claudia (2018) '22.juli-fortellinger og forhandlingen om hva terroren skal bety for fremtiden [22 July narratives and negotiations about what terrorism should mean for the future]', *Tidsskrift for kulturforskning*, 17(1): 89–106.

Leonard, Cecilia H., George D. Annas, James L. Knoll IV & Terje Tørrissen (2014) 'The case of Anders Behring Breivik – Language of a lone terrorist', *Behavioral Sciences & the Law*, 32(3): 408–22.

Lerø, Magne (2012) 'Ansvar, makt og ledelse [Responsibility, power and leadership]', *Vårt Land*, 22 August.

Leucht, Brigitte, Katja Seidel & Laurent Warlouzet (2021) *The History of the European Union: Reinventing Postwar Europe* (London: Bloomsbury).

Levi, Michael & David S. Wall (2004) 'Technologies, security, and privacy in the post-9/11 European information society', *Journal of Law and Society*, 31(2): 194–220.

Lindaas, Ole A. & Kenneth A. Pettersen (2016) 'Risk analysis and black swans: Two strategies for de-blackening', *Journal of Risk Research*, 19(10): 1231–45.

Lippmann, Walter (1937) *The Good Society* (New York: Transaction Publishers).

Løvlie, Anders (2019) 'Criminal insanity: Concepts and evidence', *Bergen Journal of Criminal Law & Criminal Justice*, 7(1): 78–96.

Luhmann, Niklas (1995) *Social Systems* (Stanford, Calif.: Stanford University Press).

MacIntyre, Alasdair C. (2007) *After Virtue: A Study in Moral Theory* (Notre Dame: University of Notre Dame Press).

Madsen, Anders (2012) 'Et ansvar som ligger hos landets politiske ledelse [A responsibility that lies with the country's political leadership]', *Aftenposten*. Available at: www.aftenposten.no/meninger/kommentar/i/mRpeO/et-ansvar-som-ligger-hos-landets-politiske-ledelse? [Accessed 6 January 2023].

Malkki, Leena, Mats Fridlund & Daniel Sallamaa (2018) *Terrorism and Political Violence in the Nordic Countries* (London: Routledge).

Marable, Manning (2002) 'Racism in a time of terror', *Souls*, 4(1): 1–14.

Marx, Karl (1843) 'Letters from the Deutsch-Französische Jahrbücher: Marx to Ruge'. Available at: www.marxists.org/archive/marx/works/1843/letters/43_09.htm [Accessed 22 May 2023].

Marx, Karl (1844) 'Letter to Arnold Ruge', in *Karl Marx Frederick Engels Collected Works*, Volume 3, 1843–1844 (London: Lawrence and Wishart).

Marx, Karl (1970) *Critique of Hegel's 'Philosophy of Right'* (Cambridge: Cambridge University Press).

Massumi, Brian (1993) *The Politics of Everyday Fear* (Minneapolis: University of Minnesota Press).

Massumi, Brian (2010) 'The future birth of the affective fact: The political ontology of threat', in *The Affect Theory Reader*, edited by Gregg, Melissa & Gregory J. Seigworth (Durham: Duke University Press): 52–70.

Masys, Anthony J. (2022) 'Non-traditional security: A risk-centric view', in *Handbook of Security Science*, edited by Masys, Anthony J. (Stuttgart: Springer): 459–74.

McCormick, John (2020) *European Union Politics* (London: Bloomsbury Publishing).

McEwan, Ian (2016) *Atonement* (London: Vintage).

Melgård, Marie (2013) 'Derfor blir det ikke mistillit mot Regjeringen [That's why there was not a vote of no-confidence against the government]', *Aftenposten*. Available at: www.aftenposten.no/norge/i/MRn7M/derfor-blir-det-ikke-mistillit-mot-regjeringen [Accessed 5 January 2023].

Melle, Ingrid (2013) 'The Breivik case and what psychiatrists can learn from it', *World Psychiatry*, 12(1): 16–21.

Mikkelsen, Maria Sunna, Halldor Asvall & Anders Brekke (2011) 'Informasjonssvikt avdekket i 2006 [Information failure disclosed in 2006]', *nrk.no*. Available at: www.nrk.no/norge/informasjonssvikt-avdekket-i-2006-1.7744059 [Accessed 4 April 2022].

Mill, John Stuart (2002) *On Liberty, Utilitarianism and Other Essays* (Oxford: Oxford University Press).

Møller, Bjørn (2000) 'The concept of security: The pros and cons of expansion and contraction', *Joint sessions of the Peace Theories Commission and the Security and Disarmament Commission*, 18th General Conference of the International Peace Research Association (IPRA), 5–9 August, Tampere, Finland.

Morsut, Claudia (2020) 'The emergence and development of samfunnssikkerhet in Norway', in *Nordic Societal Security*, edited by Rinhard, Mark (London: Routledge): 68–90.

Nassim, Nicholas Taleb (2007) *The Black Swan: The Impact of the Highly Improbable* (London: Penguin).

Neal, Andrew W. (2008) 'Goodbye war on terror? Foucault and Butler on discourses of law, war and exceptionalism', in *Foucault on Politics, Security and War*, edited by Dillon, Michael & Andrew M. Neal (Basingstoke: Palgrave Macmillan): 43–64.

Neal, Andrew W. (2012) 'Normalization and legislative exceptionalism: Counterterrorist lawmaking and the changing times of security emergencies', *International Political Sociology*, 6(3): 260–76.

Nordanger, Dag Ø., Mari Hysing, Maj-Britt Posserud, Astri Johansen, Reidar Lundervold, Miranda Olff Jakobsen & Stormakr Kjell Mortenø (2013) 'Posttraumatic responses to the July 22, 2011 Oslo terror among Norwegian high school students', *Journal of Traumatic Stress*, 26(6): 679–85.

Nordby, Trond (2012) 'Hva betyr det å ta ansvar? [What does it mean to take responsibility?]', *NRK Ytring*. Available at: www.nrk.no/ytring/hva-betyr-det-a-ta-ansvar_-1.8874053 [Accessed 5 January 2022].

Norsk Telegrambyrå (2011) 'Avdekket rutinesvikt i 2006 – gjorde samme feil 22. juli [Discovered failure in routines in 2006 – made the same errors on 22 July]', *Bergensavisen*. Available at: www.ba.no/nyheter/avdekket-rutinesvikt-i-2006-gjorde-samme-feil-22-juli/s/1-41-5695764 [Accessed 5 January 2023].

North, Douglas C. (1990) *Institutions, Institutional Change and Economic Performance* (Cambridge: Cambridge University Press).

Norwegian Parliament (2007) *Societal Security: Cooperation and Coordination* (Oslo: Stortinget).

Norwegian Parliament (2011) Parliamentary minutes, 10 November, Oslo.

Notaker, Hallvard (2021) *Arbeiderpartiet og 22.juli [The Labour Party and 22 July]* (Oslo: Aschehoug).

NOU (1994) *Streikrett for politiet og lensmannsetaten [The Right to Strike of the Police and Sheriff's Department]* (Oslo: Statens forvaltningstjeneste).
NOU (1995) *Identitet og dialog [Identity and Dialogue]* (Oslo: Statens forvaltningstjeneste).
NOU (2000) *Et sårbart samfunn: Utfordringer for sikkerhets- og beredskapsarbeidet i samfunnet [A Vulnerable Society: Challenges for Security and Preparedness]* (Oslo: Statens forvaltningstjeneste).
NOU (2001) *Når ulykken er ute. Om organiseringen av operative rednings- og beredskapsressurser [When the Accident Has Happened: On the Organisation of Operative Rescue and Preparedness Resources]* (Oslo: Justis- og politidepartementet).
NOU (2006) *Når sikkerheten er viktigst. Beskyttelse av kritiske infrastrukturer og kritiske samfunnsfunksjoner [When Security Is Most Important: Protection of Critical Infrastructure and Critical Societal Functions]* (Oslo: Justis- og politidepartementet).
NOU (2009) *Lov om offentlige undersøkelseskommisjoner: Særskilt oppnevnte offentlige kommisjoner [Law on Public Investigative Commissions: Specially Named Public Commissions]* (Oslo: Justis- og politidepartementet).
NOU (2011) *Ny våpenlov. Gjennomgang av gjeldende våpenlovgivning og forslag til ny våpenlov [New Weapon Law: A Review of the Applicable Weapon Legislation and a Proposal for a New Weapon Law]* (Oslo: Justis- og politidepartementet).
NOU (2012) *Rapport fra 22.juli-kommisjonen [Report of the 22 July Commission]* (Oslo: Departementenes servicesenter, informationsforvaltning).
NOU (2013a) *Ett politi – rustet til å møte fremtidens utfordringer [A Police Equipped to Meet the Challenges of the Future]* (Oslo: Justis- og beredskapsdepartementet).
NOU (2013b) *Når det virkelig gjelder... Effektiv organisering av statlige forsterkningsressurser [When It Really Matters: Effective Organisation of State Reinforcement Resources]* (Oslo: Justis- og beredskapsdepartementet).
NOU (2014) *Skyldevne, sakkyndighet og samfunnsvern [Guilt, Expertise and Community Protection]* (Oslo: Justis- og beredskapsdepartementet).
NOU (2015) *Digital sårbarhet – sikkert samfunn: Beskytte enkeltmennesker og samfunn i en digitalisert verden [Digital Vulnerability – Secure Society: Protecting Individuals and Society in a Digitalised World]* (Oslo: Justis- og beredskapsdepartementet).
NOU (2016) *Samhandling for sikkerhet: Beskyttelse av grunnleggende samfunnsfunksjoner i en omskiftelig tid [Collaboration for Security: Protection of Fundamental Societal Functions in Changing Times]* (Oslo: Forsvarsdepartementet).
NOU (2017) *Politi og bevæpning: Legalitet, nødvendighet, forholdsmessighet og ansvarlighet [Police and Arming: Legality, Necessity, Proportionality and Responsibility]* (Oslo: Justis- og beredskapsdepartementet).
NOU (2018) *IKT-sikkerhet i alleedd Organisering og regulering av nasjonal IKT-sikkerhet [ICT Security at All Levels: Organisation and Regulation of National ICT Security]* (Oslo: Justis- og beredskapsdepartementet).
NOU (2019) *Når krisen inntreffer [When the Crisis Happens]* (Oslo: Justis- og beredskapsdepartementet).
Nozick, Robert (1993) *The Nature of Rationality* (Princeton: Princeton University Press).
NRK (Norwegian Broadcasting Company) (2011a) *Dagsrevyen*, 22 July, Oslo.
NRK (Norwegian Broadcasting Company) (2011b) *Dagsrevyen*, 24 July, Oslo.
NRK (Norwegian Broadcasting Company) (2011c) *Dagsrevyen*, 23 July, Oslo.

NRK (Norwegian Broadcasting Company) (2012) *Dagsnytt 18*, 13 August, Oslo.
NRK (Norwegian Broadcasting Company) (2019) 'Dagsrevyen vant Gullrutens hederspris [Dagsrevyen won the Gullruten honorary prize]', nrk.no. Available at: www.nrk.no/kultur/dagsrevyen-vant-gullrutens-hederspris-1.14547402 [Accessed 4 April 2022].
Nykvist, Kato (2012) 'Kunsten å skyve på ansvar [The art of passing responsibility]', *Nationen*. Available at: www.nationen.no/article/kunsten-a-skyve-pa-ansvar [Accessed 5 January 2023].
OECD (Organisation for Economic Cooperation and Development) (2016) *Development Aid in 2015 Continues to Grow despite Costs for In-Donor Refugees* (Paris: Organization for Economic Cooperation and Development).
Oliveira Martins, Bruno, Kristoffer Lidén & Maria Gabrielsen Jumbert (2022) 'Border security and the digitalisation of sovereignty: Insights from EU borderwork', *European Security*, 31(3): 475–94.
OPM (Office of the Prime Minister) (Statsministerenskontor) (2011), 12 August, Oslo.
Østli, Kjetil Stensvik (2013) *Rettferdighet er bare et ord – 22.juli og rettskaen mot Anders Behring Breivik [Justice Is Only a Word: 22 July and the Trial of Anders Behring Breivik]* (Oslo: Cappelen Damm).
Parsons, Talcott (1977) *Social Systems and the Evolution of Action Theory* (New York: Free Press).
Parsons, Talcott (1991) *The Social System* (London: Routledge).
Philo, Chris (2012) 'Security of geography/geography of security', *Transactions of the Institute of British Geographers*, 37(1): 1–7.
Poovey, Mary (1998) *A History of the Modern Fact: Problems of Knowledge in the Sciences of Wealth and Society* (Chicago: University of Chicago Press).
Poppe, Erik (2018) *Utøya 22 July* (Oslo: Paradox Film 7).
Preiser, Rika, Reinette Biggs, Alta De Vos & Carl Folke (2018) 'Social-ecological systems as complex adaptive systems', *Ecology and Society*, 23(4): 111–32.
Pursiainen, Christer (2018) 'Critical infrastructure resilience: A Nordic model in the making?', *International Journal of Disaster Risk Reduction*, 27: 632–41.
Rafoss, Tore Witsø (2015) 'Meningsløs terror og meningsfylt fellesskap: Stoltenbergs taler etter 22.juli [Senseless terror and meaningful community: Stoltenberg's speeches after 22 July]', *Sosiologisk Tidsskrift*, 23(1–2): 6–28.
Rancière, Jacques (2009) *The Aesthetic Unconscious* (Cambridge: Polity).
Rancière, Jacques (2013a) *Aisthesis: Scenes from the Aesthetic Regime of Art* (London/New York: Verso).
Rancière, Jacques (2013b) *The Politics of Aesthetics: The Distribution of the Sensible* (London: Zed Books).
Rawls, John (1971) *A Theory of Justice* (Cambridge, Mass.: Harvard University Press).
Reid, Julian (2006) *The Biopolitics of the War on Terror: Life Struggles, Liberal Modernity, and the Defence of Logistical Societies* (Manchester: Manchester University Press).
Reid, Julian (2013) 'Interrogating the neoliberal biopolitics of the sustainable development–resilience nexus', *International Political Sociology*, 7(4): 353–67.
Renn, Ortwin (2008) *Risk Governance. Coping with Uncertainty in a Complex World* (London: Earthscan).
Richards, Barry (2014) 'What drove Anders Breivik?', *Contexts*, 13(4): 42–7.
Ricœur, Paul (2000 [1995]) *The Just* (Chicago: University of Chicago Press).

Roe, Paul (2008) 'The "value" of positive security', *Review of International Studies*, 34(4): 777–94.

Rothschild, Emma (1995) 'What is security?', *Daedalus*, 124(3): 53–98.

Rousseau, Jean-Jacques (1997) *The Social Contract and Other Later Political Writings* (Cambridge: Cambridge University Press).

Rus, Katarina, Vojko Kilar & David Koren (2018) 'Resilience assessment of complex urban systems to natural disasters: A new literature review', *International Journal of Disaster Risk Reduction*, 31: 311–30.

Rustad, Per Asle & Tom Bakkeli (2011) 'Skulle stenge terror-gaten [Intended to close the terror street]', Verdens Gang (VG), 24 July.

Sætre, Jonas & Annemarte Moland (2011) 'Psykiaterne i full split om Breiviks helsetilstand [Psychiatrists in full split about Breivik's health]', *nrk.no*. Available at: www.nrk.no/norge/full-psykiatristrid-om-breivik-1.7925636 [Accessed January 2023].

Sætre, Jonas, Siv Sandvik & Kristine Hirsti (2012) 'Mæland trekker seg fra stillingen [Mæland resigns his position]', *nrk.no*. Available at: www.nrk.no/norge/maelandtrekker-seg-fra-stillingen-1.8284422 [Accessed 4 October 2023].

Sagarin, Rafe (2010) 'Natural security: What can we learn from 3.5 billion years of life on earth?' Available at: https://papers.ssrn.com/sol3/papers.cfm?abstract_id=1669735 [Accessed 4 October 2023].

Salvesen, Geir (2011) 'Tverrpolitisk enighet om en 22.juli-kommisjon [Across-the-aisle political agreement on 22 July Commission]', *Aftenposten*, 27 July.

Sandel, Michael J. (1984) *Liberalism and Its Critics* (New York: New York University Press).

Sandvik, Siv (2012) 'Gjørv: Vikitigere å se endringer enn å plasere ansvar [Gjørv: More important to see changes than to place responsibility]', *nrk.no*. Available at: www.nrk.no/norge/gjorv_-jeg-er-utalmodig-1.8382349 [Accessed 14 April 2022].

Sandvik, Siv & David Vojislav Krekling (2012) 'Jeg beklager på det aller sterkeste [I sincerely apologise]', 26 November, *nrk.no*. Available at: www.nrk.no/norge/storberget_-_-jeg-beklager-1.8406200 [Accessed 29 May 2020].

Schmid, Alex (2004) 'Terrorism: The definitional problem', *Case Western Reserve Journal of International Law*, 36(2). Available at: https://scholarlycommons.law.case.edu/jil/vol36/iss2/8.

Seibel, Wolfgang (2015) 'Studying hybrids: Sectors and mechanisms', *Organization Studies*, 36(6): 697–712.

Seierstad, Åsne (2015) *One of Us: The Story of Anders Breivik and the Massacre in Norway* (New York: Farrar, Straus & Giroux).

Shearman, Peter & Matthew Sussex (2004) *European Security after 9/11* (London: Ashgate).

Shepherd, Laura (2008) *Gender, Violence and Security: Discourse as Practice* (London: Bloomsbury Publishing).

Siedentorp, Larry (2014) *Inventing the Individual: The Origins of Western Liberalism* (London: Penguin).

Simons, Jon (2014) 'Aestheticisation of politics: From fascism to radical democracy', *Journal for Cultural Research*, 12(13): 207–29.

Simonsen, Marie (2012) 'Det store ansvaret [The big responsibility]', Dagbladet. Available at: www.dagbladet.no/kultur/det-store-ansvaret/63052652 [Accessed 6 January 2023].

Skafjeld, Anette & Nora Brønseth (2015) 'Nye Utøya tar form [New Utøya takes shape]', *nrk.no*. Available at: www.nrk.no/osloogviken/nye-utoya-tar-form-1.12225436 [Accessed 5 January 2023].
Skålevåg, Svein Atle (2016) *Utilregnelighet: En Historie om Rett og Medisin [Unaccountability: A History of Law and Medicine]* (Oslo: Pax Forlag).
Skaug, Ole Martin & Øistein Svelle (2011) 'Ingen krav til de som kjøper kunstgjødsel [No requirements to those who purchase artificial fertiliser]', *E24*. Available at: https://e24.no/naeringsliv/i/yvBed2/ingen-krav-til-de-som-kjoeper-kunstgjoedsel [Accessed 5 January 2023].
Skjeseth, Alf (2011) '1 av 4 kjenner rammede [1 in 4 knew someone affected]', *Klassekampen*, 19 August.
Smith, Anthony D. (1991) *National Identity* (Reno: University of Nevada Press).
Smith, Anthony D. (1992) *Ethnicity and Nationalism* (New York: E.J. Brill).
Smith, Anthony D. (2003) *Chosen Peoples: Sacred Sources of National Identity* (Oxford: Oxford University Press).
Smith, Steve (2005) 'The contested concept of security', in *Critical Security Studies and World Politics*, edited by Booth, Kenneth (Boulder: Lynne Rienner): 27–62.
Solberg, Hella (2011) 'Da folket tok Norge tilbake [When the people took back Norway]', *Verdens Gang* (VG), 25 July.
Sørheim, Synne & Torgeir Husby (2011) *Rettspsykiatrisk erklæring til Oslo Tingrett [Court psychiatric declaration to the Oslo District Court]* (Oslo: Oslo Tingrett).
Sparke, Matthew B. (2006) 'A neoliberal nexus: Economy, security and the biopolitics of citizenship on the border', *Political Geography*, 25(2): 151–80.
SSB (Statistisk sentralbyrå) (2019) Befolkning [Population]. Available at: www.ssb.no/statbank/table/05231/tableViewLayout1/ [Accessed 5 January 2023].
Stanghelle, Harald (2012) 'Den avkledde makten [Power exposed]', *Aftenposten*, 14 August.
Stanton, Jessica A. (2016) 'Terrorism, civil war, and insurgency', in *The Oxford Handbook of Terrorism*, edited by Chenoweth, Erica (Oxford: Oxford University Press): 348–65.
Steele, Brent J. (2013) *Alternative Accountabilities in Global Politics: The Scars of Violence* (London: Routledge).
Stengers, Isabelle (2000) *The Invention of Modern Science* (Minneapolis: University of Minnesota Press).
Stiegler, Bernard (2014) *The Re-Enchantment of the World: The Value of Spirit against Industrial Populism* (London: Bloomsbury Academics).
Stoltenberg, Jens (2011a) '22.juli-kommisjonen: Statsministerens innledning til pressekonferanse, 12 August 2011 [22 July Commission: The Prime Minister's comments to the press conference, 12 August 2011]' (Oslo: Statsministers kontor). Available at https://www.regjeringen.no/no/dokumentarkiv/stoltenberg-ii/smk/lyd-og-bilde/2011/pressekonferanse11/id652286/ [Accessed 18 October 2023].
Stoltenberg, Jens (2011b) 'Statsministerens tale til rosetoget etter terroren 22.07.11 [The Prime Minister's speech to the Rose March after the terrorist attack, 22.07.2011]', *nrk.no*. Available at: www.nrk.no/video/PS*43214 [Accessed 4 April 2022].
Stoltenberg, Jens (2011c) 'Tale ved nasjonal minnemarkering for 22.7.2011 [Speech at the national memorial service for 22.7.2011]' (Oslo, Statsministers kontor).
Stoltenberg, Jens (2011d) 'Tale i Oslo Domkirke [Speech in Oslo Cathedral]' (Oslo, Statsministers kontor).
Stortinget (2012a) 'Redegjørelse av statsministeren og justis- og beredskapsministeren om regjeringens oppfølging av rapporten fra 22. juli-kommisjon [Statement

by the Prime Minister and the Minister of Justice and Preparedness on the government's follow-up of the 22 July Commission report]', Oslo.

Stortinget (2012b) 'Innstilling fra kontroll- og konstitusjonskomiteen om redegjørelse av statsministeren og justis- og beredskapsministeren i Stortingets møte 28. august 2012 om regjeringens oppfølging av rapporten fra 22. julikommisjonen [Resolution from the Control and Constitution Committee on the statement of the Prime Minister and Minister of Justice in the Parliamentary session 28 August 2012 on the government's follow-up of the Report of the 22 July Commission]', Oslo.

Strand, Tron & Anders Haga (2018) 'Arbeiderpartiet: Politikere og Utøyaoverlevende er blitt truet på livet [Labour Party: Politicians and Utøya survivors have received death threats]', *Aftenposten*, 21 March.

Striegher, Jason-Leigh (2015) 'Violent-extremism: An examination of a definitional dilemma', *8th Australian Security and Intelligence Conference*, Perth, Western Australia: 75–86.

Stuart, Douglas T. (2008) *Creating the National Security State: A History of the Law that Transformed America* (Princeton: Princeton University Press).

Svaar, Peter (2018) 'Listhaug har slettet Facebook-innlegg [Listhaug has deleted Facebook post]', 14 March, nrk.no. Available at: www.nrk.no/norge/listhaug-sletter-omstridt-facebook-innlegg-1.13961460 [Accessed 2 January 2023].

Svendsen, Maiken, Oda Elise Svelstad, Helga Tunheim, Per Håkon Solber & Hallvard Norum (2020) 'Minnested har kostet nesten 59 millioner så langt [The memorial has cost nearly 59 million so far]', 15 May, nrk.no. Available at: www.nrk.no/kultur/22.-juli-minnestedet-blir-pa-utoykaia-1.15012461 [Accessed 11 September 2023].

Syse, Henrik (ed.) (2018) *Norge etter 22. juli: Forhandlinger om verdier, identiteter og et motstandsdyktig samfunn [Norway after 22 July: Negotiations on Values, Identities and a Resilient Society]* (Oslo: Nordic Open Access Scholarly Publishing).

Szpyra, Ryszard (2014) 'Military security within the framework of security studies: Research results', *Connections*, 13(3): 59–82.

Talking Heads & Demme, Jonathan (1984) *Stop Making Sense!* (Los Angeles: Arnold Stiefel Company).

Talsnes, Anne (2020) 'Minnesteder et debatt [Memorials and debate]'. Available at: www.22julisenteret.no/no/aktuelt/artikler/minnesteder-og-debatt [Accessed 5 January 2023].

Taylor, Charles (1992) *The Ethics of Authenticity* (Cambridge: Harvard University Press).

Thunberg, Greta (2019) 'I want you to panic', *The Guardian*. Available at: www.theguardian.com/science/video/2019/jan/25/i-want-you-to-panic-16-year-old-greta-thunberg-issues-climate-warning-at-davos-video [Accessed 27 April 2023].

Thue, Magnus (2012) 'Ansvar og 22.juli [Responsibility and 22 July]', *Minerva*. Available at: www.minervanett.no/ansvar-og-22-juli/135160 [Accessed 29 May 2020].

Tjernshaugen, Karen (2012) 'Vil ikke si om politidirektøren har tillit [Will not say whether the Police Director has her confidence]', *Aftenposten*, 16 August.

Tørrissen, Terje & Agnar Aspaas (2012) 'Rettspsykiatrisk erklæring til Oslo Tingrett [Court psychiatric declaration to the Oslo District Court].' Available at: www.coursehero.com/file/25322541/Psychiatric-Report-2012-04-10pdf [Accessed 8 January 2023].

Torset, Nina Selbo (2018) 'Utøya-overlevende etter Sanners 22. juli-kommentar: «Jeg føler du spytter på meg» [Utøya survivors after Sanner's 22 July comment: "I feel as though you are spitting on me"]', *Aftenposten*, 3 November. Available at: www.aftenposten.no/norge/i/8w7kyQ/utoeya-overlevende-etter-sanners-22-juli-kommentar-jeg-foeler-du-spytter-paa-meg [Accessed 8 January 2023].

Torset, Nina Selbo, Alf Ole Ask & Bjørn Egil Halvorsen (2018) 'Støre om Listhaugs terror-melding: Trist og opprørende [Støre on Listhaug's terrorism post: Sad and outrageous]', *Aftenposten*, 10 March. Available at: www.aftenposten.no/norge/i/wE0QOo/stoere-om-listhaugs-terror-melding-trist-og-opproerende [Accessed 8 January 2023].

Tusicisny, Andrej (2007) 'Security communities and their values: Taking masses seriously', *International Political Science Review*, 28(4): 425–49.

Tveita, Jan (2008) 'Vårt sårbare samfunn [Our vulnerable society]', *Aktuell Sikkerhet*. Available at: www.aktuellsikkerhet.no/aktuell-sikkerhet-leder-fra-papirutgaven-lederkommentar/vart-sarbare-samfunn/108175 [Accessed 6 May 2008].

Ullman, Richard (1983) 'Redfining security', *International Security*, 8(1): 129–53.

UN (United Nations) (1946) *Charter of the United Nations*, Article 51. Available at: https://legal.un.org/repertory/art51.shtml [Accessed 5 January 2023].

UNDP (United Nations Development Programme) (1994) *Human Development Report 1994* (Oxford: Oxford University Press).

Ungar, Michael (2018) 'Systemic resilience: Principles and processes for a science of change in contexts of adversity', *Ecology and Society*, 23(4): 34.

Vallen, Snorre (2021) *Utøyakortet [The Utøya Card]* (Oslo: Cappelen Damm).

Van Ham, Peter (2001) 'Security and culture, or, why NATO won't last', *Security Dialogue*, 32(4): 393–406.

Virilio, Paul (1986) *Speed and Politics: An Essay on Dromology* (New York: Semiotext).

Waage, Hilde Henriksen (2002) 'Explaining the Oslo backchannel: Norway's political past in the Middle East', *The Middle East Journal*, 56(4): 597–615.

Wæver, Ole (1996) 'European security identities', *Journal of Common Market Studies*, 34(1): 103–32.

Wæver, Ole (1997) *Concepts of Security* (Copenhagen: University of Copenhagen).

Wæver, Ole (2011) 'Politics, security, theory', *Security Dialogue*, 42(4–5): 465–80.

Wæver, Ole (2012) 'Security: A conceptual history for international relations' (unpublished).

Wagner, Peter (1994) *A Sociology of Modernity: Liberty and Discipline* (London: Routledge).

Waldron, Jeremy (2011) 'Safety and security', *Nebraska Law Review*, 85. Available at: https://digitalcommons.unl.edu/nlr/vol85/iss2/5 [Accessed 8 January 2023].

Walker, R.B.J. (1993) *Inside/Outside: International Relations as Political Theory* (Cambridge: Cambridge University Press).

Walker, R.B.J. (1997) 'The subject of security', in *Critical Security Studies: Concepts and Cases*, edited by Krause, Keith & Michael C. Williams (London: Routledge): 61–82.

Walters, William (2010) 'Migration and security', in *The Routledge Handbook of New Security Studies*, edited by Burgess, J. Peter (London/New York: Routledge): 229–40.

Weber, Max (2004) 'Science as vocation', in *The Vocation Lectures*, edited by Owen, David S. & Tracy B. Strong (London: Hackett Publishing): 1–31.

Weber, Max (2013) *Economy and Society* (Berkeley: University of California Press).

Weber, Max (2019 [1921]) *Economy and Society: A New Translation* (Cambridge: Harvard University Press).
Wernersen, Camilla & Helle Therese Kongsrud (2011) 'Har ønsket det lenge [Has wanted it for a long time]', *nrk.no*. Available at: www.nrk.no/norge/knut-storberget-gar-av-1.7872072 [Accessed 4 January 2023].
Wetherell, Margaret (2012) *Affect and Emotion: A New Social Science Understanding* (London: SAGE).
Wiggen, Mette (2012) 'Rethinking anti-immigration rhetoric after the Oslo and Utøya terror attacks', *New Political Science* 34(4): 585–604.
Wilkinson, Paul (2006) *Terrorism versus Democracy: The Liberal State Response* (London: Routledge).
Williams, Michael C. (1998) 'Identity and the politics of security', *Alternatives*, 4(2): 204–55.
Williams, Michael C. (2007) *Culture and Security: Symbolic Power and the Politics of International Security* (London: Routledge).
Winge, Åge (2011) 'Politiet ønsket ikke spesialsoldater [Police did not want special forces soldiers]', *Adresseavisen*. Available at: www.adressa.no/nyheter/innenriks/2011/07/25/Politiet-ønsket-ikke-spesialsoldater-853665.ece [Accessed 4 January 2023].
Wittgenstein, Ludvig (1961) *Tractatus Logicus Philosophicus* (London: Routledge & Kegan Paul).
Wolff, Katharina & Svein Larsen (2014) 'Can terrorism make us feel safer? Risk perceptions and worries before and after the July 22nd attacks', *Annals of Tourism Research*, 44: 200–09.
Wollebæk, Dag, Bernard Enjolras, Kari Steen-Johnsen & Guro Ødegård (2011) *Hva gjør terroren med oss som sivilsamfunn? [What Does Terror Do to Us as Civil Society?]* (Oslo/Bergen: Senter for forskning på sivilsamfunn og frivillig sektor).
Wollebæk, Dag, Bernard Enjolras, Kari Steen-Johnsen & Guro Ødegård (2012) 'After Utøya: How a high-trust society reacts to terror: Trust and civic engagement in the aftermath of July 22', *Political Science & Politics*, 45(1): 32–7.
Zakariassen, Gaute & Kirsti Haga Honningsøy (2011) 'Oppretter egen terrorkommisjon [Sets up its own commission on terror]', *nrk.no*. Available at: www.nrk.no/norge/oppretter-egen-22_7-kommisjon-1.7729462 [Accessed 4 April 2022].
Zamora, Daniel (2016) 'Foucault, the excluded, and the neoliberal erosion of the State', in *Foucault and Neoliberalism*, edited by Zamora, Daniel & Michael C. Behrent (Cambridge: Polity).
Zeh, Julie (2004) *Spieltrieb [Gaming Instinct]* (Berling: Schöffling & Co).
Žižek, Slavoj (2008) *Violence: Six Sideways Reflections* (New York: Picador).

Index

11 March 2004 Madrid
    bombings 50, 65
11 September 2001 attacks 10, 21, 36,
    45, 50, 51, 59, 60, 62, 65, 70,
    72, 106, 112, 124–9, 130, 143,
    183, 186
    Commission 10
22 July Commission 4, 5, 7, 34, 47,
    119, 139, 155–88, 193, 203,
    219–32, 247, 254, 255–7
7 July 2005 London bombings 65
9/11 see 11 September 2001 attacks

Aasrund, Rigmor 222
Adenauer, Konrad 66
Adorno, Theodor W. 43
aesthetics 25, 30, 31, 40–4
    see also affect and Burke, Edmund
        and Rancière, Jacques
affect 6, 15, 30, 42, 47, 218
    see also aesthetics
Afghanistan 138, 143
Aftenposten 153, 223, 235, 254
Anderson, Benedict 147, 180
Andreassen, Odd G. 90
Anundsen, Anders 222
apparatus 5, 10, 19, 45, 51, 112, 115,
    122, 128, 143, 151, 177, 184,
    189, 192, 223, 246, 254
assemblage 12, 19, 95, 169, 205

Beck, Ulrich 87, 108, 201
Benjamin, Walter 42, 148
biopolitics 34
    see also Foucault, Michel and
        governmentality

Bloch, Ernst 43
Brecht, Bertolt 43
Breivik, Anders Behring 1, 3, 4, 46,
    136, 139, 144, 167, 171, 176,
    203, 252–4
    trial 2, 233–49
Brundtland, Gro 136
bureaucracy 7, 10, 12–22, 32, 47, 48,
    57, 112, 115, 122, 124, 130,
    142, 157, 165, 169, 194, 198,
    200, 210, 228, 247, 255
    see also Marx, Karl and rationality
        and Weber, Max
Burke, Edmund 40–2
Bush Jr, George W. 62
    Bush II Administration 125
    see also war on terror
Butler, Judith 34

citizenship 199, 235, 251
    see also democracy
Cold War 53, 63, 74, 90–3, 98,
    110–11, 129, 145
    post- 63, 131, 146
    see also concept of the Cold War
        under security
Commission on Emergency
    Preparedness 111–13, 121
    see also Commission on
        Vulnerability
Commission on 22 July 2011
    see 22 July 2011
        Commission
Commission on Vulnerability 89–105,
    107–12, 126, 176, 206
    see also societal under security

community 5, 6, 45, 46, 48, 60, 101, 113, 120, 125, 144, 158, 166, 182, 201, 205, 211
   imagined 113, 142, 171, 180, 199
   of Norwegians 46, 47, 164
complexity theory 197, 210
conservatism 146
Control and Constitutional Committee see Control and Constitutional Committee *under* Norwegian Parliament
crisis management 8, 10, 15, 16, 23, 116, 118, 121–4, 168, 169, 186, 190, 192, 193, 196, 197, 202, 233, 247
cultural Marxism 166, 234
   see also Breivik, Anders Behring

Dagsrevyen 135, 144, 147, 152
Dahlberg, Jonas 245
de Wilde, Jaap 107
defence
   civil 9, 92, 114, 118, 123–4, 129, 248
      see also civil *under* preparedness
   policy 62, 93, 100, 123
   of society 6, 92, 167
   see also Norwegian Ministry of Defence
democracy 2, 4, 6, 13, 16, 32, 36, 100, 142, 143, 147, 149, 151, 153, 154, 157, 158, 166, 167, 168, 172, 174, 188, 199, 224, 234, 236, 242, 245, 246, 249
   see also citizenship
   direct 17
   liberal 36, 202
   social 16, 20, 99, 162, 193, 199, 226
Der Derian, James 16, 60
Dillon, Michael 36, 37
disenchantment 7, 15, 20, 23, 30, 32–5, 48, 109, 255, 257
   see also enchantment *and* Weber, Max
domination 17, 36
   see also Weber, Max
Durkheim, Émile 131

enchantment 6, 7, 11, 16, 21, 23, 45, 48, 226, 249, 250
   see also disenchantment *and* Weber, Max
Europe 5, 16, 62, 63, 65–8, 70, 73, 111, 168, 171, 214, 237, 238, 240
European Union 5, 61, 66, 155, 190
extremism 36, 37, 47, 247
   violent 36–8, 47

Faremø, Grete 224, 227, 228
Foucault, Michel 13, 20, 21
France 42
Freud, Sigmund 32–4
Friedman, Milton 35, 150

Gjørv, Alexandra Bech 254
Gjørv Commission see 22 July 2011 Commission
globalisation 38, 52, 54, 58, 61, 73, 110, 112
governmentality 6, 201, 206, 218
   see also biopolitics *and* Foucault, Michel
Graeber, David 6, 16
grief 32–5, 55, 144, 151, 152, 159, 171, 175
   see also mourning
   national 153–4

Habermas, Jürgen 147
Hareid, Knut Arild 222
Hayek, Friedrich 35, 150
Hegel, Georg Wilhelm Friedrich 17, 137, 256
Hobbes, Thomas 35, 149
humanity 2, 6, 42, 46, 48, 57, 73, 80, 86, 141, 143, 144, 165

identity 33, 38, 44, 108, 113, 131, 139, 163, 166, 177, 201, 205
   national 131, 164

Kant, Immanuel 33, 41–2, 86, 119, 189, 236
Killengreen, Ingelin 227

Knights Templar Europe 237–8
see also Breivik, Anders Behring

liberalism 36, 38, 46–7
see also neoliberalism
life
  governance of 36
  itself 52, 72, 99, 102, 156
  way of 24, 70, 138, 171, 252
Lippmann, Walter 150
Locke, John 35, 149
Longinus 43
Luhmann, Niklas 96, 180
Lukács, Georg 43

Mæland, Øystein 222, 227, 228
Marx, Karl 16–17
melancholy see Freud, Sigmund and mourning
Memory Wound 245
  see also memorialisation of *under* Oslo/Utøya attacks
militarisation 92, 124, 153, 154
Mill, John Stuart 230
mourning 32–4

neoliberalism 21, 35–6, 217
North Atlantic Treaty Organisation 6, 92, 127–9, 138, 246
Norwegian Labour Party 1, 157, 227, 228, 250–1
  Youth Organisation 1, 23, 136, 145, 152, 244–6, 251
Norwegian Ministry of Defence 93, 124, 125, 129, 155, 225
Norwegian Ministry of Justice 32, 88, 96, 123, 125, 128, 169, 186–90, 194, 203, 210, 212, 227, 247
Norwegian National Security Authority 168, 183, 200, 202, 209
Norwegian Parliament 23, 92–3, 123, 147, 156, 186, 194, 224, 227, 229–33, 247, 254
  Control and Constitutional Committee 222, 231
  see also Anundsen, Anders

Norwegian Police 32, 125, 145, 153, 155, 222–8, 232, 237, 247, 248, 254
Nordre Buskerud Police Department 117
North Buskerud Police Department 32
Oslo District Police 239
Security Service 168, 200, 222, 224, 247
Søndre Buskerud Police Department 237
Nozick, Robert 149

Organisation for Economic Cooperation and Development 135
Oslo/Utøya attacks
  memorialisation of 244–6

Parsons, Talcott 96, 180
Pentagon see 11 September 2001 attacks
Poppe, Erik 251
preparedness
  civil 40, 91–3, 94, 96, 123–4
prevention 24, 38, 179, 186, 190–3, 201
protection 38, 56, 62, 69, 71, 74–7, 91, 92–3, 97, 100, 116, 168, 169, 173, 183, 207–9, 212, 223

Rancière, Jacques 43
rationality 5, 13, 16, 18, 20, 21, 25, 30, 31, 40, 42, 43, 66, 70, 84, 102, 123, 141, 150, 159, 160, 180, 187, 217–18, 219, 243, 244
  instrumental 14, 15, 217, 218
  value 217
  see also bureaucracy *and* Weber, Max
Rawls, John 119, 149
Reid, Julian 36, 37
resilience 95, 96, 108, 111, 115, 168, 180, 207, 213, 233
  societal 39, 96

responsibility
  administrative 182–3
  legal 140, 176, 183, 224,
    233–5, 239
  moral 138, 151, 183,
    233–5, 239
  political 187, 226, 232, 233–5
  principle of 122–4, 183–5, 194–6,
    197, 210, 211, 233
  taking of 76, 215, 221, 225, 227,
    230, 232
Ricardo, David 35
rights 3, 10, 11, 62, 107, 120, 142,
  147, 149, 157, 163, 199, 231,
  249, 251, 252
risk
  analysis 8, 15, 40, 75, 79, 83, 102,
    199–202
  management 58, 101, 102, 124,
    199–202
  studies 83–4
  and vulnerability 117, 127, 188,
    203, 210
Rose March 2, 4, 153
  see also national *under* grief *and*
    memorialisation *under* Oslo/
    Utøya attacks *and* mourning
Rousseau, Jean-Jacques 119
Russia 91, 128

Schmitt, Carl 255
securitisation 160, 179, 182
security
  concept of the Cold War 38, 89,
    90, 110
  homeland 190
  human 38, 53, 59, 163
  international 110
  national 38, 52, 53, 56, 57, 59, 74,
    100, 101, 106, 186, 251
  societal 5–7, 9, 15, 52, 54, 56, 59,
    64, 89–90, 91, 93, 95–131,
    143–4, 146, 159, 182, 186–90,
    192–8, 202–14, 223, 248
  studies 9, 53, 84, 87
  technologies 51, 59–63, 67
Smith, Adam 35, 147
social contract 47, 63, 142, 150,
  177, 204

society
  attack on 147
  liberal 2, 4, 38, 39, 47, 70, 108
  open 36, 97, 137, 143, 154
Solberg government 5
Solberg, Erna 157, 158, 222, 247
spiritualisation 16, 86, 140
Stoltenberg government 190, 227, 246
  II 5, 157, 227
Stoltenberg, Jens 6, 136, 139, 144,
  154, 158, 221, 229, 232, 246,
  247, 254
Storberget, Knut 139, 223–4, 227
Støre, Jonas Gahr 157, 251
sublime 40–4
surveillance 2, 5, 62, 63, 65, 74, 86,
  106, 146, 168, 173, 202,
  247, 248

Taleb, Nassim Nicholas 75
terrorism
  counter- 5, 247
  experience of 23, 24, 30, 31,
    33, 44
  studies 8, 30
  see also 11 September 2001 attacks
    and 11 March 2004 Madrid
    bombings *and* 7 July 2005
    London bombings *and* Oslo/
    Utøya attacks

uncertainty 3–6, 16, 34, 57, 64–5,
  75–9, 88, 100, 113, 135–41,
  147, 166, 171, 175, 185, 189,
  190, 220, 221, 229, 241, 250
United Nations 61, 224
  Development Programme 53
United States 2, 10, 50, 51, 56, 62,
  63, 65, 111, 112, 127, 128,
  146, 168
  Department of Homeland
    Security 190
  Patriot Act 5, 106
  population 252

values
  societal 90, 96, 97–101, 102, 107,
    129, 145, 146, 151, 153, 155,
    167, 169, 208

violence
   neoliberal 35–9
   political 36, 41, 45, 202
   see also extremism *and* neoliberalism

Wæver, Ole 107
Walker, Rob B. J. 80
war on terror 45, 47, 51, 65, 125
Weber, Max 6, 13, 17–21, 217–18
   see also enchantment *and* rationality
Widerborg, Nico 245

Willoch, Kåre 89, 125
Wilson principles 110, 111
Wittgenstein, Ludwig 11, 12
World Trade Center *see* 11 September 2001 attacks
World War I 35, 42, 43
   post- 110
World War II 1, 42, 43, 53, 56, 66, 154, 199
   post- 6, 56, 159

EU authorised representative for GPSR:
Easy Access System Europe, Mustamäe tee 50,
10621 Tallinn, Estonia
gpsr.requests@easproject.com

www.ingramcontent.com/pod-product-compliance
Lightning Source LLC
Chambersburg PA
CBHW052057300426
44117CB00013B/2177